More ...

ADAM SMIT...

"[*Adam Smith's America*] illuminates how the ways that readers approach
a text become part of that text's story."
—REBECCA BRENNER GRAHAM, *Slate*

"An excellent book."
—BRANKO MILANOVIC, Substack newsletter
"Global Inequality and More 3.0"

"[A] provocative analysis of Scottish moral philosopher Adam Smith's
influence on U.S. politics and business. . . . A rewarding reconsideration
of an influential thinker."
—*Publishers Weekly*

"Even if Chicago, the Heritage Foundation, and other right-leaning entities
have tried to seize [Smith] for their cause, Liu examines the possibility that
he may be 'closer to the values of the contemporary left'—thus are the many
ambiguities in his work. A bracing study not just of Smith's ideas, but
also of how scholars and activists have used (and misused) them."
—*Kirkus Reviews*

"Lucid and compelling. . . . An impressively researched and deftly
executed book."
—ROBIN DOUGLASS, *Global Intellectual History*

"*Adam Smith's America* is a fascinating exploration of the politics of political
economy. It illuminates how economic ideas have been used and reimagined
over two centuries of American history, and is at the same time an important
inquiry into political disputes over markets, states, and moral values."
—EMMA ROTHSCHILD, author of *An Infinite History:
The Story of a Family in France over Three Centuries*

"Adam Smith was a moral philosopher well aware of the quirks of human
psychology. So how is it that in America he wound up as the poster
child for a free-market order that rests on false assumptions about human
hyperrationality? This fascinating story is very important, very instructive,
and has never been told. Glory Liu tells it with great verve and great charm."
—J. BRADFORD DeLONG, author of *Slouching towards Utopia:
An Economic History of the Twentieth Century*

"Adam Smith's *Wealth of Nations* has long been a touchstone of American thought, powering conversations about markets and politics alike. Yet its message has been continually reinvented since the eighteenth century. In this lively reception history, Glory Liu explains how and why Smith turned into such a potent political weapon—and what impact the rewriting of his legacy, largely untethered from the text itself, has had on political economic thought in the United States to this day."
—SOPHIA ROSENFELD, author of *Democracy and Truth: A Short History*

"Adam Smith's journey from Kirkcaldy to Chicago was a long, winding, and fascinating one, as Glory Liu brilliantly demonstrates. *Adam Smith's America* draws on a vast array of source material to make that rarest of things, a genuinely new contribution to the field."
—DENNIS C. RASMUSSEN, author of *Fears of a Setting Sun: The Disillusionment of America's Founders*

"Few thinkers have inspired such a tangle of conflicting interpretations as Adam Smith. Glory Liu incisively cuts through this thicket, providing a lucid and engaging tour through more than two hundred years of American writings on political economy. *Adam Smith's America* shows that while the meaning of Smith's work remains fraught with ambiguities, his reception reveals much about the ideals and imaginations of his readers."
—ANGUS BURGIN, author of *The Great Persuasion: Reinventing Free Markets since the Depression*

"Glory Liu's engaging and thorough study tells an important story that has largely gone untold. Her documentation of the complex and often surprising reception of Adam Smith in American politics and economics from his day to ours will be of interest both to students and to advanced scholars—and indeed to anyone who may have wondered what all the fuss over Smith is all about!"
—RYAN PATRICK HANLEY, author of *Our Great Purpose: Adam Smith on Living a Better Life*

ADAM SMITH'S AMERICA

Adam Smith's America

HOW A SCOTTISH PHILOSOPHER
BECAME AN ICON OF
AMERICAN CAPITALISM

GLORY M. LIU

PRINCETON UNIVERSITY PRESS

PRINCETON & OXFORD

Published by Princeton University Press
41 William Street, Princeton, New Jersey 08540
99 Banbury Road, Oxford OX2 6JX

press.princeton.edu

All Rights Reserved

First paperback printing, 2024
Paperback ISBN 978-0-691-24086-2
Cloth ISBN 978-0-691-20381-2
ISBN (e-book) 978-0-691-24087-9

Library of Congress Control Number: 2022939557

British Library Cataloging-in-Publication Data is available

Editorial: Rob Tempio and Chloe Coy
Production Editorial: Karen Carter
Jacket/Cover Design: Hollis Duncan Graphic Design
Production: Erin Suydam
Publicity: Kate Farquhar-Thomson and James Schneider
Copyeditor: Michelle Garceau Hawkins

This book has been composed in Arno Pro

Printed in the United States of America

To all my teachers.

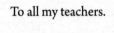

CONTENTS

ILLUSTRATIONS

Works of Adam Smith

All works belong to the standard Glasgow Edition of the Works and Correspondence of Adam Smith, republished by the Liberty Fund unless otherwise noted. With the exception of the *Correspondence* of Adam Smith, I have used the standard abbreviations.

Account   Dugald Stewart, *Account of the Life and Writings of Adam Smith, LL.D.* in *Essays on Philosophical Subjects*, ed. W.P.D. Wightman and J.C. Bryce. Indianapolis, IN: Liberty Fund, 1980.

Corr   *The Correspondence of Adam Smith*, ed. E.C. Mossner and I.S. Ross. Indianapolis, IN: Liberty Fund, 1987.

EPS   *Essays on Philosophical Subjects*, ed. W.P.D. Wightman and J.C. Bryce. Indianapolis, IN: Liberty Fund, 1980.

Lectures   *Lectures on Justice, Police, Revenue, and Arms*, ed. Edwin Cannan. Oxford: Clarendon Press, 1896.

LJ(A)   "Lectures on Jurisprudence," report of 1762–3, in *Lectures on Jurisprudence*, ed. R.L.Meek, D.D. Raphael, and P.G. Stein. Indianapolis, IN: Liberty Fund, 1982.

LJ(B)   "Jurisprudence or Notes from the Lectures on Justice, Police, Revenue, and Arms delivered in the University of Glasgow by Adam Smith, Professor of Moral Philosophy, report dated 1766," in *Lectures on Jurisprudence*, ed. R.L.Meek, D.D. Raphael, and P.G. Stein. Indianapolis, IN: Liberty Fund, 1982.

LRBL   *Lectures on Rhetoric and Belles Lettres*, ed. J.C. Bryce. Indianapolis, IN: Liberty Fund, 1985.

TMS   *The Theory of Moral Sentiments*, ed. D.D. Raphael and A.L. Macfie. Indianapolis, IN: Liberty Fund, 1982.

WN   *An Inquiry into the Nature and Causes of the Wealth of Nations*, ed. R.H. Campbell, A.S. Skinner, and W.B. Todd. 2 vols. Indianapolis, IN: Liberty Fund, 1981.

PROLOGUE

WHO IS ADAM SMITH?

To most people, Adam Smith is the father of economics, the author of *An Inquiry into the Nature and Causes of the Wealth of Nations* (1776), the ingenious Scotsman who revealed the workings of the "invisible hand"—the idea that individuals pursuing their self-interest could promote the public good without intention or direction. This version of Adam Smith pervades political and intellectual life in America and around the world. The Adam Smith Society, for example, offers an intellectual and professional network for business students to discuss and debate "foundational ideas" of capitalism such as "individual liberty, limited government, and free enterprise." American prosperity, the Society believes, depends on future business leaders' ability to "continue this tradition of promoting free markets"—a tradition that ostensibly begins with the society's namesake.[1] Smith is often the inspiration for conservative ideology, such as that of the American Enterprise Institute, which hopes to "stitch together a more robust, compelling, and inclusive center-right moral and economic agenda," or the Adam Smith Foundation, a non-profit based in Missouri that promotes values such as "working to stop needless regulations," "fighting waste and abuse of taxpayer dollars," and "working to restrain activist judges."[2] From trade

1. The Adam Smith Society, accessed October 18, 2021, https://www.adamsmithsociety.com/html/our-history.html.

2. Ryan Streeter, "Free Trade and Decadence, Old and New," *American Enterprise Institute*, July 20, 2020, sec. Society and Culture, https://www.aei.org/articles/free-trade-and-decadence-old-and-new/. Founded in 2007, The Adam Smith Foundation's activities are somewhat hard to trace. At the time of publication, their homepage adamsmithfoundation.org was no longer functional, but the organization showed signs of life on Twitter as recent as 2018. For an internet

wars to energy policy, Adam Smith is shorthand for the virtues of free markets and the vices of government intervention in economic affairs. "Adam Smith Doesn't Like U.S. Trade Policy," ran one *Forbes* headline in 2018 in response to new tariffs on Chinese imports, while another described President Donald J. Trump's attempt to stall the closures of nuclear and coal plants as a dangerous act of "stepping on Adam Smith's Invisible Hand."[3]

Smith's reputation as an economist is towering. Economists across different subfields have laid claim to Smith's legacy in behavioral economics, development economics, "mainline" economics, and most recently "humanomics."[4] *The Wealth of Nations* has been assigned on over 5,000 college syllabi nationwide, primarily in economics, but also in history, political science, business, philosophy, literature, sociology, anthropology, religion, and law. In 2021, *The Wealth of Nations* ranked forty-fourth among millions of books assigned in college courses, putting it ahead of John Stuart Mill's *On Liberty*, Alexis De Tocqueville's *Democracy in America*, and even Shakespeare's *Hamlet*. Meanwhile, Smith's first work, *The Theory of Moral Sentiments*, ranked far below, appearing on just over 1,000 syllabi.[5]

---

archive of their former webpage, as of October 18, 2021 see https://web.archive.org/web/20160303182623/http://www.adamsmithfoundation.com/index.php.

3. Stuart Anderson, "Adam Smith Doesn't Like U.S. Trade Policy," *Forbes*, July 18, 2018, https://www.forbes.com/sites/stuartanderson/2018/07/18/adam-smith-doesnt-like-u-s-trade-policy/; Peter Kelly-Detwiler, "Stepping on Adam Smith's Invisible Hand: Trump's Unwarranted Intervention in Power Markets," *Forbes*, June 4, 2018, https://www.forbes.com/sites/peterdetwiler/2018/06/04/stepping-on-adam-smiths-invisible-hand-trumps-unwarranted-intervention-in-power-markets/.

4. Nava Ashraf, Colin F. Camerer, and George Loewenstein, "Adam Smith, Behavioral Economist," *Journal of Economic Perspectives* 19, no. 3 (2005), 131–45; William Easterly, "Progress by Consent: Adam Smith as Development Economist," *The Review of Austrian Economics*, September 10, 2021; Stefanie Haeffele-Balch, Virgil Henry Storr, and Peter J. Boettke, eds., *Mainline Economics: Six Nobel Lectures in the Tradition of Adam Smith* (Arlington, VA: Mercatus Center at George Mason University, 2016); Vernon Smith and Bart Wilson, *Humanomics: Moral Sentiments and the Wealth of Nations for the Twenty-First Century* (Cambridge: Cambridge University Press, 2019).

5. For latest rankings of works on college syllabi, see the Open Syllabus Project, as of August 2021 https://opensyllabus.org/results-list/titles?size=50.

Despite all this, a persistent theme of Smith scholarship of the last several decades has been that Adam Smith was *not* an economist, or at least not merely an economist. Rather, he is remembered as an ambitious social scientist of the Enlightenment, whose *The Wealth of Nations* was but one part of a larger "science of man." This science sought to reveal and explain the hidden forces that governed human behavior and human society. In *The Theory of Moral Sentiments*, published in 1759, seventeen years before *The Wealth of Nations*, Smith explored how and why people learn moral behavior through the process of imaginative projection and sympathetic exchange. Smith also planned a work on the general principles of law and government, as well as a history of literature, philosophy, poetry, and rhetoric, both of which he never completed and ultimately had destroyed before his death in 1790. However, Smith did save a few essays for posthumous publication. Moreover, with the later discovery of student notebooks in 1895 and 1958, readers have been able to access Smith's lost ideas as they were recorded by his students in his lectures on rhetoric and jurisprudence. Today, readers can appreciate the immense range of Smith's teaching and writings, which were not limited only to economics and moral philosophy, but also included topics such as theories of language, polite learning, the history of science, literary and artistic criticism, poetry, law, and government. Given the breadth and richness of Smith's *oeuvre*, it is hardly surprising that intellectual historians, political theorists, and social scientists often complain that distorted notions of self-interest, free markets, and "the invisible hand" have eclipsed Smith's moral philosophy, jurisprudence, and more, and that Smith has become little more than an emblem for think tanks or a historical sound bite in textbooks. Yet few scholars have asked—let alone answered—the question of how and why these reductive, sloganized, and often politicized versions of Smith came about in the first place.

This book is about who Adam Smith was and who he became in America. It charts how Americans have read, taught, debated, and used Smith's ideas throughout history. It shows how Smith's reputation as the "father of economics" is an historical invention and that the foundational status of *The Wealth of Nations* is a belated construction. More importantly, though, this book tries to make sense of the political work that engaging with Smith has done throughout history and what the implications for our political and economic thinking are. Repeated contestation over Smith's original intentions, his method, and the contemporary import of his ideas has provided opportunities for past and present readers to define the relationship between ethics and economics, between politics and the economy, between past thought and present action.

————

Works on Adam Smith often begin with Smith's biography, and this book is no exception. This is not simply to present Smith's life as a sequence of events and ideas but rather to demonstrate how Smith's biography conditions the reception of his ideas and the invention of his legacy. Despite the volume of work Smith left behind, we know surprisingly little of his life, a fact that is irksome and puzzling to many of Smith's biographers and interpreters. The paucity of biographical detail has meant that what is reconstructed of Smith's life usually results from trying to reconstruct Smith's mind. Add to that Smith's most infamous act of deliberate destruction—the burning of his unpublished manuscripts—and one has the perfect recipe for an historical and intellectual enigma.

Most of Smith's biographers, historians, and admirers agree upon several key biographical details.[6] Smith was born in 1723 (the only recorded date we have is of his baptism on June 5, 1723) in Kirkcaldy, Scotland, a small seaside town ten miles north of Edinburgh. Smith's father, also named Adam Smith, had made a secure living as the Controller

6. Among the most authoritative modern biographical accounts of Adam Smith are John Rae, *Life of Adam Smith* (London: Macmillan, 1895); Ian Simpson Ross, *The Life of Adam Smith*, 2nd ed. (Oxford: Oxford University Press, 2010); Nicholas Phillipson, *Adam Smith: An Enlightened Life* (London: Penguin Books, 2010). James Buchan's introductory chapter on the biography of Adam Smith in Ryan Patrick Hanley, ed., *Adam Smith: His Life, Thought, and Legacy* (Princeton, NJ: Princeton University Press, 2016) also provides a succinct overview of Smith's life as well as the history of writing Smith's biography.

of Customs at Kirkcaldy. Adam Smith senior had been married to Lilias Drummond, who gave birth to a son, Hugh, but then died young sometime between 1716 or 1718. Smith senior remarried to Margaret Douglas, but he died in January of 1723, six months before the birth of their son, Adam Smith. Margaret Douglas devoted the rest of her life to being with her son; they were separated only briefly when he traveled, and she lived with him until her death in 1784 at age 90.

Smith grew up in Kirkcaldy, attending a burgh school and then entering Glasgow University at age fourteen in 1737, where he was drawn into the intellectual orbit of the formidable and charismatic Francis Hutcheson, professor of moral philosophy. In 1740, Smith was awarded a Snell Exhibition prize (a scholarship that paid for future studies with the expectation that he would become a clergyman of the Episcopalian Church) and departed for Balliol College at Oxford University, where he spent six years. We know virtually nothing of what Smith's life was like at Oxford, only that the experience seemed mediocre at best. Smith made a pointed—and scathing—remark about Oxford professors in *The Wealth of Nations* many years later, writing that the professors there have, "for these many years, given up altogether even the pretence [*sic*] of teaching."[7] General anti-Scots sentiment as well as pro-Jacobite and Roman Catholic adherents would have made Oxford an unpleasant environment for the Scottish, Whiggish, Protestant Smith. Nevertheless, Smith excelled in his studies; one of his professors commented that Smith was "a very fine boy as any we have."[8]

Smith left Oxford for Scotland in 1746. We know nothing of what happened between then and 1748, when he reappeared in Edinburgh as a freelance lecturer sponsored by Henry Home and soon-to-be member of parliament James Oswald. Home and Oswald believed that Smith would enrich the subjects of rhetoric, belles-lettres, and the moral philosophy of Smith's predecessors such as Francis Hutcheson and David Hume. Between 1748 and 1751, Smith delivered a series of lectures on the topics of rhetoric and jurisprudence; unfortunately, no lecture

---

7. *WN* V.i.f.8, 761.

8. Quoted in Ross, *The Life of Adam Smith*, 55.

notes, student notes, or texts have survived. This time period, including these lectures and the intellectual exposure Smith gained, played a formative role in his later professional career and writing. Moreover, it was during this time in Edinburgh that Smith met and formed a lifelong friendship with one of his greatest intellectual influences, David Hume.[9]

In 1751 Smith began preparing for a new position to which he had been elected, the Chair of Logic and Metaphysics at the University of Glasgow; he would inherit Francis Hutcheson's Chair of Moral Philosophy in 1752. Smith's lectures were of great renown. Though he was not the most "graceful" speaker, his manner was "plain and unaffected; and, as he seemed to be always interested in the subject, he never failed to interest his hearers," his student John Millar recalled. Students adored Smith, not just as a professor but as an amiable man who had "nothing of that formal stiffness and Pedantry which is too often found in Professors."[10] In addition to his professorial duties, Smith took part in university administration; in 1787 he was elected Lord Rector. Smith spent 13 years as a professor at the University of Glasgow, a time he would later reflect on as "by far the most useful, and therefore as by far the happiest and most honourable period of my life."[11]

In 1759, while still at Glasgow, Smith published his first major work, *The Theory of Moral Sentiments*. As the title suggests, Smith's primary aim was to offer an explanatory theory of moral sentiments, that is, how and why humans learn moral behavior and form moral judgments. For Smith, the answer was found in one concept: sympathy. Sympathy was a capacity to feel with and feel for others; it was both the mechanism by which we try to understand our fellow human beings—first by imagining *ourselves* in their position, seeing things from their perspective, and in turn, seeing ourselves—as well as the object of our desires. The work

9. For a serious and riveting double intellectual biography of the Hume–Smith friendship, see Dennis C. Rasmussen, *The Infidel and the Professor: David Hume, Adam Smith, and the Friendship That Shaped Modern Thought* (Princeton, NJ: Princeton University Press, 2017).

10. Stewart, *Account*, I.21 and R.S. Walker, *Correspondence of James Boswell and John Johnson of Grange.* (New York, NY: McGraw Hill, 1966), p. 7. The latter is quoted in Phillipson, *Adam Smith*, 134–35.

11. Adam Smith to Dr. Archibald Davidson, 16 Nov. 1787, *Corr.*, p. 274; Stewart, *Account*, V.10.

was immediately successful in Scotland as well as in London. Thanks in part to David Hume, who touted Smith's work among men of influence, *The Theory of Moral Sentiments* caught the eye of Charles Townshend, the soon-to-be Chancellor of the Exchequer of Great Britain. Townshend was evidently so taken by the work that he offered Smith a position as tutor for his stepson, the Duke of Buccleuch. It was a lucrative position—Smith received a handsome sum of £500 a year as the young Duke's tutor and a pension of £300 a year for the remainder of his life.

More important than the money, however, was the intellectual exposure that the position afforded Smith. Between 1764 and 1766, he traveled with the Duke to Toulouse, Geneva, Paris, and London where Smith encountered some of the most illustrious figures of the Enlightenment, among them Voltaire, François Quesnay, the Marquis de Mirabeau, and even Benjamin Franklin. Despite his terrible French, Smith was a welcome guest amongst these great luminaries.[12] Smith and the young Duke formed a lasting friendship, but the pace of life on tour was evidently too slow for the professor. While in Toulouse, Smith wrote to David Hume:

> The Progress, indeed, we have made is not very great. The Duke is acquainted with no French man whatever. I cannot cultivate the acquaintance of the few with whom I am acquainted, as I cannot bring them to our house and am not always at liberty to go to theirs. The Life which I led at Glasgow was a pleasurable, dissipated life in

12. Smith's famous awkwardness, mannerisms, and even physical appearance are subjects of much scholarly amusement. "He speaks harshly, with big teeth, and he's ugly as the devil. He's Mr. Smith, author of a book I haven't read," wrote one French novelist who met Smith in 1766. Apparently after meeting Smith, Voltaire wrote that "This Smith is an excellent man! We have nothing to compare with him, and I am embarrassed for my dear compatriots." These vignettes come from sources such as Madam Riccoboni to Robert Liston, in *Mme Riccoboni's letters to David Hume, David Garrick, and sir Robert Liston, 1764–1783*, ed. James C Nicholls (Oxford: Voltaire Foundation at the Taylor Institution, 1976), 71 and Voltaire, *Oeuvres Complètes*, ed. Beaumarchais, 70 vols. (Kehl: Imprimerie de la Société Littéraire-Typographique, 1784–1789), 21:1.71 and are quoted in Jerry Z. Muller, *Adam Smith in His Time and Ours: Designing the Decent Society* (Princeton, NJ: Princeton University Press, 1993), 15; Dennis Rasmussen, *The Problems and Promise of Commercial Society: Adam Smith's Response to Rousseau* (University Park, PA: Penn State Press, 2008), 53.

comparison of that which I lead here at Present. I have begun to write a book in order to pass away the time. You may believe I have very little to do.[13]

That book was *The Wealth of Nations*.

Published on March 9, 1776, *The Wealth of Nations* enlarged the "science of man" that Smith had begun in *The Theory of Moral Sentiments* by bringing to life his "science of political oeconomy." Over roughly a thousand pages, Smith argued that national wealth was measured not in money, but rather in the productive power of labor. He explained how wealth was accumulated and how it flowed, but he also showed how, throughout history, human institutions thwarted the natural order of things, stunting growth and hindering political and social progress. Most famously, Smith viciously attacked the commercial system of Great Britain, from what he saw as its illogical foundations of mercantilism to its destructive imperial projects run by an elite merchant class that had captured the state. Smith thus stood directly opposite James Steuart, whose *Inquiry into the Principles of Political Oeconomy* had appeared nine years earlier and who advocated state intervention in economic affairs, specifically the promotion of exports and taxes on imports so as to obtain a favorable balance of trade. At the same time, Smith's theory of national wealth and his arguments for free trade were critiques of his French counterparts like Quesnay and the physiocrats, who believed that wealth derived from agriculture alone, and that free trade could be directly imposed on societies. For Smith, manufacturing and commercial exchange also contributed to economic growth, and free trade would be the result of gradual reform, not revolutionary idealism. Though *The Wealth of Nations* would eventually become famous, even infamous, for its attack on mercantilism and its call for free trade, Smith devoted the most space to the fifth and final book in which he traced the emergence of modern states and outlined the political principles of sound policy and management of the modern economy. Despite its intimidating size, as well as the complexity and contentiousness of

13. Adam Smith to David Hume, July 1764. *Corr.*, p. 102.

its subject, *The Wealth of Nations* became a bestseller, with five editions printed within Smith's lifetime.[14]

The last fifteen years or so of Smith's life were filled with steady, quiet work in his native Scotland. He settled in Edinburgh at Panmure House with his mother, Margaret Douglas, his cousin Janet Douglas, and nine-year-old cousin and heir David Douglas. Smith took up a post in the Edinburgh Customs Board in 1777. The thought of Smith, the supposed prophet of free trade, collecting duties on imported goods and enforcing laws against smuggling is baffling at first, but Smith gave no indication that such a post went against his personal convictions. In his spare time (he only worked four days a week at the Customs House), Smith continued to revise *The Theory of Moral Sentiments* and *The Wealth of Nations*. Moreover, as mentioned previously, he had two other great works "upon the anvil," one of which was a "sort of theory and History of Law and Government" that he never completed.[15]

These were also years marked by sadness. His closest friend and mentor, David Hume, passed away in August of 1776, just a few months after *The Wealth of Nations* debuted. His mother, Margaret Douglas, with whom he lived for much of his life, passed away in 1784; his cousin Jane Douglas, who also lived with them, died in 1788. As his circle of loved ones slowly diminished, so too did Smith's energy. In the same letter to the Duc de la Rochefoucault in which Smith hinted at his works in progress, Smith expressed a profound personal weariness. "But the indolence of old age," he wrote, "tho' I struggle violently against it, I feel coming fast upon me, and whether I shall ever be able to finish either is extremely uncertain."[16] In the last years of his life, Smith continued to view himself as an extremely slow writer who would rather not see new editions of his works published without *all* of his revisions included. In 1788 Smith wrote to the London bookseller Thomas Cadell,

14. Richard B. Sher, *The Enlightenment and the Book: Scottish Authors and Their Publishers in Eighteenth-Century Britain, Ireland, and America* (Chicago IL: University of Chicago Press, 2010), 236–37.

15. Adam Smith to Le Duc de la Rochefoucauld, 1 Nov. 1785, *Corr.*, p. 286–287.

16. Adam Smith to Le Duc de la Rochefoucauld, 1 Nov. 1785, *Corr.*, p. 286–287.

As I consider my tenure of this life as extremely precarious, and am very uncertain whether I shall live to finish several other works which I have projected and in which I have made some progress, the best thing, I think, I can do is to leave those I have already published in the best and most perfect state behind me.[17]

Days before he died, Smith ordered all other remaining unfinished manuscripts burned. Only a handful of essays, which included his now-famous *History of Astronomy* and essays on ancient metaphysics and "the imitative arts" were spared and published posthumously. Smith passed away on July 17, 1790, and is buried in Edinburgh's Canongate Churchyard.

Given the relative lack of detail on Smith's life, biographers have been left with a daunting task: to take what otherwise appears to be an ordinary story of a man of letters and turn it into something extraordinary. Compared to some of his more dramatic contemporaries, Smith's life is mesmerizingly mundane. He had no major falling-outs with his intellectual interlocutors (Hume and Rousseau); he did not produce an outpouring of paranoid ravings or leave behind any orphaned children (again, Rousseau); nor did he traverse both the American and French Revolutions and narrowly escape the guillotine (Thomas Paine). Smith never even married, and barely appears to have had even a fleeting moment of romantic interest.[18] Even the second-hand stories of Smith's absent-mindedness, his abduction by roaming gypsies at a young age, and his endearing awkwardness are but bite-sized pieces of Smith

17. Smith continues in the letter, "I am a slow a very slow workman, who do and undo everything I write at least half a dozen of times before I can be tolerably pleased with it; and tho' I have now, I think, brought my work within compass, yet it will be the month of June before I shall be able to send it to you. I have told you already, and I need not tell you again, that I mean to make you a present of all my Additions. I must beg, therefore, that no new edition of that book may be published before that time." Letter from Adam Smith to Thomas Cadell, 15 Mar. 1788. *Corr.*, p. 311.

18. That Smith never married is both an accepted fact of Smith's life and indicative of its relative mundaneness. Ross writes, "It is to be feared that the biographer can do little more with the topic of Smith's sex life than contribute a footnote to the history of sublimation." Ross, *The Life of Adam Smith*, 228.

legend and lore.[19] Smith's correspondence is meager compared to other great Enlightenment-Era thinkers: Benjamin Franklin wrote or received over 15,000 letters in his lifetime; Voltaire's correspondence amounts to an astonishing 19,000 letters. Even on the lower end, Condorcet's correspondence includes some 2,000 letters (most unpublished), and David Hume's correspondence contains around 500 letters. The *Correspondence of Adam Smith*, meanwhile, contains just over 300 letters. Even finding an image of Smith is a struggle. The only surviving images are two medallions by John Tassie, and two sketches by the Scottish caricaturist John Kay. In Kay's earliest image of Smith (sketched in 1787, see Fig. 0.1), Smith wears a broad-brimmed hat, holds a handful of flowers in one hand, and has his cane propped on his right shoulder like a musket. Kay sketched Smith's portrait between Alexander Gordon, Lord Rockville, the Senator of the College of Justice, and George Brown, Commissioner of the Board of Excise for Scotland, who both gaze into the circle in which Smith is inscribed. In Kay's rendering, Smith literally inhabits his own bubble.[20]

Imagining Smith as isolated in his own world aligns with a common narrative that suggests Smith was unconcerned with his reception and reputation, despite his fastidiousness and perfectionist tendencies. Especially with regards to *The Wealth of Nations*, Smith thought himself "rather lucky than otherwise" that he was "much less abused than [he] had reason to respect," compared to the uproar he caused writing a

19. Nearly every major biographical account relishes accounts of Smith's absent-mindedness. One unverified anecdote, for example, recalls Smith giving a tour to Charles Townshend at a local tannery, and falling into a tanning pit while he was "talking warmly on his favourite subject, the division of labour." Ross, *The Life of Adam Smith*, 160. Others include Smith's tendency to talk to himself incessantly, wandering in his reveries clad in his nightgown. Robert L. Heilbroner, *The Worldly Philosophers: The Lives, Times, and Ideas of the Great Economic Thinkers*. Rev. 7th ed. (New York, NY: Simon & Schuster, 1999), 42, 45. According to Nicholas Phillipson, Smith's last years of his life as a public figure generated an abundance of mythmaking around these quirks. Phillipson, *Adam Smith*, 260.

20. John Kay made two sketches of Adam Smith—the one described in 1787, and one in 1790 entitled "The Author of the Wealth of Nations," the latter of which depicts Smith by himself. The only other portraits we have of Smith that were created during his lifetime are the medallions by James Tassie, after which many sketches and paintings were created posthumously.

FIG. 0.1. Alexander Gordon, Lord Rockville (left); Adam Smith (center);
George Brown (right) by John Kay, 1787. © National Portrait Gallery, London.
This is the earliest known sketch of Smith by John Kay.

"very harmless Sheet of paper" regarding the late David Hume.[21] In another letter to his publisher Strahan, Smith sarcastically commented, "I had almost forgot I was the Author of the enquiry concerning the Wealth of Nations," and that it was only upon learning that the work was

21. Letter from Adam Smith to Andreas Holt, 26 October 1780, *Corr.*, 251. The offending sheet of paper was a letter dated November 9, 1776, to William Strahan, Smith's publisher (*Corr.*,

being translated into Danish that he became aware of the reach of his work.[22] That Smith never actively recruited his own disciples or sought followers further reinforces the idea that he was not in the business of self-consciously constructing a tradition.[23]

But the tradition-making, myth-making, and re-inventions of Adam Smith and his ideas began almost immediately after his death in 1790. Smith's reputation and influence had already traversed across national borders in the last quarter of the eighteenth century, and his international reputation invites us to think critically about what makes his American reception distinctive. In Great Britain, writers such as James Steuart (1707–1780) and Josiah Tucker (1713–1799) preceded Smith on matters political economy. Steuart's *An Inquiry into the Principles of Political Oeconomy* (1767) had received high praise from reviewers and had been considered the "principal reference on economics" for the *Encyclopedia Britannica*. Sales of Steuart's work were disappointing, however, and that did not bode well for Smith's *The Wealth of Nations* ten years later. Though Smith's work became an "unlikely best seller," *The Wealth of Nations* was not the sole cause of Smith's rise to fame.[24] As Salim Rashid has argued, the success of Smith's works and his personal fame were highly contingent upon the good graces of close friends who were intellectual heavyweights (such as David Hume and John Millar) and admirers in Parliament such as William Pitt, Charles James Fox, and

---

p. 217–221), which was subsequently published. Smith's intent in writing the letter was more than just supplementing Hume's autobiography by providing an account of the last few months of his life. While Smith was cautious in not painting a portrait of Hume that would offend religious zealots even more, the letter nevertheless portrayed Hume as an iconic philosopher and "unashamed pagan who had faced death cheerfully." See Phillipson, *Adam Smith*, 244; Rasmussen, *The Problems and Promise of Commercial Society*; Rasmussen, *The Infidel and the Professor*.

22. Letter from Adam Smith to William Strahan, October 26, 1780. *Corr.*, no. 207.

23. Teichgraeber III, "Adam Smith and Tradition: The Wealth of Nations before Malthus," in Stefan Collini, Richard Whatmore, and Brian Young, eds., *Economy, Polity, and Society: British Intellectual History 1750–1950* (Cambridge: Cambridge University Press, 2000), 90.

24. Salim Rashid, "Adam Smith's Rise to Fame: A Reexamination of the Evidence," *The Eighteenth Century* 23, no. 1 (1982), 71, 79–85; Sher, *The Enlightenment and the Book*, 236, Appendix Table 2, 636.

Lord Shelburne.[25] Thus, Smith's later reputation as the founder of political economy is neither historically accurate nor was it inevitable.

Moreover, Smith's uptake in late-eighteenth and early-nineteenth century British party politics enabled *The Wealth of Nations* to outlive its time. The introduction of ideas from political economic texts played a significant role in shaping political discourse, and it had the potential to reinvent the reputation of an author like Smith. Kirk Willis has shown how personal friends and acquaintances of Smith's, students of economic or financial policy, and radical and Foxite Whigs (followers of the prominent MP Charles James Fox) cited Smith in eighteenth-century parliamentary debate, but with little interest in a deeper examination of the principles or implications of his ideas. Rather, Smith was quoted as "just another technical expert."[26] This type of usage was central to Smith's posthumous reputation; it showed how Smith's ideas could be useful tools on the one hand, or wielded as dangerous political and ideological weapons on the other.

The French Revolution had the greatest immediate impact on Smith's European reception. In both France and Great Britain, proponents on all sides used Smith's ideas to support opposing views on morals and politics before, during, and after the Revolution.[27] *The Wealth of Nations* had already become famous not long after its publication, and it had been translated into French five times by 1786.[28] Radical constitutional reformers like Emmanuel Joseph Sieyes were among the first to take hold of Smith's ideas, especially Smith's evaluations of different states' capacities to promote liberty and protect private property.[29] After 1789,

25. Rashid, "Adam Smith's Rise to Fame."

26. Kirk Willis, "The Role in Parliament of the Economic Ideas of Adam Smith, 1776–1800," *History of Political Economy* 11, no. 4 (November 1979), 509–10.

27. Richard Whatmore, "Adam Smith's Role in the French Revolution," *Past & Present*, no. 175 (2002), 88.

28. Gilbert Faccarello and Philippe Steiner, "The Diffusion of the Work of Adam Smith in the French Language: An Outline History," *Économies et Sociétés*, no. 10 (1995), 5–30. Reprinted in Keith Tribe and Hiroshi Mizuta, eds., *A Critical Bibliography of Adam Smith* (London: Pickering & Chatto, 2002), 61–119.

29. For a detailed analysis of Sieyes' reading of Smith, see Whatmore, "Adam Smith's Role in the French Revolution," 75–83.

figures like the Marquis de Condorcet turned Smith's ideas into the "voice of revolution," demanding that extracts of *The Wealth of Nations* be published alongside critiques of the work in order to promote reason and stave off civil conflict.[30] Smith's association with French revolutionary zeal, sedition, and dissenting public opinion travelled back to England. After Smith's death in 1790, obituaries noted that his ideas had drawn attention to "subjects that unfortunately have become too popular in most countries of Europe."[31] Following the Reign of Terror, Smith's *The Theory of Moral Sentiments* captivated the French.[32] This revived interest in Smith's moral theory reflected a growing public concern with the transformation of popular culture and public mores, cultivating sympathetic relations between rich and poor, and a desire to understand the morality of law from an impartial standpoint.[33]

Meanwhile, German readers of Adam Smith in the eighteenth century appeared only mildly enthusiastic about his works.[34] The early

30. Richard Whatmore, "Adam Smith's Role in the French Revolution," 83–89.

31. *The Times*, August 16, 1790, p. 4. For more on the British reception of the revolutionary interpretation of Smith, see also Emma Rothschild, "Adam Smith and Conservative Economics," *The Economic History Review* 45, no. 1 (February 1992), 75.

32. The belated success of Smith's *The Theory of Moral Sentiments* is somewhat surprising since the work did not do very well in its early lifetime in France. Faccarello and Steiner, "The Diffusion of the Work of Adam Smith in the French Language," 10.

33. For more on the reception of *The Theory of Moral Sentiments* after 1789 in France, see also Ruth Scurr, "Inequality and Political Stability from Ancien Régime to Revolution: The Reception of Adam Smith's *Theory of Moral Sentiments* in France," *History of European Ideas* 35, no. 4 (December 2009), 441–49; Laurie Bréban and Jean Dellemotte, "From One Form of Sympathy to Another: Sophie de Grouchy's Translation of and Commentary on Adam Smith's Theory of Moral Sentiments," Working Paper (HAL Open Science, April 4, 2016), accessed January 25, 2018, https://econpapers.repec.org/paper/halwpaper/hal-01435828.htm; Sandrine Bergés and Eric Schliesser, eds., *Sophie de Grouchy's Letters on Sympathy: A Critical Engagement with Adam Smith's The Theory of Moral Sentiments* (New York: Oxford University Press, 2019); Kathleen McCrudden, "Sophie de Grouchy as an Activist Interpreter of Adam Smith," in Paul Sagar, ed., *Interpreting Adam Smith: Critical Essays* (Cambridge: Cambridge University Press, forthcoming).

34. Keith Tribe is the authoritative scholar on Smith's German reception. See Keith Tribe, *Governing Economy: The Reformation of German Economic Discourse, 1750–1840* (Cambridge: Cambridge University Press, 1988), chap. 7; Keith Tribe, *Strategies of Economic Order: German Economic Discourse, 1750–1950* (Cambridge: Cambridge University Press, 1995), 25–33.

reception of Smith's *The Wealth of Nations* was largely overshadowed by the prevailing influence of the French physiocrats such as the Marquis de Mirabeau, Richard Cantillon, and François Quesnay. Furthermore, in contrast to Great Britain, James Steuart's *Principles of Political Oeconomy* was better known and more widely cited in Germany than Smith's *The Wealth of Nations*. Two rather poor German translations (one appearing between 1776 and 1779, the second in 1794) partially explain the lukewarm reception but do not completely account for Smith's lackluster performance among German audiences. Of greater importance were the demands that German readers brought to extant theories of political economy. For instance, James Steuart's economic nationalism was more easily assimilable to the emerging tradition of German cameralism, or the science of administration, than Smith's "system of natural liberty." Interest in *The Wealth of Nations* dissipated almost as quickly as it appeared. As Keith Tribe has documented, between the 1780s and 1790s, "the work was all but ignored by those professionally concerned with the issues that it addressed."[35] After 1790, encounters with Smith's works changed quite dramatically in Germany; there was a "growing receptiveness" to Smith's *The Wealth of Nations* as a canonical work of political economy. However, Tribe's analysis suggests that this growing receptiveness was "due not to the intrinsic merits of *Wealth of Nations* as the charter for a new economy," but rather, as in England and in France, due to a changing political and intellectual tide that brought with it the renewed interest in natural law and critical philosophy.[36]

Against this backdrop of the French Revolution's denouement, political contestation over economic knowledge in Britain, and the growing marketplace of political and economic ideas across Europe, we must place the first major work of Smith reinvention: Dugald Stewart's *Account of the Life and Writings of Adam Smith, LL.D.* Serving the role of both eulogy (it was read aloud before the Royal Society of Edinburgh in 1793) and biography (it was published in the *Transactions* of the Royal Society in 1794 and again in 1795 alongside the works that Smith had

35. Tribe, *Governing Economy*, 145.
36. Tribe, *Governing Economy*, 150.

saved from the flames), Stewart's *Account* is, in a word, "frustrating." Not only does Stewart leave a number of subjects unaddressed, his portrait of Smith is deliberately defensive.[37] That is, Stewart was fully aware of Smith's associations with dangerous ideas, not just those of the French Revolution, but also those belonging to radical constitutional reformers in Scotland and England. Thus, his main concern was to dissociate Adam Smith from revolutionary tendencies and to neutralize the overly political connotations of political economy. Stewart minimized the relationship between Adam Smith and his French influences and readers, while magnifying the personal qualities of Smith as a teacher, mentor, and polite but endearingly absent-minded genius. Portraying Smith as a "retiring, innocuous sort of person" and political economy as an "innocuous, technical sort of subject" helped construct a politically safe legacy for Smith during politically dangerous times.[38]

Perhaps of greater consequence was Stewart's reorientation of Smith's politics, or rather, Stewart's separation of Smith's politics from his political economy. In order to distance Smith from the revolutionary obsession with political liberty that had plagued France and parts of Great Britain, Stewart separated Smith's concept of political liberty from commercial liberty—freedom of trade and industry which Smith ferociously advocated—to prove that liberty was not always desirable. Under certain circumstances, political liberty could be "the means of accomplishing [a people's] own ruin" as the Revolution in France and subsequent Terror demonstrated.[39] Stewart downplayed Smith's more politically subversive moments, and shone a spotlight on what he thought was one of "the most important opinions in *The Wealth of Nations*:" that "Little else is requisite to carry a state to the highest degree

37. James Buchan, "The Biography of Adam Smith," in *Adam Smith: His Life, Thought, and Legacy*, ed. Ryan Patrick Hanley (Princeton, NJ: Princeton University Press, 2016), 10, 11. As James Buchan comments, "Stewart also set several hares racing, which his successors have endeavored to run down, long after they had passed under the hedge. What did Smith do or think in those six years at Oxford in the 1740s? What happened to those elements of his 'Jurisprudence' lectures that did not make it into the *Wealth of Nations*? And what, precisely, were the manuscripts burned that day in Smith's bedroom at Panmure house . . . ?"

38. Rothschild, "Adam Smith and Conservative Economics," 81–82.

39. Stewart, *Account*, IV.5.

of opulence from the lowest barbarism, but peace, easy taxes, and a tolerable administration of justice; all the rest being brought about by the natural course of things."[40] For these reasons, many intellectual historians see Stewart's portrait as marking the beginning of Smith's association with conservative economics.[41]

Thus, Smith's early reception in Europe reveals the contingencies of his reputation and impact. Receptions and translations of Smith's *The Wealth of Nations* in several non-English speaking countries—China, Denmark, India, Japan, Russia, and Spain to name a few—suggest a similar story.[42] No single interpretation of either *The Theory of Moral Sentiments* or *The Wealth of Nations* dominates, nor are their meanings stable over time. Reading and engaging with Smith's works is hardly a passive or neutral transmission process; instead, it is an active process of charging his ideas with—or in some cases, defusing them of—political value that suits the particular needs of the reader at a particular time.[43]

While scholarship on the global reception and diffusion of Smith's ideas has grown, there is surprisingly little on Smith in the United States. This is perhaps even more surprising given the vast scholarship on the

40. Stewart, *Account*, IV.25.

41. My analysis in this paragraph and use of the word "conservative" is with intentional reference to Emma Rothschild's work on Smith's association with conservative economics. Rothschild provides no concrete definition of "conservative" in her work, but her concluding paragraph provides a way to understand Smith's association with conservatism with regards to notions of freedom. A "revolutionary" or "radical" interpretation of Smith is one that sees him as championing a multifaceted conception of freedom that consists "in not being interfered with by others: in any aspect of life, and by any outside forces (churches, parishes overseers, corporations, customs inspectors, national governments, masters, proprietors)." By contrast, a "conservative" construction of Smith is much narrower and is stripped of that multifaceted quality: freedom was little more "than the freedom not to be interfered with in one side of one's life (the economic), and by one outside force (national government)." Rothschild, "Adam Smith and Conservative Economics," 94.

42. Two major edited volumes have been published on Smith's global reception: Cheng-Chung Lai, ed., *Adam Smith Across Nations: Translations and Receptions of The Wealth of Nations* (Oxford: Clarendon Press, 2000); Hiroshi Mizuta and Chuhei Sugiyama, *Adam Smith: International Perspectives* (London: Palgrave Macmillan UK, 1993).

43. Here I borrow the idea of a non-neutral transmission process in reception history from Jennifer Ratner-Rosenhagen, *American Nietzsche: A History of an Icon and His Ideas* (Chicago, IL: University of Chicago Press, 2012), 26.

influence of the Scottish Enlightenment during the American Founding Era.[44] Moving forward nearly two hundred years, scholars primarily in the history of economic thought have drawn out the role of Smith's ideas in twentieth-century economics broadly construed.[45] By looking at Smith's American reception through a wider historical lens, this book hopes to offer a greater sense of continuity as well as change over time. Yet, this book also aspires to do more than fill a scholarly lacuna. While I do not presume that there is anything uniquely American about this story, I argue there is great historical value in understanding the reasons why readers in a certain place are continually returning to the same text again and again.

What first interested me in Adam Smith's reception history is the gulf between the popular caricatures of Smith on the one hand, and his reputation among most scholars on the other. How, when, and why did

44. One notable exception is Samuel Fleischacker's important essay on Adam Smith and the Founders, which situated Smith's early reception within the context of the transatlantic Enlightenment and broadened standards of detecting Smith's influence through close textual analysis. For Fleischacker, the similarities "between the concerns, arguments, and language of Smith and those of the generation that established the American republic" provide ample evidence of Smith's extensive influence in the Founders' thinking on decidedly "American" issues—standing armies, separation of church and state, political factions, and the relationship between private interest and public good. Samuel Fleischacker, "Adam Smith's Reception among the American Founders, 1776–1790," *The William and Mary Quarterly* 59, no. 4 (2002), 897–924.

45. I engage with this literature in more detail in Chapters 5 and 6, but a few key references are worth noting. On the use of Smith's ideas, especially the "invisible hand" metaphor in twentieth-century economics, see Steven G. Medema, "Adam Smith and the Chicago School," in *The Elgar Companion to the Chicago School of Economics*, ed. Ross B. Emmett (Cheltenham: Edward Elgar, 2010), 40–51; Gavin Kennedy, "Paul Samuelson and the Invention of the Modern Economics of the Invisible Hand," *History of Economic Ideas* 18, no. 3 (2010), 105–19; Gavin Kennedy, "Adam Smith and the Role of the Metaphor of an Invisible Hand," *Economic Affairs* 31, no. 1 (March 2011), 53–57; Daniel Stedman Jones, *Masters of the Universe: Hayek, Friedman, and the Birth of Neoliberal Politics* (Princeton, NJ: Princeton University Press, 2012); Angus Burgin, *The Great Persuasion: Reinventing Free Markets Since the Depression* (Cambridge, MA: Harvard University Press, 2012); Warren J. Samuels, Marianne F. Johnson, and William W. Perry, eds., *Erasing the Invisible Hand: Essays on an Elusive and Misused Concept in Economics* (Cambridge: Cambridge University Press, 2014); Franz F. Eiffe, "Amartya Sen Reading Adam Smith," *History of Economics Review* 51, no. 1 (January 2010), 1–23; Vivian Walsh, "Smith after Sen," *Review of Political Economy* 12, no. 1 (January 2000), 5–26.

Smith become known primarily as an economist—specifically, a free-market economist—rather than as an enlightenment moral philosopher? Among the many canonical thinkers that one can reference, why do people continue to return to Adam Smith? Reception history can help us answer these questions. It helps us understand how and why some ideas become powerful and politically meaningful, while others fall to the wayside, but more generally, reception history can reveal how certain ways of thinking and ways of approaching a text come into being. It can shed light on some of the reasons why *The Wealth of Nations* became such an important and common departure point for the formation of American political economy, and why it became a politicized text. Reception history can help explain why some past readers were relatively uninterested in *The Theory of Moral Sentiments* for most of its afterlife, while many readers today see it as essential to understanding Smith's historical importance and practical relevance. There is something about Smith's works themselves—whether it is his literary talents or the perennial nature of the inquiries which he pursued—that have enabled them to speak across time, to seem so familiar more than two hundred years after they were written. I argue, however, that this sense of timelessness and familiarity is not an inherent feature of Smith's texts, but rather, something that is made, invented, and preserved by readers over time.

ADAM SMITH'S AMERICA

Introduction

ADAM SMITH'S AMERICA offers a new way to understand the meaning and significance of Adam Smith's ideas through the eyes of his past readers. It shows how Smith's American reception teaches us just as much, if not more, about the political, ideological, and methodological commitments that those ideas were recruited to serve as they teach us about Smith himself.

During the Founding Era, an elite cadre of American figures saw Smith's works as contributions to the Enlightenment science of man. His writings were broadly useful because they distilled general, universal principles of man and society which could be set into motion as part of the "science of the legislator" in the project of nation-building. Not until the 1820s would Americans begin to treat political economy as more than just a branch of statecraft; not until then did it become a science worthy of pursuing in its own right. In their efforts to outline a science of political economy that was fit for American circumstances, writers, educators, and popular figures also invented Smith's authoritative status. By designating *The Wealth of Nations* as the origin point of the science of political economy, American political economists turned Smith into a figure who simultaneously commanded reverence and inspired criticism.

Debates over free trade throughout the nineteenth century transformed the terms on which Americans engaged with Smith's ideas. In the hands of free trade proponents, *The Wealth of Nations* became a political weapon that defended the scientific legitimacy of free trade politics; in the hands of opponents, on the other hand, Smith's ideas represented an outmoded, dangerous, and un-American vision of national wealth and glory. Late-nineteenth-century debates in the economics profession, though they never fully stripped Smith of his associations with free trade, raised new questions about the political relevance of his works. Arguments about the correct socio-ethical orientation of economics were projected onto Smith. "New Generation" economists saw Smith's methodological eclecticism and political theory as an antidote to the extremisms of laissez-faire on the one hand and socialism on the other.

Yet the complexity and pluralism of those readings would be overshadowed by the influence of the so-called Chicago School's distillation of Smith's ideas into a popular and powerful myth: that rational self-interest is the only valid premise for the analysis of human behavior, and that only the invisible hand of the market, not the heavy hand of government, could guarantee personal and political freedom. This version of Adam Smith has become so recognizable in scholarship and in the public imagination that few have questioned its origins and purpose. I argue that the "Chicago Smith" was a deliberate construction and product of its time and place. Chicago economists over different generations repeatedly turned to Smith's ideas to construct the content of a new liberal creed and to defend a unique analytic method, but they did so in ways that ultimately diminished, if not excluded, other interpretations of Smith and his ideas. In the last quarter of the twentieth century, though, major attempts were made to push back on the "Chicago Smith" and to recover Smith as a political and moral thinker in his own right.

This book treats reception history as the line between intention and impact. Reception explains the difference between what Smith might have originally meant or intended, and what subsequent readers *made* of his ideas. Thus, I am less interested in providing a definitive account of what Smith originally intended or meant than I am in elucidating the demands that his readers have brought to his works and how that colored the lessons they have extracted from them. I adopt the language used by a number of historians of encountering, confronting, interpreting, and even appropriating to make clear that reception is a process of active creation, invention, and transformation.[1] Taking reception history seriously requires that we try to see different possibilities for a text in different times and places. We have to excavate and study the layers of historical accretions on and around an author and his or her ideas to understand how they served purposes that might be radically different from the ones they serve today.

One of the central arguments of this book is that successive constructions of Smith's significance and import often tell us less about the content of Smith's ideas themselves, and more about the grounds on which his interpreters believed his authority rested. In the eighteenth century, America's Founders saw Smith's ideas about banking, factions, the division of labor, and sympathy as useful because they appealed to enlightenment sensibilities about how to understand the governing dynamics of man in society. In the nineteenth century, assumptions about the scientific, timeless insights of his science of political economy enabled Smith's ideas to exert newfound power in political debate. Perhaps most famously, The Chicago School used Smith to represent a belief in the scientific rationality of markets in opposition to the messy irrationality of politics. That view has since been challenged, predominantly by historians of political thought and political philosophers who have argued that Smith's distinctiveness lies not just in his economic thought, but in his moral philosophy. In other words, the value of Smith's ideas has always been political. However, in contrast to being inherent in the texts, much of the political value stems from different assumptions about the objectivity and normativity of the science he supposedly invented. What I explore in this book, then, are the different ways in which

1. I am particularly indebted to the pioneering work of Jennifer Ratner-Rosenhagen in her *American Nietzsche*, as well as Daniel T. Rodgers, *As a City on a Hill: The Story of America's Most Famous Lay Sermon*, (Princeton, NJ: Princeton University Press 2018); Emily Jones, *Edmund Burke and the Invention of Modern Conservatism, 1830–1914: An Intellectual History*, (Oxford: Oxford University Press, 2017). My ideas and methods in this book have also benefitted immensely from—and indeed were inspired by—repeated conversations with Claire Rydell Arcenas and her forthcoming book, *America's Philosopher: John Locke in American Intellectual Life* (Chicago, IL: Chicago University Press, forthcoming), and Andrew Hartman and his forthcoming book on Karl Marx's American reception, *Marx in America* (Chicago, IL: Chicago University Press, forthcoming).

Americans constructed meaning out of Smith's texts and what they hoped they could gain—conceptually and politically—from doing so.

Smith's reception in America is a story about what I call "the politics of political economy." This phrase, as I see it, has two meanings. First, immediate political and economic circumstances shape the kinds of ideas that are produced and the way those ideas are consumed. This is obvious but worth restating, if only because political economic ideas—especially Smith's ideas—are often seen as transcending the time and place for which they were originally written. But the second meaning is this: political economy is a language of authority. It is a language constructed by people in positions of power who hold competing conceptions of what American political economy looks like and how one ought to go about understanding it. The way in which various readers, writers, and speakers have portrayed Smith, used his ideas, and made claims about his importance are discursive choices. These portrayals can be used as tools or weapons, and as such, they can reveal as much as they can conceal. For instance, in the antebellum free trade debates, the insistence on Smith's authority as "the founder of the science" by legislators from the Cotton South cast the issue of trade in the universalizing language of political economy, thereby averting—though ultimately unsuccessfully—the polarizing language of slavery, and occluding the fact that a national economy built on "free trade" depended on the most unfree of labor. The Chicago School's Smith relied on a conceptualization of free markets as not only freedom-enhancing but also scientifically and objectively validated; but leaning into the outsized role of self-interest and the invisible hand deliberately minimized the importance of other forces and institutions beyond the market—forces and institutions which Smith himself discussed at length in *The Theory of Moral Sentiments* and *The Lectures on Jurisprudence*.

Claims about Smith's contribution, his relevance or irrelevance to contemporary issues, his approach to political economy and (or even *as*) moral philosophy are political statements, whether about the scientific validity of free trade, the rationality of free markets over state direction, or even the morality of market societies. The impulse to portray political economy and economics, especially Smith's version of economics, as an objective science is deeply embedded in the history and politics of the discipline. And this has consequences for how *The Theory of Moral Sentiments* and other of Smith's works are incorporated—or ignored—into the discursive frameworks used to describe and understand the entanglement of politics and the modern economy.

Importantly, the reception history I chart here is selective rather than comprehensive. That is to say, this book does not try to track down and trace every reference or instance of using Smith. At the same time, it is not a history of reading Smith. Of course, reading is an important aspect of this history, and I refer to most of my primary subjects as Smith's readers. Book history and readership studies—book production and book sales, catalogues and subscription lists, publication and republication, circulation, dissemination, and the like—are part of this history, but they are not constitutive of it. Instead, this book documents what might be called inflection points in the process of canonization. Chapter 1 opens in the Founding Era, when Americans were reading Smith's works during his own lifetime and shortly after his death. Smith's works represented an enlightened way of thinking about man in society, but Americans were more interested in the usefulness of Smith's ideas for the art of statecraft than they were in deploying his intellectual authority. Smith, in other words, was not yet "ADAM SMITH." While much of my survey of this period synthesizes existing scholarship, it nevertheless provides an important prelude—and contrast—to what follows.

Adam Smith's authority as the agreed-upon founder of political economy crystallized in the early nineteenth century with the development of academic political economy in the United States, the subject of Chapter 2. Chapter 3 draws on and substantially reworks an essay published as "'The Apostle of Free Trade:' Adam Smith and the nineteenth-century American trade debates," and shows how uses of Smith's intellectual authority became an explicitly political statement in debates about free trade throughout the nineteenth century.[2] Canonized as the

2. Glory M. Liu, "'The Apostle of Free Trade:' Adam Smith and the Nineteenth-Century American Trade Debates," *History of European Ideas* 44, no. 2 (February 2018), 210–23.

"apostle of free trade," Smith became a political symbol that politicians sought either to align themselves with or distance themselves from. However, by the late 1880s, this tendency to use Smith, and the language of political economy more generally, polemically caused rifts to widen within the economics profession. Chapter 4 shows how a new generation of progressive economists began to challenge this image of Smith as a laissez-faire dogmatist. Shifting political concerns as well as bibliographical discoveries—most importantly, the *Lectures on Jurisprudence*—made doubtful the earlier, one-dimensional views of Smith as a materialist and apologist for laissez-faire. After the Great Depression, the rise of the powerhouse of the Chicago School of economics transformed Smith into a theorist of the universal axiom of self-interest and the miracle of free markets. This is a major turning point which I explore across Chapters 5 and 6, which jointly expand upon an earlier essay published in *Modern Intellectual History*.[3] But the caricature of Smith as a would-be member of the Chicago economics department drew forth criticism, sparking not only the first wave of revisionist scholarship, but also a neoconservative critique of market society. I explore these themes in Chapter 7.

In each chapter I focus on some of the dominant questions, issues, and intellectual debates of the time, and show how those questions shaped the way Americans engaged with Smith in that particular period. I have intentionally made these historiographic choices with an eye toward some of the central interpretive problems and themes that have defined scholarship on Smith over time: his role as the "founder" of economics (Chapter 2), his status as a free trade symbol (Chapter 3), the "Adam Smith Problem" (Chapter 4), his reputation as a "Chicago-style economics professor *avant la lettre*" and association with the free-market politics of the American right (Chapters 5 and 6), and efforts to recover a thicker conception of his politics and moral vision of capitalism (Chapter 7). In tracing the origins of these aspects of Smith's posthumous reputation, I seek to complicate, rather than to settle or debunk

3. Glory M. Liu, "Rethinking the 'Chicago Smith' Problem: Adam Smith and the Chicago School, 1929–1980," *Modern Intellectual History* 17, no. 4 (2020), 1041–68.

their mythological quality. Put another way, this book does not try to "save" Adam Smith by holding the line against anachronism, abuse, ahistorical readings, and the like. That work, done primarily by Smith experts across a variety of fields, is undeniably important for our understanding of Smith and his ideas, as I discuss in Chapter 7 and elsewhere in the book. But that is not one of my primary aims here. As scholars have noted, the history of Smith is full of ahistorical, anachronistic, attenuated readings. Nevertheless, we would do well to understand what purpose those readings have served and what consequences they have had—not just for how Smith's works are read, but how they shape discourse around politics and economics.[4]

A particular challenge of writing the reception history of Adam Smith in America is that he was not the stuff of legends for quite some time. Moreover, many of Smith's American commentators were parochial figures, and even the more well-known—such as the Founders or Milton Friedman—did not produce theoretically rich, thick commentary on Smith for the ages. Thus, the subjects and sources on which I base my study point toward what Sarah E. Igo calls a "free-range intellectual history," or at least a *freer*-range intellectual history. The meaning and implications of Smith's ideas have often been publicly debated and claimed; they have shaped popular notions of Smith and have been popularly shaped as well.[5] The people who have participated in these debates and made these claims are of a wide array: from founding statesmen to rank-and-file legislators; academic economists and social theorists to public intellectuals and critics. In the eighteenth century, major political and economic treatises shed light on the immediate practical importance of Smith's ideas, while book histories, reviews, and literary

4. Rodgers, *As a City on a Hill*; Rothschild, "Adam Smith and Conservative Economics;" Richard Teichgraeber III, "Adam Smith and Tradition: The Wealth of Nations before Malthus," in *Economy, Polity, and Society*, ed. Stefan Collini, Richard Whatmore, and Brian Young (Cambridge: Cambridge University Press, 2000), 85–104; Richard F. Teichgraeber, "'Less Abused than I Had Reason to Expect': The Reception of *The Wealth of Nations* in Britain, 1776–90," *The Historical Journal* 30, no. 02 (1987), 337–66; Keith Tribe, "Adam Smith: Critical Theorist?," *Journal of Economic Literature* 37, no. 2 (1999), 609–32.

5. Sarah E. Igo, "Toward a Free-Range Intellectual History," in Joel Isaac et al., *The Worlds of American Intellectual History* (Oxford: Oxford University Press, 2016), 324–42.

publications reveal the diffuse, eclectic, and even protean nature of political economy and moral philosophy at the time. In the chapters on academic political economy (Chapters 2 and 4), the extremely well-documented histories of economic thought and economics education have provided a strong foundation for understanding Smith's role in the development of economics as a discipline. Alongside this literature, I turn to a wide range of published materials—textbooks, journal articles, review essays, and the like—as well as archival materials such as student notebooks, professors' lecture notes, course syllabi and catalogues. Together, these sources offer a closer look at the patterns and processes that shaped understandings of Smith's significance. In Chapter 3 on free trade, I rely heavily on records of Congressional debates such as the *Annals of Congress*, the *Register of Debates, Congressional Globe*, and the *Congressional Record*. Local newspapers often reprinted and summarized speeches from the Congress floor, while major literary magazines like *The North American Review* offered insights into contemporary political and economic issues with an academic sensibility. Finally, the chapters on the Chicago School (Chapters 5 and 6) afforded me the opportunity to make the most out of archival materials, documentaries, magazine columns, and even popular iconography. What I hope this freer-range approach shows is that Smith's ideas—and ideas *about* Smith—do not always appear in clearly-marked and tidy packages, but are often messy, fragmented, and sometimes disguised.

This book is not about American "Smithians," nor does it aim to provide a balance sheet of legitimate and illegitimate legatees of Smith's ideas. As Knud Haakonssen and Donald Winch have argued, legacy attribution and evaluation not only require a "verdict" on which lines of inquiry springing from Smith are more or less productive, but also "that we can distinguish between what properly belongs to Smith and those accretions that reflect the preoccupations of his legatees." My approach, by contrast, is closer to what Haakonssen and Winch classify as the study of *fortuna*: "the reception, influence, diffusion, translation, and reputation enjoyed by Smith's writings as they have made their way into the world." However, *fortuna*, I believe, is a misnomer. Reception, influence, translation, and reputation are not passively enjoyed by

Smith's writings as they are tossed about by the winds of fortune; rather, these modes of transmission are *created* by human actors, who themselves are subject to, responding to, and even fashioning the "vicissitudes of opinion at various times and places." This is more than a matter of recapturing a "diachronic stock market valuation" over time, as Haakonssen and Winch describe; it is a way of understanding *how* and *why* certain people wanted to shape, control, or inherit Smith's legacy as they viewed it.[6]

Thus, I have adopted a particular angle when approaching my source material. Rather than relying on faint "verbal echoes," identifying arguments reminiscent of Smith's ideas, or using Smith's arguments as frameworks for interpreting those of others, I rely on direct attributions, verbatim or near-verbatim quotations, invocations, and critiques.[7] I suspect that some people will find this too narrow. However, following Keith Tribe, I emphasize that this perspective gives us a much closer view of what those who had occasion to engage with Smith saw in him and believed he represented.[8] One of the underlying assumptions of this perspective, therefore, is that there are reasons people are turning to Smith and choosing to invoke, quote, criticize, or attribute ideas to him. This book aims to show that those choices are politically significant, not necessarily because they directly influence policy outcomes, but because they give us insight into how certain ideas enter the political stream, how they are used to define the scope and method of studying

6. Knud Haakonssen and Donald Winch, "The Legacy of Adam Smith," in Knud Haakonssen, *The Cambridge Companion to Adam Smith*, Cambridge Companions to Philosophy (Cambridge: Cambridge University Press, 2006), 367.

7. Samuel Fleischacker's work on Smith's reception among the American Founders skillfully combines circumstantial evidence, metrics of readership and reception, and analysis of parallel arguments along the lines of "identifying verbal echoes." Fleischacker, "Adam Smith's Reception among the American Founders." Lisa Pace Vetter's *The Political Thought of America's Founding Feminists* (New York, NY: New York University Press, 2017) uses Smith's *Theory of Moral Sentiments* and *Lectures on Rhetoric and Belles Lettres* as a framework for understanding the contributions of early American feminist writers such as Fanny Wright, Harriet Martineau, Sarah Grimke, and Elizabeth Cady Stanton.

8. Keith Tribe, "'Das Adam Smith Problem' and the Origins of Modern Smith Scholarship," *History of European Ideas* 34, no. 4 (2008), 514–25.

politics and economics, and how they frame central issues of political economy.[9]

One unavoidable and unfortunate consequence of this book's approach and its emphasis on the process of canonization, however, is that it primarily deals with people in positions of power—whether in government, the academy, or in society more generally. The voices featured in this book are overwhelmingly white, male, affluent, and highly educated. Their disproportionate representation here is in no way intended to justify their claims to power; instead, it should serve to highlight the extent to which our understanding of Smith and the scope and tools of political economy have been defined by those with traditional forms of institutional power, often to the exclusion of the powerless and disempowered. Yet women, African American writers, labor unions, and other marginalized groups were by no means silent on Smith. For example, Harriet Martineau, a British author who spent two years in the United States, shot to fame with her wildly successful, twenty-five-volume *Illustrations of Political Economy* (1832–1834). Though dismissed as a mere popularizer of Smith and Mill's theories, women writers like Martineau were responsible for making political economy legible and more accessible to a lay audience, especially women and girls who would have been excluded from higher education.[10] Former slave and American abolitionist Frederick Douglass was also familiar with Smith's works. In one address, Douglass compared racial slavery to the "commercial fallacies long ago exposed by Adam Smith," and his analysis of slaveowners' love of pride and domination strongly echoes Smith's analysis of slavery in *The Wealth of Nations*.[11] While these stories of reception—and many

9. For an interesting take on how intellectual history can show the causal impact of ideas on policy, see Ben Jackson, "Intellectual Histories of Neo-Liberalism and their Limits," in Alec Davies, Ben Jackson, and Florence Sutcliffe-Braithwaite, eds., *A Neo-Liberal Age? Britain Since the 1970s* (London: UCL Press, 2021).

10. Bette Polkinghorn, *Adam Smith's Daughters: Eight Prominent Women Economists from the Eighteenth Century to the Present* (Cheltenham: Elgar, 1998); Valerie Sanders, Gaby Weiner, and Martineau Society, *Harriet Martineau and the Birth of Disciplines: Nineteenth-Century Intellectual Powerhouse*, (New York, NY: Routledge, 2017).

11. Frederick Douglass, "A Friendly Word to Maryland: An Address Delivered in Baltimore, Maryland, on 17 November 1864." In John W. Blassingame and John R. McKivigan, eds. *The*

others—are not featured here, they deserve to be told and I hope will be told soon.

Readers might wonder whether *America's Adam Smith* might have made more sense as a title for this book. After all, Americans, in the story I tell here, are the ones reimagining and reshaping Smith, not the other way around. It was his American interpreters and acolytes who Americanized *him*. But, the book's title hints at the ultimate irony in this story of Smith's reception: that Americans might be captive to the very ideas of an Adam Smith that *they* invented. It is Adam Smith's America now.

Frederick Douglass Papers. Series One: Speeches, Debates, and Interviews. Vol. 4: 1864–80. (New Haven, CT: Yale University Press, 1991), 48. Douglass writes in *My Bondage and My Freedom*, "If I ever wandered under the consideration, that the Almighty, in some way, ordained slavery, and willed my enslavement for his own glory, I wavered no longer. I had now penetrated the secret of all slavery and oppression, and had ascertained their true foundation to be in the pride, the power and the avarice of man. The dialogue and the speeches were all redolent of the principles of liberty, and poured floods of light on the nature and character of slavery." Frederick Douglass, *My Bondage and My Freedom*, ed. David W. Blight (New Haven, CT: Yale University Press, 2014), 128. Compare to Smith in *WN* III.ii.10, 388. "The pride of man makes him love to domineer, and nothing mortifies him so much as to be obliged to condescend to persuade his inferiors. Whenever the law allows it, and the nature of the work can afford it, therefore, he will generally prefer the service of slaves to that of freemen."

1

The Best Book Extant

"BY ALL ACCOUNTS," wrote David Hume to his best friend, Adam Smith, "your Book has been printed long ago; yet it has never yet been so much as advertised." The letter, dated February 8, 1776, anticipated the publication of Smith's *An Inquiry into the Nature and Causes of the Wealth of Nations* by almost exactly one month. "What is the Reason?" Hume asked eagerly. "If you wait till the Fate of America be decided, you may wait too long."[1]

Adam Smith's *The Wealth of Nations* appeared on bookshelves in London on March 9, 1776. Smith's words filled two handsome volumes, each roughly twelve by nine inches, and amounted to just over one thousand pages. Printed and bound, the work physically conveyed gravitas. The author's title commanded authority, but with little ceremony: "Adam Smith, LL.D. and F.R.S. Formerly Professor of Moral Philosophy in the University of Glasgow." This was an *inquiry*—not a treatise or manifesto—into the forces of national wealth, and it was written by a scientist and philosopher, not a man of letters or a pamphleteer.[2] It would be another three months and twenty-five days before the colonies declared their independence, but the fate of America was far from certain. Still, Smith managed to capture the American spirit of 1776 with

1. David Hume to Adam Smith, February 8, 1776. *Corr.*, 185.
2. Phillipson, *Adam Smith*, 214. On the significance of naming the author in print and changes in the printing of Smith's name and title, see Sher, *The Enlightenment and the Book*, 148–62, esp. 162.

its heightened sense of self-awareness and revolutionaries poised to make a mark in history:

> The persons who now govern the resolutions of what they call their continental congress, feel in themselves at this moment a degree of importance which, perhaps, the greatest subjects in Europe scarce feel. From shopkeepers, tradesmen, and attornies [sic], they are become statesmen and legislators, and are employed in contriving a new form of government for an extensive empire, which, they flatter themselves, will become, and which, indeed, seems very likely to become, one of the greatest and most formidable that ever was in the world.[3]

Some of Smith's readers thought these remarks about the American situation were of "capital importance."[4] Others were taken aback. "There are some pages about the middle of the Second Volume where you enter into a description about the measures we ought to take with respect to America, giving them a representation etc. which I wish had been omitted," wrote Hugh Blair, a prominent Scottish minister, rhetorician, and professor. Blair disagreed with Smith on a number of other issues, but he was particularly nervous about Smith's commentary on the American colonies "because it is too much like a publication for the present moment," he wrote.[5] Thomas Pownall, a British MP and former governor of the Province of Massachusetts Bay, also demurred. "I should here have proceeded to the consideration of your plans of the system, which you think Great Britain should adopt in her future conduct towards America," he wrote to Smith in a lengthy letter in September of 1776, "but the present state of events suspends all political discussion on that head." By the time Pownall wrote to Smith, it had been over year since the battle of Bunker Hill, the Declaration of Independence had been read out loud in the colonies, and the British army had begun to occupy New York City. At least from Pownall's view, the

---

3. *WN* IV.7.75, 623.
4. William Robertson to Adam Smith, 8 April 1776. *Corr.*, 192.
5. Hugh Blair to Adam Smith, 3 April 1776. *Corr.*, 188.

unfolding of events suggested that the question of the American colonies would be "at the hazard of events which force, and not reason, is to decide."[6]

Whatever anxiety Smith's brief treatment of the American situation caused, it did not appear to overshadow his overarching achievement, at least not for readers on his side of the Atlantic. "You have formed into a regular and consistent system one of the most intricate and important parts of political science," wrote William Robertson, another product of the Edinburgh enlightenment. Robertson continued, "I should think your Book will occasion a total change in several important articles both in police and finance."[7] Comparisons to Newton were implied. "I do really think," Governor Pownall wrote toward the end of his letter, "that your book . . . might become an institute, containing the *principia* of those laws of motion, by which the system of the human community is framed and doth act, AN INSTITUTE *of political œconomy*, such as I could heartily wish."[8]

On the other side of the Atlantic, this "institute of political oeconomy" was not far from the minds of shopkeepers, traders, attorneys, and would-be-statesmen as they marched towards independence and, ultimately, nationhood. Independence raised many of the same questions that Smith was tackling in *The Wealth of Nations*. What are the principles of law and government that promote security, prosperity, and happiness? How might a country engage in free commerce without becoming dependent on her rivals? How do different systems of political economy affect the virtue and character of a people? These questions pervaded American thought during the Founding Era, and they structured the terms on which Smith's American readers engaged with his ideas. Experiments in government, innovations in the science of wealth creation, new ideas about the relationship between private interest and public happiness—all of these could be enlightened pursuits through

---

6. A Letter from Governor Pownall to Adam Smith, *Corr.*, 375.

7. William Robertson to Adam Smith, 8 Apr. 1776. *Corr.*, 192.

8. A Letter from Governor Pownall to Adam Smith. *Corr.*, 375. Emphasis and capitalization in original.

the application of science, the employment of reason, and the study of history.[9]

Making sense of Smith's figurative arrival and reception in the decades leading up to and following American independence requires removing many of the contemporary blinders that often lead to overstatements of Smith's importance—for instance, the idea that *The Wealth of Nations* was "an intellectual shot heard round the world in 1776."[10] A number of scholars have corrected this view by showing how *The Wealth of Nations* received as much hostile criticism as it did accolades, that its argument for free trade did not appear to make any significant impact during Smith's lifetime, and that, overall, the work had "no immediate impact on Britain or its colonies."[11] The vast scholarship stressing the importance of the Scottish Enlightenment on American Revolutionary thought and the character of the American Enlightenment(s) more generally has been of even greater significance.[12] Even within this

9. Caroline Winterer, *American Enlightenments: Pursuing Happiness in the Age of Reason* (New Haven, CT: Yale University Press, 2016).

10. T. Sowell, "Adam Smith in Theory and Practice," in *Adam Smith and Modern Political Economy: Bicentennial Essays on The Wealth of Nations*, ed. Gerald P. O'Driscoll (Ames, IA: Iowa State University Press, 1979), 3.

11. Willis, "The Role in Parliament of the Economic Ideas of Adam Smith;" Rashid, "Adam Smith's Rise to Fame;" Teichgraeber, "'Less Abused than I Had Reason to Expect.'"

12. Among the most important works that established the connection between Scottish Enlightenment thought and American political thought in the revolutionary and early national period are Bernard Bailyn, *The Ideological Origins of the American Revolution* (Cambridge, MA: Harvard University Press, 1967); Gordon S. Wood, *The Creation of the American Republic, 1776–1787* (Chapel Hill, NC: University of North Carolina Press, 1969); Garry Wills, *Inventing America: Jefferson's Declaration of Independence*. First Mariner Books Edition (Boston, MA: Houghton Mifflin, 2002); Douglass G. Adair, *The Intellectual Origins of Jeffersonian Democracy: Republicanism, the Class Struggle, and the Virtuous Farmer*, ed. Mark E. Yellin (Oxford: Lexington Books, 2000). Together, these scholars established the importance of the civic republican tradition and the influence of Scottish Enlightenment thought on American political thought from the revolutionary period onward. This "republican synthesis," as it is known, stands opposite the thesis by Louis Hartz in his *The Liberal Tradition in America* (New York, NY: Houghton Mifflin Harcourt, 1955). Hartz boldly (and, according to many later historians, wrongly) argued that the American liberal tradition was based on a unique commitment to individual liberty, rather than to social justice and equality (as in the case of European countries). For an overview of the turn to republicanism in American historiography, see Robert E. Shalhope, "Toward a Republican Synthesis: The Emergence of an Understanding of Republicanism in American Historiography,"

narrower context the evidence on Smith is mixed. Quantitative historical studies point in different directions. According to David Lundberg and Henry May's landmark study, Smith's works—both *The Theory of Moral Sentiments* and *The Wealth of Nations*—were among the most popular works by Scottish authors between the 1760s and early 1800s; by their metrics, *The Wealth of Nations* enjoyed an American readership comparable to that of Montesquieu's *Spirit of the Laws* and exceeded that of Hume's *Essays and Treatises on Several Subjects*.[13] Other studies, however, show that Smith was not even among the top thirty-six most cited European thinkers in America.[14] Meanwhile, other scholars start

---

The William and Mary Quarterly 29, no. 1 (1972), 49–80; Daniel T. Rodgers, "Republicanism: The Career of a Concept," *The Journal of American History* 79, no. 1 (1992), 11–38. For more detailed investigations about the mechanisms of transmission between the Scottish and American Enlightenment, Daniel Walker Howe, "Why the Scottish Enlightenment Was Useful to the Framers of the American Constitution," *Comparative Studies in Society and History* 31, no. 3 (July 1989), 572–87; James T. Kloppenberg, *The Virtues of Liberalism* (New York, NY: Oxford University Press, 1998), chap. 2; Donald S. Lutz, "The Relative Influence of European Writers on Late Eighteenth-Century American Political Thought," *American Political Science Review* 78, no. 1 (March 1984), 189–97; Henry F. May, *The Enlightenment in America* (Oxford: Oxford University Press, 1978); Richard B. Sher and Jeffrey R. Smitten, eds., *Scotland and America in the Age of the Enlightenment* (Edinburgh: Edinburgh University Press, 1990); Winterer, *American Enlightenments*. For an overview of the scholarly debate on the nature of *the* or *an* American Enlightenment(s), see also Caroline Winterer, "What was the American Enlightenment?" in Isaac et al., *The Worlds of American Intellectual History*, 19–36.

13. David Lundberg and Henry F. May, "The Enlightened Reader in America," *American Quarterly* 28, no. 2 (July 1976), 262–93. Lundberg and May's study marked an important quantitative turn in the historiography of the American Enlightenment. The authors called their essay a "preliminary report" on the subject of Enlightenment authors and American libraries, and their survey consisted of an analysis of 291 libraries between 1700 and 1813. Lundberg and May's study has faced some criticism, however. For example, Mark G. Spencer provides a detailed critique of Lundberg and May's treatment of David Hume's publications, saying that their presentation of the data on Hume's works in America gives no indication of the availability of *A Treatise of Human Nature* (1739–40), *An Enquiry concerning Human Understanding* (1748), *Political Discourses* (1752), or *The Life of David Hume, Esq. Written by Himself* (1777) and is at times "downright deceptive." See Mark G Spencer, *David Hume and Eighteenth-Century America* (Cambridge: Cambridge University Press, 2012), 12–13. With regard to Smith, one may also dispute whether Smith's *The Theory of Moral Sentiments* truly belongs under the heading Common Sense philosophy.

14. Lutz, "The Relative Influence of European Writers on Late Eighteenth-Century American Political Thought."

from the assumption that the "Americanness" of Smith's topics—for instance, his controversial defense of standing armies, his proposal for resolving the colonial conflict through a fiscal union, his discussion of taxation—contributed to *The Wealth of Nations'* success among American audiences before it had impact elsewhere.[15] Thus, Smith's status among his American readers during the Founding Era remains unclear for at least two reasons. First, his works did not appear to exert "any fundamental influence" on the way Americans thought or acted, but at the same time, the works were not completely ignored or dismissed either.[16] Second, whether the magnitude of Smith's influence ought to be attributed to features of Smith's works themselves or to the needs and tastes of his American readers is a matter of divergent scholarly perspectives. Given the circumstances in which Americans encountered Smith's ideas, it is worth reconsidering what brought them to Smith and what specific value they found in his works.

For the American founders, the works of Adam Smith were guidebooks for enlightened statesmanship. In *The Wealth of Nations* James Madison found an array of general principles about the relationship between interests, institutions, and individual virtue. Alexander Hamilton mined *The Wealth of Nations* for ideas about the advantages and disadvantages of banking, public credit, and theories of economic growth. Meanwhile, John Adams used ideas from Smith's *The Theory of Moral Sentiments* to grapple with what Adams saw as a troubling sociopsychological influence of wealth in society. The eclecticism of these interpretations and uses evokes the embryonic state of political economic thinking during the late eighteenth century and reinforces the notion of political economy as a branch of political statecraft. Moreover, these understandings reveal the noticeable absence of a clear consensus around what Smith's works signified, politically speaking. Recovering these

15. Fleischacker, "Adam Smith's Reception among the American Founders;" Andrew S. Skinner, "Adam Smith and the American Revolution," *Presidential Studies Quarterly* 7, no. 2/3 (April 1977), 75–87; Sher and Smitten, *Scotland and America in the Age of the Enlightenment*; Peter McNamara, *Political Economy and Statesmanship: Smith, Hamilton, and the Foundation of the Commercial Republic* (DeKalb, IL: Northern Illinois University Press, 1997).

16. Teichgraeber, "'Less Abused than I Had Reason to Expect,'" 363–64.

extended engagements with Smith thus illuminates the conditions of possibility that existed during the Founding Era—conditions that shaped the way Americans conceptualized political economy and the way they imparted significance to Smith's ideas.

———

Adam Smith's works arrived on American shores at a time when a select group of people were searching for enlightenment, or rather, hoping to become enlightened. These self-consciously enlightened Americans believed that, with the aid of reason, they could free themselves from "non-or pre-rational modes of thought," and, more importantly, deliver the promise of human happiness. They sought enlightened approaches to everything: from politics to religion; from the way they rotated their crops, to the way they comprehended geological space and time.[17]

Smith's two main published works—*The Theory of Moral Sentiments* and *An Inquiry into the Nature and Causes of the Wealth of Nations*—blended into this flowering landscape of ideas. First published in 1759 by Andrew Millar in London and Alexander Kincaid and John Bell in Edinburgh, *The Theory of Moral Sentiments* became a bestseller in Great Britain and elsewhere in Europe.[18] Advertisements from colonial booksellers and printers reveal that Smith's work was being imported in the early 1760s and that it had obtained a critical level of prestige and popularity in the second half of the eighteenth century.[19] One advertisement in the *New-York Mercury* in 1762 described *The Theory of Moral Sentiments* in glowing terms, saying that "this Author's Discourse" was "animated by the Sentiments of Virtue" and that its ideas "[flow] along, like a full and rapid Stream . . . [carrying] the Reader thro' many entertaining Scenes of Common Life, and many curious Disquisitions of Literature, and it

17. Winterer, *American Enlightenments*.

18. Sher, *The Enlightenment and the Book*, 628.

19. Some of the most prominent colonial book-sellers advertised "Smith's Moral Sentiments" on their catalogs and lists between 1760 and 1773, including Garrat Noel (New York), David Hall (Benjamin Franklin's publishing partner in Philadelphia), John Mein (Boston), and the New York Society Library.

is universally allowed to be the best Composition of the Kind that ever appeared."[20]

Alongside the works of other eminent eighteenth-century Scottish thinkers—Lord Kames' *Elements of Criticism* (1762), Thomas Reid's *An Inquiry into the Human Mind* (1764), Dugald Stewart's *Elements of the Philosophy of the Human Mind* (1792)—Smith's *The Theory of Moral Sentiments* represented a body of moral and critical thought that Americans read to cultivate an enlightened mind. Whether by reading history, literary criticism, or works of natural science, Americans were yearning for a reason-based understanding of their physical, intellectual, and moral worlds in order to improve them. In a well-known letter written to Robert Skipwith in 1771, which included a list of books for a private library, Thomas Jefferson included *The Theory of Moral Sentiments* under the heading "Criticism on the Fine Arts."[21] The physician Elihu Hubbard Smith also recommended Smith's *The Theory of Moral Sentiments* in a letter written to his sister in 1792, exhorting her to "direct your principal attention to such writings as will assist you in forming just notions in morality and criticism."[22] In 1790, *The Universal Asylum and Columbian Magazine*, an archetypal magazine for polite and cultured gentlemen of the era, reprinted a single chapter of Smith's *The Theory of Moral Sentiments* in three installments, advertising it as an essay on the "Influence of utility in producing beauty."[23] According to Lundberg and May's study, of all the works by Scottish Common Sense authors, Smith's *The Theory of Moral Sentiments* was the most popular book on moral

20. *New-York Mercury*, 23 August 1762, 4.

21. Jefferson wrote, "If you are fond of speculation, the books under the head of Criticism, will afford you much pleasure." From Thomas Jefferson to Robert Skipwith, with a List of Books for a Private Library, 3 August 1771. *The Papers of Thomas Jefferson*, vol. 1, *1760–1776*, ed. Julian P. Boyd. (Princeton, NJ: Princeton University, 1950), 77.

22. As quoted in Sher, *The Enlightenment and the Book*, 505.

23. The reprinted chapter was "Of the Beauty which the appearance of utility bestows upon all the productions of art, and of the extensive influence of this species of beauty," *TMS* IV.i.1–11, 179–187. Interestingly, this is the chapter that contains Smith's mention of the "invisible hand" in *The Theory of Moral Sentiments*. I briefly discuss the republication of this section in the *Universal Asylum* later in this chapter.

philosophy for American readers, appearing in approximately twenty-three percent of American libraries between 1759 and 1813.[24]

While Smith's *The Wealth of Nations* attracted the readership of men of polite letters, more importantly it attracted men of power. In Great Britain, a slow but steady stream of dedicated readers made Smith the subject of public and political discussion.[25] The initial success of the work naturally caught the attention of an enterprising Scottish Philadelphian publisher, Thomas Dobson, who printed the first American edition of *The Wealth of Nations* in 1789 (Fig. 1.1). This was no light decision given the costs and risks of printing such a massive work, but his foresight paid off. A 1796 reprinting of Dobson's edition of *The Wealth of Nations* reveals the work's popularity within the first seven years of its American run.[26] Dobson's American publication of *The Wealth of Nations* also anticipated the introduction and development of courses on political economy in higher education. By the mid-1780s, Bishop James Madison was teaching the nation's first college course on political economy at the College of William and Mary and using *The Wealth of Nations* as his primary textbook.[27] Some forty years later at the University of

---

24. Lundberg and May, "The Enlightened Reader in America."

25. Sher, *The Enlightenment and the Book*, 236–37. By 1790, Smith's *The Wealth of Nations* was already in its sixth edition, with a seventh soon to come. Sher's estimates of popularity ratings are on the basis of the number of editions published in Britain through 1810. A bestseller is one that has ten or more editions printed, and Smith's *The Wealth of Nations* would reach that milestone by 1810. See Sher's Appendix Table 2, 650 and 688. On the immediate reception and fame of Smith in Great Britain, see Rashid, "Adam Smith's Rise to Fame;" Teichgraeber, "'Less Abused than I Had Reason to Expect';" Willis, "The Role in Parliament of the Economic Ideas of Adam Smith."

26. Sher, *The Enlightenment and the Book*, 556–61. On the material costs, production, and circulation of books in early America, see David Hall's "The Atlantic Economy," in Hugh Amory and David D. Hall, eds., *A History of the Book in America, Volume 1: The Colonial Book in the Atlantic World* (Chapel Hill, NC: The University of North Carolina Press, 2009), Chapter 5 ("The Atlantic World"), Part 1, 152–162; John Bidwell's "Printers' Supplies and Capitalization," in Amory and Halls, eds. A History of the Book in America, Volume 1, Chapter 5 ("The Atlantic World"), part 2, 163–183; and Elizabeth Carroll Reilly and David Hall's "Customers and the Market For Books" in Amory and Halls, eds. A History of the Book in America, Volume 1, Chapter 11 ("Practices of Reading"), part 2, 387–399.

27. There is dispute in the scholarship about the exact date when Madison introduced the course on political economy at William and Mary. John K. Whitaker writes, "Although the

Virginia, *The Wealth of Nations* would be used as the primary text in political economy from roughly 1825 to 1846.[28] The book received attention
beyond the academy too. Thomas Jefferson and James Madison both
included it on a list of recommended books for Congress in 1783; Jefferson even hailed it as "the best book extant" on political economy in
1790.[29] John Adams owned not one but two copies of *The Wealth of
Nations* (one in English and one in French), as well as a condensed version and commentary of it entitled, "The Essential Principles of the
Wealth of Nations, Illustrated, in opposition to some false doctrines of
Dr. Adam Smith, and Others" published in 1797. Lundberg and May's
study estimates that, on average, the work's readership grew steadily

---

record is slight, there does seem to be enough clear evidence to justify the belief that Madison
was the first person in North America to teach a systematic course based on *The Wealth of Nations*, and probably the first ever to teach a course that could be properly characterized as dealing
with the new science of political economy." See Whitaker, "Early Flowering in the Old Dominion: Political Economy at the College of William and Mary and the University of Virginia," in
Breaking the Academic Mould: Economists and Higher Learning in the Nineteenth Century, ed.
William J. Barber (New Brunswick, NJ: Transaction Publishers, 1993), 15–41, at 20. As for the
date at which the political economy course was introduced, we have some further details. Madison began lecturing in moral philosophy in 1784, so there is some reason to believe that the
introduction of the subject of political economy as a branch of moral philosophy could have
started as early as 1784. E.R.A. Seligman writes, "The subject of political economy was certainly
taught at William and Mary in 1801, and very probably in 1799. It was probably taught in 1798, if
the possession of a copy of the *Wealth of Nations* by a student in the college in that year may be
considered pertinent. There is no proof that the study was included in the curriculum before
that date . . . There is nothing to make us believe that it was taught, as alleged, as early as 1785—
for the argument which is used for William and Mary would equally apply to every other college
of that date where moral philosophy was taught." See Seligman, "The Early Teaching of Economics in the United States," in *Economic Essays, Contributed in Honor of John Bates Clark*, ed.
Jacob Hollander (New York, NY: The Macmillan Company, 1927), 283–320, at 301.

28. Whitaker, "Early Flowering in the Old Dominion," in *Breaking the Academic Mould*, ed.
Barber, 30–31. I discuss the development and spread of political economy courses in higher education in the nineteenth century in Chapter 2.

29. From Thomas Jefferson to Robert Skipwith, with a List of Books for a Private Library,
3 August 1771; "Report on Books for Congress, [23 January] 1783." *The Papers of James Madison*
(henceforth *PJM*) vol. 6, *1 January 1783–30 April 1783*, ed. William T. Hutchinson and William M. E.
Rachal. (Chicago, IL: University of Chicago Press, 1969), 62–115; Letter from Thomas Jefferson to
Thomas Mann Randolph, Jr., 30 May 1790. *The Papers of Thomas Jefferson*, vol. 16, *30 November 1789–4
July 1790*, ed. Julian P. Boyd. (Princeton, NJ, Princeton University Press, 1961), 448–50.

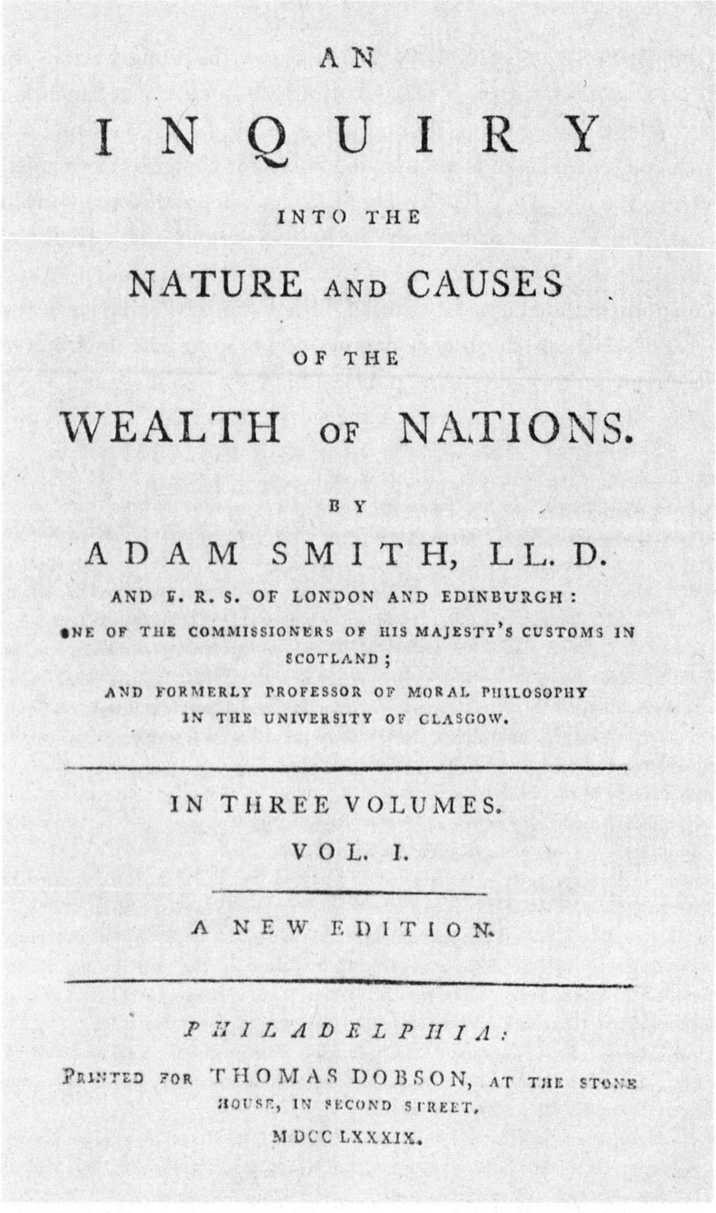

A N

I N Q U I R Y

INTO THE

NATURE AND CAUSES

OF THE

WEALTH OF NATIONS.

B Y

A D A M S M I T H, LL. D.

AND F. R. S. OF LONDON AND EDINBURGH:
ONE OF THE COMMISSIONERS OF HIS MAJESTY'S CUSTOMS IN
SCOTLAND;
AND FORMERLY PROFESSOR OF MORAL PHILOSOPHY
IN THE UNIVERSITY OF GLASGOW.

IN THREE VOLUMES.

VOL. I.

A NEW EDITION.

PHILADELPHIA:

PRINTED FOR THOMAS DOBSON, AT THE STONE
HOUSE, IN SECOND STREET.
M DCC LXXXIX.

FIG. 1.1. The title page of Thomas Dobson's first American edition of *The Wealth
of Nations*, printed in 1789. Kress Collection of Business and Economics,
Baker Library, Harvard Business School.

through 1813 and that it appeared in approximately thirty-one percent of American libraries.[30]

Other elements of Smith's corpus found their way into American intellectual life through more indirect routes. Though Smith's *Lectures on Jurisprudence*, for example, were never published during his lifetime, their contents may have been captured, distilled, and disseminated to American readers through Lord Kames's *Historical Law-Tracts* (1758). Kames sponsored and attended the first iteration of Smith's lectures in Edinburgh between 1748 and 1750, and the *Historical Law-Tracts* were known among key American figures such as Jefferson, Madison, Adams, and particularly James Wilson, who used Kames extensively in his lectures on law at the College of Philadelphia.[31] The posthumously published collection of Smith's *Essays on Philosophical Subjects* (1795) did poorly in terms of its London circulation and was unlikely to have had much uptake in America. Finally, Smith's letter to his publisher, William Strahan, after the death of David Hume was reprinted in numerous American publications, most infamously in the *United States Magazine* in 1779. Alongside an account of the death of Reverend Samuel Finley, an Irishman who immigrated to the American colonies in 1734, Smith's letter to Strahan appeared under the provocative title, "CONTRAST between the Death of a DEIST and a CHRISTIAN, David Hume, and Samuel Finley."[32]

American readers placed Smith within a larger family of eighteenth-century Scottish thinkers that included Francis Hutcheson (1694–1746), Henry Home, Lord Kames (1696–1782), Thomas Reid (1710–1796), David Hume (1711–1776), and Adam Ferguson (1723–1816). Together, these thinkers represented a distinctive way of thinking about man and society in the Age of Enlightenment. They modeled themselves after

---

30. Lundberg and May, "The Enlightened Reader in America," 288.

31. On the transmission of Smith via Kames and Wilson, see Fleischacker, "Adam Smith's Reception among the American Founders," 898–99; Iain McLean, "Adam Smith, James Wilson, and the US Constitutional Convention," in *The Adam Smith Review*, ed. Fonna Forman, vol. 8 (Abingdon: Routledge, 2015), 141–60.

32. On the publication of the "Contrast" and its impact on Hume's reputation in America, see Spencer, *David Hume and Eighteenth-Century America*, 195–202.

natural philosophers such as Isaac Newton in hopes of discovering the "connectedness of things" and outlining the universal, constant, scientific principles of the relationship among man, government, and society.[33] If human beings had an essential, unchanging nature—not unlike the fundamental particles of the physical world—then one could deduce the conditions under which they behaved differently under various political and social arrangements. Seen in this light, history was "the realm of human construction"—not the outcome of divine will "punctuated by an ascending sequence of sacred events"—and it propelled modern society forward towards greater progress.[34] History provided the essential data for the science of man. Most importantly, the purpose of this science was to guide statesmen's decisions that would ensure the stability of the republic and the flourishing of its people.[35] Few thinkers captured the spirit of this science of man and society better than David Hume:

> Mankind are [sic] so much the same, in all times and places, that history informs us of nothing new or strange in this particular. Its chief use is only *to discover the constant and universal principles of human nature*, by showing men in all varieties of circumstances and situations, and furnishing us with materials from which we may form our observations and become acquainted with the regular springs of human action and behavior. These records or wars, intrigues,

33. The word "scientist" was not coined until 1835, following the publication of Mary Somerville's *On the Connexion of the Physical Sciences*.

34. Dorothy Ross, *The Origins of American Social Science* (Cambridge: Cambridge University Press, 1991), 3.

35. Douglass Adair, "'That Politics May Be Reduced to a Science': David Hume, James Madison, and the Tenth Federalist," *Huntington Library Quarterly* 20, no. 4 (1957), 343–60; Winterer, *American Enlightenments*, 158–63. For introductions to the social theories of the Scottish Enlightenment, see Christopher J. Berry, *Social Theory of the Scottish Enlightenment* (Edinburgh: Edinburgh University Press, 1997); Alexander Broadie and Craig Smith, eds., *The Cambridge Companion to the Scottish Enlightenment*, 2nd ed., Cambridge Companions to Philosophy (Cambridge: Cambridge University Press, 2019); Gladys Bryson, *Man and Society: The Scottish Inquiry of the Eighteenth Century* (Princeton, NJ: Princeton University Press, 1945); John Robertson, *The Case for the Enlightenment: Scotland and Naples, 1680–1760* (Cambridge: Cambridge University Press, 2005); Ross, *The Origins of American Social Science*, introduction and chap. 1.

factions, and revolutions, are so many collections of experiments, by which the politician or moral philosopher fixes the principles of his science, in the same manner as the physician or natural philosopher becomes acquainted with the nature of plants, minerals, and other external objects, by the experiments which he forms concerning them. [emphasis added][36]

Understanding man's essential nature—whether naturally virtuous or vicious—was the object of moral philosophy. Explicating the origins, development, and effects of law and government, meanwhile, was the object of political science. Finally, unveiling the hidden forces of national prosperity was the object of political economy. Moral, political, and economic science, were thus inseparable from one another in their shared pursuit of human flourishing in society.

This approach to the science of man radiated outward from Scotland in the eighteenth century and left deep imprints in American intellectual life. Several figures served as direct and important conduits between Scotland and America. Benjamin Rush, the famed Philadelphia physician and educator, studied medicine at the University of Edinburgh between 1766 and 1768, and it was there that he encountered figures such as David Hume and John Witherspoon, the latter of whom he convinced to become president of the College of New Jersey (now Princeton University). A Presbyterian minister moved by the works of Francis Hutcheson and Thomas Reid, Witherspoon impressed upon many young minds (including one James Madison) the Scottish "inquiry into the nature and grounds of moral obligation by reason, as distinct from revelation."[37] Likewise, Francis Alison, a Glaswegian transplant in the American colonies, propagated a Hutchesonian approach to the

36. David Hume, "Of Liberty and Necessity." In *Enquiries Concerning the Human Understanding and Concerning the Principles of Morals by David Hume*, ed. L.A. Selby-Bigge, M.A., 2nd ed. (Oxford: Clarendon Press, 1902), 83.

37. John Witherspoon, *Lectures on Moral Philosophy*, ed. Varnum Lansing Collins, (Princeton, NJ: Princeton University Press, 1912). For more on the influences on and influence of Witherspoon in America, see Douglas Sloan, *The Scottish Enlightenment and the American College Ideal* (New York, NY: Teachers College Press, Columbia University, 1971); Peter J. Diamond, "Witherspoon, William Smith and the Scottish Philosophy in Revolutionary America," in

science of morals. Students who had the fortune to take moral philosophy from Alison at the College of Philadelphia in the 1750s could look forward to a daunting assignment: preparing an abridgement of Hutcheson's *Short Introduction to Moral Philosophy*.[38]

But Americans in Scotland (and Scotsmen in America) didn't just rehearse and replicate Scottish enlightenment thought; they adapted it for their circumstances and applied it to their unique purposes. Samuel Stanhope Smith, a student of Witherspoon's at the College of New Jersey (later the University's seventh president), launched one of the most forceful challenges to Lord Kames's theory of polygenism—that at the moment of Creation, God had created different pairs of races, suited for different climates. Drawing on observations of the experience of slaves in America, Stanhope Smith's *Essay on the Causes of the Variety of Complexion and Figure in the Human Species* (1787) put America on the map in a transatlantic debate about race-based slavery.[39] Benjamin Rush quoted *The Theory of Moral Sentiments* in a speech for the American Philosophical Society linking certain diseases to defects in the moral sense.[40] And while Scottish and other European thinkers tinkering with population statistics and predictions looked to America as a testing ground of theories of growth, Benjamin Franklin astonished readers with an incredible prediction in his essay, "Observations Concerning the Increase of Mankind, Peopling of Countries, etc.": that the population of the then-colonies would double in a mere twenty-five years. It would take European countries five hundred years to achieve that kind

---

Scotland and America in the Age of Enlightenment, 115–32; Thomas P. Miller, "John Witherspoon and Scottish Rhetoric and Moral Philosophy in America," *Rhetorica* 10, no. 4 (1992), 381–403.

38. Douglas Sloan, *The Scottish Enlightenment and the American College Ideal* (New York, NY: Teachers College Press, Columbia University, 2018), 89.

39. Winterer, *American Enlightenments*, 159–63; Sloan, *The Scottish Enlightenment and the American College Ideal*, chap. 4.

40. Benjamin Rush, *Medical Inquiries and Observations Upon the Diseases of the Mind* (Philadelphia, PA: Kimber and Richardson, 1812); Benjamin Rush, *An Inquiry into the Influence of Physical Causes upon the Moral Faculty delivered before a Meeting of the American Philosophical Society, held at Philadelphia, on the Twenty-Seventh of February, 1786* (Philadelphia, PA: Haswell, Barrington, and Haswell, 1839).

of growth—a "fact" that even Adam Smith acknowledged in *The Wealth of Nations* almost twenty years after Franklin.[41]

The diversity of ideas about human nature, institutions, and development often culminated in grand histories and sweeping narratives of progress.[42] Perhaps the most paradigmatic of these kinds of narratives was known as stadial theory, or the "four stages" theory. Evident in the work of Lord Kames and Smith in Scotland, Anne Robert Jacques Turgot and Adrien Helvétius in France, as well as Franklin and Jefferson in America, stadial theory provided an appealing framework for understanding the advancement of civilization in four consecutive stages: from hunter-gatherer societies, to nomadic shepherding states, to large agricultural societies, and, finally, to commercial nations.[43] The

41. Benjamin Franklin, "Observations Concerning the Increase of Mankind, 1751." *The Papers of Benjamin Franklin*, vol. 4, *July 1, 1750, through June 30, 1753*, ed. Leonard W. Labaree. (New Haven, CT: Yale University Press, 1961), 225–234. See also Thomas D. Eliot, "The Relations between Adam Smith and Benjamin Franklin before 1776," *Political Science Quarterly* 39, no. 1 (1924), 67–96. For Smith's population growth estimate, see *WN* I.viii.23, 87–88. Caroline Winterer has an excellent discussion about the statistics and science of population and its application to understanding the Native American population in America in her *American Enlightenments*, chap. 4.

42. On the flourishing of philosophical histories in the eighteenth century, see Caroline Winterer, "History," in *A Cultural History of Ideas in the Age of Enlightenment*, ed. Jack Censer, Cultural History of Ideas series, vol. 4, ed. Sophia Rosenfeld and Peter Struck. (London: Bloomsbury Academic Press, forthcoming).

43. Pioneering works on stadial theory in Scottish Enlightenment thought, see Ronald L. Meek, *Social Science and the Ignoble Savage* (Cambridge: Cambridge University Press, 1976); Ronald L. Meek, "Smith, Turgot, and the 'Four Stages' Theory," *History of Political Economy* 3, no. 1 (March 1971), 9–27. Subsequent work on the category of "commercial society" in Enlightenment thought emphasizes the centrality of the "four stages" as a schema or "model" for thinking about the evolution of social institutions and across history. See for example Berry, *Social Theory of the Scottish Enlightenment*; Berry, *The Idea of Commercial Society in the Scottish Enlightenment* (Edinburgh: Edinburgh University Press, 2013); Craig Smith, *Adam Smith's Political Philosophy: The Invisible Hand and Spontaneous Order*, vol. 42., Routledge Studies in Social and Political Thought (New York, NY: Routledge, 2006), chap. 4; Andrew Skinner, "Adam Smith: An Economic Interpretation of History," in *Essays on Adam Smith*, eds. Andrew S. Skinner and Thomas Wilson (Oxford: Clarendon Press, 1975), 154–178. István Hont reconstructs earlier theories of sociability and stadial theory and charts their continuity in Smith in his "The Language of Sociability and Commerce: Samuel Pufendorf and the Theoretical Foundations of the 'Four-Stages' Theory," in *The Jealousy of Trade: International Competition and the Nation State in*

inhabitants of America provided concurrent examples of these stages, too. The "lowest and rudest state of society" could be found "among the native tribes of North America," where "every man is a warrior as well as a hunter."[44] But should the hunting nations of America ever become shepherds, Smith surmised, "their neighborhood would be much more dangerous to the European colonies than it is at present."[45] The colonial settlers, however, were on a precipice. The "rapid advances of our North American colonies," Smith wrote, was "founded altogether in agriculture."[46] Whether America was hurtling towards the commercial stage—and whether that was the apogee of civilization or the beginning of demise—had yet to be determined.

What Americans inherited from the Scottish science of man, then, was not so much an anthology of political and moral maxims, but rather, an entire way of seeing, thinking, and placing themselves on the grand stage of human history. Debates over the Federal Constitution beginning in 1787 only heightened this sense of self-awareness. "Of all the memorable æras that have marked the progress of men from the savage state to the refinements of luxury," wrote the American lexicographer and educator Noah Webster in October of 1787, "that which has combined them into society, under a wise system of government, and given form to a nation, has ever been recorded and celebrated as the most important."[47] This was, after all, an "age of experiments in government."[48]

Historical Perspective (Cambridge, MA: Belknap Press of Harvard University Press, 2005), 159–184.

44. *WN* V.i.a.1–2, 689–690.

45. *WN* V.i.a.6, 692.

46. *WN* III.iv.19, 422.

47. [Noah Webster] A Citizen of America, "An Examination into the Leading Principles of the Federal Constitution," in *The Debate on the Constitution: Federalist and Antifederalist Speeches, Articles, and Letters During the Struggle over Ratification. Part 1*, ed. Bernard Bailyn (New York, NY: The Library of America, 1993), 129–163 at 129.

48. The phrase "age of experiments in government" was famously used by Thomas Jefferson in a letter to John Adams in 1796 after reflecting on the failures of the 1784 Committee of the States, and also witnessing the French Revolution of 1789 and its aftermath. Thomas Jefferson to John Adams, 28 February 1796. *The Papers of Thomas Jefferson*, vol. 28, *1 January 1794–29 February 1796*, ed. John Catanzariti. (Princeton, NJ: Princeton University Press, 2000), 618–619.

Whereas other nations were "driven together by fear and necessity," America would be different. Their new constitution would reflect the "wisdom of all ages," the collective wisdom of "the legislators of antiquity," and the "opinions and interests of the millions." Americans would build "an *empire of reason*."[49]

Among the many building blocks for this empire was, of course, Adam Smith's *The Wealth of Nations*. Webster himself had read the book in 1784 and had adopted it as one of his primary references on economic issues.[50] Alexander Hamilton allegedly prepared a commentary on *The Wealth of Nations* when he was a delegate to the Continental Congress in 1783.[51] Strewn across the debates over the Constitution, including *The Federalist Papers*, are a handful of references to Smith and *The Wealth of Nations*.[52] Nicholas Collin, a Swedish pastor in Philadelphia, wrote as "A Foreign Spectator" and urged Americans to consider "how federal sentiments must be acquired by education, manners, laws, morals, and religion" and how those might be "promoted by civil institutions" (above all others, the federal Constitution). "Ye political architects!" Collin exhorted, "exert all your skill; poise your centers of gravity; calculate the weights and bearings; Consult the plans of Montesquieu, Harrington, Stuart [sic], Hume, Smith, and others," he continued. And yet Collin wanted Americans to do more than just read and consult these plans. By invoking the works of Montesquieu, Hume, Smith, and

49. Webster, "An Examination into the Leading Principles of the Federal Constitution," 129. Italics in original.

50. Harlow G. Unger, *Noah Webster: The Life and Times of an American Patriot* (New York, NY: John Wiley & Sons, 1998), 72.

51. Clinton Rossiter, *Alexander Hamilton and the Constitution*. (New York, NY: Harcourt, Brace, & World, 1964), 306 n. 26. See also "Introductory Note: Report on Manufactures," in *The Papers of Alexander Hamilton* (henceforth *PAH*), vol. 10, *December 1791–January 1792*, ed. Harold C. Syrett (New York, NY: Columbia University Press, 1966), 1–15.

52. In addition to the example provided by Nicholas Collin, see the essay by "Civis Rusticus" in reply to George Mason's "Objections," in *The Debate on the Constitution: Federalist and Antifederalist Speeches, Articles, and Letters During the Struggle over Ratification, part 1*, ed. Bernard Bailyn (New York, NY: The Library of America, 1993) 353–362. The author also refers to Hume and William Paley in the essay. Fleischacker briefly discusses Civic Rusticus's mention of "Dr. Smith" in "Adam Smith's Reception among the Founders," 902.

other thinkers, he urged America's "political architects" to use those ideas to construct something new. Americans should aspire to "ameliorate and innoble [sic] them therefore by all means," Collin proclaimed, to "improve their solidarity, firmness, cohesion; animate them with the generous spirit of true freedom: make them say—*here we are, place us where we suit best: that is the post of honor, whether in the lowest part of the foundation, or in the towering arch.*"[53]

Among those ennobling architects was James Madison, whose writings in *The Federalist Papers* reveal the depth of his engagement with Smith's ideas as well as his clever repurposing of them. Though often regarded as founding texts of American political theory, the eighty-five articles that comprised *The Federalist Papers* were blazing partisan essays intended to persuade the delegates from New York state to ratify the new U.S. Constitution. Madison's *Federalist 10*, perhaps the most famous of all the essays, redefined the very idea of a republic both in terms of scope as well as institutions. A republic, Madison contended, was defined first by its system of representation that would "refine and enlarge the public views," and second by its size. A republic, unlike a democracy, had a "greater number of citizens and extent of territory" under its jurisdiction. While it has been widely established that he was primarily influenced by the philosophy of David Hume, less appreciated is Madison's interpretation and adaptation of Smith's ideas.[54]

53. [Nicholas Collin], A Foreign Spectator, "An Essay on the Means of Promoting Federal Sentiments in the United States" XV. Reprinted in *Friends of the Constitution: Writings of the "Other" Federalists, 1787–1788*, eds. Colleen E. Sheehan and Gary L. McDowell (Indianapolis, IN: Liberty Fund, 1998), 406–440 at 425–426, available at *https://oll.libertyfund.org/titles/2069*. Italics in original.

54. The influence of David Hume on the political thought of James Madison, particularly in *Federalist 10* is a longstanding debate. Douglas Adair's 1957 essay, "'That Politics May Be Reduced to a Science:' David Hume, James Madison, and the Tenth Federalist," is often cited as *the* essay that established this strong link between Madison and Hume. Other major works in this vein include Garry Wills, *Explaining America: The Federalist* (New York, NY: Penguin Books, 2001); Roy Branson, "James Madison and the Scottish Enlightenment," *Journal of the History of Ideas* 40, no. 2 (1979), 235–50; Stanley Elkins and Eric McKitrick, *The Age of Federalism: The Early American Republic, 1788–1800* (New York, NY: Oxford University Press, 1995). Those who have challenged Adair's thesis include Lance Banning, *The Sacred Fire of Liberty: James Madison and the Founding of the Federal Republic* (New York, NY: Cornell University Press, 1995);

Where Smith in *The Wealth of Nations* illustrated a general principle about the connection between human behavior and human institutions in one arena, Madison transposed that principle into a different one. For example, Smith argued that the diffusion and proliferation of many religious sects would reduce the likelihood of religious enthusiasm, fanaticism, and civil conflict. Instead of instituting an established religion—which was Hume's solution to the problem of religious sectarianism—Smith argued that allowing society to be divided into "two or three hundred, or perhaps into as many thousand small sects, of which no one could be considerable enough to disturb the publick tranquility" would force religious groups to vie for adherence, thereby reducing the danger any one sect posed. Competition amongst religious factions would, according to Smith, lead to "candour and moderation" and reduce "popular superstition and enthusiasm."[55]

As Samuel Fleischacker has observed, Madison extended and adapted Smith's idea in two powerful instances in *Federalist 10*.[56] The first was Madison's analysis and classification of the source of factions. In the first book of *The Wealth of Nations*, Smith provided a definition of national wealth and showed how the "whole annual produce of the land and labour of every country . . . naturally divides itself" among three parts: rent, wages, and profit. Those three divisions were the bases of the "three different orders of people:" those who lived by rent (landowners), those who lived by wages (laborers), and those who lived by profit (merchants). These were, according to Smith, "the three great,

---

Edmund S. Morgan, "Safety in Numbers: Madison, Hume, and the Tenth 'Federalist,'" *Huntington Library Quarterly* 49, no. 2 (1986), 95–112. In his article, "Adam Smith's Reception among the American Founders," Fleischacker argues that "it is remarkable that neither Adair nor any of the many scholars who have relied on his work ever extended an investigation of Madison's reading of Hume to Smith. Hume and Smith have such similar views on so many topics in moral, political, and economic philosophy that the extension seems a natural one . . . This omission is especially surprising [given] that Adair eventually faced a problem—to which Smith would have given him a solution—in tracing Madison's argument to Hume." For an overwhelmingly comprehensive list of all works that engage with this debate, see Spencer, *Hume in Eighteenth-Century America*, Chapter 6, especially note 11 (which spans 3 pages) and note 15.

55. *WN* V.i.g.8, 793.

56. Fleischacker, "Adam Smith's Reception among the American Founders."

original and constituent orders of every civilized society."[57] Importantly, Smith foresaw the potential for cooperation and conflict stemming from these different "orders". The proprietors of land (the landed aristocracy), whose income came from rents, generally shared interests with laborers in increasing economic prosperity. However, the voices of laborers—whose interest was "strictly connected with that of society"—were often neglected. Most pernicious of all, merchants and master manufacturers ("whose interest is never exactly the same with that of the publick," Smith claimed) have "generally an interest to deceive and even oppress the publick" and "upon many occasions, both deceived it and oppressed it."[58]

Madison's schema for classifying competing interests in *Federalist 10* is strikingly similar. "A landed interest, a manufacturing interest, a mercantile interest, a monied interest . . . grow up of necessity in civilized nations, and divide them into different classes," according to Madison. He continued, the "most common and durable source of factions, has been the various and unequal distribution of property." Competing economic interests based on the "most frivolous and fanciful distinctions" were enough to "kindle their unfriendly passions, and excite their most violent conflicts." Creditors were pitted against debtors, landholders against the landless. What is more, Madison's rhetoric reverberates with Smith's concerns about the political consequences of economic divisions. It would be wrong for someone with a vested interest to be the judge of his own cause, "Yet the parties are and must be themselves the judges," Madison conceded, "and the most numerous party, or, in other words, the most powerful faction must be expected to prevail."[59] That conflict over whose interests would prevail was inevitable, and the public would bear the burden of biased judgment.[60]

57. *WN* I.xi.p.7, 265.

58. *WN* I.xi.p.8–10, 265–267.

59. Madison, *Federalist 10*, in *The Federalist with Letters of "Brutus,"* ed. Terence Bell (Cambridge: Cambridge University Press, 2003), 42.

60. For a compelling analysis of Smith's classifications as a heuristic for political judgment, see Alexandra Oprea, "Adam Smith on Political Judgment: Revisiting the Political Theory of the Wealth of Nations," *The Journal of Politics*. Published online December 3, 2021: 1–15.

The second instance where Madison adapted Smith's ideas is in one of the most famous arguments in *Federalist 10*: that a multiplicity of political factions was much less dangerous in a large republic than it was in a small one. In a small republic, according to Madison, there would naturally be fewer "distinct parties and interests;" and, as a result, it would be easier for any one of those parties to "concert and execute their plans of oppression." But, "Extend the sphere" of the republic, Madison argued, "and you take in a greater variety of parties and interests; you make it less probable that a majority of the whole will have a common motive to invade the rights of other citizens."[61] Here, Madison enlisted the same logic of Smith's analysis of religious sects: the more factions there were, the more competition there would be among them, and the less dangerous any one of them would be to the republic.[62] Regardless of whether Madison was ultimately more influenced by Hume or by Smith, his use of Smith is distinctive. Madison did not

61. Madison continues, "Or if such a common motive exists, it will be more difficult for all who feel it to discover their own strength, and to act in unison with each other." *Federalist 10*, 45.

62. For an extended discussion and analysis of the verbal parallels between Madison's argument in *Federalist 10* and Smith's defense of disestablishment, Fleischacker, "Adam Smith's Reception among the American Founders, 1776–1790," 909–13, 921–23; Alexander Broadie and Craig Smith, eds., "The Impact on America" in *The Cambridge Companion to the Scottish Enlightenment*, 2nd ed., Cambridge Companions to Philosophy (Cambridge: Cambridge University Press, 2019), 320–24, available at https://doi.org/10.1017/9781108355063. I agree with Fleischacker that one of the reasons the Madison-Smith connection has been overlooked is likely a misunderstanding of Smith's "invisible hand." This is not so much a misunderstanding of the precise usage of the "invisible hand" (which occurs in a different chapter in *The Wealth of Nations*) so much as it is a misunderstanding of the *logic* underneath it. Fleischacker writes, "The point of Smith's invisible hand accounts of social phenomena was that individuals generally promoted the public good whether or not they intended to do so. The point was supposed to hold regardless of whether the individual's own interest was furthered, harmed, or left alone by his or her actions: individuals would promote the public good even when in doing so *defeated* their own interest." What happened to religious sects in Smith's analysis, according to Fleischacker, followed the second pattern; they would try to compete for adherents by tempering their doctrines. "This would be good for society, but it would be an abandonment of what the sects took to be their own good ... In one sense, the logic of the market was inverted— competition weakened, rather than strengthened, the relevant 'product.' In another sense, the logic of the two cases was the same: competition resulted in a good for society," Fleischacker, "Adam Smith's Reception among the American Founders, 1776–1790," 911, 912. Emphasis in original.

simply quote Smith or invoke his name; instead, he repurposed the underlying logic of Smith's ideas in a new political argument. Smith's analysis of the material bases of interest groups underlined the pervasive threat of political factionalism in a republic. By adapting Smith's analysis of competition among religious sects to an analysis of political factions, Madison demonstrated how the aspirations of a virtuous republic did not have to rely on perfectly virtuous citizens.[63]

———

The Founders' aspirational empire of reason extended well beyond the design of the main pillars of federalism. Even after the ratification of the federal Constitution in 1788, there was no guarantee that it would last. "The federal government *appears* to be a mighty sovereign," wrote Nicholas Collin, the same "foreign spectator" who spurred the Constitutional delegates to rear "*a grand temple of federal liberty*" with the mighty stones of Montesquieu, Harrington, Steuart, Hume, and Smith. "But it is a Hercules in the cradle, surrounded by serpents."[64] The United States had only just become a sovereign nation and already faced several new threats. Expansion of US territory increased the risk of armed conflict with other colonial powers as well as with Native Americans. Commercial relations with the former mother country were souring, and the rumblings of revolution in France raised grave concerns about whether the US was obligated—or even capable—of aiding in the revolutionary effort. Then there was the question of how the nation would finance expansion, war, and public goods. When George Washington was inaugurated in April of 1789, he inherited a country with no stable currency, a debt that amounted to 54,124,464 dollars and 56 cents, and no surefire way of financing it. It quickly became clear that in order to activate the full powers of the national government, a strong economic edifice had

63. Fleischacker, "Adam Smith's Reception among the American Founders," 915.

64. For "*grand temple*," (emphases in original), see [Nicholas Collin] A Foreign Spectator, "An Essay on the Means of Promoting Federal Sentiments in the United States" XV, 426. The famous "Hercules in the cradle" imagery is quoted in Max Edling, *A Hercules in the Cradle* (Chicago, IL: Chicago University Press, 2014), 1.

to be erected first.[65] Federalists and anti-Federalists alike thundered about how the government would fund debt, how it would raise revenue and regulate commerce, and how each of these tasks would affect the character of the nation.

Rising to meet these challenges was Alexander Hamilton, Madison's indefatigable coauthor of *The Federalist Papers*, Washington's Treasury Secretary, and precocious finance engineer. Hamilton, too, had thought the United States a young "Hercules in the cradle," but he also would see to it that the young American Hercules was armed and strengthened.[66] He elucidated his elaborate plan to modernize American financial and political institutions across three major works written between 1789 and 1791: the "Report Relative to a Provision for the Support of Public Credit" (1790), the "Second Report on the Further Provision Necessary for Establishing Public Credit" (1790), and the "Report on the Subject of Manufactures" (1791). Hamilton framed each of these works within a rallying cry for political and economic unity and a bold vision of the United States as a competitive commercial power. Expanding public credit was vital in order "to promote the increasing respectability of the American name, to answer the calls of justice . . . to cement more closely the union of the states . . . [and] to establish public order

65. Key works on the importance of fiscal matters in the Constitutional debates and the development of American state capacity include Roger H. Brown, *Redeeming the Republic: Federalists, Taxation, and the Origins of the Constitution* (Baltimore, MD: The Johns Hopkins University Press, 1993); Edling, *A Hercules in the Cradle*; E. James Ferguson, *The Power of the Purse: A History of American Public Finance, 1776–1790*, Published for the Omohundro Institute of Early American History and Culture, Williamsburg, Virginia (Chapel Hill, NC: The University of North Carolina Press, 2014); Woody Holton, *Unruly Americans and the Origins of the Constitution* (New York, NY: Hill and Wang, 2007); Thomas K. McCraw, *The Founders and Finance: How Hamilton, Gallatin, and Other Immigrants Forged a New Economy* (Cambridge, MA: Belknap Press, 2014); Richard Sylla, "Hamilton and the Federalist Financial Revolution, 1789–1795," *The New York Journal of American History* 65, no. 2 (2004), 32–39; Mark Somos, "'A Price Would Be Set Not Only upon Our Friendship, but upon Our Neutrality:' Alexander Hamilton's Political Economy and Early American State-Building," *Studies across Disciplines in the Humanities and Social Sciences, Helsinki Collegium for Advanced Studies* 10 (2011), 184–211.

66. From Alexander Hamilton to George Washington, [14] April 1794. *PAH*, vol. 16, *February 1794–July 1794*, ed. Harold C. Syrett, (New York, NY: Columbia University Press, 1972), 261–280 at 272.

on the basis of an upright and liberal policy."[67] National debt, Hamilton believed, could be the "powerfull [sic] cement of our nation."[68] The benefits of a National Bank were also undeniable to Hamilton: "Industry is increased, commodities are multiplied, agriculture and manufactures flourish, and here consist true wealth and prosperity of a state."[69]

While Hamilton's objectives in these reports appear in abstract and highly technical language—debt financing, credit creation, discriminatory interest rates, manufacturing subsidies—his overall mission was political. Hamilton was determined to convince the public that the political fate of the nation was inextricably tied to its financial straits, and that only by activating certain powers of the national government would the nation have a viable future. To that end, he set into motion the principles from what was then known as the science of political economy.

At the time Hamilton began preparing his treatises, political economy had only just begun to coalesce into a body of systematic thought. In the Anglophone world, James Steuart's *Principles of Political Oeconomy* (1767), which antedated Smith's *The Wealth of Nations* by nearly a decade, outlined the principles and purpose of political economy in a straightforward, pragmatic manner. "Oeconomy in general is the art of providing for all the wants of a family, with prudence and frugality," Steuart asserted in the first chapter of the work. "What oeconomy is in a family, political economy is in a state . . . The great art therefore of political economy is, first to adapt the different operations of it to the spirit, manners, habits, and customs of the people, and afterwards to model these circumstances so, [sic] as to be able to introduce a set of new and more useful institutions."[70] Like the science of politics, the

67. "Report Relative to a Provision for the Support of Public Credit" (henceforth, "Report on Public Credit"). 9 January 1790. *PAH* vol. 6, *December 1789–August 1790*, ed. Harold C. Syrett. (New York, NY: Columbia University Press, 1962), 65–110 at 70.

68. Alexander Hamilton to Robert Morris, 30 April 1781. *PAH* vol. 2, 1779–1781, 604–635 at 618.

69. Alexander Hamilton to Robert Morris, 30 April 1781. *PAH* vol. 2, 635.

70. James Steuart, *Inquiry into the Principles of Political Oeconomy* (henceforth, *Principles of Political Oeconomy*) (London: A. Millar and T. Cadell, 1767), 1–2.

science of political economy relied on observation and history—not scripture or divine revelation—to distill principles of wealth creation and management for a nation. For Steuart, a shrewd reader and practitioner of political economy would therefore be able to "[extract] the principles of this science from *observation* and *reflection*," and remove himself, as far as possible, from his local prejudices.[71] In this sense, the derivation of general principles from the particular experiences of different nations made political economy a science. Adam Smith, too, offered a succinct definition of the science of political economy. It was "a branch of the science of a statesman or legislator" which had two intertwined aims: to provide revenue and subsistence for the people, and to provide revenue for the state sufficient for public services. The science of political economy was a branch of statesmanship which proposed "to enrich both the people and the sovereign."[72] Relying on history, reason, and observation made political economy unmistakably scientific; its agenda, however, was neither apolitical nor amoral, but "expansive, urgent, and fundamental to the creation of social happiness."[73]

Hamilton saturated his three major reports with insights from this science. He had extensively studied works such as David Hume's *Political Discourses* (1752), Wydham Beawe's *Lex Mercatoria Rediviva* (1754), Malachy Postelthwayt's *The Universal Dictionary of Trade and Commerce* (1757), Adam Anderson's *Origin of Commerce* (1764), James Steuart's *Principles of Political Oeconomy* (1767), and Adam Smith's *The Wealth of Nations*. Hamilton had consulted the works of Jacques Necker, a Genevan banker and finance minister to King Louis XVI of France, and had relied heavily on the experience and wisdom of Robert Morris, the famed American financier who established the short-lived Bank of North America in 1781.[74] While Hamilton's uses of ideas from Smith's

71. Steuart, *Principles of Political Oeconomy*, 3. Italics in original.

72. *WN*, IV.i.1, 428.

73. Winterer, *American Enlightenments*, 197.

74. On Hamilton's sources in the "Report on Public Credit," "Report on the National Bank," and the "Report on Manufactures," see the editors' "Introductory Note to the Second Report on the Further Provision Necessary for Establishing Public Credit," *PAH*, vol. 7, *September 1790–January 1791*, ed. Harold C. Syrett. (New York, NY: Columbia University Press, 1963),

The Wealth of Nations relative to other sources were by no means exceptional, they illustrate how an American statesman interpreted and challenged competing theories of economic growth in projecting his own
vision of the nation's future.

In a number of cases, Hamilton simply cribbed from *The Wealth of
Nations* to spell out his economic logic and persuade his readers. In the
"Report on the National Bank," for example, Hamilton borrowed
Smith's distinction between "dead" and "live" stock to illustrate how
banks did more than circulate precious metals. Banks stimulated
investment—something that had far greater impact on the wealth of a
nation than the quantity of coin. Once money was deposited in banks,
gold and silver became the basis for circulating currency; money thus
took on an "active and productive quality" and facilitated circulation,
investment, and growth.[75] Hamilton also shared Smith's deep-seated
skepticism of government management of banks. British government
officials had "never been famous for good oeconomy," and their public
management of a national bank would therefore "be a good deal more
doubtful," Smith put diplomatically.[76] Hamilton echoed Smith's suspicion of government management. Under a "feeble or too sanguine

---

236–256. Hamilton's correspondence also reveals his appetite for reading books on the subject
of finance. See, for example, Alexander Hamilton to Colonel Timothy Pickering, April 20, 1781.
PAH, vol. 2, *1779–1781*, ed. Harold C. Syrett. (New York, NY: Columbia University Press, 1961),
595–596; Letter from Angelica Church to Alexander Hamilton, 4 February 1790. *PAH*, vol. 6,
December 1789–August 1790, ed. Harold C. Syrett. (New York, NY: Columbia University
Press, 1962), 245; Alexander Hamilton to Robert Morris, 30 April 1781, *PAH* vol. 2, *1779–1781*,
ed. Harold C. Syrett. (New York, NY: Columbia University Press, 1961), 604–635.

75. Alexander Hamilton, "Second Report on the Further Provision Necessary for Establishing Public Credit" (henceforth, "Report on a National Bank") in *PAH*, vol. 7, 306–307, 314, 308.
Cf. *WN* II.ii.86, 320: "It is not by augmenting the capital of the country, but [rather] by rendering
a greater part of that capital *active* and productive than would otherwise be so, that the most
judicious operations of banking can increase the industry of the country . . . The judicious operations of banking enable him to convert *this dead stock into active and productive stock*; into
materials to work upon, into tools to work with, and into provisions and subsistence to work
for; into stock which produces something both to himself and to his country by rendering a
greater part of that capital *active and productive* than would be so, that the most judicious operations of banking can *increase the industry of a country*," (emphases added).

76. *WN* V.ii.a.4, 818.

administration," private money would be dangerously liable to "being too much influenced by public necessity." For Hamilton, public confidence in the integrity of a national bank depended on its structure: "that it shall be under a private not a public Direction, under the guidance of individual interest, not of public policy."[77]

The clearest references to Smith's political economy appeared in Hamilton's "Report on Manufacturers," written in December of 1791.[78] Originally drafted in response to a request from Washington and the House of Representatives to prepare a report on the "encouragement and promotion of such manufactories [sic]," the Report went far beyond proposals for small-scale domestic manufacturing, tariffs, subsidies, trade regulations, and the like.[79] From his largely European source base, Hamilton reconstructed an ongoing debate about political economy in order to project an audacious vision of American political and economic prowess. The Report opens with a summary of one of the most prominent political-economic worldviews of the time: that national wealth came solely from the produce of the land. "In every country (say those who entertain them)," Hamilton wrote, "Agriculture is the most beneficial and *productive* object of human industry," and "the cultivation of the earth" ought to be "the most certain source of national supply . . . the immediate and chief source of subsistence to man," and a mode of subsistence "most favorable to the freedom and independence of the human mind." The popularity of this view was in no small part due to its suitability to the American context, Hamilton surmised. "This position, generally, if not universally true, applies with peculiar emphasis to the United States, on account of their immense tracts of fertile territory, uninhabited and unimproved."[80]

77. "Report on a National Bank," *PAH* vol. 7, 331.

78. An extensive compilation of parallel passages between Smith's *The Wealth of Nations* and Hamilton's "Report on Manufactures" can be found in Edward G. Bourne, "Alexander Hamilton and Adam Smith," *The Quarterly Journal of Economics* 8, no. 3 (April 1894), 328–44.

79. "Alexander Hamilton's Final Version of the Report on the Subject of Manufactures," (henceforth, "Report on Manufactures,") in *PAH* vol. 10, 230–340, note 125.

80. *PAH* vol. 10, 230–340 at 231. Italics in original.

The position Hamilton was reconstructing originated among a group of eighteenth-century French thinkers referred to as the *économistes*, but better known as the physiocrats. Thinkers such as François Quesnay, the Marquis de Mirabeau, and Anne-Robert-Jacques Turgot believed that certain natural laws, or principles of order and social progress, could be enacted on society. Among the most important of these natural laws was that the land and those who worked it were the only productive engines of society and therefore the only legitimate bases of national wealth. Hence, the more well-known appellation associated with these thinkers was physiocracy—literally, the "rule of nature." The physiocrats were considered to be among the first political economists, but, more importantly, they were recognized for instigating a program of radical political and economic change in eighteenth-century France. By demanding sweeping changes in economic policy, such as lower taxes on farmers and the complete free trade of staple crops (especially grain), the physiocrats espoused a revolutionary overhaul of the previous regime's mercantile policies. The notion of laissez-faire was not a rejection of all state powers in favor of market forces, but rather a rejection of what the physiocrats believed to be "unnatural" restraints on the rule of nature.[81]

There is little evidence that Hamilton actually read the works of the Quesnay, Turgot, and the others. Instead, what is more likely is that he relied heavily on Smith's critique of the physiocrats to both reconstruct and refute their position. This was not unusual at the time. Smith's *The Wealth of Nations* was the best-known work of political economy written

---

81. For an introduction to the political and economic philosophy of the physiocrats, see Ronald L. Meek, *The Economics of Physiocracy: Essays and Translations* (Cambridge, MA: Harvard University Press, 1963); T.J. Hochstrasser, "Physiocracy and the Politics of Laissez-Faire," in *The Cambridge History of Eighteenth-Century Political Thought*, ed. Mark Goldie and Mark Wokler (Cambridge: Cambridge University Press, 2006), 419–42; Keith Tribe, *Continental Political Economy From the Physiocrats to the Marginal Revolution* (Cambridge: Cambridge University Press, 2003). Detailed treatments of the physiocrats in a transatlantic context (specifically the exchange between France and America) include Manuela Albertone, *National Identity and the Agrarian Republic: The Transatlantic Commerce of Ideas between America and France* (Surrey, England: Ashgate, 2014); Drew R. McCoy, *The Elusive Republic: Political Economy in Jeffersonian America* (Chapel Hill, NC: The University of North Carolina Press, 1996), chap. 1.

in English that would have made the ideas of the *économistes* available to an audience that might not have read French.[82] In Book IV of *The Wealth of Nations*, Smith outlined with great detail the assumptions and elements of "that system which represents the produce of land as the sole source of the revenue and wealth of every country." Such a system had "never been adopted by any nation," Smith admitted, but "exist[ed] only in the speculations of a few men of great learning and ingenuity in France."[83] Smith praised the physiocrats for their ideas, which were, in his estimation, "perhaps the nearest approximation to the truth that has yet been published upon the subject of political oeconomy." But he ultimately concluded that their doctrines were "too narrow and confined" in supposing that agricultural labor *alone* was productive.[84]

The physiocratic doctrine had a powerful grip on America. The space that Hamilton devoted to it—even if only to controvert the theory—speaks to the influence of his philosophical and political opponents, embodied most notably in thinkers like Benjamin Franklin and Thomas Jefferson.[85] These American physiocrats clung to an image of America as a republic of virtuous, independent, and happy farmers. "Agriculture,"

82. Benjamin Vaughan, for example, admitted that "Smith has an express section explaining the System of the *Oeconomistes* which much instructed me." As quoted in Winterer, *American Enlightenments*, 205.

83. *WN*, IV.ix.2, 663.

84. *WN* IV.ix.38, 679. For a detailed discussion of Smith's relation to the physiocratic school, see Hont, *Jealousy of Trade*, 361–74. Hont argues that Smith made it clear that he believed that the physiocrats' prescriptions were overly "utopian, oppressive, and unnatural," even if they were striving to undo the mercantilist policies of the Colbertist regime that preceded them. Smith's worry, then, was that though the *économistes* were motivated by good intentions—a desire for greater freedom and prosperity—they "set out to promote it in a way that, according to Smith, was by its very nature 'obliged' to turn the political system into tyranny." Hont contends that "Smith's critique of the exaggerated agricultural bias of Physiocracy was in effect the key to his demonstration of the fundamental political and philosophical folly underlying the entire French project of perfect liberty." See also Hochstrasser, "Physiocracy and the Politics of Laissez-Faire."

85. Franklin had been welcomed into the physiocrats' circle in 1767 during a short visit to Paris. Jefferson, who was minister to France from 1785–1789, was also a deep admirer of Condorcet's works and his bookshelves contained many of the physiocrats' works. See Albertone, *National Identity and the Agrarian Republic*, 84–89.

wrote Franklin in 1769, is "the only honest Way; wherein Man receives a real Increase of the Seed thrown into the Ground, in a kind of continual Miracle wrought by the Hand of God in his Favour, as a Reward for his innocent Life, and virtuous Industry." Commerce, meanwhile, was "generally *Cheating*". Farming preserved and promoted the virtues of independence, self-sufficiency, and a "happy mediocrity" through the "restrained and rational use of goods."[86]

The virtues of farming were also social and political. "Cultivators of the earth are the most valuable citizens," Jefferson wrote in 1785. According to Jefferson, an agricultural way of life guaranteed that citizens would be wedded to the "liberty and interests" of the republic "by the most lasting bands," thereby immunizing the republic to tyranny and corruption.[87] Large-scale manufacturing and extensive commerce, in contrast, would introduce the twin vices of luxury and poverty and thereby endanger the moral fabric of republican government; they would thrust America onto the "unnatural and retrograde" European trajectory of development and ensnare her in costly and corrupting wars.[88] Such was the tenor of the discourse of political economy. Still in its infancy, political economy was highly attuned to the moral dimensions of economic life and "had not yet been sacrificed to the hubris of those who would claim to make economics into a 'non-moral' science."[89]

86. Benjamin Franklin, "Positions to be Examined, 4 April 1769." *The Papers of Benjamin Franklin*, vol. 16, *January 1 through December 31, 1769*, ed. William B. Willcox, (New Haven, CT: Yale University Press 1972, 107–109. Emphasis in original. The "Positions" is a working paper of sorts that Franklin wrote to develop ideas about the relationship between labor, agriculture, manufacturing, and commerce. As the editors of the paper note, Franklin expressed some approval of British nonimportation agreements and their beneficial effects for American manufacturing. Franklin was not, however, ready "to abandon the mercantilist system in favor of the theory of free trade then being discussed in France, and developed in Scotland by Lord Kames's' protégé, Adam Smith." Ibid., 107. On Franklin's physiocracy, see Albertone, *National Identity and the Agrarian Republic*, chap. 4.

87. Thomas Jefferson, Letter to John Jay, Paris, Aug. 23, 1785. *The Papers of Thomas Jefferson*, vol. 8, *25 February–31 October 1785*, ed. Julian P. Boyd. (Princeton, NJ: Princeton University Press, 1953), 426–428.

88. McCoy, *The Elusive Republic*, 178. On Jefferson and the physiocrats, see Albertone, *National Identity and the Agrarian Republic*, chap. 3.

89. McCoy, *The Elusive Republic*, 6.

However, by the mid–1780s, it had become clear that some degree of manufacturing and commerce was vital for the country to survive; the question was how much was really necessary.[90] Unlike his Jeffersonian opponents, Alexander Hamilton believed manufacturing was crucial for maintaining independence and solvency, and he leveraged ideas from Smith's *The Wealth of Nations* to scrutinize the doctrines of the physiocrats and their American adherents in order to promote a vision of the United States as a globally-competitive manufacturing nation.

Hamilton's first target in the "Report on Manufactures" was the assumption that agriculture was "not only, the most productive, but the only productive species of industry." This seductive belief, that agricultural production had *"intrinsically a strong claim to pre-eminence over every other kind of industry,"* had been "conceded without hesitation," he asserted.[91] Conventional physiocratic wisdom held that manufacturers were unproductive because they consumed more than they produced. Manufactures could increase the wealth of society only indirectly by saving. Smith recapitulated the physiocratic view in these terms:

> Artificers, manufacturers and merchants can augment the revenue and wealth of their society, by parsimony only; or, as is expressed in this system [the agricultural system], by privation . . . Unless, therefore, they annually save some part of [their funds] . . . the revenue and wealth of their society can never be in the smallest degree augmented by means of their industry.[92]

Hamilton summarized this view in almost exactly the same terms: only by "saving, or *parsimony* not the positive *productiveness* of their labour" could artificers and manufacturers "augment the revenue of the Society."[93]

Hamilton's rebuttal is also a near-verbatim restatement of three key points from Smith's critique of the physiocrats. First, while artificers and

90. McCoy, *The Elusive Republic*, chap. 4.

91. "Report on Manufactures," *PAH*, vol. 10, 236. Italics in original.

92. *WN* IV.ix.13, 668.

93. "Report on Manufactures," *PAH*, vol. 10, 237. Italics in original. Hamilton repeats this point on 238.

manufacturers might not produce more than they consume, their consumption could nevertheless substantially increase the value of goods in the market, and in some cases double their value.[94] Second, the argument that only "parsimony and privation" would increase national wealth applied equally to farmers as it did to manufacturers.[95] Third and most importantly, Hamilton offered an alternative conception of national wealth and its production. National wealth could only be increased in two ways: by unleashing the productive powers of labor through specialization, or by increasing the absolute quantity of labor.[96] On this final point, Hamilton borrowed Smith's three-pronged explanation of how the division of labor increased productivity: first, by increasing dexterity of workers; second, by saving time; and third, by introducing machinery.[97] By laying bare what he saw as the flawed

94. Compare the two passages. "Though the value of what the artificer produces, therefore, should not at any one moment of time be supposed greater than the value he consumes, yet at every moment of time the actually existing value of goods in the market is, in consequence of what he produces, greater than it otherwise would be," WN IV.ix.32, 676. Hamilton: "And though the increment of value produced by the classes of Artificers should at no time exceed the value of the produce of the land consumed by them, yet there would be at every moment, in consequence of their labour, a greater value of goods in the market than would exist independent of it." "Report on Manufactures," PAH vol. 10, 238.

95. Smith: "Fourthly, farmers and country labourers can no more augment, without parsimony, the real revenue, the annual produce of the land and labour of their society, than artificers, manufacturers and merchants," WN, IV.ix.34, 676. Hamilton: "That the position, that Artificers can augment the revenue of a Society, only by parsimony, is true, in no other sense than in one, which is equally applicable to Husbandmen or Cultivators." "Report on Manufactures," PAH vol. 10, 238.

96. Smith: "The annual produce of land and labour of any society can be augmented only in two ways; either, first, by some improvement in the productive powers of the useful labour actually maintained within it; or, secondly, by some increase in the quantity of that labour." WN IV.ix.34, 676. Hamilton "That the annual produce of the land and labour of a country can only be increased in two ways—by some improvement in the *productive powers* of the useful labour, which actually exists within it, or by some increase in the quantity of such labour." "Report on Manufactures," PAH vol. 10, 239. Emphasis in original.

97. The similarity between the two passages in Smith and the "Report on Manufactures" is striking. Smith: "This great increase of the quantity of work, which, *in consequence of the division of labour*, the same number of people are capable of performing, *is owing to three different circumstances*; first, to the *increase of dexterity* in every particular workman; secondly, to the *saving of the time* which is commonly lost in passing from one species of work to another; and lastly, to *the invention of a great number of machines which facilitate and abridge labour*, and enable one man

premises of the physiocratic system and illuminating the true forces of productivity, Hamilton sought to prove the "utility of Artificers or Manufacturers" in a nation and, from there, to promote their growth by activating the powers of the national government.

In Hamilton's mind, the most important levers of economic growth that the government could pull were high taxes on imports (tariffs) and subsidies (known as "bounties"). The "Report on Manufactures" included an itemized list of increased duties on twenty-one foreign products, and he described bounties as "one of the most efficacious means of encouraging manufactures, and . . . in some views . . . the best."[98] Subsidies for nascent industries were more likely to increase the chances of profit, reduce the risk of loss and scarcity, and enlarge the market for domestic producers.[99] Smith famously devoted an entire chapter of *The Wealth of Nations* to the "unreasonableness of those Restraints" that stemmed from "national prejudice and animosity." Smith argued that bounties diminished rather than expanded domestic markets and stunted population growth and productivity. Hamilton, however, viewed them as "not only the best, but the only proper expedient" for encouraging both agriculture and manufacturing; they were "especially essential" for new industries that faced foreign competition.[100] Hamilton

---

to do the work of many." *WN* I.i.5, 17 (emphases added). Hamilton: "It has justly been observed that there is scarcely anything of greater moment in the economy of a nation than the *proper division of labor, which arises principally from three circumstances*. 1st—the *greater skill and dexterity* naturally resulting from a constant and undivided application to a single object . . . 2nd. *The oeconomy of time*—by avoiding the loss of it, incident to a frequent transition from one operation to another of a different nature . . . 3rd. *An extension of the use of Machinery.*" (emphases added) "Report on Manufactures," *PAH* vol. 10, 249–251.

98. "Report on Manufactures," *PAH* vol. 10, 298.

99. "Report on Manufactures," *PAH* vol. 10, 299; see also Douglas A. Irwin, *Clashing over Commerce: A History of US Trade Policy* (Chicago, IL: University of Chicago Press, 2017), 80–88.

100. "Report on Manufactures," *PAH* vol. 10, 300. Smith's analysis of the effects of the bounties on corn is as follows: "The corn bounty, it is to be observed, as well as every other bounty upon exportation, imposes two different taxes upon the people; first, the tax which they are obliged to contribute, in order to pay the bounty; and secondly, the tax which arises from the advanced price of the commodity in the home-market . . . In this particular commodity, therefore, this second tax, is by much the heaviest of the two. . . . So very heavy a tax upon the first necessary of life, must

derived his position not from abstract theory, but rather from experience and observation. "Experience teaches," Hamilton wrote, "that men are often so much governed by what they are accustomed to see and practice, that the simplest and most obvious improvements, in the [most] ordinary occupations, are adopted with hesitation reluctance and by slow gradations."[101] Attaining the object of political economy—national wealth and public happiness—"may therefore require the incitement and patronage of government."[102]

Why would Hamilton quote so extensively from Smith's *The Wealth of Nations* if the specific policies in his "Report" ultimately were opposed to Smith's "system of perfect liberty?" The significance of Hamilton's reliance of Smith's *The Wealth of Nations* in the "Report on Manufactures" has puzzled scholars.[103] On the one hand, the political directive of the

---

either reduce the subsistence of the laboring poor, or it must occasion some augmentation in their pecuniary wages, proportionable to that in the pecuniary price of their subsistence. So far as it operates in the other, it must reduce the ability of the employers of the poor, to employ so great a number as they otherwise might do, and must, so far, tend to restrain the industry of the country. The extraordinary expectation of corn, therefore, occasioned by the bounty, not only, in every particular year, diminishes the home, just as much as it extends the foreign market and consumption, but, by restraining the population and industry of the country, its final tendency is to stunt and restrain the gradual extension of the home-market; and thereby, in the long run, rather to diminish, than to augment, the whole market and consumption of corn." *WN* IV.v.a.8, 508–9.

101. "Report on Manufactures," *PAH* vol. 10, 266.

102. "Report on Manufactures," *PAH* vol. 10, 267.

103. Louis M. Hacker has argued that there has been an "unbroken tradition of misinterpretation" of Hamilton: that Hamilton was an avid protectionist and nationalist, rather than (as Hacker suggests), someone who saw government assistance of infant industries "as an expedient necessary only because new, young, and underdeveloped nations were unequal in a race where the more powerful nations had every advantage for the very reason that their governments used intervention on their behalf . . . He follows Adam Smith so plainly and completely that one can only express wonder that the Hamilton text has been misunderstood for so long." Louis M. (Louis Morton) Hacker, *Alexander Hamilton in the American Tradition* (New York, NY: McGraw-Hill, 1957), 12. Ron Chernow expresses a similar view about the Hamilton-Smith connection in Ron Chernow, *Alexander Hamilton* (New York, NY: Penguin Books, 2005), 375–77. One of the earliest articulations of this view is found in Bourne, "Alexander Hamilton and Adam Smith." Bourne contends that Hamilton may have "concealed" the source of his ideas (i.e., Smith) for reasons of "political expediency," since "The citation of an English writer on Political Economy would have weakened rather than strengthened his case." More recently,

Report aimed to dismantle Smith's proposition "that Industry, if left to itself, will naturally find its way to the most useful and profitable employment." A list of "very cogent reasons" could be summoned against this hypothesis—the risks of starting a new enterprise, the "strong influence of habit and the spirit of imitation," the high barriers to entry that new businesses faced in a competitive market—each of which necessitated the additional support of some trusted investor.[104]

On the other hand, Hamilton's rejection of the physiocratic doctrine and his temperate view of free trade suggest a closer affinity to Smith's own position. Hamilton admitted that "a free exchange, mutually beneficial" between nations would support the "full vigour" of industries. If it were the case that liberty of industry and commerce was "the prevailing system of nations," there might not need to be the "zealous pursuits of manufactures" in the United States. But this was not the case. Free trade, from Hamilton's viewpoint, was "far from characterizing the general policy of Nations. The prevalent one has been regulated by an opposite spirit."[105] This mirrors Smith who argued that to wish for a system of free trade was "as absurd as to expect that an Oceana or Utopia should ever be established."[106] In a global environment of hostile nations, maintaining political and economic independence demanded that America first would have to imitate her rivals before she could transcend them.

Hamilton's extensive engagement with Smith reveals the intricacies of how major American thinkers were developing an original political economic strategy in the late eighteenth century. European sources, including but not limited to Smith's *The Wealth of Nations*, provided the conceptual tools to understand the science of wealth creation, but those

---

Mark Somos has laid out a nuanced and compelling argument about how Hamilton's views in the "Report on Manufactures" are embedded in a larger foreign relations argument centered on neutrality and a strong executive. See Somos, "'A Price Would Be Set Not Only upon Our Friendship, but upon Our Neutrality:' Alexander Hamilton's Political Economy and Early American State-Building."

104. "Report on Manufactures," *PAH* vol. 10, 266.
105. "Report on Manufactures," *PAH* vol. 10, 262.
106. *WN* IV.ii.43, 471.

tools had to be reshaped in the American context. Unencumbered by the legacy of the *ancien régime* and free from the fetters of the British mercantile system, American thinkers could design their political-economic institutions afresh. In this context, Smith's proposals in *The Wealth of Nations* "had the best chance of success" in a fledgling nation.[107]

Whether in institutional design or the enactment of specific policies, however, the success of Smith's proposals was not the only indicator of his importance in the Early National period. Hamilton's repurposing of *The Wealth of Nations* in the "Report on Manufactures," like Madison's use of Smith in *Federalist 10*, shows how Americans could reimagine their futures through the kaleidoscope of the science of political economy. For some, like the Jeffersonians, the science of political economy revealed the promises of an agricultural republic shielded from the corrupting forces of commerce and luxury. For others, like Alexander Hamilton, the science of political economy pointed to the invigorating—not enervating—powers of manufacturing and commerce; it also proved the necessity of strong initiative from the national government. Thus, the prevalence of Smith's ideas among American statesmen speaks not so much to Smith's singular importance, but rather, to the widespread conviction that the science of political economy provided an indispensable roadmap for a polity, economy, and society on the cusp of transformation.

In the end, however, applying the science of political economy was a matter of raw politics. Hamilton's proposal for the federal government to assume state debts in "Report on Public Credit" caused an immediate uproar. Senator William Maclay, who along with Robert Morris represented Pennsylvania as its first senatorial pair, condemned Hamilton's bill as a "villainous business" that would create "the most abandoned system of speculation ever broached in our country."[108] Representative James Jackson from Georgia exclaimed, "My soul rises indignant at the avaricious and immoral turpitude" of speculators, whom he called

107. Fleischacker, "Adam Smith's Reception among the American Founders," 903–5.
108. Not only that, Maclay was disgusted also by Hamilton's Anglophilia and scorned Hamilton's report as one "in the style of a British minister." As quoted in Chernow, *Alexander Hamilton*, 302.

"rapacious wolves seeking whom they may devour, and preying upon the misfortunes of their fellow-men."[109] When Jefferson returned from Paris in March of 1790, he described the political commotion as "the most bitter and angry contest ever known in Congress before or since the union of the states."[110]

Even those who were once Hamilton's closest allies tried to dismantle his elaborate financial machinations. James Madison had spurned the idea of government-directed economic growth even before Hamilton had drafted the "Report on Manufactures," but the rift between the one-time coauthors began widening in 1789. "I own myself the friend to a very free system of commerce," Madison proclaimed in Congress, alluding to Smith's *The Wealth of Nations*, "and hold it as truth, that commercial shackles are generally unjust, oppressive, and impolitic."[111] He also turned one of Hamilton's weapons against him, invoking one

109. *Annals of Congress*, House of Representatives, 1st Congress, 2nd Session. January 28, 1790, 1132 and 1137. See also Broadus Mitchell, *Alexander Hamilton: The National Adventure, 1788–1804* (New York, NY: Macmillan, 1962), 45.

110. Thomas Jefferson, *Complete Anas of Thomas Jefferson*, ed. Franklin B. Sawvel. (New York, NY: Round Table Press, 1903), 32.

111. "Import and Tonnage Duties, 9 April 1789," *PJM* vol. 12, eds. Charles F. Hobson et al. (Charlottesville, VA: University of Virginia Press, 1979), 69–74 at 70–71. Madison reveals his fondness for Smith's political economy, perhaps lending further proof for Fleischacker's thesis that Madison was "the most Smithian" thinker of the Founders. Madison paraphrases the underlying logic of the "invisible hand" passage in Book IV of *The Wealth of Nations*: "that if industry and labor are left to take their own course, they will generally be directed to those objects which are the most productive, and this in a more certain and direct manner than the wisdom of the most enlightened legislature could point out." The day before, Madison delivered a similar, but shorter speech on the same subject, stating that the general regulation of commerce "ought to be as free as the policy of nations will admit." See "Import and Tonnage Duties, 8 April 1789," *PJM* vol. 12, 64–66. Madison did make important exceptions to free trade, however. For example, if the US were to abide by a policy of free trade while others did not, such a policy could be detrimental to American commercial interests at home and abroad. "If America was to leave her ports perfectly free, and make no discrimination between vessels owned by her citizens and those owned by foreigners, while other nations make this discrimination, it is obvious that such a policy would go to exclude American shipping altogether from foreign ports, and she would be materially affected in one of her most important interests." *PJM*, vol. 12, 72. On April 21, 1789, Madison also stated "I am a friend to free commerce, and at the same time a friend to such regulations as are calculated to promote our own interests, and this on national principles," *PJM*, vol 12, 99.

of "the most enlightened patrons of banks, particularly . . . Smith on the Wealth of Nations" to highlight the disadvantages of a national bank.[112] Perhaps most frustrating for Hamilton was Madison's brazen opposition to the federal assumption of state debts. Four times in 1790, Madison corralled other representatives to thwart the assumption proposal, earning him the nickname, "the Big Knife."[113]

Determination to undo the Hamiltonian edifice and to restore faith in the idea of an agricultural republic marked the Jefferson presidency and the decade that followed. The Louisiana Purchase of 1803 was a professed failsafe measure of agrarian republicanism. The vast expanse of western territory would foster the expansion of virtuous farming and erode the mercantile spirit, while access to navigable ports would ensure that there would be just enough access to foreign markets for agricultural surplus. The infamous embargo of 1807 attempted to enforce this economic and moral order on an international scale. Though it partially served a diplomatic aim by penalizing Great Britain for its wartime blockade against the American continent, the 1807 embargo was also an expressive act of rejecting foreign luxury and endorsing a "peaceable coercion" of agricultural prosperity.[114] Writing in 1816, Jefferson held fast to his belief that agriculture was America's "distinguishing feature." Commercial entanglements and the manufacturing ploys of Hamilton—"a man whose mind was really powerful, but chained by the native partialities to every thing English," as Jefferson described him— were incompatible with a nation so "essentially agricultural, & insulated by the nature from the abusive governments of the old world."[115]

112. "The Bank Bill," in *PJM*, vol. 13, ed. Charles F. Hobson and Robert A. Rutland. (Charlottesville, VA: University Press of Virginia), 372–382 at 373.

113. Chernow, *Alexander Hamilton*, 322.

114. McCoy, *The Elusive Republic*, 222. McCoy writes, "The basic purpose of commercial coercion was to liberate American commerce from devastating foreign restrictions in order to underwrite and secure the prosperity of an agricultural republic. Ibid., 223. See also Albertone, *National Identity and the Agrarian Republic*, chap. 3.

115. "Thomas Jefferson to William H. Crawford, 20 June 1816," *The Papers of Thomas Jefferson*, Retirement Series, vol. 10, *May 1816 to 18 January 1817*, ed. J. Jefferson Looney. (Princeton, NJ: Princeton University Press, 2013), 173–176 at 174.

The realities of politics assailed Jefferson's idealism, however. West-ern expansion into untrodden territory demanded an aggressive foreign policy, and the embargo crippled the American economy over a fourteen-month period.[116] During James Madison's presidency, re-newed conflict with Great Britain in 1812 exposed the fragility of foreign trade relations. Even after the war ended in 1815, new political-economic issues—heightened debates about the tariff, monetary policy, and, of course, slavery—continually placed the United States in precarity and revived longstanding debates over the proper origins and management of national wealth.

Antagonism toward the Hamiltonian system was expressed in less explicitly political ways as well. Despite maintaining a cool and cordial relationship with Treasury Secretary Hamilton during the Washington administration, John Adams often complained in private of Hamilton's hypocrisy, his "proud, Spirited, conceited, aspiring" ambitions, and his "Puppy head" pleas.[117] After his term as president and long after the National Bank received its charter from the federal government, Adams criticized Hamilton savagely, calling him a "Creature . . . in a delirium of Ambition," who had been "blown up with <Ambition> Vanity by the Tories," and in his quest to become president, Hamilton "hated every Man young or old, who stood in his Way, or could in any manner eclipse his laurels or rival his Pretensions."[118] The problems of moneyed interest in politics were a given, but Adams was more preoccupied with a set of moral vices—ambition, greed, vanity, the desire for superiority—which could make wealth socially insidious. One major source of inspiration

116. Douglas Irwin estimates that the Jefferson embargo cost the United States approxi-mately five percent of its Gross National Product at the time. Douglas A. Irwin, "The Welfare Cost of Autarky: Evidence from the Jeffersonian Trade Embargo, 1807–09," *Review of Interna-tional Economics* 13, no. 4 (2005), 631–45.

117. Letter from John Adams to Abigail Adams, January 9, 1797. [electronic edition] *Adams Family Papers: An Electronic Archive*. Massachusetts Historical Society. http://masshist.org /digitaladams.

118. "From John Adams to Benjamin Rush, 25 January 1806," *Founders Online*, National Ar-chives, http://founders.archives.gov/documents/Adams/99-02-02-5119 (last update: 2016-03-28). This is an Early Access document from *The Adams Papers*. It is not an authoritative final version.

for Adams in this respect was a well-known and eccentric work of the Enlightenment: Adam Smith's *The Theory of Moral Sentiments*.

———

When Smith's *The Theory of Moral Sentiments* first appeared in 1759, reactions ranged from generous commendations to philosophical puzzlement. On the one hand, Smith's closest friends and admirers lauded the text's ingenuity, perspicuous style, captivating illustrations, and lucid presentation of different systems of moral philosophy. Edmund Burke expressed how convinced he was of the "solidity and Truth" of Smith's theory. He praised Smith for his "elegant Painting of the manners and passions" and the way in which Smith captured those "natural movements of the mind" with "happy illustrations from ordinary life."[119] Even the most "superficial and careless Reader, though incapable of forming a just judgment of our Author's system," *The Monthly Review* speculated, would be pleased with Smith's "agreeable manner of illustrating his argument, [and] by the frequent appeals he makes to fact and experience."[120]

On the other hand, some of Smith's readers found the style and substance of *The Theory of Moral Sentiments* distracting and even deceptive. Burke complained to Smith in private correspondence that for all of its sublime illustrations, the work was "rather a little too diffuse" in some places.[121] George Ridpath, a bookish Scots churchman, found *The Theory of Moral Sentiments* exasperating. "What is new in it is perhaps of no great moment in itself, and is neither distinctly explained nor clearly established," Ridpath wrote in his diary in October of 1759. Smith was clearly "a man of knowledge and of genius," but one who Ridpath believed had overindulged in "playing everywhere the orator" and who been led "quite astray from that study of accuracy, precision, and

119. Letter from Edmund Burke to Adam Smith, 10 September 1759. *Corr.*, 46–47. Burke was also the purported author of a (very complimentary) review of *TMS* published in the *Annual Register*, vol. 2 (1759).

120. *The Monthly Review*, vol. 20, (July 1759), 2.

121. Letter from Edmund Burke to Adam Smith, 10 September 1759. *Corr*, 47.

clearness." To Ridpath's disappointment, Smith's resulting work spun out "to the tedious length of 400 pages what in my opinion might be delivered as fully and with far more energy and perspicuity in 20."[122]

If one plumbed deep enough, the main problem with *The Theory of Moral Sentiments* seemed to be that Smith's theory simply could not be correct. "I have always thought Dr Smith's System of Sympathy wrong," wrote Thomas Reid, Smith's successor in Moral Philosophy at the University of Glasgow. [123] For Reid, Smith's theory that "all Our moral Sentiments are resolved into Sympathy" was either incomplete or circular reasoning. Sympathy, according to Reid, was inextricably linked to self-love, affection, and esteem for others; as such, our own self-love, affection, and esteem could not be said to be the product of sympathy.[124] Lord Kames also found Smith's reliance on sympathetic imagination far-fetched. "That a man should conceive himself to be another, is no slight effort of imagination," he commented, but to make sympathy depend on such a "ductile imagination" would exclude people whom Kames called "dull people and illiterate rustics."[125] In Kames's reading, sympathy was not the final arbiter of our moral conduct; it had to proceed from some other natural, universal principle of human behavior. That Smith failed to provide an adequate account of the origin of sympathy was the starting point of arguably one of the most notable responses to *The Theory of Moral Sentiments* in France: Sophie de Grouchy's *Letters on Sympathy*, published in 1798 alongside her

122. *Diary of George Ridpath, 1755–1761* (Edinburgh: The University Press by T. & A. Constable, 1922), pp. 273–6. Reprinted in *On Moral Sentiments: Contemporary Responses to Adam Smith*, ed. John Reeder (Bristol: Thoemmes Press, 1997), 30–32.

123. Letter from Thomas Reid to Lord Kames, 30 October 1778. From Ian S. Ross, ed. "Unpublished Letters from Thomas Reid to Lord Kames, 1762–1782," in *Texas Studies in Literature and Language* 7, no. 1 (1965), 17–65, Reprinted in John Reeder, *On Moral Sentiments: Contemporary Responses to Adam Smith* (Bristol: Thoemmes Press, 1997), 65–68 at 66

124. Thomas Reid, "A Sketch of Dr Smith's Theory of Morals," in "Thomas Reid on Adam Smith's Theory of Moralsm" eds. J.C. Stewart-Robertson and David Fate Norton, *Journal of the History of Ideas* 45 (1984), 310–21. Reprinted in Reeder, *On Moral Sentiments*, 69–99 at 70.

125. Henry Home, Lord Kames, *Essays on the Principles of Morality and Natural Religion*, 3rd edition (Edinburgh: Liberty Fund, 1779), chapter 11. Reprinted in Reeder, *On Moral Sentiments*, 61–63.

translation of Smith's work. In De Grouchy's critical engagement with *The Theory of Moral Sentiments*, sympathy was not purely an imaginative experience, but fundamentally an embodied one that could be traced to early physiological memories of pain and pleasure.[126]

By the time of Dugald Stewart's ascendancy in the nineteenth century, Smith's *The Theory of Moral Sentiments* was past its prime. Stewart extolled Smith's writing and ingenuity, but he expressed dissatisfaction with Smith's theory of sympathy. *The Theory of Moral Sentiments* was a fine work of "*practical* morality," Stewart argued, but it obscured the metaphysical problems at the heart of moral science— Where did sympathy come from? Is sympathy different from affection, love, or benevolence?—and blurred the lines between descriptive and normative content.[127] Such mixed assessments also characterized the American readings of *The Theory of Moral Sentiments*. Americans' readings of Smith's *The Theory of Moral Sentiments* turned not only on the philosophical solidity of its arguments, but also on the particular needs of American academic moralism in the late eighteenth and early nineteenth centuries.

Like the science of political economy, American moral science was eclectic, especially in institutions of higher learning. Professors of moral philosophy, often also the college president, assumed the responsibility of instructing the consciences of students and setting them on the path of right and moral leadership. The professors' goal was not only to describe man's moral nature and his relation to the moral universe, but also to prescribe the ends and duties toward which human actions should

126. De Grouchy's engagements with Smith and her extension of his moral psychology are, thankfully, beginning to be appreciated. See Bergés and Schliesser, *Sophie de Grouchy's Letters on Sympathy*; Scurr, "Inequality and Political Stability from Ancien Régime to Revolution," McCrudden, "Sophie de Grouchy as an activist interpreter of Adam Smith," forthcoming.

127. Dugald Stewart, "Of Sympathy," and "Note C. Smith's Moral Theory," from *The Philosophy of the Active and Moral Powers of Man* (1828), in *The Collected Works of Dugald Stewart*, ed. Sir William Hamilton vol. 6, (Edinburgh: Thomas Constable and Co.; Boston: Little, Brown, and Co., 1854–60), 328–33 and 407–14. Reprinted in Reeder, *On Moral Sentiments*, 121–35. Emphasis in original. For an extensive compilation of criticisms of *The Theory of Moral Sentiments* in Great Britain, France, and Germany, see Daniel B. Klein, "Dissing *The Theory of Moral Sentiments*: Twenty-Six Critics, from 1765 to 1949," *Econ Journal Watch* 15, no. 2 (2018), 201.

BEST BOOK EXTANT 55

be directed.[128] Thus, their choice of texts, philosophies, and ideas to teach reflects how they used the tools of moral science to shape the virtue and character of America's educated class. Among the most important works for instructional purposes were those of the Scottish Enlightenment and the later Scottish Common Sense writers, which remained pillars of moral philosophy curriculum through the antebellum period. John Witherspoon, for example, relied heavily on Francis Hutcheson's *System of Moral Philosophy* in teaching his course at the College of New Jersey, and he highlighted the different accounts of virtue from thinkers such as Archibald Campbell, Adam Smith, and David Hume.[129] The teachings of Francis Alison and William Smith of the College of Philadelphia were also indebted to Scottish authors such as Francis Hutcheson, William Fordyce, and George Turnbull.[130] At Harvard, figures such as Levi Frisbie, Levi Hedge, James Walker, and Francis Bowen turned the Common Sense ideas of Thomas Reid and his disciples into the metaphysical foundations of their Unitarian moralism.[131]

Though by no means uniform in their treatment of Scottish authors, American moralists found a common language and method with which to demystify and explain the principles of human nature and virtue. Scottish philosophy furnished the moralists with the concept of the moral sense and insisted on an inductive approach to understanding the human mind.[132] Most importantly, the writings of Scottish philosophers

128. Donald H. Meyer, *The Instructed Conscience: The Shaping of the American National Ethic* (Philadelphia, PA: University of Pennsylvania Press, 1972), 4; Daniel Walker Howe, *The Unitarian Conscience: Harvard Moral Philosophy, 1805–1861* (Cambridge, MA: Harvard University Press, 1970), 2.

129. John Witherspoon, *Lectures on Moral Philosophy*, ed. Varnum Lansing Collins (Princeton, NJ: Princeton University Press, 1912), 23–26.

130. Diamond, "Witherspoon, William Smith and the Scottish Philosophy in Revolutionary America," 115.

131. As Daniel Walker Howe contends, "nowhere else was Scottish common sense philosophy accepted so enthusiastically or unqualifiedly as at Harvard." Howe, *The Unitarian Conscience*, 31.

132. For a lengthier discussion of the heterogeneous role of Scottish Common Sense philosophy in America, see Diamond, "Witherspoon and the Scottish Philosophy in Revolutionary America," as well as Shannon Stimson, "'A Jury of the Country': Common Sense Philosophy and the Jurisprudence of James Wilson," in *Scotland and America in the Age of Enlightenment*,

were malleable to pedagogical and ideological demands of an American society intensely preoccupied with cultivating practical morality and proving God's divine will. For John Witherspoon, it was only by following the dictates of a conscience "enlightened by reason, experience, and every way by which we can be supposed to learn the will of our Maker" could men perform the duties that were "productive of the greatest good."[133]

And yet, *The Theory of Moral Sentiments* sat awkwardly in this picture. Witherspoon's lectures, for example, reduced Smith's theory of sympathy to nothing more than "a new phraseology for the moral sense," and Francis Alison appears to have made little of incorporating *The Theory of Moral Sentiments* alongside his teaching of Hutcheson in the 1760s.[134] Major book publishers wielded immense influence on the broader market of ideas in print. William Young, a prominent publisher based in Philadelphia, published the first American editions of Thomas Reid's *Essay on the Intellectual Powers of Man* and *Essays on the Active Powers of Man* in 1792, as well as Dugald Stewart's *Elements of the Philosophy of the Human Mind* in 1793. Convinced that Reid and Stewart's philosophies were antidotes to the poison of Humean skepticism, Young hoped that the American publication of their works would provide a firm foundation for moral education in the new republic. By doing so, Young transformed common sense philosophy into "a commodity that was not only purchased and used, but literally remade, in America," and in turn, he almost single-handedly established the template for moral philosophy curriculum for decades.[135] Incidentally, it was one that all but eclipsed Smith's *The Theory of Moral Sentiments*.

The problem with Smith's *The Theory of Moral Sentiments*, at least for American readers, was philosophical as much as it was pedagogical.

193–208. Sophia Rosenfeld, *Common Sense: A Political History*. (Cambridge, MA: Harvard University Press, 2011).

133. Witherspoon, *Lectures on Moral Philosophy*, 30.

134. Witherspoon, *Lectures on Moral Philosophy*, 25–26; Mark Somos notes that Francis Alison's lectures drew mostly from Hutcheson, but by 1760–1761 Alison had started incorporating Smith's *The Theory of Moral Sentiments*. Mark Somos, *American States of Nature: The Origins of Independence, 1761–1775* (New York, NY: Oxford University Press, 2019), 40–43.

135. Sher, *The Enlightenment and the Book*, 567.

Beyond the fact that it was not the best-suited text for instruction (Hutcheson, Reid, and Stewart earned that honor), Smith's theory that moral rules could be deduced from sympathy appeared philosophically unsound. A single—but lengthy—review essay on *The Theory of Moral Sentiments*, written by Levi Frisbie and published in *The North American Review* in 1819, reveals this peculiar stance. Frisbie, the inaugural Alford Professor of Moral Philosophy at Harvard, remarked that Smith's theory, despite "the uncommon ingenuity" of its presentation, "[had] not, so far as we know, been formally examined by any writer," and, what is more, "seems to have been adopted by none."[136] Much of Frisbie's critique of *The Theory of Moral Sentiments* echoed that of Smith's later contemporaries. The "whole difficulty of the problem" of sympathy, Frisbie contended, was that it was non-foundational, perhaps even anti-foundational. Over the span of a densely packed, twenty-six-page review, Frisbie interrogated Smith's theory from a multitude of angles. If sympathy is foundational to moral action, how is it that we can identify so many instances of moral approval without sympathy? When we enter into the feelings of virtuous people, is our satisfaction increased by sympathy, or is it founded on some other, prior form of moral approval? Why does Smith's impartial spectator substitute sympathy with action for affection when making moral evaluations?

Smith's failure to satisfactorily answer these questions—and many others—led Frisbie to essentially reject his science of morals, notwithstanding the "ingenuity, acuteness, and eloquence" with which the work was written.[137] Though overflowing with rich and colorful illustrations, *The Theory of Moral Sentiments* lacked the precision necessary for a work of true philosophy. "The style is often vague and diffuse, and rather that of a popular essay, than a philosophical discussion," Frisbie commented, and the copious examples were "better suited to enforce received truth, than to settle what is doubtful, or elucidate what is obscure." Such errors

136. "Reviewed Work(s), The Theory of Moral Sentiments;—or an Essay towards an Analysis of the principles, by which men naturally judge concerning the conduct and character, first of their neighbors and afterwards of themselves. By Adam Smith, LL.D. F.R.S. Boston, Well & Lilly, 1817," *The North American Review*, 8.23 (March 1819), 372.

137. "Reviewed Work(s), The Theory of Moral Sentiments," 394.

of style produced errors of reasoning, which, according to Frisbie, explained why "so many rise from the perusal of Dr. Smith's work with the conviction that it cannot be true, without being able to point out where-in the fallacy lies."[138]

Though academic moralists may have been less than enthusiastic about Smith's theory of sympathy and morality, revisiting their encounters with *The Theory of Moral Sentiments* enables us to more clearly reconstruct their intellectual worlds. Academic moralists used the works of Francis Hutcheson, Adam Smith, Thomas Reid, and Dugald Stewart as powerful lenses that brought into focus the epistemological and sentimental bases of moral action. Additionally, American readers of Scottish moral philosophy were searching for more than intellectual stimulation or interpretive conclusions about morality. They were searching for moral instruction that was independent of theology, but supportive of religion; scientifically derived, and straightforwardly practicable.[139] This earnest desire for moral improvement pervaded American life; one's morals, conduct, and character were believed to have profound influence on the broader happiness and virtue of the community.

———

"Ever keep in mind my son that virtue is the dignity of Humane nature," Abigail Adams wrote her son, Charles, in 1786. "Tho as individuals each may think himself too unimportant to effect so desirable an event," she beseeched, "yet every one is accountable for his conduct and none so insignificant as not to have some influence." She prodded Charles to review the characters of history and the consequences of their actions, and to "Behold the Havock and devastation of Rapine cruelty Luxery avarice and ambition." In order to cultivate virtue and to ward off vice, Abigail recommended a series of "valuable Books" on "an other course of reading," namely, moral philosophy: Henry Grove's *A System of Moral Philosophy* (1749), Joseph Butler's *The Analogy of Religion* (1785), Adam

138. "Reviewed Work(s), The Theory of Moral Sentiments," 395.
139. Meyer, *The Instructed Conscience*, xi–xii.

Smith's *The Theory of Moral Sentiments* (1759), and Isaac Watts' *The Improvement of the Mind* (1741).[140] Later that year, John Quincy Adams noted in his diary that he had checked out Smith's *The Theory of Moral Sentiments* (along with Edmund Burke's essay on the sublime and beautiful and a book on algebra) from the Harvard College library.[141] By the end of 1786, word of Smith's work on moral sentiments appeared to have reached other members of the Adams family. In a December letter to her aunt, Lucy Cranch expressed her fondness for the Adamses by quoting *The Theory of Moral Sentiments*: "the cheif [sic] part of human happiness, consists in the consciousness of being beloved."[142] By 1790, John Adams called attention to a "sett [sic] of Scotch Writers" that he believed warranted a young John Quincy's "Attention in a very high Degree." Among those writers and works were Kames's *Elements of Criticism* and *Historical Law Tracts*, Steuart's *Principles of Political Oeconomy*, and Smith's *The Theory of Moral Sentiments* and *The Wealth of Nations*.[143]

Private moral life became a matter of public discussion for the most assiduous reader of the Adams family, John Adams. Having held a long-standing fascination with the workings of the human psyche, John Adams immersed himself in literature, history, and works of moral philosophy not just for his own moral edification, but also to distill a theory of aristocracy that at the time went against the grain of prevailing republican sentiments. Between 1787 and 1791, Adams penned two major

140. Abigail Adams to Charles Adams, ca. 16 February 1786. The Adams Family Correspondence, volume 7. *Adams Papers*, Digital Edition, available at http://www.masshist.org/publications/adams-papers/index.php/view/ADMS-04-07-02-0016#sn=18.

141. Diary of John Quincy Adams, vol. 2 November 17, 1786. *Adams Papers*, Digital Edition, available at http://www.masshist.org/publications/adams-papers/index.php/view/ADMS-03-02-02-0001-0010-0017#sn=7.

142. *TMS* I.ii.5.1, 41. The letter continues: "I believes he says true, the greatest pleasure I ever feel is derived from a consciousness that there are those, who feel a friendship for me and who I have reason to think are interested in my happiness." Lucy Cranch to Abigail Adams, December 7, 1786. *Adams Family Correspondence*, volume 7. *Adams Papers*, Digital Edition, available at http://www.masshist.org/publications/adams-papers/index.php/view/ADMS-04-07-02-0156#sn=8.

143. John Adams to John Quincy Adams. February 19, 1790. *Adams Family Correspondence*, volume 9 *Adams Papers*, Digital Edition, available at http://www.masshist.org/publications/adams-papers/index.php/view/ADMS-04-09-02-0010#sn=10.

works that would eventually set him apart as a political scientist par excellence, though an anomalous one at that: *A Defence of the Constitutions of Government of the United States* (1787) and *Discourses on Davila* (1790–1791). The former led to charges of Adams's alleged monarchical sympathies; the latter, written between 1790 and 1791, did little to rectify those accusations. The last essay of the *Discourses*, published in April of 1791, so angered Adams's political opponents that he had to abruptly halt the publication of any further essays.[144]

Adams's musings on politics during the 1780s and 1790s has bedeviled scholarly attempts to place him in a single tradition. Some scholars have read the *Defence* and *Discourses*, works of the "mature" Adams, as betrayals of revolutionary ideals and hallmarks of Adams's reactionary conservatism.[145] Others have treated Adams as the American personification of an unbroken tradition in classical republican political thought.[146] Still others see Adams as a liberal constitutional thinker, much like James Madison, who was anxious about securing natural rights and designing sound institutions to corral men's passions.[147]

144. Zoltán Haraszti, *John Adams and the Prophets of Progress* (Cambridge, MA: Harvard University Press, 1952), 156; Haraszti, "The 32nd Discourse on Davila," *The William and Mary Quarterly* 11, no. 1 (1954), 89. The planned but incomplete thirty-third essay is printed in Sara Georgini et al., eds. *The Papers of John Adams, vol. 20: June 1789–February 1971* (Cambridge, MA: Belknap, 2020), 339–343.

145. For this interpretation of John Adams as a reactionary or conservative defender of oligarchy, see Joyce Appleby, *Liberalism and Republicanism in the Historical Imagination* (Cambridge, MA: Harvard University Press, 1992); Russell Kirk, *The Conservative Mind from Burke to Eliot* (Washington, D.C.: Regnery Publications, 1986).

146. J.G.A. Pocock, for example, called Adams's *Defence* "perhaps the last major work of political theory written within the unmodified tradition of classical republicanism." J. G. A. Pocock, *The Machiavellian Moment: Florentine Political Thought and the Atlantic Republican Tradition* (Princeton, NJ: Princeton University Press, 1975), 526. Adam Lebovitz advances a significant revision to these existing interpretations of Adams's thought, arguing that Adams's *Defence* provided the most important template not only for the Massachusetts state constitution, but also exerted profound influence on French constitutional thought after the Revolution. Adam Lebovitz, *Colossus: Constitutional Theory in France and America, 1776–1799* (Cambridge, MA: Harvard University Press, forthcoming).

147. According to Luke Mayville, the most comprehensive study of Adams's political thought along these lines is C. Bradley Thompson, *John Adams and the Spirit of Liberty* (Lawrence, KS: University Press of Kansas, 1998). For a concise review of different approaches to the

Whatever the case may be, it is clear that Adams's strident political commitments moved him "in a direction that eventually left him isolated from the main line of American intellectual development," as the historian Gordon Wood writes.[148]

No small part of this frustration arises from Adams's *Discourses on Davila*. Published as a series of essays in the Federalist periodical *The Gazette of the United States* between April of 1790 and April of 1791, *Discourses* appeared against a backdrop of political and intellectual turmoil. Hamilton's financial plans were dividing Congress and kindling fears about the emergence of a class of seditious financiers. Meanwhile, the revolution in France had garnered enough American sympathy to unsettle people like Adams, who watched with fear as the French were "morally and constitutionally entering unchartered territory."[149] Channeling his anxieties, Adams intended to provide a translation and commentary of Enrico Caterino Davila's *Historia delle guerre civili di Francia*, a seventeenth-century Italian historian's account of the sixteenth-century French civil wars. Many essays were straight translations of Davila's work, but fourteen were devoted to Adams's "useful reflections" on human moral psychology. Thus, *Discourses* is best read as a complement or extension of Adams's analysis in the *Defence*.[150] Whereas the *Defence* showed the persistence of oligarchic threats to republics throughout history, *Discourses* delved into the moral-psychological foundations of that threat. And where Adams' contemporary critics—notably Thomas Jefferson and John Taylor of

---

political thought of John Adams, see Mayville's precis in Luke Mayville, *John Adams and the Fear of American Oligarchy* (Princeton, NJ: Princeton University Press, 2016), 9–14.

148. Wood, *The Creation of the American Republic, 1776–1787*, 569.

149. Mayville, *John Adams and the Fear of American Oligarchy*, 99.

150. In a series of letters to John Taylor, Adams described himself feeling "all the ridicule of hinting at my poor *four volumes* of 'Defence and Discourses on Davila,' after quoting Mariana, Harrington, Sidney, and Montesquieu," (emphasis added). The *Defence* was three volumes, but this characterization suggests Adams saw both the *Defence* and *Discourses* as making up the same (four-volume) project. In a letter to his son Thomas Boylston, Adams himself expressed his wish that "The Discourses on Davila were collected and printed as a fourth Volume, for they are in reality a Key to the whole." See the editorial note in the *Papers of John Adams*, vol. 20, 337–339.

Caroline—failed to recognize how aristocratic power could not simply be willed away with democratic reforms, Adams set out to prove how obstinate and dangerous a natural aristocracy was to republican government.

A closer examination of Adams's use of eighteenth-century moral philosophy, especially Smith's *The Theory of Moral Sentiments*, reveals a striking and underappreciated originality in Adams's political thought. As Luke Mayville has powerfully demonstrated, Adams's preoccupation with aristocracy—and its malignant twin, oligarchy—in the *Defence* and *Discourses* reveals not a fondness for, but rather a grave fear of, oligarchic power in American society. While democratic-republican reformers like Jefferson believed that America would weed out the roots of ancient and corrupt oligarchic institutions and cultivate the seeds of a truly meritocratic and virtuous elite, Adams was doubtful. According to Adams, the deep, social psychological roots of authority would give rise to a "natural aristocracy" not of the wise, talented, and virtuous, but rather of the beautiful, well-born, and wealthy. What is more, this natural aristocracy would not only survive, but thrive if left unchecked, all to the detriment of the republic. Adams approached moral philosophy as more than an academic guide to the human psyche. He made it a crucial link between the "phenomena of social life and the problems of political power" that enabled him to advance a unique conception of oligarchy.[151]

Of the various sources that Adams used to animate *Discourses*, Adam Smith's *The Theory of Moral Sentiments* stands out.[152] The portions of *The Theory of Moral Sentiments* upon which Adams relied provided the framework for Adams's analysis of oligarchy. Several of the essays contain extensive paraphrasing or verbatim quotations from the work of a "great writer" (Adams never mentioned Smith by name). First, Adams shared Smith's view that the desire for sympathy and fellow-feeling was

151. Mayville, *John Adams and the Fear of American Oligarchy*, 101.

152. Scholars have noted that in addition to *The Theory of Moral Sentiments*, Adams drew on different works by Shakespeare, Alexander Pope, and the English poet William Young. See Haraszti, *John Adams and the Prophets of Progress*, 170–72; Mayville, *John Adams and the Fear of American Oligarchy*, 100.

both a defining feature of human nature and also a source of disparate social power.

> From whence, then, arises that emulation which runs through all the different ranks of men, and what are the advantages which we proposed by that great human purpose of life which we call bettering our condition? . . . To be observed, to be attended to, to be taken notice of with sympathy, complacency, and approbation, are all the advantages which we can propose to derive from it.[153]

Adams echoed Smith in his own observation that of all the passions, sentiments, and dispositions that animated human society, none was "more essential or remarkable, than the *passion for distinction*." The "desire to be observed, considered, esteemed, praised, beloved, and admired by his fellows," was, according to Adams, "one of the earliest, as well as keenest dispositions discovered in the heart of man."[154] This need for social approval and recognition manifested itself in different ways: in the "desire to excel another" through the practice of virtue (emulation), in the thirst for power (ambition), and in the apprehension of others' success (jealousy).

Smith's observation that the desire for approval, sympathy, and distinction was lopsided also resonated with Adams. "It is because mankind are [*sic*] disposed to sympathize more entirely with our joy than with our sorrow," Smith wrote, "that we make parade of our riches, and conceal our poverty." Though this sympathetic asymmetry was natural insofar as it was an inevitable and immovable feature of human psychology, it was exacerbated by social inequalities. For Smith,

> [A rich man] glories in his riches, because he feels that they naturally draw upon him the attention of the world, and that mankind are disposed to go along with him in all those agreeable emotions with

153. *TMS*, I.iii.2.1, 50.

154. John Adams, *Discourses on Davila; A Series of Papers on Political History. By an American Citizen*, in *The Works of John Adams, Second President of the United States: with A Life of the Author, Notes and Illustrations, by his Grandson Charles Francis Adams*, vol. 6 (Boston, MA: Charles C. Little and James Brown, 1851), 232. Italics in original. (Henceforth, Adams, *Discourses*.)

which the advantages of his situation so readily inspire him. At the thought of this, his heart seems to swell and dilate itself within him, and he is fonder of his wealth, upon this account, than for all the other advantages it procures him. The poor man, on the contrary, is ashamed of his poverty. He feels that it either places him out of the sight of mankind, or, that if they take any notice of him, they have, however, scarce any fellow-feeling with the misery and distress which he suffers.[155]

Echoing Smith's theory, Adams wondered,

Why do we make an ostentatious display of riches? . . . or, in better words, why should the rich man glory in his riches? . . . Why, on the other hand, should any man be ashamed to make known his poverty? Why should those who have been rich, or educated in the houses of the rich, entertain such an aversion, or be agitated with such terror, at the prospect of losing their property? . . . The poor man's conscience is clear; yet he is ashamed . . . He feels himself out of the sight of others, groping in the dark. Mankind take no notice of him.[156]

Following Smith, Adams was convinced that men valued wealth not for its intrinsic value, but rather for its instrumental value in earning social recognition and distinction. "The answer to all these questions is," Adams asserted, "*because riches attract the attention, consideration, and congratulations of mankind.*"[157]

Adams's central insight was the connection he made between the asymmetries both in sympathy and in power. For Adams, people were disposed to "consider the condition of the great in all those delusive colors, in which the imagination can paint and gild in it," and they felt a peculiar sympathy with those "who are already powerful, celebrated,

155. *TMS*, I.iii.2.1,50–51. In Essay VII of the *Discourses*, Adams follows Smith's language closely: "Providence, which has placed one thing over against another, in the moral as well as physical world, has surprisingly accommodated the qualities of men to answer one another. There is a remarkable disposition in mankind to congratulate with others in their joys and prosperity, more than to sympathize with them in their sorrows and adversity." Adams, *Discourses*, 253.

156. Adams, *Discourses*, 237–239.

157. Adams, *Discourses*, 238. Emphasis in original.

and rich."[158] What Adams called the "qualities of fortune"—one's birth, wealth, beauty—seemed everywhere to "glitter with the brightest lustre in the eyes of the world."[159] So strong was this sympathy with the rich, argued Adams, that it would override that inner voice "which seems to intimate, that real merit should govern the world," and that men of wisdom, talent, virtue, and "real merit" would be rewarded. However, the majority of people would be less concerned with real merit, and instead, "apply themselves to seek for honor" in more tangible, immediate ways: "by displaying their taste and address, their wealth and magnificence, their ancient parchments, and statues, and the virtues of their ancestors."[160] In other words, Adams feared that the goods of fortune would determine who had power—not just in terms of the formal structures of law and government, but in terms of people's ability to "stand out, to be recognized, and to evoke favorable public sentiments."[161] In such a society, wondered Adams, "what chance has humble, modest, obscure, and poor merit in such a scramble?"[162]

The *Discourses on Davila* is an extraordinary example of how a major American political figure not only read, but repurposed the ideas from eighteenth-century moral science in new ways. Adams found in *The Theory of Moral Sentiments* a way to render visible the hidden mechanisms by which wealth translated into power—ones that were fixed firmly not in the institutions of government, but rather in the workings of the human mind. Harnessing the language of Smith's moral sentiments allowed Adams to articulate a chronic worry that he believed his contemporaries were ignoring. Jefferson's aspirations for educating a mass public so that they might select the "veritable aristoi" were

158. Adams, *Discourses*, 257. Again, Adams's language parallels Smith's very closely: "When we consider the condition of the great, in those delusive colours in which the imagination is apt to paint it, it seems to be almost the abstract idea of a perfect and happy state. It is the very state which, in all our waking dreams and idle reveries, we had sketched out to ourselves as the final object of all our desires. We feel, therefore, a peculiar sympathy with the satisfaction of those who are in it." *TMS* I.iii.2.2, 51–52.

159. Adams, *Discourses*, 242.

160. Adams, *Discourses*, 249–250.

161. Mayville, *John Adams and the Fear of American Oligarchy*, 118.

162. Adams, *Discourses*, 250.

hopeless idealism when met with the power of wealth, in Adams's eyes.[163] Wealth, Adams contended, would continue to attract sympathy, admiration, and respect, over and above what could be gained by men of virtue and talent. Adams warned that even in the great age of experiments in government, elite domination would persist, especially outside the formal sphere of politics.

———

Between the second half of the eighteenth century and the first decades of the nineteenth, the Scottish "science of man" was being made American—not only in terms of American book culture, but also in terms of politics, finance, and moral philosophy. Equipped with a progressive view of history and a secular faith in the power of human reason, America's political and intellectual leaders embraced their unprecedented position as the architects of a new nation. Not content with passively reading works of history, philosophy, and politics, they actively adapted and applied knowledge from the enlightenment science of man in their various endeavors, from defending the size and strength of the federal government, to directing the course of economic growth or warning against the sinister effects of wealth in society. The works of Adam Smith provided an array of concepts applicable to these efforts as well as an overarching method for pursuing them. For James Madison, Smith's *The Wealth of Nations* provided the political-economic logic of competition behind one of the most powerful arguments in *Federalist 10*. For Alexander Hamilton, *The Wealth of Nations* served as an encyclopedic guide to the science of wealth creation. He refashioned and used its summary of the physiocratic doctrine, its history of banking practices, and its theory of economic growth to scaffold a forward-

163. Jefferson's discussion of the "veritable aristoi" and the "Psuedo-aristoi" is in his letter to Adams, October 28, 1813, in *The Adams-Jefferson Letters: The Complete Correspondence between Thomas Jefferson and Abigail and John Adams*, ed. Lester J. Cappon (Chapel Hill, NC: University of North Carolina Press, 1959), 387–392 at 387. Adams responded to Jefferson, saying that his "distinction between natural and artificial Aristocracy does not appear to me well founded." Adams to Jefferson, November 15, 1813 in *The Adams-Jefferson Letters*, 397–402 at 400.

looking agenda of political and economic nationalism. And for John Adams, Smith's *The Theory of Moral Sentiments* called attention to the way the human mind transformed wealth into a deceptive and yet inescapable source of power. In the eyes of these readers and thinkers, Smith's works proved useful resources that helped identify and outline paths toward private and public happiness.

The particular American needs during this era thus delimited the importance and applications of Smith's works. In their quest to justify and critique different visions of American society, figures like Hamilton, Madison, and Adams sought out systematic, comprehensive, universal, and enlightened ways of thinking on matters that Smith addressed at length in his two major works. Ideas from both *The Theory of Moral Sentiments* and *The Wealth of Nations* suited those needs, though no more so than those of other major thinkers. The Founders were not constrained either by assumptions about Smith's authorial intentions or by beliefs about the normative implications of Smith's moral philosophy or the politics of Smith's political economy. It was possible, as Hamilton's use of Smith's ideas in the "Report on Manufactures" shows, to separate and make use of Smith's ideas without necessarily endorsing their political implications. It was also possible to reject Smith's theory of sympathy as a philosophically robust theory of morality on the one hand, while using it as an explanatory account of why people sought wealth and distinction on the other.

These early engagements with Smith underscore two things. First, within the context of the enlightenment science of man, political economy was still an emergent discourse. However, it was one whose ultimate aim was to inform and recommend to the public a *way of thinking* about the forces that govern human society. The Founders' uses of Smith's ideas demonstrate how they absorbed the nature and purpose of Smith's works. As works of science, the texts organized and connected explanatory principles of human society; and as works of public thought, they aimed to guide social and political practices.[164] On these

164. Eric Schliesser, *Adam Smith: Systematic Philosopher and Public Thinker* (Oxford: Oxford University Press, 2017).

terms, Smith's science of a legislator was brought to life in the words and practices of his American readers.

Second, the Founders read Smith's works as neither political ideologies nor as defined moral stances. This is worth emphasizing because it highlights the absence of a singular, definitive Smith image. At least in the writings examined here, figures like Madison, Hamilton, and Adams "rarely paused to elaborate upon the maxims from which [they] drew support."[165] As was conventional, these men were more inclined to take political ideas "wherever [they] found them, and [make] each one fit into a philosophy" that suited their particular political beliefs and needs; they freely borrowed, adapted, paraphrased, and quoted from Smith's works without appealing to Smith's authority. They were eager to prove, as the biographer Clinton Rossiter put it, that they were men who used their brains rather than their bookshelves.[166] This is not to say that Smith's works were altogether unimportant, or, in a slightly less deflationary tone, that Smith's works gained historical significance simply because they were read or acclaimed as works that *ought* to be read.[167] Rather, it is to suggest that Smith's authority, whether on matters of political economy or moral philosophy, had yet to become an intellectual currency that gave ideas prestige, legitimacy, and power. It would not be long before that transpired.

165. Rossiter, *Alexander Hamilton and the Constitution*, 115.
166. Rossiter, *Alexander Hamilton and the Constitution*, 118, 119–20.
167. Teichgraeber, "'Less Abused than I Had Reason to Expect,'" 339.

2

Whence He Is Called
Its Founder

JOSEPH SHELTON WATSON (1780–1805) was a keen student at the College of William and Mary. His letters to his brother, David, depict the colorful experiences and emotions of a young man living away from home, perhaps for the first time. Learning Latin and French alongside reading the works of Paine, Locke, and Rousseau was tedious, but enlightening. The pageants of modern politics from the death of Washington to the election of 1800 filled him with a mix of fascination and weariness. And the "frolick" of a group of students after a large "oister supper"—they pulled down the fences of several inhabitants, hoping to "put the town to rights"—positively horrified him.[1] In one letter from 1801, between a profession of faith in republican government and a trailing note about his ambitions to construct an "Air-baloon," Watson updated his brother on the progression of his studies at William and Mary. "My studies, tho considerably more easy and agreeable than they were last year, require of me, notwithstanding, considerable labour and exertion." He continued, "Few sciences, if any, are more abstruse and intricate than that of political economy. Yet the extensive information, the comprehensive and powerful talents of Smith, have thrown upon the

1. Letter from Joseph Shelton Watson to David Johnson. "Letters from William and Mary College, 1798–1801," *Virginia Magazine of History and Biography* 29, no. 2 (April 1921), 164.

subject a light which I believe no other man could have given."[2] The Smith to whom Watson was referring was none other than Adam Smith.

Teaching Smith's *The Wealth of Nations* at the College of William and Mary in the late eighteenth and early nineteenth centuries was an anomaly. At the time Watson attended, William and Mary was probably the only major institution of higher learning that offered a course on political economy.[3] While Smith's *The Wealth of Nations* was likely one of if not the best-known text on political economy at the time, there were good reasons why people might not have deemed it suitable as an instructional text. Besides its near-prohibitory length (the 1789 Dobson edition, for instance, was three volumes amounting to just over 1,100 pages), its organization was not necessarily straightforward, its lengthy statistical digressions were uninspiring, and, on top of that, Smith's critical views of established religion might not have been particularly welcome among most American colleges in the early 1800s.[4] Since colonial times, higher education had been the product of religious interests. With the exception of the University of Pennsylvania, all of the major northeast colonial colleges had denominational affiliations and missions. Most students would have been preparing for careers in ministry or law and, therefore, studied a limited range of subjects deemed appropriate for those careers—theology, classics, biblical studies, and perhaps some mathematics and philosophy—and instructors found little reason to deviate from inherited patterns of teaching.[5] Thus, while books like *The Wealth of Nations* might have been eagerly read by statesmen as practical handbooks, the distinctly modern science of political economy lay outside the prescribed boundaries of an otherwise deeply moralistic education system.

2. Letter from Joseph Shelton Watson to David Johnson. "Letters from William and Mary College, 1798–1801," 166.

3. See note 27 in Chapter 1.

4. Michael O'Connor speculates that these factors likely prevented Smith's early adoption among colleges in the northeast specifically. However, given the early date at which Watson appears to have encountered Smith, I have expanded his inference here. See Michael Joseph Lalor O'Connor, *Origins of Academic Economics in the United States* (New York, NY: Columbia University Press, 1944), 113–14.

5. Meyer, *The Instructed Conscience*; Howe, *The Unitarian Conscience*.

Watson's brief encounter with Smith's *The Wealth of Nations* anticipated many of the changes in the way that Americans thought about the
abstruse and intricate science of political economy in the nineteenth
century. If Americans in the late eighteenth century were mostly consumers of European authorities on political economic science, by the
1820s Americans had become producers who were formulating their
own treatises, principles, and contributions to the science. Americans
began to treat sources from across the Atlantic not as a "rigid and mo-
nistic system," but rather as a reconfigurable mosaic of ideas that had to
be reinterpreted, challenged, and adapted in light of their own realities.[6]
In addition, the expansion and democratization of American education
during the antebellum decades made instruction on political economy
increasingly important for a growing body of students seeking a secular
and practical education. These overlapping intellectual environments
provided fertile ground in which American writers, students, and educators could uncover the kernels of Smith's ideas and transplant them
in new and prolific ways.

Americans thought with, through, and against Smith's *The Wealth of
Nations* in ways that not only shaped the work and its author's wider
reputation, but also defined the parameters of a larger debate around
the content, scope, and aims of the science of political economy. By the
1830s, Smith and his works had acquired a foundational status among
American readers. However, the significance of *The Wealth of Nation's*
reputation as the "foundation and text-book" of political economy signified more than Smith's canonization. Smith's American interpreters
began to think about the distance between Smith's time and their own.
They postulated the extent of *The Wealth of Nation's* timelessness, but
they also saw ways in which it was bound by its late-eighteenth-century
context. In making claims about what or which aspects of Smith were
scientific truths that transcended the times for which it was written,
Smith's American admirers and critics alike began establishing a pattern
for evaluating Smith's legacy. In their contests to become regarded as

---

6. Paul Keith Conkin, *Prophets of Prosperity: America's First Political Economists* (Bloomington, IN: Indiana University Press, 1980), 40, 16.

Smith's legitimate followers, these American readers were also making implicit claims about the mode of thinking that most suited American political and economic needs.

———

No longer just the "science of the legislator" as Adam Smith labeled it in 1776, political economy in the nineteenth century was reformulated as a scientific inquiry worth pursuing as an end in itself. It was a science because it carried a presumption of empirical validity. It was political because the unit of analysis was not the management of a private household, but rather an entire nation and its people. Moreover, political economy was considered a branch of moral philosophy because a full understanding of the principles of political economy required instruction of one's duties and obligations in society.[7] Early American political economists strove to develop a mode of inquiry that would uphold American political and economic independence as well as account for the differences between American and European experiences. "Here in America," one writer for *The North American Review* proclaimed in 1823, "the class of professed philosophical writers cannot be said to exist, and the duty of directing the opinions of their fellow-citizens on all subjects necessarily devolves on some class of professional or practical men."[8] Unlike Europe, where there were "much more lofty and solid" class barriers, in America it was "not uncommon to meet with intelligent individuals" whose vocations—manufacturing, farming, or trading—made them intimately acquainted with the "great pursuits in question" in political economy. At least in America, political economy existed in the vernacular. Moreover, the author observed, while political economy was *practiced* by this class of "practical" men in America, it was *produced* by lawmakers. Figures like Alexander

7. Conkin, *Prophets of Prosperity*, ix.

8. "Review: Considérations sur l'Industrie et la Législation sous le Rapport de leur Influence sur la Richesse des Etats, et Examen Critique des Principaux Ouvrages, Qui ont paru sur l'Economie Politique by Louis Say," *The North American Review*, 17, no. 41 (1823), 424–36 at 425–26. (henceforth, "Review: Considérations sur l'Industrie et la Législation").

Hamilton and Albert Gallatin were responsible for reducing "all the affairs of life to principle and [unfolding] . . . the abstract rule, by which they are to be settled."[9] However, it was clear that a new class of not just practical but also "philosophical" political economists had begun to emerge.

Among the first major commentaries on American economic issues was John Taylor of Caroline's texts *Arator* (1813) and *An Inquiry into the Principles and Policy of the Government of the United States* (1814). Published in the midst of war with Great Britain, Taylor reignited the debate over the prospects of agriculture versus manufacturing in the new nation. Though many of his beliefs in the benefits of trade can be traced to Smith, Taylor was more of an embodiment of the Jeffersonian conviction "that the prosperity of our country [depends] upon a competent share of agricultural and political knowledge." Agriculture was "the guardian of liberty, as well as the mother of wealth," and Taylor believed that it had to be secured against the "political frauds" of government.[10] More urgently, agricultural interests had to be defended against what Taylor decried as "the promise of the manufacturing mania." "What!" he scoffed, "Secure our independence by bankers and capitalists?" Taylor feared that banking, manufacturing, and commercial dealings would turn honest American farmers into "swindlers" and "dependents on a master capitalist for daily bread."[11] His thought amplified the broader social and intellectual currents of an agro-republican movement. The establishment of agricultural societies and a surge in agriculture-focused periodicals such as *The Agricultural Museum* and *The New England Farmer* in the first half of the nineteenth century reveal how many Americans remained deeply attached to the Jeffersonian vision of an enlightened agricultural republic.[12]

Caught between the ideas from the Old World and the prospects of the New, early American political economists hoped to carve out their own intellectual territory, but they did so with the tools of a "common

9. "Review: Considérations sur l'Industrie et la Législation," 426.

10. John Taylor, *Arator, Being a Series of Agricultural Essays, Practical and Political: In Sixty-Four Numbers* (Petersburg, VA: Whitworth & Yancey, 1818), iii, vi.

11. Taylor, *Arator*, 23–24.

12. Winterer, *American Enlightenments*, 218.

but borrowed intellectual heritage."[13] A pantheon of European writers provided different models for a science of national wealth, and American thinkers freely adopted ideas that seemed to fit the United States' political and economic circumstances, while rejecting those that did not. For example, Malthusianism—the view that population would outstrip the food supply, that wages would be driven to subsistence levels—was "undeniable" in theory but had "no applicability to the present state of human affairs" in America.[14] As one American writer for *The North American Review* wrote, "owing to the vast extent of our attainable and unsettled land, the Malthusian doctrine . . . has never obtained much currency among us."[15] Americans also harbored doubts about David Ricardo (1772–1823), despite the initial success of his *Principles of Political Economy and Taxation*, first published in 1817. Ricardo's *Principles* was greeted with eagerness at first. The work was generally admired for its analytic style and more precise definitions of rent and labor, but there were other factors that kept it from gaining the same intellectual and cultural cache as Smith's texts. *Principles* was intimidatingly dense and poorly written, making it "not easy fare for layman" and ill-suited as a college text. Thomas Jefferson predicted that the work would "not stand the test of time and trial," and that the nature of rent "is not to be proved by such muddy reasoning as that of Ricardo." Jefferson predicted that Ricardo's reputation would "fall as soon as it comes to be read."[16]

13. Conkin, *Prophets of Prosperity*, xi.

14. "Review of Principles of Political Economy, with Some of Their Applications to Social Philosophy by John Stuart Mill," *The North American Review* 67, no. 141 (1848), 396.

15. "Review of Principles of Political Economy, with Some of Their Applications to Social Philosophy," *The North American Review* 98, no. 202 (1864), 271. An earlier review of John Stuart Mill's *Principles of Political Economy* in 1848 expressed a similarly dismissive attitude towards Malthusianism: "We say that Malthusianism, in this simple form, is undeniable, and yet that it has no applicability to the present state of human affairs, and we have no immediate concern in establishing its truth or falsehood." "Review of Principles of Political Economy, with Some of Their Applications to Social Philosophy by John Stuart Mill," *The North American Review* 67, no. 141 (1848), 370–419 at 396.

16. Conkin, *Prophets of Prosperity*, 111; O'Connor, *Origins of Academic Economics in the United States*, 150. "Thomas Jefferson to Joseph Milligan, 12 January 1819." *The Papers of Thomas Jefferson, Retirement Series*, vol. 13, *22 April 1818 to 31 January 1819*, ed. J. Jefferson Looney (Princeton, NJ:

In contrast to the gloomy presentiments of Ricardo and Malthus, a new school of French thinkers known as the *idéologues* found an increasingly receptive American audience. Inspired by Smith's *The Wealth of Nations*, thinkers such as Jean-Baptiste Say, Pierre Samuel du Pont de Nemours, and Antoine Louise Claude Destutt de Tracy introduced a new ideology in the most literal sense: a science of ideas that would be the basis of a new social and political order.[17] One of the most significant products of the *idéologues* was Jean-Baptiste Say's *Traité d'economie politique* (or *Treatise on Political Economy*), first published in 1803, and translated into English by Charles Prinsep in 1821. Say's *Treatise* quickly became a standard textbook for teaching political economy at schools such as Harvard, the University of Virginia, and Dartmouth. A sanguine work that reaffirmed the principles of free trade, Says' *Treatise* offered a powerful prescription that neutralized the bleak predictions of Malthus and Ricardo. The preface of the work reinforced a narrative of American exceptionalism: "The old states of Europe are cankered with prejudices and bad habits;" Say wrote to the English editor of his *Treatise*, "it is America who will teach them the height of prosperity which may be reached when governments follow the counsels of reason, and do not *cost* too much."[18]

Say's *Treatise on Political Economy* became an important mechanism by which Adam Smith's reputation as the "father of political economy" was disseminated in America. "Many principles strictly correct had often been advanced prior to the time of Dr. Smith; he, however, was

---

Princeton University Press, 2016), 573. The eminent historian Dorothy Ross has made a similar argument about the fate of Malthus and Ricardo in America: "In political economy Americans preferred Smith's optimism to the somber theories of Malthus and Ricardo that had emerged from early industrial poverty and conflict. The liberal-republican formulation of American exceptionalism was closer to the moral world of the Scottish Enlightenment than to the classical liberalism of contemporary Britain." Ross, *The Origins of American Social Science*, 49.

17. H.M. Drucker, *The Political Uses of Ideology* (London: Palgrave Macmillan, 1974); Winterer, *American Enlightenments*, 219–22.

18. Jean-Baptiste Say, *A Treatise on Political Economy, or, the Production, Distribution and Consumption of Wealth, Translated from the Fourth Edition of the French*, ed. Clement C. Biddle, trans. C.R. Prinsep, 3rd ed. (Philadelphia, PA: John Grigg, 1827), xvi–xvii. Emphasis in original.

the first author who established their truth," Say claimed. Smith had furnished his readers with "the true method of detecting errors," and in doing so, had endowed political economy with "the new mode of scientific investigation" that started not from abstract principles, but from observable facts.[19] At the same time, Say's *Treatise* established one of the main lines of criticism of *The Wealth of Nations*. For all of its achievements, *The Wealth of Nations* was still a primitive and convoluted text, or, to use Say's words, "an immethodical assemblage of the soundest principles of Political Economy, supported by luminous illustrations, and of the most ingenious researches in Statistics . . . but . . . an irregular mass of curious and original speculations and of known and demonstrated truths."[20] Smith, in Say's view, had not sufficiently maintained a distinction between the science of a legislator and the science of political economy—the former belonging to the art of politics, the latter an exact science concerned only with natural laws of production, distribution, and consumption of national wealth. Aiming to separate his work from Smith's, Say streamlined definitions and organized his work into a clear-cut, three-part structure: the production, distribution, and consumption of wealth. Furthermore, unlike *The Wealth of Nations* whose intended audiences were highly-educated citizens either in or aspiring to public office, Say addressed his *Treatise* to a much broader readership of ordinary, less-educated readers.[21] The *Treatise* became one of the most popular choices for college courses on political economy. It was used at Yale from roughly 1827 until the appearance of Francis Wayland's text in 1837, *Elements of Political Economy* (which itself relied on Say's work as its organizational backbone), at Harvard through the 1850s, and at Dartmouth until 1870. Between the time of its initial publication and 1880, the text had been reprinted eight times in France and at least twenty-six times in the United States.[22]

19. Say, *A Treatise on Political Economy*, xxxix.

20. Say, *A Treatise on Political Economy*, xxii.

21. Roger E. Backhouse and Keith Tribe, *The History of Economics: A Course for Students and Teachers* (Newcastle upon Tyne: Agenda Publishing, 2017), 99–100.

22. O'Connor, *Origins of Academic Economics in the United States*, 125, 172–74; Backhouse and Tribe, *The History of Economics*, 105. It is worth noting that not everyone liked Say's *Treatise*.

The accessibility of Say's *Treatise* made it an especially effective tool not only for teaching political economy but also for assessing Smith's importance in the science. Thomas Jefferson, one of the most avid readers of Francophone political works, was the most prominent figure in this line of reception from Smith to Say to American readers. "If your views on political inquiry go further to the subjects of money and commerce," Jefferson wrote to John Norvell in 1807, "Smith's wealth of nations is the best book to be read, unless Say's Political economy can be had."[23] By 1817, Jefferson was fully convinced of the superiority of French economic thought and had published a translation of Destutt de Tracy's *A Treatise on Political Economy*, a work which Jefferson believed shone "with all the lights of his predecessors [the *économistes*]" but with "more discussion and greater maturity of subject." In the "Prospectus" of the work, Jefferson declared the *économistes* to be the first thinkers to turn political economy into the "form of a regular science." Adam Smith, meanwhile, was merely the first *English* thinker to publish a system of political economy, but his work, while "admitted to be able, and of the first degree of merit," was "prolix and tedious."[24]

This classical restatement of Smith's contributions found an early foothold in the South. Thomas Cooper, president of the College of South Carolina from 1820 to 1834, recommended the works of Malthus, Ricardo, and the Scottish economist John Ramsay McCulloch for advanced study, but reminded his students to never forget "that they must begin with Adam Smith." He argued that the physiocrats were perhaps the first to seriously treat political economy as a science, but it was Smith's *The Wealth of Nations* that "created an era in the science; and . . . contributed more than any other [work] to make known the principles

Caleb Cushing, a tutor at Harvard, for example, criticized Harvard for using a book "so confused in its arrangement, so mistaken in fundamental doctrines, and teaching opinions prejudicial to the welfare of this country" in its course. As quoted in O'Connor, *Origins of Academic Economics in the United States*, 44.

23. Thomas Jefferson to John Norvell. June 14, 1807. *Writings*, 1176.

24. "Prospectus," in Antoine Louis Claude Comte Destutt de Tracy, *A Treatise on Political Economy*, trans. Thomas Jefferson (Georgetown, D.C.: Joseph Milligan, 1817), iv.

of political economy and to impress on the public mind the importance that ought to be attached to them."[25] Thomas Dew, professor at the College of William and Mary, also used Smith's *The Wealth of Nations* as a textbook from around 1827 to 1830, as did George Tucker at the University of Virginia.[26] Their reliance on and praise for Smith, however, were not politically neutral—Cooper, Dew, and Tucker were early and staunch defenders of free trade politics in the South. Dew's one-sided *Lectures on the Restrictive System* (1829), contrary to what its title suggests, was a sustained defense of political economy as the political-economic system of free trade along the lines of the physiocrats and Adam Smith. The fourth and final part of his lectures served merely to prove how "the establishment of the restrictive system in almost all countries" ran "contrary to the best established principles of our science."[27] Similarly, Cooper's passing remarks on Smith's contributions focused almost entirely on the underlying principles of free trade. Smith had "clearly shewn," Cooper wrote, "that human labor employed in conferring utility or value on some material object, is the sole foundation of all wealth, individual and national." This principle underwrote the policy of free trade, that "it is in every case sound policy to leave individuals to pursue their own interest in their own way," that regulations of international commerce or forced channels of industry were "injurious to the rights of individuals," and "adverse to the progress of *real* opulence and lasting prosperity."[28] The science which Smith created, therefore, delegitimated what Cooper scorned as the "disgraceful act called the Tariff Law!" passed in the United States just four years prior and reinforced his utilitarian view of government—that *"the government which is effective at the least expense to the people, is the best government."*[29]

25. Thomas Cooper, *Lectures on the Elements of Political Economy* (Columbia, SC: M'Morris & Wilson, 1829), v, 13–15.

26. O'Connor, *Origins of Academic Economics in the United States*, 50–51.

27. Thomas Roderick Dew, *Lectures on the Restrictive System* (Richmond, VA: Samuel Shepherd & Company, 1829), 3.

28. Cooper, *Lectures on the Elements of Political Economy*, 15. Emphasis in original. Here, Cooper actually quotes J.R. McCulloch's *Discourses* on Smith.

29. Cooper, *Lectures on the Elements of Political Economy*, 15, iv–v. Emphasis in original. I discuss at length the uses of Smith in free trade debates in Chapter 3. For an extended

Opposite Say and the Southern school of Cooper and Dew stood figures such as Daniel Raymond, one of America's first and most vocal critics of Smith. In Raymond's mind, Smith's political economy represented a delusional and inconsistent view of nationhood and national wealth. "The fundamental error," according to Raymond, was that Smith and "most other writers" perpetuated a definition of national wealth that failed to adequately distinguish between private and public wealth. According to Raymond's reading, Smith naively assumed that national wealth was indivisible, but this left too much room for "a distinction between a nation and a fractional part of a nation." The interests of the merchants were at odds with the general public, and often the interests of the "agriculturalists, manufacturers, and every other class of the community" were pitted against each other as well as the general will. Smith's apparent neglect of a harmony of national interest, therefore, reduced his work into a treatise on individual—not national—wealth, which Raymond saw as "degrading the dignity of the science of political economy into a paltry science of dollars and cents!"[30] For Raymond, the science of political economy ought to be a project on the scale of national politics. A firm nationalist with little attachment to state or regional identity, Raymond saw the need for a "strong, positive, and righteous government." In terms of economic policy, this meant not only having a firm grasp of which streams of individual wealth flowed "*from* or *into*" the wider stream of national wealth, but also having an active government that could "either . . . turn their currents or cut them off" when necessary.[31]

But it was Smith's inconsistency and ambiguity that frustrated Raymond the most. Smith "sometimes adopts the agricultural system as to

discussion of Cooper and Dew's contributions to political economy and political thought, see Conkin, *Prophets of Prosperity*, chap. 6; O'Connor, *Origins of Academic Economics in the United States*, 48–63; Michael D. Bordo and William H. Phillips, "Faithful Index to the Ambitions and Fortunes of the State: The Development of Political Economy at South Carolina College," in *Breaking the Academic Mould*, ed. Barber.

30. Daniel Raymond, *The Elements of Political Economy, in Two Parts*, 2nd ed. Vol. 1 (Baltimore, MD: Lucas, Jun. and E.J. Coale, 1823), 155–56.

31. Raymond, *The Elements of Political Economy*, 168. Emphasis in original.; Conkin, *Prophets of Prosperity*, chap. 4.

one subject, and the mercantile theory as to another," Raymond wrote, "yet in the main he opposes both, but does not suggest any system of his own system, unless 'no system,' be his system."[32] Raymond read Book IV of *The Wealth of Nations* not as Smith's lengthy reconstruction and systematic critique of both the British mercantile regime and the physiocrats, but rather as evidence that Smith could not make up his mind or provide an alternative "system" of political economy in their place. "The systems which he [Smith] attacked undoubtedly contained many errors, and he deserves credit for having exposed them, but he certainly is not entitled to the credit of having devised a theory of political economy," Raymond wrote. Smith's system of "no restriction or legislation" was nothing short of an "absurdity" of "not legislating at all, and permitting every man to pursue his interest in his own way," eventually devolving into "a state of nature."[33] Raymond's critique of Smith was sobering. While at times Raymond opined that "no man was ever capable of writing with more clearness, perspicuity, and force, than Adam Smith," at other times, he found Smith's celebrated work to be "unintelligible," "confused," and "indistinct," especially around the definitions of capital and stock. These lapses in clarity were more than stylistic complaints; in Raymond's opinion, they exposed the fundamental unsoundness of Smith's main ideas. "When Adam Smith, therefore, does not write with clearness and force," Raymond argued, "it is because he has imperfect and erroneous views of the subject he is endeavouring to enforce."[34]

Raymond's works left deep impressions on the German émigré Friedrich List who would become one of the most influential political economic thinkers in America in the 1830s and 1840s. A predecessor of the German Historical School, List found his adopted country to be the perfect context in which to work out a contrarian approach to the science of political economy. In 1827, List published his *Outlines of American Political Economy*, a series of letters written to Charles J. Ingersoll,

---

32. Raymond, *The Elements of Political Economy*, 161.
33. Raymond, *The Elements of Political Economy*, 163–64.
34. Raymond, *The Elements of Political Economy*, 154–55.

then Vice President of the Pennsylvania Society for the Promotion of Manufactures. List wanted to "lay the axe to the root of the tree, by declaring the system of Adam Smith and Co. to be erroneous" and pleaded for support for the study of what he called "the American System."[35] The system of Adam Smith and his followers failed to understand the contingencies of national political economy, according to List. "Not taking into consideration the different state of power, constitution, wants and culture of the different nations," List argued, *The Wealth of Nations* was little more than "a mere treatise on the question, how the economy of individuals and of mankind would stand, if the human race were not separated into nations."[36] Adam Smith created a "*cosmopolitical economy*"—one that blurred the lines between national boundaries and that refused to acknowledge the exigencies of national interests. The American System that List outlined rejected the cosmopolitan ideal of free trade as an imperialist agenda, and instead embraced a Hamiltonian project of economic nationalism and independence through the protection and encouragement of domestic industry. This was a true political economy that recognized how the United States had to "follow its own course in developing its productive powers."[37]

Thus, for List, Smith's idea of timelessness and truth was a dangerous deception. The talents of Smith, Say, and their followers, according to List, "enabled them to give their castles in the air the appearance of strong, well founded buildings . . . too elevated to be questioned by future generations."[38] Economic nationalists like List cautioned against this trans-historical or ahistorical reading of Smith, whose cosmopolitan vision would send the United States down the wrong path of

35. Georg Friedrich List, *Outlines of American Political Economy* (Philadelphia, PA: Samuel Parker, 1827), 6.

36. List, *Outlines of American Political Economy*, 7.

37. List, *Outlines of American Political Economy*, 24. Emphasis in original. On the impact of List on early American political economy, see Marc-William Palen, *The "Conspiracy" of Free Trade: The Anglo-American Struggle over Empire and Economic Globalization, 1846–1896* (Cambridge: Cambridge University Press, 2016); Tribe, *Strategies of Economic Order*, chap. 3; Joseph Dorfman, *The Economic Mind in American Civilization*, vol. 2, Reprint edition (New York, NY: August M. Kelley, 1966), 575–84.

38. List, *Outlines of American Political Economy*, 5.

economic development. Americans ought to rue the day that an historian would reflect on American decline in the following way:

> They were a great people, they were in every respect in the way to
> become the first people on earth, but they became weak and died—
> trusting in the infallibility of two books imported into the country;
> one from Scotland, the other from France; books, the general failure of
> which was shortly afterwards acknowledged by every individual.[39]

With the exception of Say's *Treatise*, the works of Raymond, Cooper,
and List were an unusual mixture of high intellectualism and popular
polemic, sweeping histories of economic thought and chaotic imma-
nent critiques. List's brand of economic nationalism would eventually
become a political movement, garnering a major following among the
proponents of the American System, a topic I cover in Chapter 3. Despite their vastly different styles and political outlooks, they all used
Smith's *The Wealth of Nations* as an instrument to give structure and
substance to their own contributions. Some, like Cooper, treated
Smith's political economy as the scientific foundation for laissez-faire.
Others, like Raymond and List, used Smith's work as a foil for devising
an alternative paradigm of national political economy. Moreover, in
their attempts to evaluate the scientific merits of Smith's work, they
began to politicize Smith's contributions. Caleb Cushing, for example,
published a critique of Smith's *The Wealth of Nations* and Say's *Treatise*
in order to expose "the fallacy, not of every thing in the Inquiry, which
is open to exception; but chiefly of doctrines, which it is conceived are
of tendency injurious to the welfare of our country." Writing as "A
Friend of Domestic Industry," Cushing presented an itemized list refuting twenty-eight specific arguments in *The Wealth of Nations* in hopes
of refuting "the authority of Adam Smith [who] has so frequently been
urged."[40] Such criticisms were almost guaranteed to be met with animated responses, like that of the free-trade leaning *The North American*

---

39. List, *Outlines of American Political Economy*, 6.

40. Caleb Cushing, *Summary of the Practical Principles of Political Economy: With Observations on Smith's Wealth of Nations and Say's Political Economy* (Cambridge: Hilliard and Metcalf,
1826), 45.

Review, which called Cushing's pamphlet "of dubious import," characterized by "precipitancy, imperfect examination" and a dispatch of "a
series of aphorisms." Rushing to Smith's defense, the author then declared Smith "one of the master spirits of his age" and that any errors in
his works were not those of "a hasty decision, or of a feeble grasp of his
subject," but rather, "mere specks on the bright mirror of [his] fame."[41]

Thus, in Smith's shadow a tradition started to emerge. Americans
began self-consciously seeing themselves—or were seen by others—as
either followers of Smith's principles or as opponents who nevertheless
saw the need to take Smith's ideas seriously, if only to openly refute
them.[42] Even before academic political economy reached maturity,
Americans were sharply aware that they were actively shaping Smith's
legacy. His reputation was being sustained, as one writer for *The North
American Review* put it, not "through the blindness and indifference of
those who have followed him," but rather with "the care and acumen,
which succeeding writers have bestowed on *Wealth of Nations*."[43]

———

Throughout the 1820s and 1830s, the college classroom became the most
important site in which educated Americans learned from and about

41. "Review: Summary of the Practical Principles of Political Economy, with Observations
on Smith's Wealth of Nations, and Say's Political Economy by A Friend of Domestic Industry,"
The North American Review 23, no. 53 (1826), 465–66.

42. This is an adaptation from Stefan Collini's four stages theory (so to speak) of the process
by which an author becomes a "classic." The first stage is that in which the "pronouncement and
the positions he took in his lifetime" are still considered part of live debate on substantive issues.
The second stage, which I have used here, is that in which "later writers, and to a lesser extent,
politicians still regard themselves, or are regarded by others, as applying his principles (or, conversely, as thinking it still a worthwhile contribution to current political debate to controvert them)."
In the third stage the author has become an "authority, or, more nebulously, a symbol or part of a
tradition" which might be useful in broad cultural terms "and perhaps at certain moments in more
immediate political terms, to invoke and align oneself with (or, conversely, distance oneself from);"
and in the fourth stage, "the author has "ostensibly no current political resonance," but has attained
a classic status or is an object of pure scholarly inquiry. Stefan Collini, *Public Moralists: Political
Thought and Intellectual Life in Britain, 1850–1930* (Oxford: Clarendon Press, 1991), 317–19.

43. "Review: Considérations sur l'Industrie et la Législation," 427.

Adam Smith. The changes in college curriculum which made these encounters with Smith possible reflected the large-scale transformations
occurring in American society. As the nation expanded westward, the
number of higher education institutions multiplied. Between 1800 and
1850, the number of colleges in the United States increased from roughly
twenty institutions clustered in the Northeast to over two hundred, the
majority of which were founded after 1830 and were scattered across the
South and West. Moreover, the proportion of denominationally-
affiliated institutions dropped from around seventy percent of colleges
in the 1800s to about thirty percent in 1850. Expansion of white male
suffrage was accompanied by a doubling of the portion of American
men who attended college between 1800 and 1850.[44] The country pried
its way into new territory and stretched the mileage of its roads, water,
and railways. Meanwhile, a new class of "self-made men" began to enter
into politics—a change welcomed by some, reviled by others. The economic and political populism of the Jacksonian era led to emboldened
demands for curricular reform in American colleges, especially for instruction in "relevant" subjects such as the natural sciences, law, ethics,
and political economy.[45] Dartmouth College pushed for curricular reform in 1816, hoping to include courses on "science and government and
political economy," though the changes were not implemented until
nearly a decade later. Harvard, Columbia, and Princeton introduced
courses in political economy between 1817 and 1819, though they remained
limited in scope within the broader subject of moral philosophy.[46] The
University of Virginia, chartered in 1819, made political economy a key
subject, and when classes began in 1825, Smith's *The Wealth of Nations*

44. Of course, the college-educated white male population was still a tiny fraction of the
American population. According to Caroline Winterer, the percentage of white males aged
15–20 who attended college rose from about 0.6 percent in 1800 to about 1.2 percent in 1860.
Caroline Winterer, *The Culture of Classicism: Ancient Greece and Rome in American Intellectual
Life, 1780–1910* (Baltimore, MD: The Johns Hopkins University Press, 2004), 44–45.

45. Winterer, *The Culture of Classicism*; *Breaking the Academic Mould*, ed. Barber, 5–6.

46. O'Connor, *Origins of Academic Economics in the United States*, 98–103. Francis Bowen,
professor of moral philosophy at Harvard, in 1882 wrote that "I do not think Pol. Economy was
taught at all in this College before 1800, probably not before 1816." Letter from Francis Bowen
to G.B. Diswell, esq. Harvard University Archives, Francis Bowen Papers. HUG 1232.300.

was a core textbook. Francis Wayland, the fourth president of Brown University, introduced political economy courses for senior-level students between 1827 and 1828; he would later write one of the best-selling textbooks on political economy in the United States. By 1830, most major academic institutions offered some form of instruction in political economy.[47]

The formalization of academic political economy in the antebellum college played a critical role in crystallizing and disseminating Smith's historical and scientific significance. Those in positions of power—especially university presidents, who almost always taught the political economy curriculum and who often wrote the textbooks—established which of Smith's ideas were worth teaching, instilling, revising, or refuting. An explosion of textbooks between 1825 and 1850 evinces the academic fervor of distilling, organizing, and publicizing the fundamentals of the field: John McVickar's *Principles of Political Economy* (1825), Willard Phillips's *A Manual of Political Economy* (1828), Samuel P. Newman's *Elements of Political Economy* (1835), Henry C. Carey's *Principles of Political Economy* (1837), and Francis Wayland's *Elements of Political Economy* (1837) were just some of the most well-known works. Textbook authors were less interested in putting forth their own theoretical contributions than in presenting material "in such order as would be most likely to render them serviceable either to the general student, or to the practical merchant," as Wayland professed in his *Elements*.[48] Wayland's text, which was preceded by his earlier best-selling work, *Elements of Moral Science* in 1835, quickly became one of the most widely-used textbooks and went through eighteen editions before 1861.[49] Even as the

47. Barber, "Political Economy and the Academic Setting before 1900: An Introduction" *Breaking the Academic Mould*, ed. Barber, 1–14 at 6; Conkin, *Prophets of Prosperity*; Michael O'Brien, *Conjectures of Order: Intellectual Life and the American South, 1810–1860* (Chapel Hill, NC: The University of North Carolina Press, 2004), chap. 17; O'Connor, *Origins of Academic Economics in the United States*, 100.

48. Francis Wayland, *The Elements of Political Economy*, 2nd ed. (New York, NY: Robinson and Franklin, 1838), iii.

49. William J. Barber, "Political Economy from the Top Down: Brown University," in *Breaking the Academic Mould*, ed. Barber, 73–78; Conkin, *Prophets of Prosperity*, 116–18; O'Connor, *Origins of Academic Economics in the United States*, 172–190.

education landscape expanded and the reservoir of teaching sources brimmed, there were relatively few changes to the overall outline and content of political economy curriculum. Their patterns of instruction, especially at colleges in the northeast, were designed to engrain the practical and moral importance of political economic science in a student's mind, and as such remained relatively stable through the 1860s.

Typically, colleges offered students a course in political economy in their senior year. By that point, students would have completed or been in the process of completing their course in moral philosophy, which would have provided them with a general ethical framework for thinking about social issues. Political economy, therefore, was an extension of that matrix. Especially in the northeast, political economy courses were usually taught by the university president, who was almost always a minister or preacher. Francis Wayland, a Baptist minister and the fourth president of Brown University, articulated this relationship between the science of political economy and moral philosophy as a study of the divine will of God. As he wrote in his landmark *Elements of Political Economy*, "By Science . . . we mean a systematic arrangement of the laws which God has established, so far as they have been discovered, of any department of human knowledge." To Wayland, it was obvious that political economy had certain "determinate laws." "Every one, for instance," the preacher stipulated, "knows that no man can grow rich, without industry and frugality."[50] Especially in the northeastern clerical schools, then, the science of political economy qua moral philosophy was a handmaiden of religion; the study of the systematic arrangement of the laws of nature—even the laws that governed economic activity—revealed the divine will of God and instructed one's highest moral faculty to follow its dictates. In the South, where secular tendencies resisted the strong theological connection, political economy was nevertheless treated as having an important formative role.[51] "Every well educated

50. Wayland, *Elements of Political Economy*, 15.

51. On the relationship between moral philosophy and political economy and religion, see Paul Heyne, "Clerical Laissez-Faire: A Case Study in Theological Economics," in *Are Economists Basically Immoral? And Other Essays on Economics, Ethics, and Religion*, ed. Geoffrey Brennan and A.M.C. Waterman (Indianapolis, IN: Liberty Fund, 2008), 238–64; Howe, *The Unitarian*

young man throughout the United States, considers himself as a politician;" stated Thomas Cooper, one of the earliest American political
economists. With an eye to the future leaders of the nation, early writers
on the subject were convinced that "without some elementary notions
relating to this modern branch of knowledge," those gentlemen "would
be but ill prepared for the duties which some years hence he may be
called to undertake."[52] Knowledge of national wealth, many believed,
lay at the "foundation of national intelligence, and indeed of all true
national greatness."[53]

The first task of the course was to define the science of political economy. For Francis Wayland at Brown, political economy was "the science
of Wealth," and "frequently styled the science of <u>national</u> wealth,"
(though Wayland admitted this definition was perhaps too limited).[54]
John McVickar, professor of moral philosophy, rhetoric, and belles
lettres at Columbia, offered a multiplicity of popular and analytic definitions with which his students could grapple. Political economy could
be styled as a "Science of Exchanges," or, more precisely, a science of
"Maxima and Minima or That Science which teaches to obtain the maximum of Good with the minimum of Expenditures."[55] Past thinkers
such as Smith illustrated the advantages and disadvantages of certain

---

Conscience; Meyer, *The Instructed Conscience*; *Breaking the Academic Mould*, ed. Barber;
O'Connor, *Origins of Academic Economics in the United States*.

52. Cooper, *Lectures on the Elements of Political Economy*, iii–iv.

53. "Lectures on the Elements of Political Economy. By Thomas Cooper, M.D. President of
the South Carolina College, and Professor of Chemistry and Political Economy. Columbia, S.C.
1826, 8vo. Pp. 280." *The North American Review*, vol. 25 (October 1827), 408–425 at 409.

54. Wayland's Elements of Moral Philosophy, Lecture notes written by a student, 1834–35.
Francis Wayland Papers, Box 15, Folder 6. Underlining in original. The same definition is noted
in the papers of John Larkin Lincoln, Lectures on Political Economy (1836) Brown University,
MS–1M–2, Box 30. This definition comes directly from Wayland's *Elements of Political Economy*
(1838, p. 15), "Political Economy is *the Science of Wealth*. It is sometimes defined the Science of
National Wealth. This definition seems not, however, sufficiently comprehensive; inasmuch as,
the laws which govern the creation of wealth are essentially the same, whether they are considered in respect to man as an *individual*, or to man as a *society*," (emphasis in original).

55. The student writes, "This last is the best Definition." Wheelock H. Parmly, Notes with Professor McVickar, 1841–1842. Columbia University, Columbiana Manuscripts, Series 1 Item 24.

definitions. Money, according to Smith, was "but one of the forms of Wealth, and one of the least items in National Wealth."[56] Students then learned that Smith defined wealth in terms of "Exchangeable value embodied in Material Product," and, in doing so, rejected the centuries-old doctrine that "Gold and Silver were considered as Wealth par excellence." But Smith's definition raised questions for future practitioners of the science to resolve: "What is wealth? Is it moral, intellectual, or material wealth?" McVickar posed to his students at Columbia (fig. 2.1). Smith was wanting in formal definitions and instead regarded wealth "as the returns to labor a material form having exchangeable value." Accordingly, this was "defective because [it was] confined to material objects."[57]

The introductory lectures often included a brief historical overview that traced the emergence of political economy as a form of scientific inquiry. Professors started in ancient times, discussing old beliefs about war and conquest, occasionally gesturing to Aristotle or Cicero. They then turned to medieval prejudices against the accumulation of gold and silver, and finally to early mercantilist thought, which paved the way for Smith's *The Wealth of Nations*. Though it was widely recognized that other writers like James Steuart and the physiocrats preceded him, Smith earned special recognition for being the first to give "the order of Science to the scattered truths of Political Economy." In addition to his "General Soundness," his "high liberal and demonstrative principles," and his "Common Sense," Smith earned his special status as the first to truly systematize the science of political economy.[58] *The Wealth of Nations* was "the first attempt to constitute political economy into a science," the prestigious literary magazine *The North American Review* claimed in 1823, and the "numerous criticisms made upon him [Smith] by successors" did not so much erode as it did reinforce its importance.[59] New

56. Wheelock H. Parmly, Notes with Professor McVickar, 1841–1842. Columbia University, Columbiana Manuscripts, Series 1 Item 24.

57. Lectures from Professor John McVickar on Political Economy. Taken by Edward Courtlandt Babcock, class of 1849. Columbia University, Columbiana Manuscripts, Series 1 Item 89.

58. Wheelock H. Parmly, Notes with Professor McVickar, 1841–1842. Columbia University, Columbiana Manuscripts, Series 1 Item 24.

59. "Review: Considérations sur l'Industrie et la Législation," 427.

works were sometimes viewed as having done "little more than translate and arrange Smith," while others were criticized for either "departing from the principles of Smith, or [regarding] them as of little importance" and having "thrown confusion around the general plan" of their work.[60] "The great work of Adam Smith, which created the science of Political Economy," *The North American Review* wrote in 1831,

> is still the foundation and text-book of this branch of learning, and is in fact almost the only truly original and valuable treatise, which we have upon it. It is one of those standard productions, in which a master-mind, capable of grasping the whole domain of science and letters, has directed its great powers and resources with indefatigable perseverance to the illustration of a single subject. . . . The inquirer will there find the great and simple principles which constitute the basis of the science, distinctly stated in the most elegant language, proved and illustrated by curious and instructive details of facts, and followed out in to the most important, and generally most correct practical conclusions.[61]

It is important to remember that at this point in its development, academic political economy relied primarily on descriptive illustrations and explanations, rather than mathematics or statistics. Style and substance, therefore, went hand in hand; the composition of the textbook as well as the elocutionary abilities of the lecturer facilitated the student's ability to comprehend and properly assess the scientific merits of its principles. Smith's literary talents were often seen as standard-setting. His famous illustration of the pin factory in Book I of *The Wealth of Nations*, for example, provided one of the most fundamental lessons in political economy: "By constantly pursuing the same operation, [a] degree of skill is acquired, which is impossible in those whose labor is employed in several operations," John Larkin Lincoln noted in Francis Wayland's course. "Adam Smith observes that a smith, accustomed to

---

60. "Review of *A Manual of Political Economy, with Particular Reference to the Institutions, Resources and Condition of the United States*, by Willard Phillips," *The North American Review* 32, no. 70 (1831), 220.

61. "Review of *A Manual of Political Economy*," 216–17.

make nails, but whose regular business is not nail-making, can make only 800 or 1,000 a day—but a boy who attends nothing else, can make 2,300."[62] The division of labor unleashed the productive powers of human industry by increasing the dexterity of workers, saving time that would have otherwise been lost in switching from one task to another, and introducing machinery. These were the same three points that Hamilton seized from Smith and used in his "Report on Manufactures" in 1791. Smith had so "admirably illustrated" the division of labor, and his lively painting of the pin-factory had become so well-known that Harvard professor Francis Bowen didn't even bother repeating the point in his 1856 *Principles of Political Economy*.[63]

One complaint, however, was that Smith's rich and illuminating descriptions sacrificed scientific accuracy and precision. It was not uncommon, for example, to encounter the criticism that Smith had "most unreasonably exaggerated the beneficial effects of a division of labor." But these were errors in the "looseness of language, which must necessarily creep into the first essays on a moral science" and seemed forgivable given the embryonic state of the science in Smith's time.[64] The real problem, though, pertained to the whole enterprise: there appeared to be endless possibilities for new definitions, illustrations, and proofs of value, utility, cost, price, labor, production, consumption, and all the other conceptual elements of political economy. "And thus the science of political economy dwindles into a miserable logomachy;" wrote one frustrated author in 1838, "and the reader, instead of making progress in

62. John Larkin Lincoln, Lectures on Political Economy, dated 1836. Brown University, MS–1M–2, Box 30. The same lesson is recorded in student notes on Wayland's Elements of Moral Philosophy (1834–35), Wayland Papers Box 15 Folder 6; Edward Andrew Bennett, Lectures on Political Economy (1836), MS–1M–2 Box 11; and William Henry Potter, Lectures on Political Economy (1836), MS–1M–2 Box 37.

63. "The advantages of Simple Coöperation, which was formerly regarded as the only kind of Division of Labor, have been so admirably illustrated by Adam Smith. Passing over, as it is so well known, his illustration from pin-making, I adopt an example of the effects produced by the division of labor that is given by M. Say, in a passage translated by Mr. Mill." Francis Bowen, *The Principles of Political Economy Applied to the Condition: The Resources, and the Institutions of the American People* (Boston, MA: Little, Brown, and Company, 1856), 57.

64. "Review: Considérations sur l'Industrie et la Législation," 431.

the principles on which a nation is to be made great, and rich, and happy, finds himself involved in grammatical subtilties [sic] and verbal disquisitions."[65] One major point of contention in this verbal mêlée was Smith's untenable distinction between productive and unproductive labor. "A distinction has been drawn in all ages between the productive and unproductive classes of Society," John McVickar stipulated in his lecture course on political economy at Columbia. "Smith says All who are engaged directly or indirectly in furnishing productions (material) and bringing them to the consumer are productive. All others Unproductive." This was undoubtedly an unpopular assertion. Clergymen, ministers, lawyers, politicians, and—not least—professors would all have been considered unproductive labor by Smith's definition. By contrast, "Ricardo And his School say All are productive classes, who are freely supported by community. Beggars, thieves, etc. are of course excluded." The verdict? "The School of Ricardo is doubtless in the Right." The comparison between Smith and Ricardo was a powerful tool for showing how different modes of argumentation led to different conclusions (see fig. 2.2). Ricardo's thought was "marked by metaphysical abstractions," while Smith was more "statistical;" Ricardo was "analytic," while Smith was "practical." Other of Smith's assertions could be defeated with one swift blow from the professor. Smith defined rent as "the payment demanded by the Landlord, in return for his monopoly Right," while Ricardo "maintained that 'Rent grows up with and arises from the wants of Society'" ("Ricardo is without doubt Right.").[66]

By 1850, Adam Smith's *The Wealth of Nations* had been all but eclipsed as a classroom textbook. English versions of Say's *Treatise* had dominated Harvard's coursework between 1831 and 1850 until it was replaced by John Stuart Mill's *Principles of Political Economy*, first published in 1848. Wayland's *Elements* was the standard assigned text at Brown, Yale,

65. "Principles of Political Economy. Part the First. Of the Laws of the Production and Distribution of Wealth by Henry C. Carey," *The North American Review* 47, no. 100 (1838), 75.

66. Wheelock H. Parmly, Notes with Professor McVickar, 1841–1842. Columbia University, Columbiana Manuscripts, Series 1 Item 24. Similar lessons appear in Lectures from Professor John McVickar on Political Economy. Taken by Edward Courtlandt Babcock, class of 1849. Columbia University, Columbiana Manuscripts, Series 1 Item 89.

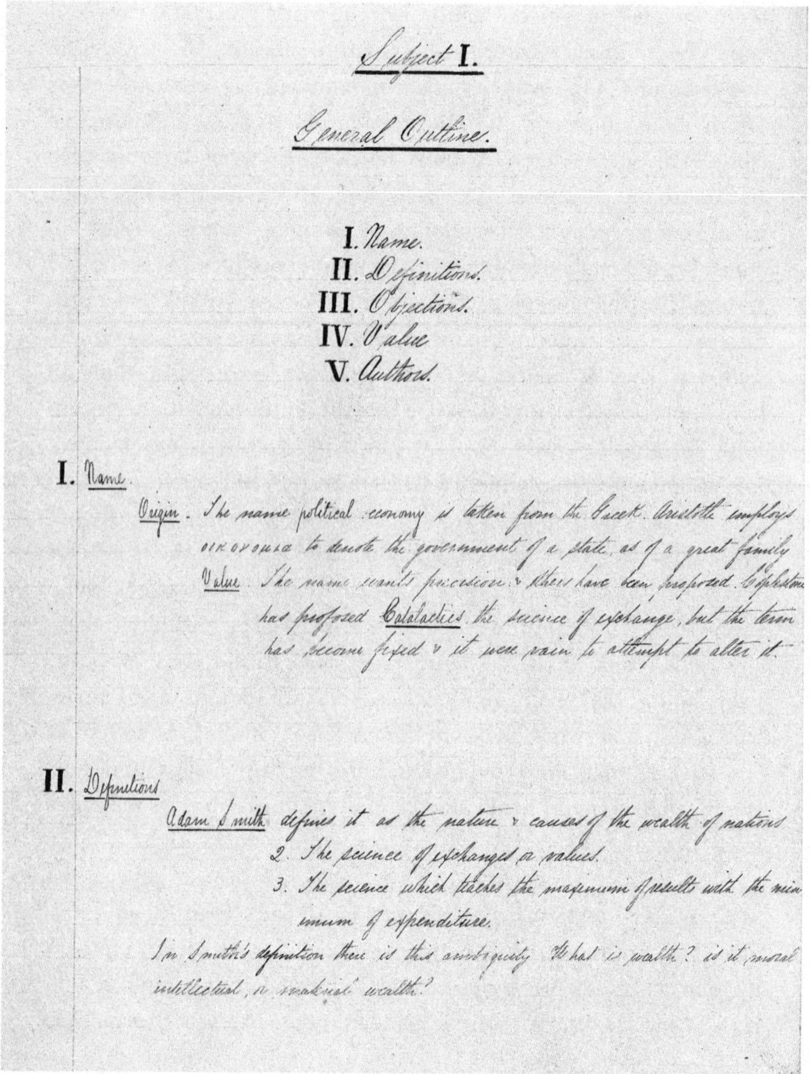

Subject I.

General Outline.

I. Name.
II. Definitions.
III. Objections.
IV. Value
V. Authors.

I. Name.

Origin. The name political economy is taken from the Greek. Aristotle employs οικονομια to denote the government of a state, as of a great family

Value. The name wants precision & others have been proposed. Wheatstone has proposed Catalactics the science of exchange, but the term has become fixed & it were vain to attempt to alter it.

II. Definitions

Adam Smith defines it as the nature & causes of the wealth of nations
2. The science of exchanges or values.
3. The science which teaches the maximum of results with the minimum of expenditure.
In Smith's definition there is this ambiguity. What is wealth? is it moral intellectual, or material wealth?

FIG. 2.1. The first lesson in a typical college course on political economy usually covered the definition of "the science of political economy." Here, the student notes, "In Smith's definition there is this ambiguity. What is wealth? Is it moral intellectual, or material wealth?" University Archives, Rare Book & Manuscript Library, Columbia University Libraries.

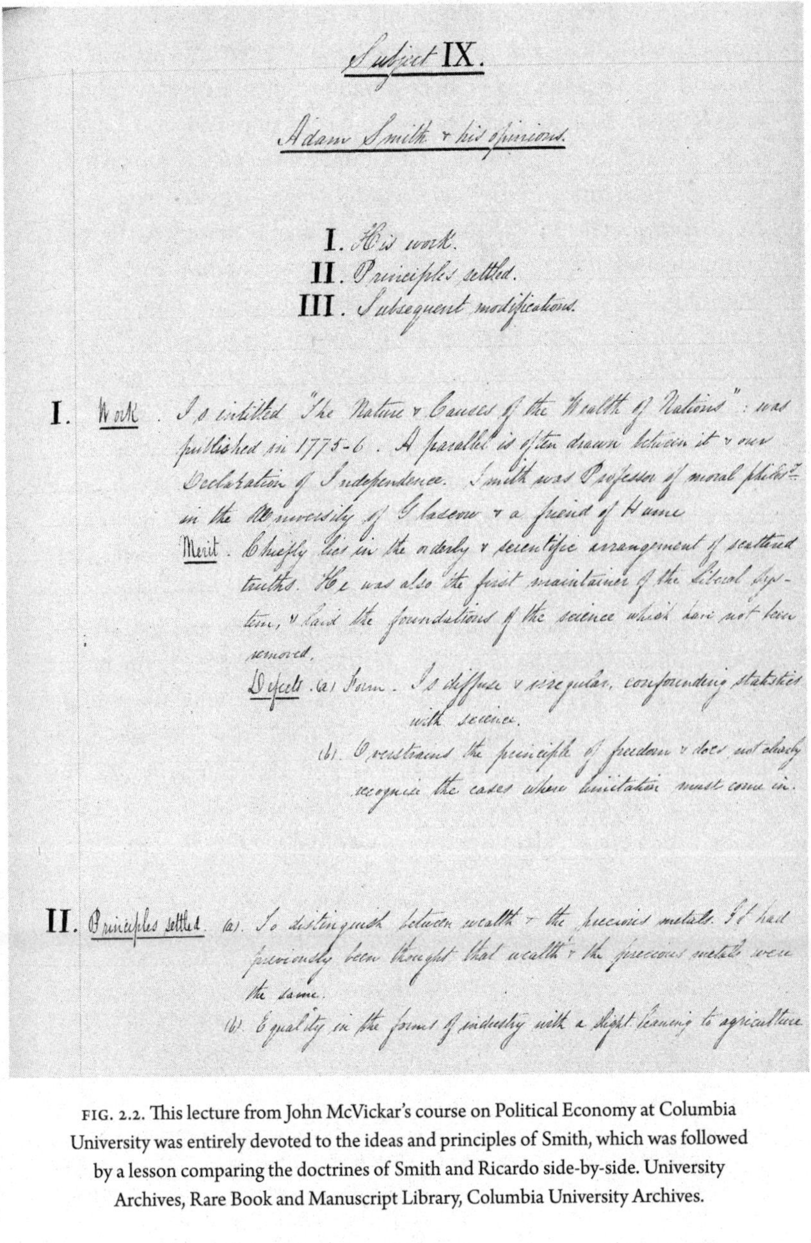

Subject IX.

Adam Smith & his opinions.

I. His work.
II. Principles settled.
III. Subsequent modifications.

I. Work. Is entitled "The Nature & Causes of the Wealth of Nations": was published in 1775-6. A parallel is often drawn between it & our Declaration of Independence. Smith was Professor of moral philos. in the University of Glasgow & a friend of Hume.

Merit. Chiefly lies in the orderly & scientific arrangement of scattered truths. He was also the first maintainer of the Liberal System, & laid the foundations of the science which have not been removed.

Defect. (a) Form. Is diffuse & irregular, confounding statistics with science.

(b) Overstrains the principle of freedom & does not clearly recognise the cases where limitation must come in.

II. Principles settled. (a) To distinguish between wealth & the precious metals. It had previously been thought that wealth & the precious metals were the same.

(b) Equality in the forms of industry with a slight leaning to agriculture.

FIG. 2.2. This lecture from John McVickar's course on Political Economy at Columbia University was entirely devoted to the ideas and principles of Smith, which was followed by a lesson comparing the doctrines of Smith and Ricardo side-by-side. University Archives, Rare Book and Manuscript Library, Columbia University Archives.

and Dartmouth beginning in 1837, and at the University of Virginia—where Smith's *The Wealth of Nations* had been a staple until the 1840s—the works of Say, Mill, and Francis Bowen became the most prominent texts.[67] Smith became valued less for the content of his contributions to economic theory, and more for his importance as an historical mile-marker. When Mill's *Principles of Political Economy* debuted in 1848, *The North American Review* hailed it as "unquestionably the ablest, the most comprehensive, and the most satisfactory exposition of the whole science of political economy that has appeared since the days of Adam Smith." Such an extraordinary accomplishment was Mill's that his book "ought to take its place by the side of *The Wealth of Nations* in the library of every well-informed man, both in the Old and the New World."[68]

Smith slowly faded into the background of curricula, but he never fully disappeared. Instead, as writers became more aware of the distance between their own time and Smith's, they began to historicize Smith's contributions. "As circumstances vary from age to age, as well as between different countries," Francis Bowen wrote in his *Principles of Political Economy*, "it is continually necessary to review and modify the leading doctrines of the science . . . If Adam Smith were living in our own day, it may be doubted whether he would be the uncompromising advocate that he was, of the principles of Free Trade." This was more than making good historical practice part of economics, though. For Bowen, an advocate of the American System, emphasizing the conditions under which certain ideas arose was a way to downplay the theoretical

67. These observations are collected from various course catalogues of the different colleges from roughly 1825–1914. Michael O'Connor reaches a similar conclusion about the dominance of Say's *Treatise*, especially in the Northeast, between roughly 1821 (when the English translation appeared) and 1837 (when Wayland's *Elements* was published). On the use of Adam Smith's text in the Northeast—or lack thereof—O'Connor makes an interesting argument: "The *Wealth of Nations* is long, somewhat contradictory, not strictly organized, and by 1812 and 1825 it seemed to some Americans to be 'needlessly loaded' with statistical details . . . Possibly a factor which decided its rejection in the North was the content of the book, a content which has been amply discussed in the extensive literature on Smith." O'Connor also suggests about how Smith's deism and criticism of clerical associates of the British ruling class may have appeared, at least to American audiences, an improper motive for the distinction between the unproductive and productive classes. O'Connor, *Origins of Academic Economics in the United States*, 111–13.

68. "Review of Principles of Political Economy, with Some of Their Applications to Social Philosophy by John Stuart Mill," 419.

underpinnings of free trade that could be traced to the founder of political economy. According to Bowen, Smith's ideas "flourished at a time when the system of monopolies and restraints was in full action and vigor," which explained why Smith "should utter an earnest protest against these odious restrictions and monopolies, and carry his argument against them too far, by neglecting to mention the exceptions and limitations to which his own principles were liable."[69] This way of selectively historicizing Smith's contributions was a powerful argumentative strategy for proponents of the American System.

Thus, at least among academic audiences, Adam Smith's *The Wealth of Nations* was an amorphous text. As course curricula and textbooks were becoming standardized, certain ideas were codified and principles established within the frameworks of the new science: Smith's labor theory of value was disproven; his definitions of stock, capital, and wealth were vague and obsolete; his distinction between unproductive and productive labor was incorrect; and the division of labor, as central as it was to understanding the production of national wealth, was probably exaggerated. But, while Smith's scientific merits were limited, his historical importance remained indisputable. Educators and authors continued to praise *The Wealth of Nations* for its inimitable style, and, above all, for its ambitious attempt at giving form, structure, and scientific value to political economy. As one writer put it, "if we even admit, that the work of Smith contains some errors of considerable importance . . . it must still be regarded, and will probably remain for a long time, the standard treatise on the science of Political Economy."[70] If there was one factor that played an outsized role in extending the afterlife of Adam Smith, perhaps it was simply the conviction of Smith's readers that *The Wealth of Nations* had outlasted—and would continue to outlast—its own history.

———

Postbellum America witnessed societal changes on an unprecedented scale. Between 1860 and 1890, the population of the country exploded

69. Bowen, *The Principles of Political Economy*, vi.
70. "Review of Phillips' Manual of Political Economy," 217.

from over 41 million to close to 76 million people. New questions arose around the political and economic integration of 4 million former slaves, now freedmen and freedwomen. Cities transformed: their populations grew more than five times (from roughly 6 million to over 30 million urban residents); their sidewalks were paved, illuminated with gas lamps, and marked with the signs of public sanitation systems. Territories stretched from the Atlantic to the Pacific, and, following the California Gold Rush in the mid-nineteenth century, immigrants of different races, ethnicities, and religions populated its vast expanses. The Civil War had torn the nation apart, but the completion of the Transcontinental Railroad in 1869 was reconnecting it in an altogether different way. The floodgates of new political movements were opened: the rise of the anti-gold standard Greenback Party in the 1870s prefigured populist movements; the temperance and women's suffrage movements gained momentum between the 1870s and 1880s; and memberships in organized labor movements continued to swell into the 1890s. This new America in the latter half of the nineteenth century encapsulated the conflicting forces of new industrial capitalism in its heyday: immense wealth and widening inequality, victory over slavery followed by the oppression of wage labor, an influx of diversity and the seeds of nativism. Demographically, materially, culturally, and intellectually, the United States was a different nation.[71]

71. Richard White offers one of the best general accounts of Reconstruction and Gilded Age history in his *The Republic for Which It Stands: The United States during Reconstruction and the Gilded Age, 1865–1896*, Oxford History of the United States (New York, NY: Oxford University Press, 2017). White's impressive volume, as well as his earlier work, *Railroaded: The Transcontinentals and the Making of Modern America* (New York, NY: W.W. Norton & Co, 2011) are representative contributions to an important body of historical scholarship that reinterprets the promises and failings of Reconstruction. Eric Foner, *Reconstruction: America's Unfinished Revolution, 1863–1877* (New York, NY: Harper & Row, 1988) is also considered a landmark contribution. See also Steven Hahn, *A Nation under Our Feet: Black Political Struggles in the Rural South from Slavery to the Great Migration* (Cambridge, MA: Harvard University Press, 2003); Heather Cox Richardson, *The Death of Reconstruction: Race, Labor, and Politics in the Post-Civil War North, 1865–1901* (Cambridge, MA: Harvard University Press, 2001); Mark W. Summers, *The Ordeal of the Reunion A New History of Reconstruction*, The Littlefield History of the Civil War Era (Chapel Hill, NC: The University of North Carolina Press, 2014); T. J. Jackson Lears, *Rebirth of a Nation: The Making of a Modern America, 1877–1920* (New York, NY: HarperCollins,

Concomitant with these seismic social shifts were major changes in the structure of higher education. The Morrill Act of 1862 enabled the expansion of state-funded higher education institutions that offered training in agriculture, engineering, mechanical arts, applied sciences, and other "practical" studies. Enrollment in "modern" disciplines—modern languages, modern history, modern social science—increased, crowding out antiquated disciplines such as Classics. The enrollment of women and Black men slowly but steadily increased, thanks to new institutions such as Vassar College (an all-women's college founded in 1865), Fisk, and Howard University (the latter two both historically Black colleges founded in 1866 and 1867, respectively). Postgraduate and professional degrees were now being offered, and universities became hubs of academic professionalization.[72]

Between 1865 and 1900, academic political economy was redefined in three major ways. The first was the gradual separation of political economy from its parent discipline, moral philosophy. Political economy became a separate course outside philosophy in 1879 at Harvard, though it wasn't until the 1890s that political economy moved from moral philosophy to the School of Historical Sciences at the University of Virginia. In 1879, lectures in political economy at Brown University explicitly enumerated reasons why political economy "must be discriminated from other sciences having affinity with it," including political science, social science, and especially moral science.[73] With sufficient historical distance from the earlier generation of academic moralists

---

2009). For the linking of Reconstruction to the Gilded Age, see also Rebecca Edwards, *New Spirits: Americans in the Gilded Age, 1865–1905* (New York, NY: Oxford University Press, 2006); T. J. Jackson Lears, *No Place of Grace: Antimodernism and the Transformation of American Culture, 1880–1920* (Chicago, IL: University of Chicago Press, 1994).

72. Winterer, *The Culture of Classicism*, 99–100; Barber, "Political Economy and the Academic Setting before 1900," 10–14.

73. Edward Stowe Adams, Lectures in Political Economy by T. Whiting Bancroft (1879). Brown University Archives, MS–1M–2 Box 8. The three points distinguishing moral science from political economy were: "1. Moral science deals with questions of duty. P.E. with questions of profit. 2. Moral Science defines mutual obligation. P.E. ascertains mutual advantages. 3. Moral Science based of right. P.E. on ideas of expedience; yet the two have important parts of contact."

(such as Wayland, Bowen, and McVickar), and, at an even greater distance, the "founders" (Smith, Say, and the classical economists), post-bellum political economists went out of their way to explicitly redefine political economy as a *modern* science. True, the science of wealth related to the "chief practical interests of man," but the science itself "is one of modern origin." There was no science of political economy in ancient Greece, nor in the Middle Ages. Even in the first instance of systematic political economy—Smith's publication of *The Wealth of Nations*—the science was still primitive because it was "created as a branch of moral philosophy," noted one student at Brown.[74] Major advancements in commerce, technology, and industry since Smith's era had provided the literal wealth of the modern age, and it was the task of political economists to investigate its causes and consequences.

The second major development in academic political economy was specialization. While in the antebellum period it had been relatively easy for an ordinary reader to become as well-versed as an expert in technical subjects ranging from the tariff to land policy, postbellum political economy required much more specialized training.[75] Political economy in the academy demanded that students master a core theoretical approach to the science before proceeding to detailed studies of a variety of topical issues. The rise of the elective system showcased the

74. Henry Hilliard Earl, Lectures on Political Economy (Diman, 1865), Brown University Archives, MS–1M–2 Box 19; Cary C. Bradford, Lectures on Political Economy (Diman, 1875–1877), Brown University Archives, MS–1M–2 Box 13 vol. 3. Similar language can be found in Professor Richmond M. Smith's political economy lectures at Columbia University in 1886: "Political Economy is of recent date; within the century, it has developed to its present state. The ancients had no systematic course in this study. In Greece, art and philosophy occupied most of the time of men; in Rome, all attention was given to the extension of military power; in the Middle Ages, activity in industry and commerce declined under the influence of the time but was revived by a series of discoveries, opening new fields of work. The discovery of the compass, of America, of a new route to the Cape of Good Hope, etc., suddenly revived the dead industry and men began to consider the questions of economy, and the West became rich." Political Economy: Historical and Practical. Lectures delivered by Prof. Richmond M. Smith to the class of 1886. Columbia University Archives, Columbiana Manuscripts, Series 1 Item 69.

75. Conkin, *Prophets of Prosperity*, 313. Byrd L. Jones, "A Quest for National Leadership: Institutionalization of Economics at Harvard," in *Breaking the Academic Mould*, ed. Barber, 120–22.

range and depth with which students could apply their newly acquired knowledge.[76] By the 1890s at Harvard, students could take courses on bimetallism, labor arbitration, the economic history of Europe and America, the history of tariff legislation, the management and ownership of railways, and the social and economic conditions of workingmen in the United States. Academics saw specialization as serving two purposes. It not only increased the reputation of political economy as a "full-time scientific investigation," it also broadened their audience at a time when the public was growing more and more aware of the fact that major national issues were, at their core, economic in nature.[77]

Finally, new influences, rival schools of thought, and the rise of popular proselytizers heightened debates about the relationship between science and social reform. Prior to the 1860s, the European influence on American political thought was mostly British and French, but during the 1870s the ideas and approaches of German economists became much more prominent. Cohorts of young American men flocked to Germany for advanced training from the mid–1870s to 1890s, a time when the heavyweights of the younger German Historical School, Adolph Wagner and Gustav Schmoller, were reaching their apogee. Preaching a re-historicized, re-moralized version of economics, Wagner and Schmoller were arguably the most influential thinkers who "[drove] home to American students the historical relativity of all economic doctrines." They rejected the notion of economics as a "timeless" and universal science, and instead, "defended the need to think historically, contextually, and empirically about economic policy."[78] This broad commitment to a loose "historical method" served as the veneer for the

76. A.W. Coats's pyramid analogy illustrates the purpose and success of the elective system quite nicely: The "broadening of the base and a narrowing at the top of the educational pyramid" generated "a process whereby the range of offerings spread outward to embrace new subjects . . . and upward into more advanced, specialized study and research." A.W. Coats, "The Educational Revolution and the Professionalization of American Economics," in *Breaking the Academic Mould*, ed. Barber, 340–375 at 343.

77. Joseph Dorfman, *The Economic Mind in American Civilization*, vol. 3 (New York, NY: The Viking Press, 1949), 49.

78. Daniel T. Rodgers, *Atlantic Crossings: Social Politics in a Progressive Age* (Cambridge, MA: Harvard University Press, 1998), 92.

much more active, social policy-oriented intentions of German econo-mists. Most German economists were civil servants, appointed at uni-versities to teach law students, and they directed their students towards the application of economic theory in the analysis of contemporary socio-economic data for social policy.[79] Above all, the German econo-mists defended the state not as a regulator, but as the main shelter of economic life.[80] Upon returning home, a new generation of German-trained American economists selectively imported their knowledge from abroad. Lecture formats, the subjects of elective courses, new scholarly publications, and graduate programs all bore the hallmarks of German economics education. In 1885, the economists Richard T. Ely of the Johns Hopkins University, E.R.A. Seligman of Columbia, and Henry C. Adams of Cornell founded the American Economics Associa-tion (AEA), modeled after the German Verein für Socialpolitik (Union for Social Policy). The AEA marked the beginnings of professionaliza-tion within the social sciences, but it also was a marker of growing fis-sures in the discipline. Ely, whom many considered a German academic socialist in an American suit, was eventually forced to abandon his pro-gressive vision for the society and restate the AEA's mission in terms of a more neutral, scholarly agenda. In 1894, Ely stood on trial at the Uni-versity of Wisconsin-Madison for allegedly teaching socialist ideas; the trial became the starting point for the first serious discussions around academic freedom in the United States.

79. Backhouse and Tribe, *The History of Economics*, 174–75, 182–83; Simon J. Cook and Keith Tribe, "Historical Economics," in Gilbert Faccarello and Heinz D. Kurz, *Handbook on the History of Economic Analysis. Volume II, Schools of Thought in Economics* (Cheltenham: Edward Elgar Publishing, 2016), 295–312.

80. Rodgers, *Atlantic Crossings*, 91. For a helpful account of the development of the younger German Historical School see Bruce Caldwell, *Hayek's Challenge: An Intellectual Biography of F.A. Hayek* (Chicago, IL: University of Chicago Press, 2004), 48–63. For more on the develop-ment of American economics in the late nineteenth century, see Coats, "The Educational Revo-lution and the Professionalization of American Economics;" Dorfman, Joseph, *The Economic Mind in American Civilization*; Joseph Dorfman, "The Role of the German Historical School in American Economic Thought," *The American Economic Review* 45, no. 2 (1955), 17–28; Tribe, *Strategies of Economic Order: German Economic Discourse, 1750–1950* (Cambridge: Cambridge University Press, 1995).

New voices also amplified debates beyond the walls of the academy. During the 1880s William Graham Sumner and Henry George surfaced as the most vocal representatives of opposing sides of the conflict between capital and labor in the nineteenth century. Sumner's incendiary *What the Social Classes Owe One Another* (1883) became the iconic text of organized capital, declaring the independent capitalist as the "Forgotten Man" of American society. At the other end, Henry George's *Progress and Poverty* (1879) became the manifesto of labor movements, and George became the figurehead of a wider political movement— Georgism—centered on his signature idea, the single tax. *Progress and Poverty* opened with a survey of the most well-known texts—Smith, Ricardo, McCulloch, Mill, Wayland, and Carey—in order to deconstruct the conceptual foundations of political economy. Most authors, George argued, had confounded *wealth* with *capital*, and they had fallen into the further error of assuming that wages were drawn from capital. Both fundamental errors had origins in Smith, and George did not hesitate to deploy colorful metaphors to describe Smith's "vulgar errors." "If they, one after another, have followed Dr. Adam Smith, as boys play 'follow my leader,' jumping where he jumped, and falling where he fell," George commented, referring to Smith's theory of wages and compensation, "it has been that there was a fence where he jumped and a hole where he fell." This was the first "great misstep" which led political economy "into the jungle, instead of upon the mountain tops," wrote George.[81]

---

81. Henry George, *Progress and Poverty: An Enquiry into the Cause of Industrial Depressions, and of Increase of Want with Increase of Wealth. The Remedy* (New York, NY: Sterling Publishing, 1879), 142, 146. George's contributions to political economy deserve far more treatment than what I have managed here. The literature on his social and political philosophy is relatively sparse. One of the earliest comprehensive treatments of George's life, works, and thought is George Raymond Geiger, *The Philosophy of Henry George* (New York, NY: The Macmillan Company, 1933). See also John L. Thomas, *Alternative America: Henry George, Edward Bellamy, Henry Demarest Lloyd and the Adversary Tradition* (Cambridge, MA: Harvard University Press, 1983). Jeffrey Sklansky's important and intricate analysis of both Sumner and George treats the two as mile-markers of the birth of a new theory of society in the crisis of postbellum America. Jeffrey Sklansky, *The Soul's Economy: Market Society and Selfhood in American Thought, 1820–1920* (Chapel Hill, NC: University of North Carolina Press, 2002).

George wanted to explode the theories of Smith, but at the same time, he saw the possibility for something new to emerge from its ashes. George's aim, as he stated in the book's preface, was to "unite the truth perceived by the school of Smith and Ricardo to the truth perceived by the schools of Proudhon and Lasalle; to show that *laissez faire* [sic] (in its full true meaning) opens the way to a realization of the noble dreams of socialism."[82] As part of that noble dream, George wanted to completely reconfigure the common (mis)conception of capital. The central conceptual claim of the work was that land was a source of capital valued not for its natural productive powers, but rather for its facilitative powers. From transportation to exchange, the workings of the market all took place on land. George's achievement, therefore, was to redefine land and labor as distinctively "social rather than natural resources."[83] *Progress and Poverty* quickly outsold all previous works of political economy and even most popular novels in both the United States and England.[84]

As these challenges to American political economy were mounted from within and from without, the economics profession began to turn inward. Writing in 1876, Charles Franklin Dunbar, who had been appointed head of Harvard's department of economics in 1871, viewed recent developments with disappointment and anxiety. Economics in the United States had become too preoccupied with explaining actual material conditions and trying to seek practical solutions to economic problems in Dunbar's mind. At the level of practice, this meant too much emphasis was placed on writing textbooks replete with watered-down principles, rather than the discovery of new scientific theories. While in the last decade there was "a marked and salutary revival of interest in economic discussion" on topical issues, American economics had "done nothing towards developing the theory of political economy," Dunbar wrote in a retrospective essay for *The North American Review*.[85] The superfluity of political economic vocabulary drawn from "popular

---

82. George, *Progress and Poverty*, xi. Italics in original.

83. Sklansky, *The Soul's Economy*, 123.

84. Sklansky, *The Soul's Economy*, 115.

85. Charles F. Dunbar, "Economic Science in America, 1776–1876," *The North American Review* 122, no. 250 (January 1876), 136–37, 140.

discourse" made the science "peculiarly liable to equivocal use," and, more worryingly, vitiated "the whole process of reasoning" that scholars had for so long worked to build.[86]

The larger problem with this emphasis on application over theory, according to Dunbar, was that it misled the public and mischaracterized the discipline of political economy as ideological. "Indeed," Dunbar complained, "the strongly practical direction given to every pursuit in American life has not only served to turn our statesmen and scholars away from work in the field of political economy, but has also given a marked character to such work as they have done in that field." Statesmen looked not to the scientific laws and systematic works of theory, but instead to the "pamphlets and occasional essays" of popular economists like Henry George, which risked leading people "into some serious misconceptions as to the direct bearing of economic laws."[87] Dunbar's worry about the public perception of economists as little more than partisan ideologues in professorial robes was justifiable. The practice of appointing chairs specifically to teach the doctrine of free trade or protectionism was still in place when Dunbar wrote. Prior to the Civil War, finding intellectual respectability for the doctrine of protectionism "was an uphill battle," but in the latter half of the nineteenth century, it was not uncommon for courses to require equal treatment of protectionist and free trade ideas.[88] Even new generation economists like Ely criticized these arcane academic arrangements. "It has been so generally felt that professors of political economy in America were more advocates of existing institutions," Ely claimed, "that the masses have turned away from them in angry impatience, and have been prejudiced even against the important and unassailable doctrines which they did teach."[89] Thus, these trends—the move away from moral philosophy, increased specialization, and professionalization—were shaped by larger currents in

86. Dunbar, "Economic Science in America," 148.

87. Dunbar, "Economic Science in America," 147.

88. Judith L. Goldstein, *Ideas, Interests, and American Trade Policy* (Ithaca, NY: Cornell University Press, 1993), 26, 33, 86–88.

89. Richard T. Ely, "Political Economy in America," *The North American Review*, 144 no. 363 (Feb. 1887), 113–119 at 116.

public intellectual and political life in the late nineteenth century. Striving for scientific status and prestige, the "old" science of political economy was giving way to the "new" science of economics—the latter of which strove to be "free from theological, ethical, historical, and sociological encumbrances, and above all, free from the blemishes of missionary zeal and partisanship."[90]

How the profession of economics defined its present and envisioned its future required reckoning with its past. In this quest for self-definition, academic political economists simultaneously glorified and historicized Adam Smith. As discussed earlier in this chapter, distinguishing political economy from other types of science often required identifying the features that made it a modern science and pinpointing the moment when it was founded. Adam Smith was very frequently, if not universally, acknowledged as its founder in this regard. It "[w]ell may be said of Adam Smith," recorded one student at Brown University in 1865, "that this solitary Scotchman has by the publication of one single work contributed more towards the happiness of man that has been effected by the united abilities of all the statesmen & legislators from History has preserved an account."[91] But this image of Smith as a founding father was also historically bounded. Smith published *The Wealth of Nations* in 1776 and became "the first systematic writer on the subject, whence he is called its founder"—that much was obvious. But Smith was also "influenced by the circumstances of his time;" his advocacy of free trade was "necessary in his time" because he witnessed how a monarchical government "interfered with a man's actions at every step" and "how the rise of industry was hindered by the rules." An historical understanding of Smith and the trajectory of political economy as a science revealed that the principle of laissez-faire was "simply an historic principle dating from Adam Smith . . . when a paternal government and an absolute monarchy were the curse of industry," and it was a mistake for political

90. Coats, "The Educational Revolution and the Professionalization of American Economics," 364.

91. Henry Hilliard Earl, Lectures on Political Economy (Professor Diman, 1865), Brown University Archives, MS–1M–2 Box 19.

economists to take "this temporary principle as an absolute law."[92] Smith, in short, became squarely part of political economy's past.

Making Smith part of the past, however, was not necessarily in service of recovering Smith's original intentions or providing an integrated account of Smith's works. Nor was historicizing Smith incompatible with attributing to him an enduring relevance, even almost a hundred years later. The publication of the first two volumes of the English historian Henry Thomas Buckle's *History of Civilization in England* in 1861 made this abundantly clear. Despite its title, Buckle's *History* was not history strictly speaking, but rather his philosophy of history and science. History, for Buckle, simply provided evidence for his proposition that progress was measured in the discovery and diffusion of scientific knowledge, and that a "spirit of skepticism" against prevailing truths had to prevail in order to allow a "spirit of investigation" to come into full flower. Buckle saw this dynamic relationship between skepticism and enlightenment most powerfully exemplified in Adam Smith, but his treatment of Smith is striking for two reasons. First, Buckle paid close attention to Smith's *The Theory of Moral Sentiments* and *The Wealth of Nations* not as separate or disjointed contributions, but rather as "two divisions of a single subject." Smith, Buckle explained, saw that "all of us are sympathetic as well as selfish," and that "no attempt has hitherto been made to analyze the intellect of Adam Smith, by considering his two great works as the opposite, but yet the compensatory, parts of a single scheme."[93] When read as two parts of a unified whole, the works illustrated the uniqueness and limitations of Smith's method of inquiry—a method that relied heavily on deduction from first principles, but elaborated those premises with so many examples drawn from observation that each argument led "to a conclusion which approximates to truth."[94]

92. Political Economy: Historical and Practical. Lectures delivered by Professor Richmond M. Smith to the class of 1886. Columbia University Archives, Columbiana Manuscripts, Series 1 Item 69.

93. Henry Thomas Buckle, *History of Civilization in England*, Vol. 2 (London, West Strand: Parker, Son, and Bourn, 1861), 432, 433, 457.

94. Buckle, *History of Civilization in England*, Vol. 2, 434.

Buckle's obsession with philosophical method animated his idiosyn-cratic reconstruction of *The Theory of Moral Sentiments* and *The Wealth of Nations*. Proceeding from the premise of the "universal impulse which is called Sympathy" allowed Smith to explain "a vast number of social phenomena:" sympathy with the rich, loyalty, custom, and fashion; as well as the establishment of norms of rewards and punishment. From this "bold hypothesis," Buckle claimed, Smith leveled the idea that self-ishness was the only principle of human nature. "At one stroke," Smith "so narrowed the field of inquiry, as to exclude from it all considerations of selfishness as a primary principle, and only to admit its greatest an-tagonist, sympathy."[95] But *The Theory of Moral Sentiments* did not com-plete Smith's science, and Smith had seen the necessity to elevate the status of questions regarding human nature to the level of science through "separate and fragmentary investigation," as Buckle put it. Thus was the impulse for Smith's second great work, *The Wealth of Nations*. Buckle had no shortage of glowing verbiage when it came to *The Wealth of Nations*. He cloaked Smith in the garb of a prophet who descended into "that dense and disorderly mass" of institutional history, trade trea-ties, banking technicalities, poor-laws, and colonial disturbances, only to bring "symmetry, method, and law" to the subjects, and "at his touch, anarchy disappeared, and darkness was succeeded by light."[96] "No single man ever took so great a step upon so important a subject," Buckle wrote, and "no single work which is now preserved, contains so many views, which were novel at the time, but which subsequent experience has ratified."[97] The "striking generalizations" in *The Wealth of Nations*, he admitted, were "far from containing the whole truth," but more important than their objective truth was the explanatory power of Smith's reasoning. Starting from the "dictates of unalloyed selfishness," Smith explained "many other circumstances which society presents, and which at first sight appear incongruous."[98] According to Buckle, the relation between *The Theory of Moral Sentiments* and *The Wealth of*

95. Buckle, *History of Civilization in England*, Vol. 2, 438, 440.
96. Buckle, *History of Civilization in England*, Vol. 2, 442, 445.
97. Buckle, *History of Civilization in England*, Vol. 2, 446.
98. Buckle, *History of Civilization in England*, Vol. 2, 452.

Nations, therefore, was not one of inter-textual content or substantive relation, but rather of method. Accounting for the substantive shift between the premises of *The Theory of Moral Sentiments* and *The Wealth of Nations*, however, would not be something scholars attended to for more than two decades.[99]

What is perhaps most striking about Buckle's observations on Smith is that they were almost completely ignored in America. Aside from echoing Buckle's praise for Smith in the college classroom, American readers of Buckle remained unconvinced by the grand narrative of his *History*.[100] "Evidently this is a sketch of a system of philosophy, and not a project of writing history," wrote *The North American Review* in 1861. The reviewer accused Buckle of dogmatically following his own philosophy such that he "ransacks all history, literature, and science for proofs and illustrations of his preconceived opinion."[101] The author rejected Buckle's assessment that the defining feature of Smith's accomplishment was his reliance on the deductive method. "The truth of the matter is that both Hume and Adam Smith simply reasoned on the facts before them, just as Bacon did," wrote another author. For Buckle to have attempted to chart the progress of history in different countries "smacks, in short, of the pretentious mouthing of the philister, rather than of the genuine accents of the philosopher."[102] In short, if there

99. Here of course I refer to the infamous Das Adam Smith Problem, the reception of which is central to my discussion in Chapter 4.

100. It appears Buckle's assessment was repeated in lectures on Political Economy at Brown in 1865: "Still greater advance was made in the 18th century by the labors of the French economists who advocated unrestricted freedom of trade, & in England by the essays of Hume, till at length in 1776 by the publication of the 'Wealth of Nations,' Adam Smith established P.E. [political economy] as a science. Looking at its ultimate results the 'Wealth of Nations' says Buckle, is probably the most important book that has ever been written. Well may it be said of Adam Smith & said too without fear of contradiction that this solitary Scotchman has by the publication of one single work contributed more towards the happiness of man that has been effected by the united abilities of all the statesmen & legislators from History has preserved an account." Henry Hilliard Earl, Lectures on Political Economy (Diman, 1865) Brown University, MS–1M–2 Box 19.

101. "Review: Buckle's *History of Civilization in England* (volumes 1 and 2)," *The North American Review*, 93 (1861), 519–559 at 522.

102. J. H. Stirling, "Review: *History of Civilization in England and France, Spain and Scotland* by Henry Thomas Buckle" *The North American Review* vol. 115, no 236 (1872), 65–103 at 78–79.

existed a truly "historical" account of Smith's accomplishments and nuanced reading of his works, it certainly was not to be found in Buckle's *History*.

Economics offered an alternative approach to reading Smith in history. With the growing influence of the German Historical School, some colleges expanded their offerings in the history of economic theory. Harvard offered different senior elective courses in the history of thought, one beginning with Smith and another ending with Smith. For example, in Frank Taussig's course on the history of economic thought, a contextualized reading of not only Smith but also the physiocrats, Ricardo, the disciples of the classical school, and even ancient economic thinkers provided an opportunity for students to assess different methods of reasoning and tease out the relationship between economic theories and social philosophies. Smith's works "had great influence on events of his time," but they also demonstrated the more general notion that ideas and history were reciprocal influences and that "events often influence writers & cause rise of new schools."[103] In Taussig's course, Smith was not so much worshipped as he was studied as a historical monument, and Taussig did not refrain from pointing out what aspects of Smith were outdated or misunderstood. Smith's "unmerciful" and "final stroke" against mercantilism, for example, could now be seen as "going a little too far [the] other way," and his idea that the home industry "put in motion more capital than foreign trading" was an "obsolete doctrine."[104]

Treating Smith as an artefact of the past served a broader methodological purpose. Taussig underscored how Smith's "faculty of observing and combining facts & knowledge of practical affairs" was the "distinguishing characteristic" of his approach to political economy, and it was one that was particularly admirable. At the same time, Smith's role as an eighteenth-century professor of moral philosophy and

103. This appears to be the thrust of Professor Frank Taussig of Harvard in his course Political Economy 2. Notes in Political Economy 2. Lectures by Asst. Prof. Taussig, 1887–1888 by Clarence Alfred Bunker. Harvard University Archives, HUC 8887.371.2.

104. Notes in Political Economy 2. Lectures by Asst. Prof. Taussig, 1887–1888 by Clarence Alfred Bunker. Harvard University Archives, HUC 8887.371.2.

jurisprudence made him the borderline between pre-scientific and scientific thinkers. Smith, according to Taussig, was not the original
founder of political economy but rather a great synthesizer of previous
writers. At the same time, Taussig admitted there was "as much [original]
thought and [contributions] in W. of N. as in any book ever published."
Such statements were intended not to minimize Smith's importance, but
rather to highlight the developments that would eventually take place. "No
writer," Taussig would later argue, "was so scientific as Ricardo," whose
political economy was a "strict [investigation] without regard to ethics."[105]
This argument contained an implicit acknowledgement that somehow,
in some way, Smith's political economy had sufficiently disentangled
itself from *The Theory of Moral Sentiments* and, more generally, from
the wider web of moral philosophy in the eighteenth and early nineteenth centuries.

Thus, at least among American scholars in the late 1870s and 1880s,
there was no clear consensus on what a "historical" Smith looked like.
On the one hand, Buckle's interpretation of Smith told the story of the
triumph of secular, deductive reasoning over superstition and religion
in eighteenth-century Scotland. And while Buckle endeavored to show
that the methodological unity of *The Theory of Moral Sentiments* and *The
Wealth of Nations* was the by-product of a larger historical force at work,
this broad historical narrative was by and large rejected or, at the very
least, overlooked by American readers of Buckle. On the other hand,
academic economists had their own version of an historical Smith. In
some ways, economists who tried to turn Smith into an artefact of the
past were also presuming a certain telos like Buckle. There was a scientific truth to be uncovered, and Smith represented but one point on the
long arc of history. Adam Smith and *The Wealth of Nations* receded even
further into the background of economics, and yet Smith and his works
still occupied a unique position in the minds of American academic
economists. Smith's ideas had been or would be disproved, expanded,
and revised, but readers still viewed *The Wealth of Nations* as an object

105. Notes in Political Economy 2. Lectures by Asst. Prof. Taussig, 1887–1888 by Clarence
Alfred Bunker. Harvard University Archives, HUC 8887.371.2.

of special historical value. It was valued so highly not because intellectuals unanimously believed in the intrinsic truth it contained, but because it stood as a "mile-post which [served] to measure the distance by which thought has passed [it]."[106]

———

One hundred years after its initial publication, amidst the scores of new works of political economy from both America and Europe, Smith's *The Wealth of Nations* was still regarded as one of the most important works of political economy. In the same retrospective essay on the state of the economics profession, Harvard's Charles F. Dunbar wrote that,

> the economist finds the foundations of the science . . . laid deep and solid for the first time by Adam Smith; the great men who have since carried forward the work have declared himself his followers, and in developing and extending the science have kept to the lines of discussion which he laid down with such vigor and insight a century ago.[107]

That American readers considered Smith's *The Wealth of Nations* (alongside John Stuart Mill's *Principles of Political Economy*) as the best book on political economy even in 1876, is a remarkable story not of inevitable canonization, but of continuity and resilience amidst rapid change.[108]

106. Van Buren Denslow, "American Economics," *The North American Review*, vol. 139 no. 332 (Jul 1884), 12–29 at 12.

107. Charles F. Dunbar, "Economic Science in America, 1776–1876," 124.

108. The competition put out by *The Publishers' Weekly* asked readers to submit a list of publications that were "the most standard and salable books in each branch of literature" to establish "which books and editions have, independent of local or ephemeral interest, become standard or popular works in the American market, hence safe stock for investment." *The Publishers' Weekly*. Vol. IX, no. 214, February 19, 1876, 229. See Joseph Dorfman, *The Economic Mind in American Civilization*, vol. 3 (New York, NY: The Viking Press, 1949), 81. Irwin Collier provides some insights as to how exactly this contest works in a post on the top-ten textbooks in the US. See, Irwin Collier, "Political Economy Books. Top-Ten Sellers in the U.S., 1876." February 13, 2016, Economics in the Rear-View Mirror, available at https://www.irwincollier.com /political-economy-books-top-ten-sellers-in-the-u-s-1876/.

Academic political economy in the United States had no single origin. Early political economic writers like Raymond, Cooper, and List drew inspiration from and built their reputation on the works of Smith, Ricardo, and Say. But they also saw themselves as pioneers in new intellectual territory. Though Smith had mapped out some of the terrain the writers were exploring, they often felt the need to correct, or even completely deviate from, the paths he charted. The formalization of political economy curricula in antebellum colleges was another important site for establishing the legitimacy of political economy as an academic field and for constructing certain patterns of teaching and making use of Smith's ideas. The nature of Smith's significance for instructors and students alike changed as the discipline grew and evolved. *The Wealth of Nations* transformed from being a trove of terminology, illustrations, and lessons for students to commit to memory to an historical object whose primary importance lay in the fact that it accomplished something that no other work before it had accomplished: it created not a mere study but a *science* of political economy. To the extent that Smith's American readers saw themselves as his disciples or defectors, then, it generally had to do with the degree to which they accepted or rejected the content of Smith's ideas—his definition of national wealth, rent, labor, or even the relative power of the division of labor.

American readers were also beginning to reinvent Smith's legacy on different terms. The confluence of the politics of political economy with the science of political economy in the nineteenth century enabled readers to marshal Smith's ideas as well as his intellectual authority. The political commitments of the individual reader often conditioned perceptions of Smith's scientific value—the truth of his ideas, the timeless quality of his analysis, the relevance of his policies. This was especially the case when it came to matters of free trade. Supporters of free trade seized on Smith's reputation as the great founder of the science of political economy and invoked *The Wealth of Nations* to defend their position, while those who championed the American System of protectionism tried to cast doubt on its claims and its relevance.

3

The Apostle of Free Trade

IN 1876, the Delmonico brothers' restaurant in New York City had a number of claims to fame. As one of the first French fine dining restaurants in New York City, it welcomed various luminaries from around the country and globe. It boasted the creations of its head chef, Charles Ranhofer, who allegedly invented eggs benedict, baked Alaska, and "Chicken a la king." Located at Fifth Avenue and 26th Street between glittering hotels and theaters, Delmonico's was a place to see and be seen in Manhattan. Perhaps that is why Delmonico's was the spot for a "sumptuous banquet" on December 12, 1876, which was attended by eminent public figures and intellectuals of the day including New York Secretary of State John Bigelow, editor of *The New York Evening Post* William Cullen Bryan, Professor William Graham Sumner of Yale, and Charles Franklin Dunbar, professor of political economy at Harvard. The occasion? The hundredth anniversary of the publication of *The Wealth of Nations*.

Close to a hundred attendees took part in the festivities, which had been billed as a celebration of "the principles of freedom taught in that immortal work" of Adam Smith.[1] New York free-trade journalist Parke Godwin opened the line of speakers, declaring that "It is not often that men meet to do honor to a book," but on that day they were gathered

---

1. "Adam Smith. Centennial Celebration of the Publication of 'The Wealth of Nations'—Speeches by William Cullen Bryant, Parke Godwin, David A. Wells, Professor Sumner, Mr. Atkinson and Others.," *Evening Post*, December 13, 1876. (Hereafter "Adam Smith . . . Speeches.")

together "to commemorate not a work drawn out of the mysterious wells of the imagination, but a work treating our every day affairs which has taken its place among the masterpieces of genius." Godwin hailed the eighteenth-century Scotsman as demigod who,

> saw the truth in its intrinsic force . . . grasped it in its bearings and relations, and . . . developed it with such completeness and simplicity that he made it plain to the common apprehension, that he made it the property of men in the common walks of life, and not alone of the student in his closet or the speculator in his school.[2]

Smith turned the scientific truth of free trade into common sense; that was the reason why dozens gathered "to celebrate it as one of the greatest features of our Centennial," Godwin proclaimed.[3]

Newspapers described the centennial gathering as "representative of the strongest Free Trade Sentiment in the United States." "We do not remember a Free Trade gathering for many years which afforded a clearer indication of the policy or principles maintained by those who stand at the head of this singularly vital agitation," wrote one journalist in *The Providence Evening Press*.[4] Yet even before the Delmonico's banquet, the presses extolled Adam Smith's *The Wealth of Nations* as an American gospel. The overlapping centennials of Smith's work and American Independence provided the perfect backdrop for a national celebration: to remember how far the nation had come, and to recall how Smith, like a prophet, showed the way to wealth.[5] It also provided a moment for sober reflection. "In our legislation upon commercial matters," *The New York Evening Post* wrote,

> we have violated almost every precept that Adam Smith laid down for the guidance of men and nations. We have broken the golden rule

2. "Adam Smith . . . Speeches."

3. "Adam Smith . . . Speeches."

4. "A Free Trade Synagogue," *Providence Evening Press*, December 14, 1876.

5. As one newspaper put it, "Adam Smith represents one of the prophets who, from lofty points of observation, look back over the winding, devious, dusty paths the nations have walked, and see how they have stumbled and strayed." "An Economic Centennial," *Daily Albany Argus*, April 21, 1876.

of his commercial gospel continually. We have not heeded the truth he taught, and have vainly striven to secure our own prosperity by preventing that of other men.[6]

For those who shared *The Evening Post's* beliefs, it was altogether fitting that the hundredth anniversary of Smith's magnum opus would fall at the same time as that of the nation. Perhaps, they hoped, a century of experience would have taught the nation to "appreciate as we never did before the wisdom and the righteousness of the precepts upon which Adam Smith founded his commercial philosophy."[7]

The Smith worship at Delmonico's would have been a spectacle to most ordinary Americans at the time. To start, the policy of free trade was dramatically out of sync with reality in 1876. Average tariff levels had reached historic highs since the 1820s, and the next two decades would be remembered as the most protectionist era in history. By the 1890s, the country had fully embraced the rhetoric and policy of overseas expansion, intensifying the global turn away from free trade and toward imperialism. At best, the Smith centenary celebrations might have appeared as little more than an ostentatious attempt to resuscitate a politically inert idea. But the image of Smith conjured up at the Free Trader Centennial would have been almost unrecognizable to Americans a century earlier as well. As Chapters 1 and 2 demonstrated, American statesmen in the Founding Era had made use of Smith's ideas without necessarily attaching them to a unified political agenda. While *The Wealth of Nations* was read widely and considered an important work, it did not appear to exert any fundamental influence on matters of practical politics. Moreover, the chief architects of American political economic institutions—Hamilton in particular—held a general view that free trade, though desirable in theory, was nonetheless an unattainable ideal in the real world. As one scholar put it, there is little evidence to suggest that "anyone in America took the *Wealth of Nations* to be 'the penultimate manifesto of free trade,'" at least in the eighteenth century.[8]

6. "The Adam Smith Centenary," *New York Evening Post*, December 8, 1876.

7. "The Adam Smith Centenary."

8. Teichgraeber, "'Less Abused than I Had Reason to Expect,'" 344.

In short, the late-nineteenth century image of Smith as "the apostle of free trade" in America presents a puzzle: not only had Smith become a symbol of a doctrine that was out of step with political reality, *The Wealth of Nations* appeared to be something that it had not been before, namely, a "giant machine assembled to drive home one easily understood point:" free trade.[9] How and why did this transformation take place?

Over the course of the nineteenth century, American trade policy constantly shifted in and out of the national political spotlight. Following the conclusion of the War of 1812, tariff debates dominated national politics. The tariff was a key foreign policy instrument, but it became a critical political lever for domestic policy in the 1820s and 1830s. The consequences of trade policy were entangled with questions about slavery, westward expansion, internal improvements, and the fragility of the Union. After the Civil War, tariffs reemerged as one of the central issues around which the two major political parties differentiated themselves and formed coalitions. Thus, the changing circumstances under which Americans turned to Smith shaped their use of his ideas and also their sense of his relevance to actual experience. Those who called for free trade in the antebellum Cotton South, for instance, had dramatically different reasons for invoking *The Wealth of Nations* from those who called for protectionism in the postbellum industrialized North. Yet they all found inspiration and authority in Adam Smith.

The politics of free trade in the nineteenth century fundamentally altered the way Americans engaged with Smith's ideas. One obvious consequence of this transformation was that the central message of *The Wealth of Nations* was reduced to the doctrine of free trade, while *The Theory of Moral Sentiments* was virtually ignored. On the Congress floor, legislators flattened Smith's complex, "pragmatic, distinctively self-scrutinizing" arguments into a scientific and unambiguous defense of free trade.[10] If, for Smith, the prospects of free trade were as uncertain as that of "an Oceana or Utopia," American legislators read and invoked

9. Teichgraeber, "'Less Abused than I Had Reason to Expect,'" 345.
10. Teichgraeber, "'Less Abused than I Had Reason to Expect,'" 346.

Smith *as if* free trade was a political and economic certainty. Meanwhile, politicians and agitators who championed the American System of protectionism pointed to Smith's arguments for protecting the "home market;" however, they did so not to add nuance back into Smith's own ideas, but rather to delegitimize the doctrine of free trade as inconsistent and unsound. Smith's political value, therefore, stemmed from an unspoken consensus that Smith was an—if not *the*—authority on free trade as well as a symbol whom politicians could invoke in order to align themselves with or distance themselves from.[11]

Beyond turning Smith into a pole star, reading Smith within the narrow terms of the trade debates had consequences for the status of political economic ideas within the arena of contesting politics. On the one hand, Smith's *The Wealth of Nations* could supply much-needed policy roadmaps in uncertain environments; the causal argument for free trade could be easily distilled, and it implied specific policy strategies to attain a specific goal.[12] But, on the other hand, the use of Smith's ideas—and the ideas of other academic economists more generally—in formal political debate raised questions about the validity, timelessness, and practicability of ideas in different historical contexts. Those who defended free trade could parade their arguments under the mantle of Smith's scientific and timeless truth, but those who favored protectionism could turn those ideas on their head, denouncing Smith's ideas and the whole enterprise of political economy as irrelevant, disconnected from the reality of contemporary politics, and ultimately un-American. Debates about trade policy thus reveal an ongoing and dynamic relationship between the production of economic ideas in one arena and their use in another. The doctrines of economists could be used as political and ideological weapons; however, the more politically activated Smith's ideas became, the more likely people were to doubt the

11. Here I have also adapted the "model" of canonization from Collini, *Public Moralists*, 317–19.

12. Judith Goldstein and Robert O. Keohane, *Ideas and Foreign Policy: Beliefs, Institutions, and Political Change* (Ithaca, NY: Cornell University Press, 1993).

objectivity and relevance of the science he supposedly invented.[13] And yet, these repeated challenges to his authority did not weaken Smith's reputation as one of the most transcendental thinkers but rather strengthened it.

———

Barely thirty years after the War for Independence concluded and the U.S. Constitution was ratified, the nation found itself at war with Great Britain once again. The War of 1812 began and ended with conflict over trade. Hoping to maintain its dominance over US exports—primarily cotton—Great Britain introduced trade restrictions in order to block-ade neutral trade between its formal colonies and France. The impress-ment of Americans into the British navy only added salt to the wounds of the former subjects of the British crown. The conclusion of the war in 1815 was no guarantee that the United States would be free from Brit-ish commercial domination, however. The British quickly spiked import tariffs on American goods and dumped shiploads of British manufac-tured goods on American shores. Desperate to resuscitate domestic industry and protect fledgling American industries, Congress passed the first major piece of American tariff legislation in 1816; serious fiscal pressures quickly made it clear that the tariff had to be revised. By the 1820s, a fiscal surplus and the near-elimination of national debt chal-lenged the idea that raising revenue was the primary motivation for tariff legislation. While tariffs had provided a vital stream of government revenue since the 1790s, they could also be used as a shield against for-eign rivals, or as a lever to pry open foreign markets. Thus, the grounds on which a new tariff or a revision to existing tariffs were justified

13. My argument here is inspired by and corroborates Kirk Willis's examination of Smith's ideas in eighteenth-century parliamentary debate in Great Britain. Willis describes the "twin aspects of the popularization of political economy" in parliamentary debates as involving two things: on the one hand, the intention of classical economists to make their works "easily un-derstood, readily available, and widely read by laymen," and, on the other hand, their intention that political economy be a useful science, specifically for government. Willis, "The Role in Parliament of the Economic Ideas of Adam Smith," 506

became the crux of the issue and the source of intense polarization. Between 1820 and 1850, debates over tariff policy ran almost uninterrupted; the debates in 1824 alone filled over a thousand pages in *The Annals of Congress*.[14]

There were multiple answers to the question of free trade. The most widely accepted argument in favor of free trade was that it was mutually beneficial and fostered peace and prosperity for all nations. Lower barriers to international trade meant that nations could buy products from where they were produced more cheaply, and sell products where they could fetch higher prices. Trade was not a zero-sum game, but rather, under the right conditions, it could be a positive-sum game in which all parties stood to gain. So long as individuals and industries were left to make their own decisions about how to allocate resources and invest in production, there was no need for the national government to dictate the path of national growth. This argument for free trade seemed to have the support of the great lights of the classical tradition, beginning with Adam Smith and followed by Say and the classical English economists. "A trade which is forced by means of bounties and monopolies, may be, and commonly is disadvantageous to the country in whose favour it is meant to be established," Smith wrote in Book IV of *The Wealth of Nations*. "But that trade which, without force or constraint, is naturally and regularly carried on between any two places is always advantageous, though not equally so, to both."[15]

On the other side, free trade skeptics viewed global trade as a vehicle for hostility and treachery, not for peace and prosperity. The War of 1812 showed how American manufacturers were the victims of British predation and dumping. Animated by a strong sense of economic nationalism, advocates of protectionism believed that, though global free trade was an ideal, peace and prosperity could be attained only through strong state policies that protected national industries from foreign

14. Irwin, *Clashing over Commerce*, 4, 154–55. Irwin calls these three objectives the "three Rs" of trade policy: revenue, restriction, and reciprocity. Richard C. Edwards, "Economic Sophistication in Nineteenth Century Congressional Tariff Debates," *The Journal of Economic History* 30, no. 4 (1970), 805, 837.

15. *WN* IV.iii.c.2, 489.

competition—such as high import duties, import restrictions, or subsidies for domestic producers. In the American System, "the interference of Government to secure employment" was thus "absolutely necessary to render the nation industrious," as one congressman put it in 1824.[16] And while Smith, Say, and Ricardo might not have been available to supply these arguments, the German economist Friedrich List, along with American printer-turned-popular political economist Mathew Carey, and Senator Henry C. Clay became the most influential authorities of the "American System," which Clay himself described in a three-day speech in 1832. Contrary to the belief that tariffs would plunge the nation into debt and destroy foreign markets, Clay argued that over the seven-year period since the tariff of 1824, the tariff had lifted people out of debt, increased the value of land, stimulated urban growth, and boosted imports and exports. Thus, while Clay conceded that the American System did not have the backing of esteemed theorists, it did have the backing of lived experience. "The people of the United States have justly supposed that the policy of protecting *their* industry, against *foreign* legislation and *foreign* industry, was fully settled," he proclaimed, "not by a single act, but by repeated and deliberate acts of government, performed at distant and frequent intervals."[17]

There were gradations to the various arguments for free trade and protectionism. Few free traders believed in eliminating all barriers to trade, and most believed that import duties were a vital source of government revenue that had to be kept in place. In the 1830s and 1840s, the most influential British free trade movement—Cobdenism, so named for the radical parliamentarian and leader of the Anti-Corn Law League, Richard Cobden—began gaining momentum in the American northeast, particularly in financial and manufacturing strongholds such as New York and Boston. The American version of Cobdenism also carried with it a strong moral message: free trade ought to imply not only the

16. *Annals of Congress*, 18th Congress, 1st Session, House of Representatives, (April 2, 1824), 2073.

17. Henry Clay, "The American System," in *The Senate: 1789–1989. Classic Speeches: 1830–1993*, ed. Wendy Wolff, vol. 3 (Washington, D.C.: U.S. Government Printing Office, n.d.), 88. Emphasis in original.

free movement of goods but also of labor. Several prominent abolition-ists such as George Thompson, the Massachusetts Reverend Joshua Levitt, William Lloyd Garrison, and Ralph Waldo Emerson linked free trade with abolition. Whilst the abolitionists were a radical minority in the 1840s, they were nevertheless able to build a coalition—albeit a tenuous one—with Northern protectionists upon the Republican plat-form of antislavery.[18] However, the rise of both British and American free trade movements also galvanized the opposition. Proponents of the American System increasingly began to portray the idea of free trade as a vast British conspiracy to undercut American growth and indepen-dence. "Gentlemen deceive themselves," Clay argued in his famous American System speech in 1832. "It is not free trade that they are rec-ommending to our acceptance. It is, in effect, the British colonial system that we are invited to adopt; and, if their policy prevail [sic], it will lead substantially to the recolonization of these states, under the commercial dominion of Great Britain."[19] As free trade movements continued to gain momentum on both sides of the Atlantic, arguments against them increasingly adopted an Anglophobic tone.[20]

Despite the tariff being an issue of international policy, at least on the surface, almost every American would have seen it as a bitter domestic dispute as well—and one that skirted around the issue of slavery. Whatever tariff schedules were adopted, some states or regions would win while others would lose. The Cotton South relied heavily on their exchange with England and New England, where cotton textile produc-tion took place. For cotton plantation owners, then, high tariffs on im-ported goods not only increased their cost of living, but also threatened to shrink foreign markets for raw cotton exports should the importing

18. Eric Foner, *Free Soil, Free Labor, Free Men: The Ideology of the Republican Party before the Civil War* (Oxford: Oxford University Press, 1995); Douglas A. Irwin, *Against the Tide: An Intel-lectual History of Free Trade* (Princeton, NJ: Princeton University Press, 1996); Irwin, *Clashing over Commerce*; Palen, *The "Conspiracy" of Free Trade*. On the varieties of the free-trade/free-labor ideas in Britain, see Richard Huzzey, "Free Trade, Free Labour, and Slave Sugar in Victo-rian Britain," *The Historical Journal* 53, no. 2 (2010), 359–79.

19. Clay, "The American System," 91.

20. Palen, *The "Conspiracy" of Free Trade*.

nations retaliate. On the other side, for cotton textile and woolen manufacturers in the North, a higher tax on imported British products
boosted the competitiveness of domestic production. The idea of free
trade in America during the antebellum decades was thus riddled with
contradictions. For the Cotton South, free trade was essential for the
profitability of the unfree labor in the region; tariffs were seen as a tax
on slavery itself. For cotton and woolen manufacturers in the North,
protectionism provided an opportunity to break into an emerging
"home market," but it was a market whose primary customers were
those seeking to outfit enslaved bodies in the cheapest way possible.
Thus, at stake in the tariff debates was more than the specific amount or
goods subject to taxation. The very morality and political viability of
expanding a system of political economy that depended on slavery lay
at the heart of the tariff debates.[21] These disagreements came to a head
in 1828 with the passage of a tariff that raised import duties on raw materials, especially wool, from thirty to fifty percent, a level that exporters

21. There was a good deal of nuance and heterogeneity of economic interests across regions.
For example, New England states went from being pro-free trade (due to the large commercial
shipping sector) to being very pro-tariff within the first third of the nineteenth century as
manufacturing (particularly in textiles) grew. States in the Mid-Atlantic, dominated by iron
and glass manufacturing interests, were ardently pro-tariff. States in the Midwest, meanwhile,
were "swing states" because they produced many types of raw materials (such as hemp, wool,
and grains) but were largely isolated from foreign markets in the first half of the nineteenth
century. For more on sectional interests and tariff policy in the antebellum period, see Schoen,
The Fragile Fabric of Union: Cotton, Federal Politics, and the Global Origins of the Civil War (Baltimore, MD: The Johns Hopkins University Press, 2009), chap. 3; O'Brien, *Conjectures of Order*,
chap. 17. Seth Rockman demonstrates how tariff debates from the 1820s onward implicated the
market for so-called negro cloth, i.e., cloth that was used to make clothing for slaves, in his
"Negro Cloth: Mastering the Market for Slave Clothing in Antebellum America" in Sven Beckert and Christine Desan, eds., *American Capitalism: New Histories*, Columbia Studies in the
History of U.S. Capitalism (New York, NY: Columbia University Press, 2018), 170–194. For
further analysis of the tariff debates in relation to slavery, see Brian D. Schoen, *The Fragile Fabric
of Union*, especially chap. 3; Daniel Peart, "Looking Beyond Parties and Elections: The Making
of United States Tariff Policy during the Early 1820s," *Journal of the Early Republic* 33, no. 1 (2013),
87–108; and Andrew Shankman, "Capitalism, Slavery, and the New Epoch: Mathew Carey's
1819" in *Slavery's Capitalism: A New History of American Economic Development*, eds. Sven Beckert and Seth Rockman, Reprint edition (Philadelphia, PA: University of Pennsylvania Press,
2018), 243–261.

in the South believed was prohibitory. Senator John C. Calhoun decried this "bill of abominations" as evidence of "power . . . abused by being converted into an instrument of rearing up the industry of one section of the country on the ruins of another."[22] Calhoun's essay, entitled, "South Carolina Exposition and Protest," expressed what many Southern free traders believed: that the tariff was no longer being used as an instrument for raising revenue, but rather as a tool for rewarding the North at the expense of the South. For a national policy to be so one-sided demanded the revision—indeed, the nullification—of federal law. Even years after the nullification crisis had been narrowly averted, the existential consequences of the tariff question distressed legislators. "I confess," declared Massachusetts representative Rufus Choate,

> that I have more than once during the discussion been led to fear the diversity of employment growing up in opposite extremes of this country . . . the eternal and inherent hostility which exists between free trade doctrine and measures and protective doctrine and measures; and that still deeper, still more unappeasable hostility . . . between free labor and the employers of slave labor—I say, sir, I have thought it possible . . . that these causes may sever this Union.[23]

The Congress floor became the stage where regional and party interests confronted the textbook theories of political economy. Framing the tariff question as a battle of principles and ideas enabled legislators to argue in terms scientific soundness and validity, or to appeal to vague notions of the "national economy." In 1820, Massachusetts Congressman Harrison Gray Otis characterized the tariff question as an intellectual problem that posed a difficult choice between the "pre-eminence of the agricultural and exclusive system" on the one hand, and the system of "the disciples of the celebrated Adam Smith" on the other. Deciding between free trade, protectionism, or some compromise was a matter of "the most important and complicated principles of the most difficult

22. John C. Calhoun, "Rough Draft of What is Called the South Carolina Exposition," in his *Union and Liberty: The Political Philosophy of John C. Calhoun*, ed. Ross M. Lence (Indianapolis, IN: Liberty Fund, 1992), 311–365 at 314.

23. *Register of Debates in Congress.* House of Representatives (June 13, 1832), 3525.

science—political economy—principles which had divided the opinions of the greatest men, and agitated the counsels of the wisest nations," Otis argued. And while the "judgments of the highest tribunals of the literature, and of the most enlightened statesmen" seemed to rule in favor of the celebrated Smith, Say, and Ricardo—that is, in favor of free trade—men were so apt to "refer all calamity to whatever appears to be the approximate cause" and to see tariff legislation as the direct cause of either the decline or the increase of manufacturing in the nation. Otis thus pleaded for caution; he urged fellow congressmen against ascribing unassailable authority to the principles of political economists. If there was one lesson from the ideas of political economists, Otis intimated, it was that "it was always dangerous to legislate under the influence of sudden impulses and strong excitements."[24] Other congressmen, like Pennsylvania Representative Charles J. Ingersoll, later the Vice President of the Pennsylvania Society for the Promotion of Manufactures, saw the choice between systems of political economy as a source of political stalemate. After his "laborious consultations of all the theories [I] could find," Ingersoll found himself at a loss. "I am constrained to acknowledge that these doctors disagree so much among themselves as to defy the adoption of any one system from all their commentaries," he lamented. For Ingersoll, the systems of political economy presented by figures like Smith were neither generalizable nor politically neutral. "Each one has his own favorite fund of finance, and each one combats all the rest with ability," he argued.[25] In other words, the diverging politics of those political economists ("Stewart, my Lord Lauderdale, Say, [Charles] Ganilh") made it impossible for legislators to decide on the proper course of action.

The antebellum tariff debates reveal the contested status of Adam Smith and political economic ideas more generally. While there was little doubt about Smith's importance for the science of political economy, appealing to or attempting to undercut his theories served opposing political purposes. For those who championed free trade, especially in

---

24. *Annals of Congress*, Senate, May 4, 1820, 668–669.
25. *Annals of Congress*, 13th Congress, House of Representatives, 1st session (June 29, 1813), 358.

the Cotton South, treating *The Wealth of Nations* as a compendium of scientific and objective laws legitimized a vision of a national political economy in which free trade was essential to national prosperity.[26] "I will lay down a general principle, *upon the authority of Adam Smith*," declared South Carolinian Representative George McDuffie, one of the most vocal proponents of Southern free trade,

> who, notwithstanding the terms of sweeping condemnation which have been applied to his speculations, has done more to enlighten the world of political economy than any man of modern times. He [Adam Smith] is the founder of the science. All that has been since done is but a development or modification of the principles he established.[27]

Southern free traders like McDuffie saw themselves as true disciples of modern science and professed to bring peace and prosperity at home and abroad. Smith's "great elementary principle," McDuffie expounded, was to leave labor and capital alone, to allow them to "receive direction from individual sagacity," such that they would "naturally seek, and speedily find, the most profitable employments." This theory was founded on the soundest, "most steady and immutable and powerful principles of human action:" that individuals were more capable of judging "what will promote their pecuniary interests, than the most enlightened Government can possibly be."[28] No legislation, no protective government measures would be needed to dictate the free flow of goods; indeed, McDuffie hinted, it might even be morally salubrious if the manufactured goods for which Americans seemed to have "perhaps too keen an appetite" were not actively encouraged by the government.[29] This was the simple and obvious truth of free trade: let labor and capital flow freely to the channels in which they would be most productive, without the control of government.

---

26. Schoen, *The Fragile Fabric of Union*, chap. 3; O'Brien, *Conjectures of Order*, chap. 17.

27. *Annals of Congress*, 18th Congress, 1st session, House of Representatives (April 16, 1824), 2403, emphasis added.

28. *Annals of Congress*, 18th Congress, 1st session, House of Representatives (April 16, 1824), 2403.

29. *Annals of Congress*, 18th Congress, 1st session, House of Representatives (April 16, 1824), 2404.

Legislators like McDuffie were all too aware that their arguments for free trade would be heard as nothing but sectional grievance. "It would be some consolation to me, sir," McDuffie concluded his lengthy speech in 1824, "if I could believe that the heavy impositions, which must operate so oppressively upon the part of the Union I have the honor to represent, would produce an equivalent benefit to other portions of the Union."[30] The representatives who found themselves on McDuffie's side had to bear the burden of proving both that free trade would benefit the nation as a whole, and disproving the logic of protectionism. "There never prevailed in an enlightened body so perfect a delusion," McDuffie claimed, than the doctrine of protectionism. Disguised as an effort to protect domestic industry, protectionism involved "the almost entire annihilation of foreign commerce" while also unintentionally diminishing domestic production, he argued. The irony was that while McDuffie discredited the American System as a viable way to promote the "patriotic spirit of a free people," his advocacy of the system of Adam Smith implicitly entailed the expansion of slavery.[31]

Rather than pressing on the contradictions of free trade as an ideology of the Cotton South, those in favor of protectionism directed their efforts at challenging the intellectual authority on which that ideology rested. One tactic was to confront theory with practice, as New Jersey Representative George Holcombe did in a speech in 1823. Great Britain had not become wealthy on account of the ideas of Adam Smith, he contended; rather, it was "the policy of protecting—or effectually protecting the industry of her citizens from all foreign competition" that enabled Great Britain to become wealthy and powerful. As a counterexample, in Spain, where "the doctrines of the author of *The Wealth of Nations*" operated in "full and free operation," Holcombe argued, one saw not prosperity, but rather a nation that had "sunk from the elevation of her imperial grandeur, below the level of the secondary Powers of Europe, and at length into utter bankruptcy."[32] Other protectionists

30. *Annals of Congress*, 18th Congress, 1st session, House of Representatives (April 16, 1824), 2426.

31. *Annals of Congress*, 18th Congress, 1st session, House of Representatives (April 16, 1824), 2418.

32. *Annals of Congress*, 17th Congress, 2nd session, House of Representatives, (January 30, 1823), 742.

continued to insist that free trade was nothing but a European conceit foisted upon America. "While the European nations are exporting for our use the theories of political economy recommended in the books of their writers," spoke George Cassedy of New Jersey, "the wise, the sagacious, the experienced statesmen of those very nations, are practicing upon different principles at home—the principles involved in this bill."[33] Petitioners from Oneida, New York, argued that Great Britain preached the principle of Adam Smith, but "at all times, and under every vicissitude, turned a deaf ear to the lesson, as though it were intended for other nations."[34]

All this speechifying and politicking about trade policy tested the resilience of Adam Smith's authority and compelled legislators to question the contemporary relevance of his ideas. Another rhetorical tactic of anti-free-trade politicians was to emphasize the historical constraints of Smith's wishful thinking. "I speak not lightly of the works of Adam Smith, Jean Baptiste Say, and others of the same school. They are certainly profound thinkers; and their books contain much valuable information," Lewis Williams of North Carolina professed in 1824. But Williams and others were unconvinced that the ideas of Smith, transported from another country and from another time, could be useful for Americans under the present circumstances. The works of Smith and Say left "off at the very point where commercial practice begins," Williams argued. Smith and Say fantasized about policies and nations "as they wish them to be, not as they are," and "in a word . . . [presumed] a state of things which does not exist, and which never can be brought about, but by a convention of nations."[35] Adam Smith's chief error, then, was that his ideas were superseded by history. "The doctrines of Adam Smith had a charm to the Continental Nations of Europe," argued Senator Asher Robbins from Rhode Island, and national experience "refuted his reasoning," for prosperity was built upon a practice exactly

33. *Annals of Congress*, 18th Congress, 1st session, House of Representatives (April 3, 1824), 2143.

34. The memo was read aloud in the Senate on January 7, 1818, but was originally presented to Congress in December of 1817. *Annals of Congress*, 15th Congress, 1st session, Senate, (January 7, 1818), 87.

35. *Annals of Congress*, 18th Congress, 1st session, House of Representatives (April 3, 1824), 2130.

the opposite of free trade.[36] Free-trade skeptics lampooned the ideas of political economists as "visionary," delusional, and ideological. Above all, they were ideas that history had proven wrong.

While the ideas of Smith and other writers were "frequently and ably exploded" on the Congress floor, as one congressman put it, free traders continued rushing to their defense.[37] "I have heard . . . the names of Say, [Charles] Ganilh, Adam Smith, and Ricardo, pronounced not only in terms, but in a tone, of sneering contempt, as visionary theorists, destitute of practical wisdom, and the whole clan of Scotch and Quarterly reviewers lugged in to boot," Representative John Randolph of Virginia lamented in 1824. But Randolph was adamant that these writers had timeless truths to offer. "I leave Adam Smith to the simplicity, and majesty, and strength of his own native genius which has canonized his name," Randolph continued, "a name which will be pronounced with veneration, when not one name in this House will be remembered."[38] Congressmen summoned Smith's spirit not only to reiterate the principles of free trade, but also to condemn the current state of affairs. "If Adam Smith (an authority, by the way, much contemned [sic] by a certain school of political economists in this enlightened age and country) could have risen from his grave," Representative James Hamilton Jr. of South Carolina imagined,

> this worthy philosopher would indeed have believed that the world, ever since his exit from it, had been in a slumber as profound as that which had visited his own tomb. He would have thought, with good reason, that all those anticipations of progress of truth, and the consequent extirpation of error, which he had cherished in a generous love of his species, had indeed been the idle dreams of a foolish and vain philosophy—for he would have met here the very dogmas of that school of restriction and monopoly which it had been the chief business of his valuable life to refute and overthrow.[39]

36. *Register of Debates*, 20th Congress, 1st session, Senate, (April 7, 1828), 600.

37. *Register of Debates*, 20th Congress, 1st session, House of Representatives, (April 2, 1828), 2122.

38. *Annals of Congress*, 18th Congress, 1st session, House of Representatives (April 15, 1824), 2372–2373.

39. *Annals of Congress*, 18th Congress, 1st session, House of Representatives (April 6, 1824), 2178.

Much to Hamilton's chagrin, the ghost of Adam Smith did not appear to be something that most congressman feared. They had become so accustomed to hearing appeals to Smith that some even mocked the blind devotion to the patron saint of free trade. Representative John Tod of Pennsylvania derided free traders as uncharitable and dogmatic proselytizers who accused others of not understanding "the new light of political economy" and not reading their Adam Smith. "Every man for himself, is the only thing for the country. Here it is in the book. In this way we enrich ourselves . . . and we make the nation rich, as the book shows," Tod ventriloquized. Of course, Tod's own view was that the dictates of Adam Smith would bring "nothing but prosperity to foreign nations . . . nothing but destruction and death to three-fourths of the agricultural, grain-raising, and manufacturing interest of our own country."[40] Adam Smith, in other words, would be a curse upon America.

In the 1840s, frenzied debate continued to challenge the authority and principles of Adam Smith. McDuffie, now one of South Carolina's senators, represented the most dogged contingency of Southern Democrats who believed that the eternal and objective science of political economy unquestionably legitimized the doctrine of free trade. McDuffie preached for two and a half hours at one point, waxing philosophical about the inductive process of reasoning exemplified by Adam Smith, and defending his use of "theory" from those who would stigmatize it. The principles of Adam Smith ("a very celebrated Scotch philosopher") had undergone "the most rigid examination of philosophers and statesman, and they remained unchanged and unchangeable," McDuffie avowed. However, those who were attempting "to sneer it [the doctrine of free trade] down" and promote the interests of manufactures were, in McDuffie's opinion, "manufacturing facts to suit their purpose."[41] Such rhetoric toed the line between an impassioned plea for dispassionate analysis and a dangerous accusation of a fellow congressman's dishonesty

40. *Annals of Congress*, 18th Congress, 1st session, House of Representatives, (April 7, 1824), 2222.

41. *Congressional Globe*, 28th Congress, 1st Session, Senate, (January 29, 1844), 205.

and personal integrity.[42] But McDuffie found himself vulnerable to the same accusations of ignoring facts. When Senator George Evans of Maine responded to McDuffie's speech in the same session of debate, the former questioned "whether the senator [McDuffie] has maintained or attempted to maintain a single one of his charges by reference to authentic, existing facts, by proofs, by experience." From Evans' perspective, McDuffie's arguments for free trade amounted to nothing but "positive assertions, resting upon theories, and dogmas of political economists" that were no better than the creeds of ancient philosophers draped in the seductive rhetoric of "elementary principles."[43] By exposing free trade as a theory grounded in sophistry and dogma instead of in science and truth, advocates of the American System attempted to dislodge it as a cornerstone in the American political economy.

Though politicians often debated ideas with a "tone of honest inquiry directed at discovering economic knowledge," the politics of political economy proved to be a rancorous battleground. Every issue seemed to teeter on the edge of violence, and congressmen came prepared to defend their positions not only with textbooks, but also with their fists, canes, bowie knives, and pistols.[44] Free traders and protectionists in the North and West reached a tenuous party coalition under the Republican flag of antislavery, but "free trade" appeared incongruous next to the rallying cry of "free men, free soil, and free labor." And though slavery was the presumed ideological fault line, explicit discussion over growing

42. As Joanne Freeman has documented, accusing someone of being a liar in public was effectively an explicit challenge to a duel. See Joanne Freeman, *The Field of Blood: Violence in Congress and the Road to Civil War* (New York, NY: Farrar, Straus and Giroux, 2018).

43. *Appendix to the Congressional Globe*, 28th Congress, 1st Session, Senate, (February 1844), 708.

44. Edwards, "Economic Sophistication in Nineteenth Century Congressional Tariff Debates," 836–37. Paul Conkin also argues that especially between 1820 and 1850, congressmen demonstrated remarkable expertise on even the most subtle of economic issues. "On the whole, congressmen were sophisticated consumers of even technical economic theory. In specialized areas of responsibility, such as land policy or banking, or on such pervasive issues as the tariff, they read widely and accumulated all the economic data they could find. If anything, the wealth of pro-and anti-tariff arguments offered by congressmen excelled in subtlety those offered by economists." Conkin, *Prophets of Prosperity*, 313. On physical violence in Congress during the antebellum period, see Freeman, *The Field of Blood*.

anti-slavery sentiment was off the table. In fact, between 1836 and 1844, representatives from slave-holding states attempted to pass a set of gag rules in order to silence any discussion of anti-slavery petitions on the Congress floor.[45] The passage of the Morrill Tariff in March of 1861 significantly raised import duties on goods such as pig iron and wool, thus causing rifts within the Republican party and further alienating the South. Moreover, the timing of secession in December of 1860, the passage of the tariff in early 1861, and the late adoption of the Republican party's anti-slavery platform confounded potential allies of the North's cause.[46]

The uneasy alliance between free traders and abolitionists in the North added another layer of complexity to Adam Smith's nineteenth-century reputation. Smith's reputation as the founder of political economy still preceded him, as the radical abolitionist Charles Sumner's famous "Barbarism of Slavery" speech in 1860 demonstrates. Having returned to Congress from a four-year hiatus (which he spent recovering from being brutally caned by Preston Brooks in 1856), Sumner delivered an unrelenting, blistering criticism of slavery. Slavery, Sumner argued, was fundamentally incompatible with civilization. Not only did it rest on barbaric principles—not least among them that man could own property in another man—it reduced both the slave and slave-master to barbaric practices. Sumner issued a damning indictment of the character of slave-holders, and he summoned the arguments of both political and intellectual authorities to state his case. The "*American Authority*" of Colonel Mason, a Virginia slave-master, and Thomas Jefferson spoke to the tyrannical spirit and abhorrent manners that slavery bred in American men. To the "fiery soul of Jefferson" and Mason, Sumner then added the commanding words of "*Philosophic Authority*:" John Locke, Adam Smith, and Dr. Samuel Johnson. Here, Sumner turned not to Smith's *The Wealth of Nations*, but rather to *The Theory of Moral Sentiments* for philosophical ammunition.

45. Freeman, *The Field of Blood*, chap. 4.

46. Marc Palen writes that the late adoption of an anti-slavery platform "played an integral role in confounding British opinion about the causes of southern secession, and in enhancing the possibility of British recognition of the Confederacy." Palen, *The "Conspiracy" of Free Trade*, 34.

APOSTLE OF FREE TRADE   131

Adam Smith, the founder of the science of Political Economy, who, in his work on Morals, thus utters himself: "There is not a negro from the coast of Africa who does not possess a degree of magnanimity which the soul of his sordid master is too often scarce capable of conceiving. Fortune never exerted more cruelly her empire over mankind, than when she subjected these nations of heroes to the refuse of gaols of Europe, to wretches who possess the virtues neither of the countries which they come from, nor of those which they go to, and whose levity, brutality, and baseness, so justly expose them to the contempt of the vanquished."[47]

What did it mean to have "the founder of the science of Political Economy" sanction the argument that the character of slave-masters revealed the "essential Barbarism" of slavery? For Sumner, it clearly signaled that there was a quality of unassailable truth in Smith's ideas. "With such authorities, American and Philosophic," Sumner declared, "I need not hesitate in this ungracious task; but Truth; which is mightier than Mason and Jefferson, than John Locke, Adam Smith, and Samuel Johnson, marshals the evidence in unbroken succession."[48] Wielding Smith's authority in this way would have been among the least offensive aspects of his speech. With full force, Sumner chastised slave-owners as backwards, violent, degraded people unconscious of their own barbarism. Unmoved by Sumner's words, Senator James Chesnut attempted to chasten the abolitionist's cause as cowardly, un-American, and unmanly. "After ranging over Europe, crawling through the backdoors to whine at the feet of British aristocracy, and reaping a rich harvest of contempt, the slanderer of States and men reappears in the Senate," Chesnut retorted, alluding to Sumner's return from absence. He had hoped that Sumner might have learned from his lesson in 1856, but it appeared he had not. "It has been left for this day, for this country, for the Abolitionists of Massachusetts, to deify the incarnation of malice, mendacity, and cowardice," Chesnut stated. Congressmen from both

47. *The Congressional Globe*, 36th Congress, 1st session, June 4, 1860, 2595. The passage from *The Theory of Moral Sentiments* that Sumner quoted is from *TMS* V.2.9, 206–7.
48. *The Congressional Globe*, 36th Congress, 1st session, June 4, 1860, 2595.

sides personified one of Sumner's opening lines: "this was no time for soft words or excuses." On the eve of the Civil War, Adam Smith and political economic debates on tariffs receded into the background as Americans confronted the slavery question "directly, openly, and thoroughly."[49]

The uses of Smith in the antebellum tariff debates are thus politically significant in a number of ways. First, how politicians chose to engage with Smith was conditioned on their prior commitment to free trade or to the American System. Second, the invocations and appeals to Smith on the Congress floor revealed the grounds of a particular vision for the American political economy. For free trade southerners, it was the scientific, timeless, and universal truth of Smith's theories that legitimated their vision of a national economy characterized by the free movement of goods across and within national boundaries and a harmony of interests among northern manufacturing, western agriculture, and southern cotton. These southerners were promoting "a vision of America as a dynamic agrarian nation capable of exploiting the conditions of global peace and seeking to lead the world toward the ultimate triumph of free trade."[50] But, in doing so, they were also promoting a vision whereby the gains of free trade were reaped on the backs of unfree labor. By contrast, northern protectionists expressed skepticism at the idea of basing national policy on the theories of an old thinker, revered though he was. If regional interests were to be harmonized, it would be accomplished by protective tariffs; protecting infant industries would "stimulate and liberate U.S. agriculture."[51] Ideas in the abstract were an insufficient guide for policymaking, especially when it came to facing foreign rivals in the competitive arena of global trade. Excluding the abolitionists, many northern advocates of the American System were willing to accept the persistence of slavery in the south if it meant that protective tariffs would generate a sustained, self-sufficient home market for their manufactured goods. The northerners' rejection of Smith—or at least

49. *The Congressional Globe*, 36th Congress, 1st session, June 4, 1860, 2603, 2590.
50. Schoen, *The Fragile Fabric of Union*, 55.
51. Schoen, *The Fragile Fabric of Union*, 108.

the free traders' use of Smith—represented a rejection of a particular way of imagining the integration of the American economy and the bases on which that image rested. Ultimately, Smith's importance in the antebellum tariff debates had very little to do with substantive interest in what he had to say about trade, and more to do with what his thought had come to represent: an ideological and seemingly irresolvable conflict over the politics of free trade.

———

After the Civil War, controversy over tariffs persisted, and it strained the delicate alliance between the free-trade and the protectionist wings of the Republican party. In the academy, the fracturing of political economy into the disciplines of political science and economics relegated Smith to the far-flung corners of intellectual debate. In politics, elected officials were less concerned with the validity of extant academic economic theories, and more concerned with the coalition-building power of an idea. As they debated the impact of free trade on their particular constituencies, politicians either rallied behind the gospel of Adam Smith, or dismissed the whole field of political economy as irrelevant and disconnected from politics. Postbellum politics would effectively institutionalize an era of protectionism, but in the public and political imagination, Smith's reputation as the apostle of free trade would become more resilient than ever.

Certain contours of postbellum America rendered the search for new ideas and their application an obsolete strategy in politics. The dominance of the Republican Party was virtually unchallenged from 1860 until 1874 when the Democrats finally gained control of the House of Representatives, something they had not achieved since 1859. From 1874 on, the parties locked talons and were constantly vying for power on roughly equal terms. The economic landscape of the entire country was also endlessly shape shifting. A major economic downturn in 1873, the influx of immigrants from new countries, the intermittent flares of labor strikes in the 1870s and 1880s, and the social and economic dislocations of the new industrial capitalism made it particularly challenging to build political platforms that cut across such a fractured electorate. At the same time, economic interest groups grew in size and power. Major producer interest groups began forming national organizations—such as the National Association of Wool Growers, the National Association of Wool Manufacturers, the American Iron and Steel Associates— which began exerting their influence not only by lobbying politicians in Washington, but also by distributing pamphlets and backing political candidates through campaign financing.[52] Against this backdrop of partisan competition, intense lobbying, and economic strife, the tariff was one of the few politically tractable issues that could be used "as a device to appeal to social harmony and to break the national political equipoise."[53] As a result, existing theories and ideas about tariffs and trade policy became vital coalitional glue for the major national parties by serving as focal points for their respective agendas.[54] Few issues differentiated the two parties as sharply and consistently as the tariff from the 1870s on. Trade policy became the framing device for partisan positions on the most fundamental questions of political economy: what constituted national wealth, who were the winners and losers in the American economy, whether increasing trade would make the US more or less dependent on foreign rivals, and whether the government had a duty to correct the displacements in labor and capital resulting from international trade.[55]

52. Irwin, *Clashing over Commerce*, 238–39.

53. Tom E. Terrill, *The Tariff, Politics, and American Foreign Policy, 1874–1901* (Westport, CT: Praeger, 1973), 9.

54. This claim is an adaptation of Goldstein and Keohane's framework of "ideas as coalition glue." If one views politics as a repeated game with multiple equilibria outcomes, then ideas can be critical elements of a player's strategy by alleviating "coordination problems arising from the absence of unique equilibrium solutions." According to Goldstein and Keohane, ideas as coalitional glue "serve as focal points for strategies and expectations when it is unclear what the objective criterion are for evaluating an outcome." Goldstein and Keohane, *Ideas and Foreign Policy*, 18.

55. Douglas Irwin points out that the motivation of the 1870 Republican Congress to consider changes to the tariff was primarily political rather than economic, owing to the fact that failing to address the tariff would cede political advantage to Democrats, who would insist on an even greater and undesirable tariff reform. See Irwin, *Clashing over Commerce*, 229.

Year after year, the parties volleyed the same sets of arguments for and against the tariff.[56] Republicans professed that the "imposition of duties on foreign imports shall be made not "for revenue only, but . . . such duties shall be so levied as to afford security to our diversified industries and protection to the rights and wages of the laborer," while the Democrats denounced the tariff as a "masterpiece of injustice, inequality and false pretense, which yields a dwindling and not a yearly rising revenue, [that] has impoverished many industries to subsidize a few."[57] Republicans swore that tariffs guaranteed protection of domestic industries and high wages for workers; Democrats believed that tariffs would merely increase the price of consumer goods. Republicans believed that protectionism was patriotism and doubled down on the Anglophobic argument that free trade was a vast British conspiracy to bring America down to her knees, while Democrats imbibed British Cobdenism enthusiastically, advocating free trade as a means to global peace and prosperity. After the election of 1884, the party lines were solidly drawn. Any remaining free traders who had once been Republicans now backed the Democratic candidate, Grover Cleveland, on the policy of "a tariff for revenue only," and the Republican party became the party of protectionism.[58]

With little room for policy innovation in this post-Civil War system, the ideas of political economists were useful not as roadmaps in untrodden policy territory, but as unifying partisan banners. The boom in mass media meant that news outlets eagerly propagated free trade and protectionist ideas. For every free-trade newspaper like *The New York Evening Post*, there was a protectionist counterpart like *The New York Tribune*. The English Cobden Club (founded in 1866), which had many prominent American members, was met by the Anti-Cobden Club (founded in the 1880s); the American Free Trade League (started in 1865 as a tariff reform organization) faced opposition from the Association for the

56. Irwin, *Clashing over Commerce*, 246; Palen, *The "Conspiracy" of Free Trade*.

57. Republican Party Platform of 1884 and Democratic Party Platform of 1876 in Donald Bruce Johnson and Kirk H. Porter, eds., *National Party Platforms, 1840–1968*, 4th ed. (Urbana, IL: University of Illinois Press, 1970), 72–73, 50.

58. Palen, *The "Conspiracy" of Free Trade*, 110–14; Irwin, *Clashing over Commerce*, 256–58.

Protection of American Industries (1883). In 1881, the founding of the Wharton School at the University of Pennsylvania represented an overt attempt to build an academic bastion of protectionist ideas in response to the prevailing free-trade tendencies of most academic institutions.[59]

Though free traders had academic and intellectual respectability on their side, they faced serious "rhetorical disadvantages" in trying to dismantle the arguments and appeal of protectionism.[60] "Protectionism as patriotism" had an appealing and deceptively simple logic: high tariffs protected domestic industry, which increased demand for labor, which in turn kept wages high. But rather than trying to undercut the economic logic of protectionism, hardline free traders focused on an alternative— albeit bland—approach that espoused tariff revision or a tariff for revenue only.[61] However, amidst the gradual institutionalization of protectionism, free traders returned to a trusted source for political and rhetorical fortification: Adam Smith.

To say that the American nation had "not been guided by Adam Smith's teaching," or that it had forgotten the gospel of Smith's *The Wealth of Nations* was a euphemism for the failures of protectionism.[62] Years of high tariffs in the name of protecting American industries and American workers had brought nothing but "years of languishing enterprise, years of despairing industry, years of strikes, years of contention between employers and the employed," argued William Cullen Bryan in his rousing speech at the Adam Smith centennial. "We have tried the protective system . . . we have tasted its fruits, and they are

59. Palen, *The "Conspiracy" of Free Trade*, 72–73, 106–9; Goldstein, *Ideas, Interests, and American Trade Policy*, 85–90; Coats, "The Educational Revolution and the Professionalization of American Economics," 352, 362.

60. Irwin, *Clashing over Commerce*, 244.

61. Irwin, *Clashing over Commerce*, 245. While I use the label "free trade" and "free trader" here, it should be noted that by the second half of the nineteenth century (and even in the early nineteenth century), "free trade" did *not* signify completely open borders and *no* tariff. Especially in the late nineteenth century, people who identified as "free traders" were really championing minimal tariffs for revenue only. For more on this distinction, see Palen, *The "Conspiracy" of Free Trade*, xxii–xxiv.

62. "The Adam Smith Centenary."

bitter. Let us now have a season of free exchange."[63] Redoubling their efforts to legitimize and institutionalize free trade, clubs, newspapers, and politicians breathed new life into Smith's life and legacy. In response to the shaky logic of protectionism, free traders projected the authority of their eighteenth-century hero: "one of the most unbusinesslike of mankind . . . an awkward Scotch professor, apparently choked with books and absorbed in abstractions."[64] Elaborate descriptions of Adam Smith's world-changing achievement proliferated. Smith founded a science that "demonstrates morals . . . diligence, economy, prudence, truth, and justice . . . [and] also the means of a sound and stable public prosperity."[65] He was a prophet who, with "prescient wisdom . . . brought within the focus of human vision the possibilities of future centuries, and recalled from amid decaying debris the lost records of the ages long ago."[66] This was a political message that relied not on spelling out the economic logic of free trade, but on reinforcing the timelessness of Smith's ideas and asserting discipleship.

Republicans and their protectionist allies harnessed Adam Smith's authority to their own political advantage, too. "Gentlemen, 'the markets of the world' will not come to us," Republican Congressman James O'Donnell of Michigan proclaimed in 1888. "We must rely upon the best market in the world, the home market, the market created by the people of our land—I repeat, the best market of the world," he continued. This was more than a rallying cry of economic nationalism; from O'Donnell's perspective, it was also an opportunity to delegitimize the ideas that free traders so heavily relied on. "Remember that the true saying of the great apostle of free trade, Adam Smith, who in his Wealth of Nations, makes this admission, which you all overlook," O'Donnell declared, quoting the following passage from Smith's magnum opus:

> Whatever tends to diminish in any country the number of artificers and manufacturers tends to diminish the home market, the most

63. "Adam Smith. Centennial Celebration."
64. "Adam Smith," *Patriot*, August 9, 1876.
65. "Adam Smith. Centennial Celebration."
66. "An Economic Centennial."

important of all markets, for the rude produce of the land, and thereby still further to discourage agriculture.[67]

O'Donnell's underscored the two-pronged protectionist argument that domestic markets ought to be prioritized over international markets, and that the interests of manufacturing and agriculture were aligned. Protectionism would increase the market for manufactured goods at home, increase the wages of workers, and, therefore, increase demand for agricultural products—or so the argument went. The irony, of course, is that the excerpt in which Smith appears to have conceded some legitimacy to economic nationalism foregrounded his attack on *all* systems that give preference to one branch of industry over another. For Smith, the interconnectedness of internal trade was so important to grasp precisely because it illustrated the follies of restrictive policies that promoted one sector of production through the use of "extraordinary encouragements" or "extraordinary restraints." Smith wrote,

> It is thus that every system which endeavours either, by extraordinary encouragements, to draw towards a particular species of industry a greater share of the capital of the society than what would naturally go to it; or by extraordinary restraints, to force from a particular species of industry some share of capital which would otherwise be employed in it; is in reality subversive of the great purpose which it means to promote. It retards, instead of accelerating, the progress of the society towards real wealth and greatness; and diminishes, instead of increasing, the real value of the annual produce of its land and labour.[68]

In other words, Smith argued that the means of protecting and promoting the home market was inimical to its own ends. Tariffs and other protective measures like subsidies for infant industries diverted capital

---

67. "The Tariff: The Progress of the Nation and its People. Speech of James O'Donnell of MI." *Jackson Citizen*. Jackson, MI. July 24, 1888; *WN* IV.ix.48, 686.

68. *WN* IV.ix.51, 687.

and labor away from more productive uses; even if there was a short-term boost in the productivity of both domestic manufactures and agriculture, it would still be less than if the state had not dictated the allocation of labor and capital into specific channels of the economy. However, protectionists invoking this line from *The Wealth of Nations* appeared unconcerned with either the broader context of the passage or the fact that they were overtly contradicting Smith's own argument. The argumentative strategy that Republicans deployed here relied on an "even-Smith-said-so" logic. That is, it relied on the familiar image of Smith as the "apostle of free trade" in order to expose what could be read as a major inconsistency, thereby delegitimizing the notion of free trade as a valid and practicable political ideology. This rhetorical maneuver underpinned an objection to the soundness and relevance of economic science more generally, too. "Free trade as an economic science, in the judgment of the world, is a dismal failure," Senator Justin Morrill declared in 1893. The fact that "even the highest authority on free trade declared" that diminishing manufactures would diminish domestic markets should have given free traders reason to pause.[69] "Adam Smith, despite his horror and intolerance of all protective measures," Senator Stephen Elkins argued, "made an exception in favor of the navigation act, which he regarded as a wise and patriotic law. It was in his eyes not only an act regulating commerce, but a measure of public safety."[70] That even Smith made a case for protectionism under certain circumstances eroded his intellectual authority as the icon of free traders and undermined the view that free trade was a scientifically sound and consistent policy that could be applied regardless of political and economic conditions. Thus, leveraging the apparent ambiguity, inconsistency, and even contradictions in Smith's views on free trade allowed Republicans to frame protectionism as a more politically realistic alternative.

While Republicans may have relished unveiling these Smithian foibles—even if much of their strategy relied on but a few lines stripped

---

69. *Congressional Record*, 53rd Congress, 2nd Session, Senate, (December 13, 1893), 203.

70. *Congressional Record*, 55th Congress, 1st Session, Senate, (April 5, 1897), 584.

of their broader context—Democrats were not thrown off guard. In 1886 Poindexter Dunn stated,

> Now I have seen it stated in protectionist publications that Adam Smith—and our protectionist friends never roll any morsel under their tongues with such unction as any little morsel they may get from Adam Smith— . . . that Adam Smith said that the old restrictive navigation laws of England were beneficial to her commerce and resulted in great good to England. Now let us see what Adam Smith did say.[71]

The Republican strategy could backfire, though. It was obvious that protectionists were unsuccessfully trying to undercut the bases of free trade by turning Smith into their own weapon. Once again, Democrats and Republicans found themselves face to face, fighting over Adam Smith's words, intentions, and who could claim to be a true disciple of the apostle's creed.

For Republicans, stripping Adam Smith of his iconic status was the first step towards delegitimizing the theories of free trade. Moreover, it was part of larger maneuver to discredit the very notion of relying on political economic theory and abstract ideas to inform contemporary politics. The Smith straw man that protectionists had created certainly stood for the flawed and inconsistent views of free-traders, but, more than that, it stood for a naïve attachment to antiquated ideas. The economic theories that at one time had won the hearts and minds of many legislators were now pejoratively described as the work of theorists who like "to get away from facts and from the daily routine and experience of human existence." Political economy, according to Representative John Brutzman Storm, a dissenting Democrat from Pennsylvania, was "a science based upon observation and experience," and that the definition of the science stood at odds with the way in which some congressmen were deploying it. Neither Adam Smith nor Henry George ("One very recent and popular writer") provided satisfactory answers to the

---

71. *Congressional Record,* 49th Congress, 1st Session, House of Representatives (May 22, 1886), 4813.

question of national wealth. "One scientist arbitrarily assumes that free trade was the cause, another says protection, another currency, and so on," Storm complained. This indeterminacy meant that the science of political economy stood on shaky epistemic grounds and could not be trusted to guide political affairs. Storm wanted to issue a warning against the reckless adherence to "dogmatic assumptions and propositions which can not be admitted as self-evident, nay, which are unsupported by the facts of human experience."[72]

The status of political economy, the relevance of a century-old book, the credibility of congressmen who still clung to theoretical ideas all came under fire in the closing years of the nineteenth century. Congressmen who tried to slander Smith were trying to completely unhinge political debate from the intellectual exercises of past decades and by-gone eras. Some, like Representative Storm, tried to put Adam Smith back in the eighteenth century. "When we reflect that more than a century has passed since Adam Smith wrote his Wealth of Nations," Storm stated, "we are compelled to admit that the science of political economy has not achieved a high rank in the social sciences."[73] Similarly, Representative Dalzell of Pennsylvania viewed attachment to Adam Smith as a display of ignorance about completely different economic conditions. "They forget that the political economy of Adam Smith has long since become inapplicable in many respects because of new conditions and ought to be relegated to the time for which it was written when other than modern conditions prevailed," Dalzell argued.[74] Some congressmen, like Republican Jonathan Prentiss Dolliver of Iowa, blamed contemporary woes on politicians' fondness for "dreams and visions and mysteries and speculations, drawn mostly from text-books of foreign political economists," which seemed to have supplanted the importance of the facts and experience. "And even now,"

72. *Congressional Record*, 48th Congress, 1st Session, House of Representatives, (April 28, 1884), 3502.

73. *Congressional Record*, 48th Congress, 1st Session, House of Representatives, (April 28, 1884), 3502.

74. *Congressional Record*, 55th Congress, 1st Session, House of Representatives, (March 25, 1897), 285.

Dolliver complained sorely, "we are regaled in this debate with long extracts from Adam Smith, brought into this House as novelties, as if the American people have never heard of Mr. Smith." If Smith had been right and "the people of the United States had desired to govern themselves by the wisdom of the father of English political economy," a century of American history would have proven so through its trade policy, Dolliver surmised.[75] But it hadn't.

While those who defended the works of Adam Smith saw themselves as the defenders of truth, their opponents saw them as hopelessly detached from reality and un-American. "I have studied the works of these great lights of economic science for a good many years, and I have the greatest admiration possible for the style of their composition and for the vigor of their rhetoric," admitted New York Republican Joseph Belford. Belford reminded Congress of the "copious and ample citations and quotations from Adam Smith, from Cobden, from John Bright, and the long line of English illuminants" that had been presented before them. "But," Belford continued, "I wish to say, in addition to that, 'O Lord, have mercy upon us when we must turn to English theorists to find the lines for a tariff for American workingmen and American manufacturers.'"[76] Belford's speech reflects the Anglophobic and intense economic nationalism of the Republican party in the 1890s. It also reveals how some of the initial impulses of early American political economic thinking still resonated in late-nineteenth century politics. Just as antebellum political economists saw themselves as breaking away from European models and re-defining the parameters and objectives of American prosperity, late-nineteenth century politicians' rejection of "theorism"—an attachment to abstract theories from political economy—was a defiant rejection of European ideas and historical precedent. However, unlike the politicians and political economists of the antebellum period, politicians like Belford no longer saw politics as an arena in which political economic ideas were explored, tested, and

75. *Congressional Record*, 53rd Congress, 2nd session, House of Representatives, (January 11, 1894), 737.

76. The Record also notes that applause followed these remarks. *Congressional Record*, 53rd Congress, 2nd session, House of Representatives, (March 24, 1897), 245.

applied. This was not to say that there was no room at all for textbook political economy, but rather that the lessons of the classroom had no place on the Congress floor. "In these great throbbing, pulsing days," Belford contended,

> it is not in the college lecture rooms of the world that we are to look for the bases of tariff taxation or legislation; not in the theories of the schoolmen, but in the facts of practical business, and in the long run business is very likely to get the better of theory every time.[77]

At the close of the century, the line that separated Democrats and Republicans was, on the surface, a line between those who stood behind Adam Smith and those who did not, those who cried for free trade, and those who clamored for protectionism. But underneath it was an even deeper division that could not be redrawn by simply changing policies. It was a vast gulf separating those who uncritically followed the science of political economy from those who doubted its premises, those who espoused theorizing from those who wanted to ground politics in experience, and those with a jejune attachment to Adam Smith's intellectual authority from those who wanted to challenge it.

———

On May 31st, 1876, the London Political Economy Club hosted a "grand dinner and special discussion" of Adam Smith's *The Wealth of Nations*. Though it anticipated the Delmonico's celebration by about six months, the spirit was very much the same. As *The Pall Mall Gazette* projected, the "honour of Adam Smith's memory . . . [did] not coincide with an auspicious moment in the history of the science which Adam Smith founded."[78] Not only had the political economy fallen "into low or lower esteem" in England, it seemed that in Germany and France, too,

77. *Congressional Record*, 53rd Congress, 2nd session, House of Representatives, (March 24, 1897), 245.

78. *Pall Mall Gazette*, May 30, 1876. Reprinted in the *Minutes and Proceedings of the Political Economy Club, 1821–1882* Vol. 3 (London: Printed for the Club by Unwin Brothers, Printers, 1881), 135.

thinkers were "probing the weak points" of the doctrine of free trade. Rising to the challenge, however, was the eminent Robert Lowe, former Chancellor of the Exchequer and Home Secretary, who delivered a lengthy speech recounting "how it was that [Smith] arrived at the results which have made his name immortal." In fact, "I might say, I think, without much exaggeration, that Adam Smith has been the Plato of Political Economy," he stated matter-of-factually.[79]

Much like the one in England, the Smith Centenary celebration at Delmonico's was the culmination of decades of contest over Adam Smith's authority, relevance, and legacy in American political and intellectual life. To Smith acolytes, it was high time that the world had him "honored with immortality"[80] Smith the man and Smith the idea became one; he was the personification of free trade. But to Smith cynics, Smith and his American disciples misguided the nation. "There is in the poetic temperament something which leads to the perception of love of truth, in whatever gilded and fictitious dress imagination may shape it," read one protectionist response to the banquet at Delmonico's. The quest for scientific truth was a misapprehension grounded not in reality but in the arcane ideas of a dead Scottish philosopher. Those who abided by the words of Smith could be relied on for nothing except adopting "the most absurd ideas, and [sticking] to them with sublime audacity."[81]

The centenary of *The Wealth of Nations* represented the apex of a protracted debate over Smith's position within the politics of free trade. From about 1815 to the end of the long nineteenth century, trade emerged as the primary interpretive lens through which American politicians engaged with Smith and defended contending visions of national political economy. But the reduction of *The Wealth of Nations* to a manifesto on free trade served different purposes for Smith's disciples and

79. To which Rowe added, "that Ricardo (a member of this Club) also has been its Aristotle." *Pall Mall Gazette*, May 30, 1876. Reprinted in *Minutes and Proceedings of the Political Economy Club, 1821–1882* Vol. 3, 78, 83.

80. "An Economic Centennial."

81. "The Commercial Revolution—The Results of Protecting Industry," *Cincinnati Daily Gazette*, December 23, 1876.

Smith's critics, both before and after the Civil War. On the one hand, those who saw themselves as disciples of Smith's system had a strong tendency to justify the policy of free trade on the grounds of its scientific validity and ostensible universality, as well as the intellectual prestige of its most recognizable exponent, Adam Smith. At least in the antebellum Congress, this way of defending the importance of Smith's work had one very important consequence: namely, that the discursive territory on which legislators clashed over commerce deliberately avoided and obscured the topic of slavery. On the other hand, those who saw themselves as Smith critics challenged those justificatory grounds by historicizing Smith's importance. Without demolishing Smith's authority altogether, protectionists argued that Smith's significance was confined to his time period and ought to have no privileged claim on guiding modern American trade policy. However, their attempts to co-opt Smith's status as the "apostle of free trade"—the apostle who nonetheless saw the need for protective economic measures—fell on deaf ears. The effective institutionalization of protectionism in the last quarter of the nineteenth century only triggered an even stronger counterattack from those who sought to bring about a "national reformation" with the holy sanction of Smith's *The Wealth of Nations*.[82]

82. "The Adam Smith Centenary."

4

In the Vanguard of the
New School

"IT HAS BEEN SAID that recent tendencies in political economy indicate a return to Adam Smith," wrote the economist Richard T. Ely in
1886. Just as some philosophers had made "Back to Kant" their *cri de
coeur*, Ely observed, "it has been thought that political economists ought
to find inspiration in the cry, 'Back to Adam Smith!'"[1] Perhaps Ely was
referring to those academic economists who felt that political economy
had fallen out of favor with the public and were searching for "some sort
of reorganization of the science and method."[2] Turning to the founding
father of political economy for inspiration would have been a good start.
Perhaps Ely was referring to the more partisan wings of the profession
and their popular adherents still clamoring over protectionism or free
trade. Or, perhaps he was referring to a rising generation of economists—
of which he was a part—who wanted to return economics to its human-
istic, ethical foundations. Any one of these readings, though, evoked the
varied and often conflicting valences of political economy in the final
decades of the nineteenth century.

Adam Smith was an odd fixture in the 1880s when Ely published
his short article in *Science*. On the one hand, Smith's reputation as "the

1. Richard T. Ely, "Ethics and Economics," *Science* 7, no. 175 (1886), 531.
2. Charles F. Dunbar, "The Reaction in Political Economy," *The Quarterly Journal of Economics* 1, no. 1 (1886), 1.

apostle of free trade" lived on, even though serious examinations of his arguments about trade were few and far between. On the other hand, academic political economy had long outgrown the ideas found in the well-worn pages of *The Wealth of Nations*. Political economists were no longer interested in merely identifying, clarifying, or even correcting Smith's aged views, whether about trade, money, taxation, or the essence of value.[3] There were much more complicated and urgent questions for political economists that demanded moving beyond—not back to—Adam Smith.

At the same time, there were reasons outside of immediate social and economic conditions for Americans to return to the fabled Scottish professor. Between 1894 and 1905, several key publications unveiled valuable new information about Smith's life and ideas. In 1894, James Bonar's *Catalogue of Adam Smith's Library* meticulously arranged and presented Smith's personal literary history. Combining volumes bearing Smith's book plate with reports from private holdings, Bonar's catalogue contained over 1,000 entries and estimated that Smith's library contained some 3,000 titles in English, French, Latin, Italian, and Greek (and just three German "presentation copies"). Smith aficionados in the Anglophone world could now relish the "new and large glimpse into the workroom of the great economist."[4] In 1895, John Rae's *Life of Adam Smith* appeared as the first major biography since Dugald Stewart's 1793 memorial. Though biographical material on Smith was still "somewhat scanty" even a century after his death, Rae was applauded for his detailed reconstruction of Smith's movements, surroundings, and intellectual and personal development. Another biography, this time by British journalist and editor of *The Economist* Francis W. Hirst, followed in 1904.[5]

3. Keith Tribe makes a similar observation about Smith's reputation in late-nineteenth century Great Britain. Tribe, "'Das Adam Smith Problem' and the Origins of Modern Smith Scholarship," 515.

4. A. C. Miller, "A Catalogue of the Library of Adam Smith by James Bonar," *Journal of Political Economy* 3, no. 2 (1895), 242.

5. For one fairly positive review of Rae's biography, see L. L. Price, "Life of Adam Smith by John Rae," *The Economic Journal* 5, no. 19 (1895), 384–86. Francis W. Hirst, *Adam Smith* (London: Macmillan & Company, 1904).

Perhaps the most important discovery, however, was that of Smith's *Lectures on Justice, Police, Revenue, and Arms*, first uncovered in 1895, then edited and published by the British economist Edwin Cannan in 1896. Not only were the *Lectures* vital for reconstructing Smith's history of law and government—part of that elusive manuscript he burned before his death—their existence unambiguously demonstrated that Smith had worked out many ideas in *The Wealth of Nations* as early as 1762–3, prior to his travels in France. In the eyes of many readers, the *Lectures* provided unequivocal evidence of Smith's originality and genius as a political economist.

Finally, new interpretive problems emerged that would have an irreversible impact on the way scholars studied Adam Smith. In 1897, the German economist August Oncken published a short article in *The Economic Journal* entitled "The Consistency of Adam Smith." Oncken's primary aim was to inform his Anglophone (though primarily British) readers that they were blissfully unaware of how German scholars had been reading Adam Smith and working with his ideas in a very different way.

> Are the two principal works of Adam Smith, the *Theory of Moral Sentiments* (1759) on the one hand, and the *Inquiry into the Nature and Causes of the Wealth of Nations* (1776) on the other, two entirely independent works, or are we to regard the latter simply as a continuation of the former, though published at a later date, and both as presenting, when taken together, a comprehensive exposition of his moral philosophy?[6]

If unknown to them before, "Das Adam Smith Problem" was now readily available for British and American readers to grapple with and respond to.

In the last quarter of the nineteenth century, American economists turned "back to Adam Smith" with new information in radically different times. As the United States was transforming into the world's most

---

6. August Oncken, "The Consistency of Adam Smith," *The Economic Journal* 7, no. 27 (1897), 444.

formidable industrial power, one might have expected Smith to emerge as the capitalist's patron saint or the premier apologist of laissez-faire logic. But among certain academic political economists, Smith offered a different way of thinking about the American political economy. "Those exertions of the natural liberty of a few individuals, which may endanger the liberty of the whole society, are, and ought to be, restrained by the laws of all governments," Ely wrote, quoting Smith. For Ely, Smith represented the forgotten ethical foundations of economics during a time of social and economic upheaval. "The end and purpose of economic life are held to be the greatest good of the greatest number, or of society as a whole," he argued. In Ely's opinion, it was clear that the science of political economy had foundations in social ethics, and that individual and society were mutually constitutive and "united in one purpose."[7] Meanwhile, Ely's intellectual opponents denounced his ethical orientation toward political economy. Charles F. Dunbar of Harvard, for example, responded to Ely's "Ethics and Economics" just a few months later, criticizing Ely's call for "a more effective use of the authority of the state" to fulfill some social or moral duty as "merely the infusion of emotion into economics."[8] Truth and scientific discovery—not social and moral reform—ought to be the aims of political economy; even if one wanted to improve social conditions, one had to resist the urge to mix scientific with political and moral interests. Mixing ethics with economics, in Dunbar's opinion, would destroy "the possibility of all scientific precision."[9]

The crises of American capitalism during the Progressive Era forced economists to once again reckon with a basic question about their profession: to what extent was economics directed toward what *ought* to be as opposed to what *is*? Should economics be prescriptive as well as descriptive? How can one know what "ought" to be without first discovering in some scientific manner what truly "is?" These anxieties over the ethical and political boundaries of economics conditioned the way that

7. Ely, "Ethics and Economics," 532. Quoting *WN*, II.ii.94, 324.

8. Dunbar, "The Reaction in Political Economy," 23–24.

9. Charles F. Dunbar, "The Academic Study of Political Economy," *The Quarterly Journal of Economics* 5, no. 4 (1891), 412.

economists reconstructed Smith's intentions as a moral philosopher and as a political economist. Among American economists, the meaning of the so-called Adam Smith Problem had less to do with reconciling sympathy and self-interest on a philosophical level and more to do with reconciling ethics and economics on a practical level. Their view of the consistency, compatibility, and contemporary relevance of Smith was therefore refracted through a much wider methodological debate about whether economics—and the American political economy itself— could and should be directed towards ethical ends.

———

The restructuring of the American political economy at a fundamental level marked the closing decades of the nineteenth century. The industrial growth that had begun running in the 1870s was now racing in its highest gear along more than 29,000 miles of railroad tracks. By 1890, for the first time in its history, the value of manufactured goods surpassed that of agricultural products in the United States. Jobs in the iron and steel industry had increased over one thousand percent since 1860, and by 1895 the US was the world's leading industrial power. Decades of high tariffs yielded the bulk of federal revenue and also enabled industrial tycoons to drive up domestic prices in the absence of foreign competition. While the tariff was no longer as incendiary as it was before the Civil War, trade was still a central and polarizing political issue.

Consolidation accompanied booming output. Up until the 1870s, sole-proprietorship, family-owned firms dominated the business landscape. But the 1880s saw the gradual transformation and replacement of these small-scale businesses into vertically-integrated, capital-intensive modern corporations. Trusts dominated the industrial landscape from beets to beef, sugar to steel. By 1904, some 1,800 industrial enterprises had merged into just 157 firms, with more than half of them taking more than seventy percent of their market share. At the same time, the labor force itself was simultaneously consolidating and diversifying. Immigrant labor was slowly becoming the majority of the labor force in major industries such as iron, steel, and textile production. Organized labor was galvanizing. The Knights of Labor, founded in 1869, saw its membership peak around 1886 when it unionized nearly ten percent of the nation's nonagricultural workforce, and craft unions such as the American Federation of Labor were steadily growing apace.[10]

But these were also decades of growing pains, and historians have rightly characterized the American Progressive Era as capitalism in a state of crisis. The unprecedented trajectory of the nation's economic growth was interrupted by major financial panics in 1874, 1893, and 1907. As popular sentiment linked economic slumps and falling prices to the inflexibility of gold-backed currency, the money question became unavoidable, and calls for "easy money"—government-issued greenbacks and, later, silver—became louder. In an era of mass consumer culture, the gains from growth were hardly even; by one historical estimate, over a quarter of private wealth was in the hands of the top one percent of households in the latter half of the nineteenth century. Confrontations between labor and capital were frequent and violent. Demands for the eight-hour workday gained momentum and became a central plank of labor platforms. Between 1877 and 1905, over 36,000 strikes took place, and the US National Guard had to be mobilized over three hundred times to settle "labor troubles;" in 1886 alone there were over fourteen hundred strikes. Progressive zeal was Janus-faced, however. On the one hand, growing awareness of mass poverty and inequality prompted the use of scientific methods for diagnosing and remedying social ills. Ideas about social interdependence, linked with the development of social sciences and statistics spurred the settlement house movement—led predominantly by women—as well as charity organizations and high-profile philanthropy. On the other hand, the "progressive" spirit could often be exclusionary if not outright anti-liberal and racist. The growth

10. For this background on the Gilded Age and Progressive era, I have drawn from a variety of sources, including Dorfman, *The Economic Mind In American Civilization*; Edwards, *New Spirits*; Leon Fink, *The Long Gilded Age: American Capitalism and the Lessons of a New World Order* (Philadelphia, PA: University of Pennsylvania Press, 2015); David Huyssen, *Progressive Inequality: Rich and Poor in New York, 1890–1920* (Cambridge, MA: Harvard University Press, 2014); Lukas Rieppel, *Assembling the Dinosaur* (Cambridge, MA: Harvard University Press, 2019); White, *The Republic for which It Stands*; and White, *Railroaded*.

of the Knights of Labor in the 1880s was in large part due to the mobilization of anti-Chinese sentiment; the California Workingman's Party adopted the slogan, "The Chinese Must Go!" by late 1877. Eugenics, both in theory and practice, gained traction. Academics, social reformers, and policymakers were eager to prove that American capitalism "could be altruistic as well as competitive," but such progressive social and intellectual movements were often entangled with various commitments to engineering a physically, morally, and racially improved society.[11]

The turbulence of the 1880s was no longer something that academic political economists could ignore as mere sound and fury; it called for a major reassessment of the basic assumptions and methods of political economy as a science. The rise of popular writers such as Henry George, Edward Bellamy, and Henry Demarest Lloyd gave credence to ideas once thought outlandish and radical. Professors of political economy could be summoned by Congress to advise on a given issue, as Francis Bowen of Harvard was to determine whether a double standard of currency would be viable. The establishment of the Bureau of Labor Statistics in 1884 and the Interstate Commerce Act of 1887 flirted with the

11. On "altruistic" but competitive capitalism, see Rieppel, *Assembling the Dinosaur*, 9. On the settlement movement, the best overview is Mina Julia Carson, *Settlement Folk: Social Thought and the American Settlement Movement, 1885–1930* (Chicago, IL: University of Chicago Press, 1990). Alice O'Connor's "Origins" chapter in her *Poverty Knowledge: Social Science, Social Policy, and the Poor in Twentieth-Century U.S. History*, Reprint edition (Princeton, NJ: Princeton University Press, 2002) also provides a helpful overview of the Progressive Era approach to the production of knowledge around poverty, the poor, unemployment, and wages. On Sinophobia and the labor movement, see White, *The Republic for Which it Stands*, 379–384, 518–522; Beth Lew-Williams, *The Chinese Must Go: Violence, Exclusion, and the Making of the Alien in America*, Illustrated edition (Cambridge, MA: Harvard University Press, 2018); Alexander Saxton, *The Indispensable Enemy: Labor and the Anti-Chinese Movement in California* (Berkeley, CA: University of California Press, 1971). On the relationship between eugenics and progressivism, see Michael Freeden's influential essays, "Eugenics and Progressive Thought: A Study in Ideological Affinity," *The Historical Journal* 22, no. 3 (1979), 645–71 and "Eugenics and Ideology," *The Historical Journal* 26, no. 4 (1983), 959–62. See also Ian Robert Dowbiggin, *Keeping America Sane: Psychiatry and Eugenics in the United States and Canada, 1880–1940* (Ithaca, NY: Cornell University Press, 1997); Michael B. Katz, *In the Shadow of the Poorhouse: A Social History of Welfare in America*, Tenth Anniversary Edition (New York, NY: Basic Books, 1996). On the relationship

expansion of state power to regulate labor, employment, and the rail-roads. Academic political economists, many of whom self-styled them-selves as disinterested scientists, now had to reckon with the possibility of their science being used to directly shape the relationship between state and society.

One polemical account of differences in academic opinions appeared in Richard T. Ely's 1884 essay, "The Past and Present of Political Econ-omy." Ely was the posterchild of the "new generation" economists who received their training in Germany during the 1870s; he was also a pro-ponent of the historical method. He drew fire from his colleagues not only for his outspoken socialist sympathies, but also for his heavy criti-cism of what he called the "old school." According to Ely, the old school—the past of political economy—traced its roots to the classical political economy of English economists that began with David Ricardo and was consummated in the works of John Stuart Mill. Its method was primarily idealistic, a priori, and deductive; it took "its ultimate facts, its premises, from other sciences, from common and familiar experiences, or from the declarations of consciousness" and proceeded from those premises "to evolve [into] an economic system without any further re-course to the external world, save perhaps as furnishing tests of the

---

between eugenics and economic thought specifically, see David M. Levy, "How the Dismal Science Got its Name: Debating Racial Quackery," *Journal of the History of Economic Thought* 23, no. 1 (March 2001), 5–35. Thomas C. Leonard, a historian of economic thought, has made the most explicit link between progressive economics and eugenics, which, unsurprisingly, has caused some controversy. See Thomas C. Leonard, "'More Merciful and Not Less Effective': Eugenics and American Economics in the Progressive Era," *History of Political Economy* 35, no. 4 (2003), 687–712 and *Illiberal Reformers: Race, Eugenics, and American Economics in the Progressive Era* (Princeton, NJ: Princeton University Press, 2016). Marshall I. Steinbaum and Bernard A. Weisberger's blistering critique of *Illiberal Reformers* sparked further debate about the legacy of progressive economics and contemporary ideological battles in the profession. See, Marshall I. Steinbaum and Bernard A. Weisberger, "The Intellectual Legacy of Progressive Economics: A Review Essay of Thomas C. Leonard's *Illiberal Reformers*," *Journal of Economic Literature* 55, no. 3 (2017), 1064–83; Nicola Giocoli, "The Intellectual Legacy of Progressive Hubris: A Review Essay of Thomas C. Leonard, *Illiberal Reformers: Race, Eugenics & American Economics in the Progressive Era*," *History of Economic Ideas* 25, no. 3 (2017), 157–69; Phillip W. Magness, "The Progressive Legacy Rolls On: A Critique of Steinbaum and Weisberger on *Illiberal Reformers*," *Econ Journal Watch* 15, no. 1 (2018), 20.

validity of the reasoning." According to Ely, the old school of political economists liked to draw inspiration from Adam Smith by assuming that self-interest was the universal, "animating and overwhelmingly preponderating cause of economic phenomena" and that the logical conclusion of letting unrestrained self-interest run its course was that "government should abstain from all interference in industrial life." Ultimately, the defining characteristic of the old school and its contemporary adherents was its limited scope: its sole aim was "the discovery of truth without regard to its practical application."[12]

While Ely admitted the old school's "enticing unity . . . alluring simplicity" and fondness for "mental discipline," he spared no criticism for its methods. Despite its ability to appeal "to the vanity of the average man" with its "easily managed formulas," the political economy of the past was ill-suited for the present circumstances, Ely contended. Earlier political economy was silent on industrial progress and incapable of confronting the problems which new economic developments had brought forth. In short, the political economy of the past "failed first as a guide in industrial life," Ely argued.[13] Life outside the ivory tower tested the soundness of their assumptions, and mass social movements demonstrated that self-interest was neither the sole force nor the ideal form of economic life. Thus, the conditions of the present revealed how the ideal of economic life ought to be the "union of self-interest and altruism in a broad humanitarian spirit."[14]

This broad humanitarian spirit was at the center of the "new political economy," or the present of political economy. Sometimes called "realistic," "inductive," or "German" (though Ely pointed out that its influence extended far beyond its continental origins), the new school began not with assumptions and axioms, but rather with observations. Following the example set by founders of the German Historical School— Hildebrand, Roscher, and Knies—new political economists would study present economic phenomena in light of the past. They would

12. Richard T. Ely, *The Past and the Present of Political Economy* (Baltimore, MD: The Johns Hopkins University, 1884), 8, 10, 13, 15.

13. Ely, *The Past and the Present of Political Economy*, 23.

14. Ely, *The Past and the Present of Political Economy*, 30, 35.

begin by gathering particular facts, then proceed with "observing particulars in which these facts agree among themselves," and finish by formulating generalizations. They treated economic systems as composed not of self-propelled individuals, but of individuals "inextricably and organically bound up in state and society."[15] Because the new political economists treated man "as man, and not [as] wealth" they gave the science of political economy its normative force. The political economy of the present, Ely declared, signified a change of intention from simply studying what "is" to what "ought" to be:

> [Present-day political economy] no longer permits the science to be
> used as a tool in the hands of the greedy and the avaricious for keeping down and oppressing the laboring classes. It does not acknowledge *laissez-faire* as an excuse for doing nothing while people starve, nor allow the all-sufficiency of competition as a plea for grinding the poor. It denotes a return to the grand principle of common sense and Christian precept.[16]

Ely set off a firestorm. An anonymous review in *The Nation* impugned Ely's assessment of the state of affairs in political economy, accusing him of oversimplifying the views of the old school into a pamphlet of "entertaining reading."[17] Ely also faced harsh internal rebuke from another Hopkins scholar, the mathematician Simon Newcomb. A vocal proponent of marginal utility theory pioneered by a triumvirate of economists— William Stanley Jevons, Léon Walras, and Carl Menger—in the 1860s and 1870s, Newcomb wanted to bring a more theoretical and mathematical approach to American economics.[18] Agitated by Ely's representation of the classical school in "Past and Present," Newcomb redoubled his own efforts to wage intellectual combat with Ely in an obnoxiously academic fashion. Newcomb first tried to get the Johns Hopkins President

---

15. Ely, *The Past and the Present of Political Economy*, 9, 35.

16. Ely, *The Past and the Present of Political Economy*, 64. Italics in original.

17. As quoted in Benjamin G. Rader, *The Academic Mind and Reform: The Influence of Richard T. Ely in American Life* (Lexington, KY: University of Kentucky Press, 1966), 31.

18. On Newcomb's interpretation and response to Jevons, see Dorfman, *The Economic Mind in American Civilization*, Vol. 3, 83–87.

Daniel Coit Gilman to facilitate a conversation between himself and Ely to settle their differences. Then Newcomb and Ely turned their students on one another at conferences and penned devastating reviews of the other's publications. It was in this combative mood that Ely began organizing the German-inspired American Economics Association (AEA), while the Newcomb crowd conspired to take it down.[19]

In 1886, Ely and Newcomb publicly sparred in sequential publications in *Science*. Ely's "Ethics and Economics" came out first in June and responded to the common charge that German economists and their followers confounded positive and normative aims. "Open your Mill, your Schönberg, your Wagner, your economic magazines," Ely pleaded, "and you readily discern that the course of economic thought is largely, perhaps mainly, directed to what ought to be." The new generation of economists was "new" insofar as they consciously adopted this ethical stance and deliberately pointed out "the manner in which it may be attained, and even [encouraged] people to strive for it."[20] Adopting this position did not diminish political economy's standing as a science, though. In Ely's opinion, political economy ranked somewhere between a mental science and a physical or natural science; economic life had to be understood as a product of abstract impersonal forces *and* human will. Thus, like biological scientists who study the development of living organisms by looking deep into their past, political economists, according to Ely, also had to start by looking backwards.[21]

Newcomb's response in the following issue of *Science* was impersonal and terse. "Can Economists Agree upon the Basis of Their Teachings?" the headline ran. Ely stressed "the observed facts of society and business," while Newcomb favored "the general principles of the science and the conclusions to be deductively obtained from them." In theory, these

19. Further details of the Newcomb-Ely saga can be found in Rader, *The Academic Mind and Reform*, 31–36; Ross, *The Origins of American Social Science*, chap. 4.

20. Ely, "Ethics and Economics," 530.

21. "What seems to me a more truly scientific conception is this: the economist hopes to understand industrial society so thoroughly, that he may be able to indicate the general lines of future development. It follows from all this, that the future is something which proceeds from the present, and depends largely upon forces at work in the past." Ely, "Ethics and Economics," 530.

were simply two different paths that led to the same destination: the discovery of truth. But in practice, only one class of economists had the upper hand. Though they might be ignorant of the actual conditions of the trade and commerce of specific nations and their histories, certain economists nevertheless clearly grasped the laws of supply and demand and "all the other abstract principles of economics." This type of economist was better equipped to answer any given economic question. So, when it came to teaching economics, Newcomb undeniably preferred a version of economics that taught students "how to think and investigate" from a higher level of abstraction and generality, rather than "storing [their] minds with facts."[22]

The contretemps between Ely and Newcomb paralleled the *Methodenstreit* on the other side of the Atlantic. In 1883, the Austrian economist Carl Menger published his *Investigations into the Methods of the Social Sciences*, a theoretically rich and animated work that was part methodological treatise, part polemic against Gustav Schmoller and his ilk of historical economists. On one level, Menger provided a muscular defense of a social scientific method that took the actions of atomistic economic agents as the foundation of a purely theoretical approach to economics; such a theoretical approach to the study of human social order was not only eminently possible, he argued, but superior to alternative modes of explanation than what historicists had to offer. But, on another level, Menger was rebuking what he saw as the historical school's privileging of state policy and the conflation of purely scientific political economy with its practical applications.[23] Echoes of the

22. Simon Newcomb, "Can Economists Agree upon the Basis of Their Teachings?," *Science* 8, no. 179 (1886), 26.

23. The *Methodenstreit* is a major turning point in the history of economic thought. Besides the intensely personal nature of the Menger-Schmoller dispute, the debate also precipitated the development of the Austrian school of economic thought in opposition to the German historical school. According to Bruce Caldwell, "What the *Methodenstreit* did was to create a separate Austrian *school* of economics. Simply put, Schmoller's ostracism promoted unity among the Austrians" (specifically, Menger's followers such as Eugen Böhm-Bawerk, Ludwig von Mises, Friedrich von Wieser). For a *precis* of Menger's *Investigations* as well as the terms and stakes of the *Methodenstreit* see Caldwell, *Hayek's Challenge*, chap. 3. Emphasis in original. In his recent book, Janek Wasserman situates the infamous *Methodenstreit* within the emerging

Methodenstreit reverberated in the dispute between Ely and Newcomb, though the boundaries between their methodological and political differences were fuzzier. Nonetheless, the Ely-Newcomb clash represented a broad debate about not only the method but also the policy implications of economic science. From the standpoint of Ely and the new generation economists, economic analysis and its application made up an inherently ethical task whose basic unit of analysis was the social whole. In this sense, their pronouncements were not socialist in a Marxist sense—that is, implying public ownership of capital and the ultimate displacement of capitalism—but rather in the sense that they rejected atomistic individualism and celebrated the social whole and the state as their unit of analysis.[24] But in the eyes of critics, the new generation's sympathies with labor and their socialist tendencies compromised scientific neutrality and endangered the intellectual authority of the profession.[25] Moreover, the violence of 1886 heightened the existential urgency of these methodological and political questions. The Haymarket bombing on May 4—which followed on the heels of a massive general strike and the police killing of six workers—proved that the nationwide conversation around labor and socialism could be, quite literally, explosive.[26]

By October of 1886, Charles F. Dunbar of Harvard had published his own statement in the inaugural issue of *The Quarterly Journal of Economics*, entitled "The Reaction in Political Economy," in which he attempted to minimize the difference between the old and new schools of political

debates about subjective valuation as a prelude to the birth of the Austrian school of economics. See Janek Wasserman, *The Marginal Revolutionaries: How Austrian Economists Fought the War of Ideas* (New Haven, CT: Yale University Press, 2019).

24. White, *The Republic for Which It Stands*, 451.

25. Ross, *The Origins of American Social Science*, 115.

26. For a brief account of Haymarket situated within the "Great Upheaval" and violence of Chicago politics in 1886, see White, *The Republic for Which It Stands*, 534–44. For extended reappraisals of Haymarket and the labor and anarchist movements, as well as the legacy of Haymarket, see Paul Avrich, *The Haymarket Tragedy* (Princeton, NJ: Princeton University Press, 1984); James R. Green, *Death in the Haymarket: A Story of Chicago, the First Labor Movement, and the Bombing that Divided Gilded Age America* (New York, NY: Pantheon Books, 2006). I am grateful to Abigail Modaff for guidance on this topic.

economy. To start, even the leaders of the new generation economists—
Ely chief among them—did not unanimously reject the deductive
method; in fact, deductive, abstract reasoning was in some way part of
their approach to economics. Whatever novelty there was in this "new
departure," Dunbar argued, it was "at most . . . the addition of historical
inquiry to methods of investigation already in use." The difference
between the old and new schools, therefore, was not some radical, prin-
cipled difference, but instead a difference of degree—how much weight
to assign to historical inquiry relative to deductive inquiry.[27] From
Dunbar's vantage point, the "reaction" of the new generation economists necessitated a reappraisal of some of its central claims and accusations. Among those accusations was that the doctrine of laissez-faire
was baked into economic reasoning, and, as such, threatened to make
economics the handmaiden of minimalist government. Dunbar re-
buffed this claim, arguing that one had to separate the practical applications of economics from its scientific reasoning. "The maxim of *laissez
faire*," he argued, "whatever validity we assign to it, has to do only with
the practical applications of economic reasoning, and has no place as a
part of the reasoning itself." But questioning the place of laissez-faire
was symptomatic of deeper underlying differences. Whether and how
to restrict competition or make it freer was a question that had to be
answered with "entirely independent reasoning." Not only that, but the
new movement in political economy revealed a tendency to favor the
use of state authority to achieve "higher aims than the mere enriching
of the community."[28] The problem, therefore, was that economists
failed to distinguish between two different types of questions: ethical
questions on the one hand, economic questions on the other. This need
not imply that there was no place for sympathy, humanity, or generosity
in the human order. Dunbar simply wanted to make clear that the place
for "generous emotions" was not in economic reasoning, but rather in

27. Dunbar, "The Reaction in Political Economy," 18.

28. Dunbar, "The Reaction in Political Economy," 22–23. On the "maxim of *laissez faire*,"
Dunbar actually quotes from John Elliott Cairnes's "Political Economy and Laissez-Faire," in
John Elliott Cairnes, *Essays in Political Economy. Theoretical and Applied.* (London: Macmillan
and Co., 1873), 232–264. Italics in original.

the *applications* of economic reasoning—in politics and legislation, for instance. "In short," he wrote, "the question what *ought* to be, or what we wish, must be kept clear from the question what *is*, if we wish for any trustworthy answer to either."[29]

Other economists were inclined to agree with Dunbar's view that the chasm between the deductive and inductive, the old and new school was not as wide as Ely portrayed it. Richmond Mayo-Smith, a new school adherent and the first economist appointed as professor of political science at Columbia University, surveyed the claims of both schools in his Lectures on Political Economy in 1886. He concluded that "Political Economy is both inductive and deductive" and that "Only extremists maintain that it is wholly the one or the other."[30] Even still, this conciliatory view of economic methods did not preclude disagreement over the scope and aims of political economy. As mentioned in Chapter 3, the American offspring of so-called German "historical methods" inherited not so much a body of historical knowledge, but more a commitment to the idea that economic theories were historically and socially contingent, and that the tools of economic analysis ought to be put to use in social policy. "We accept with gratitude the results of former economists, as containing much of what was true at the time," wrote Edwin Robert Anderson Seligman, a one-time student of Mayo-Smith's and later professor of political cal economy and finance at Columbia, "but we protest against the acceptance of all their principles as practical guides for the present generation."[31] Seligman defended the position that there existed an essential relation between economic theories and the external conditions of economic life. No immutable, universal truths of economics existed, he argued in an 1886 essay entitled "The Continuity of Economic Thought." Instead, the economist could hope to understand only "peculiar

---

29. Dunbar, "The Reaction in Political Economy," 24. Emphases in original.

30. Political Economy: Historical and Practical. Lectures delivered by Prof. Richmond M. Smith to the class of 1886. Columbia University Archives, Columbiana Manuscripts, Series 1 Item 69.

31. Edwin R.A. Seligman, "The Continuity of Economic Thought," in *Science Economic Discussion*, eds. Henry C. Adams et al. (New York, NY: Science Co., 1886), 1–23 at 22.

conditions of time, place, and nationality, under which the doctrines were evolved."[32]

Two important implications followed from Seligman's articulation of the historicist approach. One was that it forced his contemporary interlocutors to recognize the rise of the "new generation" of economists as a product of its own time, of a zeitgeist not confined to Germany but instead sweeping "throughout all countries whose social conditions are ripe for a change." The continuity of economic thought, therefore, lay in the fact that economic explanations, theories, and conclusions were inextricably linked to political, cultural, and social institutions of any given time. Hence, the demands of the new generation to make political economy responsive "to the exigencies of the present" was simply a continuation of the discipline's evolution. This was a plea not for radical change, but for greater awareness to the real-world forces that shaped political economy and attention to the questions that drove it.

> The paramount question of political economy to-day is the question of distribution, and in it the social problem (the question of labor, of the laborer) . . . how and in what degree the chasm between the "haves" and the "have-nots" may be bridged over; how and in what degree private initiative and governmental action may strive, separately or conjointly, to lessen the tension of industrial existence, to render the life of the largest social class indeed worth living. This and other complex problems of the present day cannot be solved by a simple adherence to the principles of a bygone generation.[33]

The second implication concerned reckoning with the past. Economics was a distinctly modern science, but some of its most familiar ideas—like laissez-faire—needed to be properly historicized. Following Seligman's historicist interpretation, laissez-faire was not an intrinsic feature of economics as a field, but rather the product of a particular time and place. A stronger grasp of the history of thought revealed that laissez-faire was absent in the Ancient Greek conception of *oikonomia*,

32. Seligman, "The Continuity of Economic Thought," 1.
33. Seligman, "The Continuity of Economic Thought," 22–23.

which was limited by the fluidity of public and private management, the lack of a distinction between labor and capital, and the primacy of the state. In the Middle Ages, the rise of towns, merchant guilds, and commerce centered economic theories on topics of usury, interest, and "reasonable price," not freedom of trade. In the early modern period, the rise of the nation-state, the discovery of the Americas, and the never-ending wars for commercial supremacy gave birth to the theories and practice of mercantilism. It was in the eighteenth century, Seligman argued, that amidst the excesses of monopoly and the oppressiveness of the state regulations of prices, "the times were ripe for a reaction—a reaction in every sphere of life, political, religious, economic."[34] The French *économistes* led the charge against the abuses of the state and the privileges of the few, with Adam Smith following closely behind them.

Seligman assigned Smith a pivotal role in his short but sweeping history of economic thought. That Smith was "the greatest of all economists," according to Seligman, was more than perfunctory praise lavished upon the father of economics. Seligman placed Smith in the context of eighteenth-century Europe on the cusp of transformation. Though he was deep in conversation with Quesnay and Turgot on the existence of natural economic laws, Smith was "no slavish follower of the physiocrats," Seligman argued, refuting a long-held claim that Smith's economic ideas were merely derivative of his French counterparts. Smith did more than borrow from the physiocrats; he invested their ideas with newfound significance by putting their arguments in dialogue with other systems of political economy. Even if Smith had not met the physiocrats, he was already "feeling the indefinable influence of the new current of thought" embodied in Hume and Cantillon, and therefore would have arrived at the same conclusions, Seligman argued.[35]

Seligman argued that Smith's most famous ideas were bound by their context. "Every one is a product of the times, of the *zeitgeist*, and the ideas of the period are unconsciously reflected in the individual,"

34. Seligman, "The Continuity of Economic Thought," 9.
35. Seligman, "The Continuity of Economic Thought," 11.

Seligman wrote. Conceived on the eve of the industrial revolution, Smith's "system of natural liberty" was not a commandment for all times, but instead a specific antidote to "official omniscience and government sciolism," a corrective to the shortcomings of mercantile commercial policy, and a revision to the physiocrats' agricultural system. The whole work of *The Wealth of Nations*, according to Seligman, "consisted in pulling down the rotten fences which obstructed the path of the artisan, the farmer, and the merchant, and we of to-day cannot be too grateful for the salutary impulse he thus gave to all economics."[36]

But Seligman also urged caution. Smith did not espouse the "doctrine" of natural liberty without qualifications, "for he possessed a far truer historical spirit than many of his successors," Seligman argued. There were crucial exceptions to non-interference in economic affairs, and Smith's documentation of history proved it. The Navigation Acts were "a measure of the wisest statesmanship," export duties were often necessary in some instances, and Smith even confessed "that the interests of individuals 'in any particular branch of trade or manufacture are always in some respects different from, and even opposite to, the interest of the public.'"[37] Moreover, Seligman thought it impolitic to assume that what was good in Smith's time would still be good in his own time. Smith's *The Wealth of Nations*, Seligman argued, was written in response to the specific problems and needs of Smith's times; it was "imperative to tear down the old"—the remnants of the mercantile system—before constructing the system of natural liberty so cherished by Smith's successors. But the problems that Seligman and his contemporaries faced were far different than the ones Smith faced; it did not make sense to continue carrying Smith's imperative to "tear down the old" in 1886. Not one but two industrial revolutions had taken place, bringing with them "problems which scarcely existed in 1776." Commerce and transportation networks had become so much more complex that they defied regulation

36. Seligman, "The Continuity of Economic Thought," 11, 13.
37. Seligman, "The Continuity of Economic Thought," 12. Quoting *WN* I.xi, 267.

"by any such simple methods of *laissez-faire* as were possible when Smith wrote."[38]

This effort to increase the distance between Smith and his successors served another purpose as well. Seligman hoped to free Smith from misinterpretation and misattribution—specifically, the misinterpretation that Smith was a doctrinaire defender of laissez-faire. "We must not make Smith responsible for the faults of his disciples," Seligman wrote. It was one thing to protest Smith's views because they were woefully inadequate and ill-suited for present times; it was another thing to "take him to task" for failing to predict the consequences of his ideas under drastically different circumstances. *The Wealth of Nations* was "by far the most important [text] ever written in the science," Seligman reassured, "but we must not, on that account, bow down blindly before its author, and meekly accept all his conclusions." Few of Seligman's professional colleagues would have questioned his supposition that, had they been alive in 1776, they "would certainly have been followers of Smith." Far more, however, would have been struck by his assertion that "did Smith live in 1886, he would no less surely have been in the vanguard of the new school."[39]

As the founder and long-time editor of *The Political Science Quarterly* beginning in 1886, Seligman was a discriminating reader of Adam Smith. An early and tepid review of Albert Delatour's *Adam Smith, sa vie, ses travaux, ses doctrines* also reveals how hard it was to impress him. "Among the thousands of books on economic subjects," Seligman nonchalantly remarked, "not one should have been devoted to a successful and adequate description of the position of the greatest mind in the history of the science." Delatour's work was "ambitious" but scarcely more successful than the host of writers who preceded him: it repeated common knowledge, threw "no new light on any of the vexed questions," and, moreover, it showed no familiarity with works beyond French commentary and "a few English works." Any student hoping to learn more about Smith would be far better consulting *The Wealth of*

---

38. Seligman, "The Continuity of Economic Thought," 13. Italics in original.
39. Seligman, "The Continuity of Economic Thought," 13.

Nations itself, which, on Seligman's estimate, was "not so much very longer than [Delatour's] series of comments."[40] Seligman similarly dismissed R.B. Haldane's short biography, *Life of Adam Smith*, as "a mere sketch, containing no new material" and whose primary contribution was its "very convenient" bibliography.[41] Even in 1910, when writing the introduction to the new Everyman's Edition of *The Wealth of Nations*, Seligman believed that "The real interpretation of Adam Smith [had] yet to be written."[42] What was lacking, in Seligman's opinion, was a broad treatment of Smith's works "considered not as the Alpha and Omega of the science, but as a single phase (although one of paramount importance) in a long evolution."[43] In other words, what was still missing was a deeply *historical* Smith.

———

Within a few years, Seligman would find something approximating a more historical Adam Smith in the works of German scholar Dr. Wilhelm Hasbach. Seligman reviewed Hasbach's two volumes (written as companion pieces) for his English readers of *The Political Science Quarterly* in 1892: *Die Allgemeinen Philosophischen Grundlagen der von François Quesnay und Adam Smith begründeten Politischen Ökonomie* (*The General Philosophic Basis of the Political Economy founded by François Quesnay and Adam Smith*) and *Untersuchungen über Adam Smith und die Entwicklung der Politischen Oekonomie* (*Investigations on Adam Smith and the Development of Political Economy*), published in 1890 and 1891, respectively. The first of these, as its title suggests, was limited to a discussion of the philosophical bases of Quesnay and Smith's ideas. By highlighting the "philosophic precursors" to Smith and Quesnay—from

40. Edwin R. A. Seligman, "Review of *Adam Smith, sa vie, ses travaux, ses doctrines*, by Albert Delatour," *Political Science Quarterly* 2, no. 1 (1887), 185–86.

41. E. R. A. Seligman, "Review of *Life of Adam Smith*, by R. B. Haldane," *Political Science Quarterly* 3, no. 1 (1888), 179.

42. Adam Smith, *The Wealth of Nations* with an introduction by Prof. Edwin R.A. Seligman. Everyman's edition, ed. Ernest Rhys, vol. 1. (London: J.M. Dent & Sons, 1910), xiii.

43. Seligman, "Review of *Adam Smith, sa vie, ses travaux, ses doctrines*," 186.

the Stoics and Epicurean ideas, down to the immediate influences of Mandeville, Hutcheson, and Helvetius—Hasbach was travelling on well-worn paths. What stood out for Seligman, though, was Hasbach's argument that Smith's political economy was "as much the child of the philosophical currents of the day, as our political economy again is dependent on the modern philosophic movement."[44] Hasbach's reading of Smith showed how philosophy and political economy were intertwined from their inception.

Seligman's review of Hasbach's *Investigations* displayed an unusual level of receptivity to an alternative reading of Adam Smith and his legacy stemming from German scholarship. Smith had always been highly visible within Anglophone scholarship, but in 1890 he was seldom the subject of deep study. With the exception of Henry Thomas Buckle's lengthy treatment of *The Theory of Moral Sentiments* and *The Wealth of Nations*, few Anglophone scholars engaged with Smith's two major works as an integrated corpus in the late-nineteenth century. As demonstrated in Chapter 2, Smith's name was firmly linked to *The Wealth of Nations* and to political economy's distant past. This association cut both ways. At best, he was worshipped as the founder of the political economy, the great genius and systematizer who gave political economy scientific value. At worst, Smith was blamed for "letting loose upon the world all the selfish propensities of the 'Economic Man'" associated with the "old political economy" of laissez-faire.[45] Either way, by 1890 it appeared that serious discussion of Smith's ideas had all but "run its course."[46]

---

44. Edwin R. A. Seligman, "Review of *Die Allgemeinen Philosophischen Grundlagen der von François Quesnay und Adam Smith begründeten Politischen Oekonomie; Untersuchungen uber Adam Smith und die Entwicklung der Politischen Oekonomie* by Wilhelm Hasbach," *Political Science Quarterly* 7, no. 3 (1892), 557.

45. M. Kaufmann, "Adam Smith and His Foreign Critics," *The Scottish Review* 10, no. 20 (1887), 390.

46. For further discussion of the state of "serious" Smith scholarship (or lack thereof) in Great Britain, see Tribe, "'Das Adam Smith Problem' and the Origins of Modern Smith Scholarship" and Alastair Su, "Reading, and Misreading, Adam Smith: Recovering Herbert Somerton Foxwell's 'Really Historical Edition' of the Wealth of Nations," working paper.

Meanwhile, German scholars had been reading Smith on a different wavelength since the 1840s. Beginning with Bruno Hildebrand's *Nationalökonomie der Gegenwart und Zukunft* (*National Economy of the Present and Future*) published in 1848, Smith was treated as something of a *Feindbegriff*: a concept, or rather, in this case, a symbol, that identified and mobilized opposition to a perceived enemy. Hildebrand charged the *Smithsche Schule* and *Smithsche System* with putting political economy on the wrong foundations. Against the backdrop of German national unification and early industrialization, Hildebrand echoed Friedrich List's ideas that Smith's political economy ignored national circumstances and that laissez-faire worked only to the benefit of disproportionately advanced nations like Great Britain, while bringing nations (including German states) that lagged behind to their knees.[47] Hildebrand thus faulted Smith for trying to make political economy too cosmopolitan and universalizing and for denying the relevance of national history, geography, and culture. But his main criticism had to do with ethics—or the lack thereof—in Smith's doctrines. By depicting individuals as egoistic, atomistic, and materialistic, Hildebrand alleged that Smith's system rested on unethical foundations and "thus consisted in a (false) depiction of individuals as unethical, and in a (false) conclusion . . . that unethical behavior was useful for economic development."[48] Moreover, he accused Smith of hyper-rationalism associated with the French Enlightenment, whose long shadow still haunted Germany.[49] Hildebrand thus laid the foundations of *Smithianismus*: a pejorative concept that stood for the culmination of useful egoism, extreme materialism, and immorality into a system of political economy. Smith, in short, had become an anti-hero: a recognizable point of reference for all criticism of "classical," "old," and distinctly English political economy.[50]

47. Leonidas Montes, "Das Adam Smith Problem: Its Origins, the Stages of the Current Debate, and One Implication for Our Understanding of Sympathy," *Journal of Economic Thought* 25, no 1 (2003), 73.

48. Emma Rothschild, "Smithianismus and Enlightenment in 19th Century Europe," working paper. (Center for History and Economics, University of Cambridge), 5.

49. On Hildebrand's critique of rationalism, see Rothschild, "Smithianismus and Enlightenment in 19th Century Europe," and Montes, "Das Adam Smith Problem," 70.

50. Montes, "Das Adam Smith Problem," 69–70.

In opposition to Smith and Smithianismus, then, Hildebrand sought a political economy that was national as opposed to cosmopolitan, historical as opposed to rational and abstract.

The tenor of German scholarship shifted in the 1870s. In 1877, August Oncken's *Adam Smith und Immanuel Kant* challenged Hildebrand's depiction of Smith as an anti-ethical thinker. Taking his cue from Buckle's *History of Civilization in England*, Oncken set out to prove that *The Theory of Moral Sentiments* and *The Wealth of Nations* were part of a wider system, and, when read together, one could reconstitute not just Smith's ethics and economics, but also his politics. Meanwhile, subsequent works in German by Lujo Brentano, Witold von Skarżyński, and Richard Zeyss continued to wrestle with the (in)compatibility of sympathy and self-interest between Smith's two major works and the sources of Smith's ideas. For Brentano and Skarżyński, Adam Smith was "himself a Physiocrat" and hardly an original thinker. Smith's time in France accounted for the substance of his most notable contributions to political economy and also accounted for the break with his earlier moral philosophy. This interpretation reinforced the argument that *The Wealth of Nations* and *The Theory of Moral Sentiments* provided completely divergent and irreconcilable pictures of human nature and conduct.[51] By contrast, for Richard Zeyss, "Das Adam Smith Problem" was misconceived from the beginning. Smith's virtue theory added greater complexity to his moral philosophy and tempered self-interest, proving that there was never a fundamental incompatibility between the ethical and economic treatises of the great Scotsman.[52]

51. The idea that Smith underwent a "mental shift" between *The Theory of Moral Sentiments* and *The Wealth of Nations* as a result of his interactions with the physiocrats in France is cheekily called the "French connection thesis." See Montes, "Das Adam Smith Problem;" Russell Nieli, "Spheres of Intimacy and the Adam Smith Problem," *Journal of the History of Ideas* 47, no. 4 (1986), 611–24.

52. For an extended reconstruction of Ocnken, Brentano, Skarżyński, and Zeyss's ideas, see Richard Teichgraeber III, "Rethinking Das Adam Smith Problem," *Journal of British Studies* 20, no. 2 (April 1981), 106–23; Tribe, "'Das Adam Smith Problem' and the Origins of Modern Smith Scholarship;" Keith Tribe, "The 'System of Natural Liberty': Natural Order in the *Wealth of Nations*," *History of European Ideas* 47, no. 4 (2021), 573–76.

Why did any of this matter for American political economists? Just as there were two opposing models for political economy—English and German, deductive and inductive, abstract and historical—there were two interpretive pathways for understanding Smith's significance in history. On the one hand, Smith's value could be purely symbolic. Smithianismus stood for a reductive interpretation of economics qua unrestrained egoism and unethical laissez-faire. The Adam Smith of Smithianismus was useful insofar as he was a recognizable representation of a system, a way of thinking that was now seen as outmoded and immoral. On the other hand, Smith had independent value as an object of historical investigation. Connecting the dots between Smith, his predecessors, and his contemporary interlocutors illuminated not only the originality of his thought, but also the compatibility of the two seemingly opposed works.

Turning back to Seligman, his 1892 review of Wilhelm Hasbach's works shows how some American economists—or at least those who had the occasion to read and comment about Smith's ideas—were interested in Smith for reasons beyond censuring Smithianismus or untangling the complicated web of Das Adam Smith Problem. Seligman glossed over Hasbach's treatment of *The Theory of Moral Sentiments*, suggesting that it "may be passed over as belonging rather to ethics than to economics." Interestingly, though, he noted Hasbach's refutation of Buckle's statement of the problem—namely that "the two great works [were] based on the opposite principles of sympathy and self-interest."[53] But that is the extent of Seligman's engagement with what would later become a defining feature of Smith scholarship. Seligman was more interested in Hasbach's attempt to trace Smith's economic principles and financial science to a long line of predecessors—Grotius, Pufendorf, Wolff, Hutcheson, Quesnay, Turgot, and many others. Identifying the origins and understanding the development of Smith's ideas were critical because doing so showed how Smith's ideas were not created in a vacuum, but rather were products of the "philosophic and economic system of the eighteenth century." The historical method vindicated

53. Seligman, "Review of *Die Allgemeinen Philosophischen Grundlagen*," 557.

Smith as a thinker, but more importantly showed "once again how impossible is the complete separation of economics from the other moral sciences."[54] This line of reception—or as the historian Emma Rothschild put it, "reception of receptions"—did more than prove the immediate and lasting influence of *The Wealth of Nations*. By exposing how the conventional wisdom about Smith, self-interest, and laissez-faire was misguided, American readers opened the possibility that Smith could have occupied "a position more progressive than the current received opinion."[55]

For an American convert to German historicism like Seligman, there was little worthwhile in Smith hagiography. "He who starts out from an apotheosis of the great Scotchman can never arrive at satisfactory conclusions," Seligman argued in his review of Delatour.[56] But the familiar German critique of Smithianismus had its shortcomings, too. For German academics, critiquing Smith served a larger purpose that resonated with the national political, intellectual, and cultural context of mid-century Germany. To criticize Smith was to criticize a wide range of associated "dangerous" ideas: the hyper-rationalism of the French revolution, free trade evangelism, and the rhetoric of universal commerce. In other words, to be opposed to Adam Smith, Emma Rothschild argues, "was to be open, at least, to the prospects for the economic and political unification of the German nation."[57] Even as the disparagement of the Smithsche Schule cooled somewhat by the 1880s, Smith and Smithianismus came to stand for a general dissatisfaction with economic man and a despairing sense of individualism in economic life. Under the critical lens of scholars dealing with the Adam Smith Problem, Smith had become a different kind of historical object—one whose discovery, or rediscovery would be largely overlooked outside of German scholarship for several decades.

54. Seligman, "Review of *Die Allgemeinen Philosophischen Grundlagen*," 557, 558.

55. Emma Rothschild, "Smithianismus and Enlightenment in 19th Century Europe,;" Tribe, "'Das Adam Smith Problem' and the Origins of Modern Smith Scholarship," 522.

56. Seligman, "Review of *Adam Smith, sa vie, ses travaux, ses doctrines*," 186.

57. Rothschild, "Smithianismus and Enlightenment in 19th Century Europe," 12.

New generation economists like Seligman and Ely thus represented a different channel of Smith's reception that had begun to open in the mid-1880s. Mired in the methodological controversies between the "old" and "new" schools of economics, they showed how it was possible to recuperate an image of Adam Smith that worked within and buttressed the historicist paradigm, while also rejecting the use of Smith as a straw-man of the "old" school. In "Past and Present," Ely acknowledged the widespread conviction that Smith had raised "Political Economy to the dignity of a deductive science"—an argument that had echoed in the halls of the Adam Smith Centenary in London. But Ely also deliberately excluded Smith from his pantheon of classical thinkers (which included the lights of Malthus, Ricardo, Nassau Senior, James and John Stuart Mill), for Adam Smith's inspirations were the ones to which "all economists trace their origin."[58] Surely there was no better time to make the case, as Seligman did, for recasting Smith in a different light: as a thinker swept up in the philosophical currents of his time, as a champion of restraints on private power, as an economist who could not be reduced to laissez-faire. In short, Smith was reimagined as a thinker in and as the vanguard of the new school to which Seligman and Ely belonged.

One of the most progressive reimaginings of Smith appeared in Ely's entry on Smith in the 1896 edition of *The Library of the World's Best Literature*, a monumental thirty-volume collection of literary extracts and short biographies compiled by Charles Dudley Warner. Ely opened with the customary exaltations of Smith appropriate for a series claiming to contain the world's best literature: "Few books in the world's history have exerted a greater influence on the course of human affairs; and on account of this one work, Adam Smith's name is familiar to all well-educated persons in every civilized land."[59] In the short space Ely devoted to surveying Smith's life and ideas, two features stand out. The first is Ely's assessment of the value of *The Theory of Moral Sentiments* in relation to Smith's *The Wealth of Nations*. To begin, Ely believed that

---

58. Ely, *The Past and the Present of Political Economy*, 9.

59. Richard T. Ely, "Adam Smith," in *Library of the World's Best Literature: Biographical Dictionary*, vol. 23, ed. Charles Dudley Warner (New York, NY: R. S. Peale and J. A. Hill, 1898), 13519.

Smith's "other writings" were ancillary to *The Wealth of Nations*, and that they were valuable "insofar as they may throw additional light upon the doctrines of this one book."[60] Nevertheless, Ely considered *The Theory of Moral Sentiments* to be an "ambitious work," not least because it was part of a larger body of work that Smith had planned, but never completed. The passage which Ely chose to reproduce for *The Library* came from the first section of Part VI of *The Theory of Moral Sentiments*, "Of the Character of the Individual, so far as it affects his own Happiness; or of Prudence." This is surprising for two reasons. First, the entirety of Part VI was added in the sixth and final edition of *The Theory of Moral Sentiments* published in 1790. Its content and tone are markedly different from the rest of the work. Whereas the earlier parts of the work rely primarily on a descriptive account of sympathy and how it operates as the foundation for moral behavior, in Part VI Smith more openly embraced both normative and descriptive analysis in his account of virtue. In its treatment of classical and Christian virtues—such as prudence, magnanimity, and beneficence—Part VI might be best understood as Smith's contribution to the eighteenth-century tradition of virtue ethics, as opposed to utilitarianism or deontological ethics.[61] Regardless of whether this was how Ely read *The Theory of Moral Sentiments* as a whole, his selections of Smith in *The Library of the World's Best Literature* capture Smith in his most prescriptive moments. Furthermore, Ely pruned the passages so that they amounted to something like a moralistic profile of "The Prudent Man" (as the passage was titled in *The Library*), rather than a more general discussion of the nature of prudence itself. Ely trimmed away Smith's introductory remarks that provided essential context for understanding the "proper business" of prudence— that is, as the virtue which governs our health, fortune, security, and our "rank and credit" among others.[62] What appears in *The Library*, then, is a picture of a moral exemplar who "studies seriously and earnestly to

60. Ely, "Adam Smith."

61. Ryan Patrick Hanley, *Adam Smith and the Character of Virtue* (Cambridge: Cambridge University Press, 2009) and also his *Our Great Purpose: Adam Smith on Living a Better Life* (Princeton, NJ: Princeton University Press, 2019).

62. *TMS* VI.i.4–5, 213.

understand whatever he professes to understand," who works with steady industry and frugality, who "lives within his income" and is "naturally contented with his situation," and who prefers the "secure tranquility" of mind over the "vain splendor of successful ambition."[63]

Ely did not believe *The Theory of Moral Sentiments* was a significant work of philosophy. He described it as a "collection of essays on the topics with which it deals"—such as propriety, merit, virtue, and duty—and said that it lacked "any profound examination of the foundation upon which the author's views rest," namely, sympathy.[64] As discussed in Chapter 1, this had been a common line of criticism of *The Theory of Moral Sentiments* since the early nineteenth century. *The Theory of Moral Sentiments* contained powerful illustrations of the experience of moral learning and moral evaluation, but its philosophical foundation—sympathy—was too thin. It was *The Wealth of Nations* that Ely considered the more serious work of philosophy. Against a "beneficent order of nature lying back of all human institutions," Ely claimed, Smith echoed the "cry of the age . . . 'back to nature.'" Nature, according to Ely, endowed man with the instinct of self-interest, which was often socially beneficial. "We must simply leave nature alone, and give fair play to natural forces to bring about the largest production of wealth," Ely summed up. His compressed analysis marked a subtle, but important departure from an unqualified defense of individual self-interest as the sole force of economic life, though. True, Smith's *The Wealth of Nations* was a "protest against restraints and restrictions," but it was not an attack on all government whatsoever. Rather, it was directed toward "what was held to be the over-government, but what subsequent history has shown to be rather the unwise and unjust government, of that period." Like Seligman's argument a decade prior, Ely wanted to temper contemporary justifications of laissez-faire by distancing and historicizing Smith. Ely's image of Smith, therefore, was refracted through the lens of his progressive and historicist commitments. Ely demonstrated how Smith's economic views derived from close observation of human

---

63. *TMS* VI.i.7–14, 213–216 reproduced in Ely, "Adam Smith," 13524–26.
64. Ely, "Adam Smith," 13521.

life, not a priori premises; how his economic positions were "far from doctrinaire" but were responding to present circumstances; how individual liberty was in accord with Smith's moral philosophy, but that under certain conditions, activating the powers of the state would be salutary for a democratic society. Ely saw no need to appeal to *The Theory of Moral Sentiments*, to reconcile sympathy and self-interest, or to make claims about the consistency of Smith's thought. Smith's political economy on its own showed how the great thinker was "warmly humanitarian, and his ruling passion was to benefit mankind."[65]

While many of Ely's recapitulations of themes of *The Wealth of Nations* were familiar ones, he was much more explicit in the way he connected Smith's views on labor to present concerns. The salience of the labor question would have been obvious to Ely's readers in 1896. From the Haymarket Riot of 1886 ten years earlier, to the Homestead and Pullman Strikes following in rapid succession in 1892 and 1894, respectively, labor disputes had only gained momentum in the 1890s. For academic economists, taking a stance on the labor question could potentially jeopardize one's career. In 1886, Henry Carter Adams's fiery speech on "The Labor Problem," delivered in the midst of the Gould railway strike, was published in the supplement of *Scientific American*. There was "no more reason for granting irresponsible control over [capital], the greatest social force of the day," Adams claimed, "than for permitting irresponsible control over the exercise of the coercive powers of government."[66] In 1887, Adams was forced out of his position at Cornell.

Despite having tempered his activist agenda after his academic freedom trial in 1894, Ely nevertheless channeled his pro-labor, activist views through Smith. Ely underscored that Smith's targets were laws that "aimed to control labor in the interest of the employer," not "laws like our modern laws" that protected the interests of the laborer. Among the extracts from *The Wealth of Nations* that Ely chose were the first thirteen paragraphs from "Of the Wages of Labor" in Book I Chapter 8,

65. Ely, "Adam Smith," 13522.

66. Henry Carter Adams, "Sibley College Lectures XI. 'The Labor Problem,'" *Scientific American Supplement*, no. 555 (August 1886), 8862.

which begins with the theory of natural wages and finishes with Smith's underwhelming observation that "workmen . . . very seldom derive any advantage from the violence of those tumultuous combinations, which . . . generally end in nothing, but the punishment or ruin of the ringleaders."[67] Alluding to Smith's statement that regulations "which favour of the workmen . . . [are] always just and equitable," Ely turned Smith's observation into an exhortation. "This ought not to be forgotten in comparing [Smith's] spirit with that of modern writers who protest against labor legislation," Ely wrote.[68] Even the opening lines of *The Wealth of Nations* reflected Smith's intentions to "make labor central and pivotal." By showing that the measure of national wealth derived not from money or land but rather labor, Smith gave the world not a labor theory of value, but a theory of the value of human labor.[69]

Taken together, Ely and Seligman's efforts to historicize Smith were attempts to both subvert the paradigm of the "old school" and realign Smith's politics with their own. Ely's Smith, especially, was hardly politically neutral; his Smith stood firmly on the side of labor and tiptoed toward the edge of socialism. Historicizing Smith's contributions in no way precluded his contemporary relevance; indeed, it was only by situating Smith's arguments in their original context first could his political commitments and intentions could be revealed in a different light. Incidentally, that light cast Smith as a forefather of humanitarian, historicist economics that conveniently aligned with the progressive, pro-labor agenda of the new generation to which Ely and others belonged.

———

It had been a hundred and five years since Adam Smith's death, and still there seemed little hope that Smith's readers would ever know what was

67. *WN* I.viii.13, 85.

68. *WN* I.x.c.61, 157–8. Ely, "Adam Smith," 13522.

69. Ely, "Adam Smith," 13523. Ely was quite clear that Smith's theory of labor value was not the foundation of socialism, though; "Rodbertus, the German socialist," Ely added, "has claimed that his socialism consists simply in an elaboration of Adam Smith's doctrine of labor; but this is undoubtedly going too far."

contained in the manuscripts he burned. They could only speculate what those two great works upon the anvil might have been. What did Adam Smith have to say about the "different branches of Literature, of Philosophy, Poetry, and Eloquence" in a philosophical history? And what was his theory and history of law and government?[70] All of that changed in 1895 when Edwin Cannan, a rising British economist, came across a most auspicious discovery. One Mr. Charles C. Maconochie approached Cannan with something "which he regarded as of considerable interest:" a manuscript report of Adam Smith's lectures on jurisprudence, inscribed with the date 1766. This was neither Cannan's first nor his last encounter with Adam Smith. In his most famous work, *A History of the Theories of Production and Distribution*, published in 1893, Cannan called *The Wealth of Nations* a "scientific and not a practical treatise" which, disappointingly for someone known as the father of political economy, borrowed heavily from the French physiocrats.[71] In 1904, he would publish what would become one of the most authoritative editions of *The Wealth of Nations*. With his publication of the *Lectures on Justice, Police, Revenue, and Arms* in 1896, Cannan played an important role in shaping subsequent interpretations of Smith's economic theories and his corpus as a whole, especially the parts that were once believed to be irrecoverable.

For Cannan, the primary value of the *Lectures* was that they proved Smith's originality as an economic thinker. In particular, they definitively disproved the "French connection" thesis: that Smith's encounter with the physiocrats caused a decisive break in his thinking, changing his worldview from one organized by sympathy to one organized by self-interest. Moreover, the lectures proved that Smith did not simply "borrow"—or more dramatically, plagiarize—from Turgot's *Reflexions on the Formation and Distribution of Riches* (1770). The content of the

---

70. Letter to the Duc de la Rochefoucault, 1 Nov 1785, *Corr.*, p. 286–287.

71. Or, as Cannan put it, Smith had "caught much of their [the physiocrats'] spirit." Edwin Cannan, *A History of the Theories of Production and Distribution in English Political Economy, from 1776 to 1848*. (London: Percival and Co., 1893), 383. See also W. Cunningham, "Review of *A History of the Theories of Production and Distribution in English Political Economy, from 1776 to 1848*, by Edwin Cannan," *The Economic Journal* 3, no. 11 (1893), 493–94.

Lectures revealed that Smith had formed many of his core economic ideas—such as the division of labor, money, prices, stock, the mercantile system, and even his history of the "progress of opulence in different nations"—before he encountered the physiocrats in France. Readers who wished for a list of corresponding passages between the *Lectures* and *The Wealth of Nations* could consult Cannan's carefully compiled "Table of Parallel Passages in the *Wealth of Nations*." As Cannan viewed them, the *Lectures* enabled readers to follow the development of *The Wealth of Nations* as it fermented in Smith's mind, and, hence, to "distinguish positively between what the original genius of its author created out of British materials on the one hand and French materials on the other."[72]

Ironically, Cannan showed little interest in what the *Lectures* revealed of Smith's proposed work on jurisprudence (what Cannan called a "doubtless far less important but still interesting question").[73] Cannan was primarily interested in separating what was original in Smith's work from what was not, rather than trying to place the *Lectures* within Smith's works as a whole.[74] He was at pains to accept that *The Wealth of Nations* could have been "a partial fulfilment of a promise to give an account of the general principles of law and government." At very least, the *Lectures* adequately filled out the last two prongs of Smith's four-pronged schema as Millar had described them: jurisprudence, police (that is, policy), revenue, and arms. "No one unacquainted with the lectures would have described the *Wealth of Nations* as a treatise on those three subjects [police, revenue, and arms] in that order," Cannan argued.[75] Cannan thus represented a vantage point that prevailed among English economists in the late-nineteenth century: they viewed *The Wealth of Nations* as the centerpiece of Smith's corpus and treated Smith's other works as playing minor supporting roles with little standalone significance. Neither John Rae, who published the landmark biography of

72. Adam Smith, *Lectures on Justice, Police, Revenue and Arms*, ed. Edwin Cannan (Oxford: Clarendon, 1896), xxiv.

73. Smith, *Lectures on Justice, Police, Revenue and Arms*, xxxi.

74. Tribe, "'Das Adam Smith Problem' and the Origins of Modern Smith Scholarship," 516.

75. Smith, *Lectures on Justice, Police, Revenue and Arms*, xxxiii.

Smith in 1895, nor James Bonar, who had compiled the catalogue of Smith's library the year prior, engaged with questions regarding the philosophical compatibility of Smith's works.[76]

The historical, literary, scientific, and philosophical significance of the *Lectures* registered relatively quickly on the other side of the Atlantic. William Caldwell, a philosopher and lecturer in the Department of Political Economy at the recently-founded University of Chicago, was the first American to review Smith's *Lectures* in *The Journal of Political Economy* in 1897. Little is known about Caldwell beyond his presence as a philosopher and economics instructor during the nascent years of the University of Chicago. A few course syllabi reveal his sympathies with German economics and the new generation, though his course in Advanced Political Economy centered around Marshall and Cairnes's texts, pillars of a burgeoning neoclassical approach to economics. Caldwell expected his students to acquire a strong historicist training, especially in his course on the history of thought. The study of the history of political economy, for instance, was not intended "merely as a means of information." With proper attention to bibliography and "the best methods of using books," students in Caldwell's class could "expect in every case [to] read portions of the great authors bearing on cardinal principles, and, by critical comment and comparison, it is hoped he may gain much in discipline and judicial insight."[77]

Caldwell's excitement over the discovery of the *Lectures* was not in short supply.

We have now all the data we shall probably ever have and probably really require, for making out complete estimates of the intellectual work of Adam Smith, who stands now—after this, as before it, and always—in impressive proportions before the world as the world's greatest economist, as the man (comparable in this respect to Kant

76. Oncken, "The Consistency of Adam Smith," 445–46; Montes, "Das Adam Smith Problem," 75.

77. The University of Chicago: Programme of Courses in Political Economy, 1892–1893 (Chicago, IL: University of Chicago Press, 1892) available at http://www.irwincollier.com/chicago-first-detailed-announcement-of-political-economy-program-1892/.

in philosophy) whose work . . . constitutes today and always will constitute the actual subject-matter of the science of political economy.[78]

Caldwell was charitable to the "loving and discriminating care" with which Cannan treated the *Lectures*, but his review drew out implications of the discovery far beyond Cannan's narrow purview.[79] Whereas Cannan underplayed the position of the *Lectures* in Smith's body of work, Caldwell elevated it. The *Lectures* did more than confirm the structure of Smith's course in moral philosophy, Caldwell thought; they gave readers a better sense of the way in which Smith thought about the nature of politics. They showed that Smith was not content with providing a narrowly economistic view of the world, nor did he see economic science at the foundation of a theory of mankind. Instead, the *Lectures* showed how Smith, "both a philosopher and a scientific investigator and teacher," saw how the principles of economic life were inseparable from and conditioned by "a still broader law—the evolution of the principle of Justice in human affairs." Understanding Smith's philosophy of justice thus provided a means for systemizing the whole of Smith's corpus. This broader understanding of Smith's lifework, with much of it devoted to the study of law and government, exposed the "absurdity and inaccuracy" of labeling Smith as a narrow-minded economist.[80]

The bolder claim that Caldwell made was that the *Lectures* placed Adam Smith among the greatest theorists of jurisprudence. Like *The Wealth of Nations*, Smith's *Lectures on Justice, Police, Revenue, and Arms* were astounding in their "breadth of conception." Smith's jurisprudence was not just free-standing positive discourse on public and private law, but also an ambitious attempt to relate the intellectual history of jurisprudence—as traced through its great writers such as Grotius, Hobbes,

78. William Caldwell, "Review of *Lectures on Justice, Police, Revenue, and Arms, Delivered in the University of Glasgow*, by Edwin Cannan and Adam Smith," *Journal of Political Economy* 5, no. 2 (1897), 251.

79. Caldwell did acknowledge that "One can see that Mr. Cannan's own attitude to Adam Smith has gained in depth and breadth since the publication of his *Theories* etc., and cannot but at the same time admire the way in which he keeps within limits his enthusiasm for the master." "Review of *Lectures on Justice, Police, Revenue, and Arms*," 251.

80. Caldwell, "Review of *Lectures on Justice, Police, Revenue, and Arms*," 252–53.

and Pufendorf—to the history of human development. Caldwell argued that one had to place Smith among the many English writers seeking an alternative to social contract theorizing in the shadow of Hobbes.[81] Smith's twin concepts of authority and utility provided an alternative explanation for why men were induced to enter into civil society and submit to authority; political obligation stemmed not from a hypothetical social contract, but from opinion. Authority stemmed from four "natural" sources: superior abilities, age, wealth, or birth. In the early stages of human society, for example, superior ability and age were the primary sources of political authority. Chieftains in a "warlike society" were men of "superior strength," while in more civilized societies leaders were chosen for "superior mental capacity." As human society developed and property was introduced, wealth and birth became new—and increasingly important—sources of authority. Utility, as Smith saw it, was some sense of the common good: "It may sometimes be for my interest to disobey [the government] and to wish government overturned," Smith wrote. "But I am sensible that other men are of a different opinion from me and would not assist me in the enterprize. I therefore submit to it's [sic] decision for the good of the whole."[82] Authority and utility were thus functions of a society's particular historical, social, and material circumstances.

According to Caldwell, this "genetico-historical account of the different systems of political and social authority" was Smith's distinctive contribution to the science of jurisprudence. Smith provided an answer to a perennial question of political theory that on the one hand avoided the abstraction and unfounded premises of Hobbesian state-of-nature

81. It is somewhat odd, however, that Caldwell noted Locke and Blackstone as among the English writers who "sought for principles other than that of a mere contract as the foundation of society." Smith directly refuted Locke in the *Lectures*. For a discussion of Smith's rejection of Locke, see István Hont, "Adam Smith's History of Law and Government as Political Theory," in *Political Judgement. Essays for John Dunn*, ed. Richard Bourke and Raymond Geuss (Cambridge: Cambridge University Press, 2009), 131–71; Paul Sagar, *The Opinion of Mankind: Sociability and the Theory of the State from Hobbes to Smith* (Princeton, NJ: Princeton University Press, 2018); Knud Haakonssen, "The Lectures on Jurisprudence," in *Adam Smith: His Life, Thought, and Legacy*, ed. Hanley, 48–66.

82. *LJ(B)* paragraphs 12–14, 401–402.

theorizing, and on the other hand satisfied "at once our reason and our sense for fact, of the general principles of law and order among men."[83] Smith showed how the state, accordingly, was not the product of a hypothetical social contract with some external moral value of its own, but rather the product of a "natural and rational evolution of human nature." This "genetico-historical" account of law and government paralleled the historical account of the development of forms of industry in Book III of *The Wealth of Nations*, Caldwell observed, proving that *The Wealth of Nations* represented but "one phase of human activity—not the ultimate and only phase" as some economists were wont to make it. History was the missing link between Smith's analysis of political and economic life, and the value of the *Lectures* was that they revealed the expansiveness of Smith's social philosophy. Whereas for someone like Cannan, the *Lectures* were instrumentally valuable because they highlighted the originality of *The Wealth of Nations* and reinforced Smith's economic genius, for Caldwell, the *Lectures* were important for a different reason: they demonstrated that Smith's original intention was not to advance an "uncritical and uncriticised view of human economic or social activity," but rather to provide an alternative way of theorizing political order, morality, and human industry as functions of particular historical and social circumstances.[84]

Caldwell's review of the *Lectures on Justice, Police, Revenue, and Arms* is remarkable for a number of reasons. As a work of Smith interpretation, it worked within the frameworks and categories of analysis available at the time while simultaneously moving beyond them. Caldwell acknowledged the work that the *Lectures* could do in dispelling the myth of Smith as a pale imitation of the physiocrats, an argument that would have satisfied the likes of a budding Marshallian like Cannan. At the same time, Caldwell resisted using the *Lectures* solely as a weapon to censure the "old school" of classical economics, though it is clear that he was more sympathetic to the new generation of historicists. The distinguishing feature of Caldwell's extensive review was its attention to

83. Caldwell, "Review of *Lectures on Justice, Police, Revenue, and Arms*," 257.
84. Caldwell, "Review of *Lectures on Justice, Police, Revenue, and Arms*," 257–58.

Smith's history of jurisprudence on Smith's own terms. Caldwell attempted to reconstruct and assess Smith's theory of jurisprudence within a much longer tradition of theorizing the nature of political obligation and the bases of political legitimacy. This not only antedates the nearest serious examination of the *Lectures* in a review written in 1899 by the Irish economist Charles Francis Bastable, but even anticipates arguments about the centrality and uniqueness of Smith's political theory by nearly a century.[85] American economists had been close followers of overseas intellectual developments, particularly German scholarship since the 1870s, but this did not necessarily imply that they also followed—let alone accepted—foreign commentary on Adam Smith.[86] Caldwell's review thus reveals the interpretive possibilities that Americans created by reading Smith not on account of, but in spite of, the interpretations emerging in England and Germany. Whether Caldwell was uninterested in or simply saw no need for pitting the *Lectures* against *The Theory of Moral Sentiments* and *The Wealth of Nations* in a test of superiority and compatibility, we cannot know for sure. What Caldwell drew forth from the *Lectures* was an understated but prescient argument about Smith's authorial intentions: that in addition to seeking out the principles that governed moral and economic life, Smith sought out a "philosophy of Justice" that would run throughout his science of man. For Caldwell, it was this philosophy of justice that enabled Smith's readers, "better than anything else, to systematize his whole intellectual work."[87]

85. Keith Tribe argues that Bastable's review in *Hermathena* published in 1899 is a rare piece of Anglophone scholarship on Smith during the 1890s that is "distinguished by its attention to German commentary. He [Bastable] opens by noting the recent extension of materials available for an understanding of the origins of political economy, noting the work of James Bonar (on Smith's library), Hollander's work on Ricardo, the new edition of Turgot's *Réflexions*, the Harvard edition of Cantillon, the edition of Quesnay's *Tableau* edited by Henry Higgs under the auspices of the British Economic Association—and the works of Schelle, Hasbach, Oncken, Baurer ands [*sic*] Knies." Tribe then suggests that the other interesting feature of Bastable's review was that it posited a different version of "Das Adam Smith Problem." See Tribe, "'Das Adam Smith Problem' and the Origins of Modern Smith Scholarship," 517.

86. Tribe writes, "The idea that one might profit from attention to foreign commentary on an English, Scottish or Irish writer was quite alien." Tribe, "'Das Adam Smith Problem' and the Origins of Modern Smith Scholarship," 517.

87. Caldwell, "Review of *Lectures on Justice, Police, Revenue, and Arms*," 253.

Caldwell's review was exceptional in its attempt to make sense of Smith's method and intentions. At least among those who had the occasion to read and review their contents, the majority of scholars still approached the Lectures from the vantage point of The Wealth of Nations. That is, their primary concern was what the Lectures could prove—or disprove—in Smith's grand systematization of economic life. Following Caldwell's review, Wilhelm Hasbach published his review of the Lectures in The Political Science Quarterly in December of 1897. Hasbach, whose German publications had been reviewed by E.R.A. Seligman several years prior, offered readers an even deeper investigation of the Lectures and their importance. On his reading, the major discrepancy to be resolved was not between The Theory of Moral Sentiments and The Wealth of Nations, but rather that between the Lectures and The Wealth of Nations. The metaphysical foundations of Smith's "policy of freedom" were virtually absent in the Lectures, with only passing references to leaving things "to their *natural course*," or the "the *natural balance* of industry."[88]

In Hasbach's reading, Smith left the metaphysical foundations of economic freedom under-baked in the Lectures, and he half-heartedly resorted to a principle of "expediency" instead—in effect, demonstrating that the policy of economic freedom was "best calculated to foster the development of wealth." In The Wealth of Nations, however, Smith developed a more thoroughgoing metaphysical theory that made individual labor the original source of the right of property in land.[89] Here is where the physiocrats came back into the picture. According to Hasbach, Smith was so under the influence of the physiocrats' obsession with natural law ("His soul was aglow with the flame that inspired the Physiocrats,") that he gradually loosened his ties to the "historico-realistic conception of law" that animated the Lectures and developed a "more friendly attitude toward Locke and Hutcheson" in their place.[90] In Hasbach's reading, therefore, the physiocrats altered the course of

88. Hasbach, quoting from the Lectures on Justice, Police, Revenue and Arms, 182 and 180. Emphasis is Hasbach's; Hasbach, "Adam Smith's Lectures on Justice, Police, Revenue and Arms," Political Science Quarterly 12, no. 4 (1897), 688. Emphases in original.

89. Hasbach, "Adam Smith's Lectures on Justice, Police, Revenue and Arms," 690, 691.

90. Hasbach, "Adam Smith's Lectures on Justice, Police, Revenue and Arms," 693.

Smith's metaphysical and economic thought; they furnished the Scotsman with a thicker metaphysical theory based in production, which provided the edifice for his overarching theory of economic liberty. But in doing so, they also led Smith away from historical thinking. Had he simply continued the line of thinking in the *Lectures*, Hasbach speculated, Smith's economic system of "natural liberty" might "not have attained its completeness; but he would have preserved the objectivity of his historical judgment and the purity of his economic perception."[91] Hasbach's deflationary reading of the *Lectures* insinuated that a truly historical Smith was perhaps irrecoverable.

The closing years of the nineteenth century opened up new opportunities for reading Adam Smith in America. The unearthing of new material, particularly the *Lectures*, silenced doubts about Smith's originality to some degree, but their discovery certainly did not settle disputes over the nature of Smith's economic thought or his original intentions. If anything, the discovery of the *Lectures* provided even more reason to reengage with Smith, to generate new problematics with the material rather than to use his ideas to resolve old ones. Did Smith occupy a more progressive position than Smithianismus made out? To what extent was Smith's historicist thinking a consistent feature of his jurisprudence and his economic theory? What did these questions and their answers reveal about the relationship between politics, ethics, and economics? New generation scholars like Ely, Seligman, and Caldwell offered different approaches to these questions. In doing so, however, they largely passed over two prominent ways of reading and using Smith in the last quarter of the nineteenth century. On the one hand, there was the Smith of Smithianismus, the totem of the "old" or "classical" school of economics and, on the other hand, the Smith of "The Adam Smith Problem," an uncomfortable mixture of sentiment and reason, ethics and economics that defied reconciliation. Instead of trying to get to the root of the philosophical compatibility between sympathy and self-interest, or dwelling further on the precise points of transmission between Smith and the physiocrats, the new generation of American

91. Hasbach, "Adam Smith's Lectures on Justice, Police, Revenue and Arms," 698.

economists forged new interpretive pathways for reading Smith that were virtually absent in other schools of thought. They saw Smith as a social scientist whose wider concern for humanity underwrote his economic theory, as a champion of the labor movement, and as a theorist who saw the need to locate law and government historically. They reinvented him as the intellectual forerunner of the kind of ethically-and historically-minded political economy that they believed American desperately needed to face the challenges of the new age.

———

In the decades following the discovery of Smith's *Lectures on Jurisprudence*, American scholars continued to reformulate the premises of Das Adam Smith Problem in a number of important works. One reworking of the terms of the Problem came from Albion Woodbury Small's *Adam Smith and Modern Sociology* (1907). Smith was first and foremost a moral philosopher, Small argued, and it was from his moral-philosophical inquiry that the study of wealth evolved as an independent, self-sustaining line of thought. According to Small, it was the mistake of subsequent interpreters—mostly economists—who inferred that the "temporary obscuration of the moral by the economic" implied the "ultimate subordination of the economic to the moral."[92] Smith's historical, moral, and political analysis defied neat categorization into the classical or historical schools, which Small saw as a reason to open a new line of inquiry, rather than foreclose old ones. Modern sociology would take up what Smith had started and what modern economics had left behind.[93]

Small was not alone in engaging in a serious reappraisal of Smith's legacy. The economist Allyn Young, for instance, took up a subject that Albion Small had hinted at in *Adam Smith and Modern Sociology*, namely, the political and social forms that attended the division of labor and the forces of economic growth. Young's seminal essay, "Increasing

92. Albion Woodbury Small, *Adam Smith and Modern Sociology: A Study in the Methodology of the Social Sciences* (Chicago: University of Chicago Press, 1907), 196–98.

93. On Small's role in the broader "sociological turn" in the late nineteenth century, see Sklansky, *The Soul's Economy*, 174–78.

Returns and Economic Progress" (1928), challenged existing notions of capitalist growth and questioned the nature of increasing returns as being the result of exogenous forces, laying the groundwork for what is now known as endogenous growth theory.[94] Between December of 1926 and February of 1927, the University of Chicago hosted a series of lectures commemorating the sesquicentennial of Smith's *The Wealth of Nations*. Though five of the six contributors were economists by profession (Glenn Morrow being the only philosopher), they were for the most part concerned with revising the idea of "Adam Smith as an Economist."[95] Judging from the range of topics covered—laissez-faire, Smith's moral philosophy, Smith's use of history, his labor theory of value, and the reception of *The Wealth of Nations* in France and Germany—scholars had reached a new high point in their understanding of the intertextual relations among Smith's works, their dissemination, and their influence. While some thinkers acknowledged the existence of Das Adam Smith Problem, they also resisted treating it as an irredeemable feature of Smith's thought. Jacob Viner, for instance, called it a "pretty term" in his highly influential essay, "Adam Smith and Laissez-Faire," while philosopher Glen Morrow dismissed the underlying hypothesis of the Problem as "impossible."[96]

The Adam Smith Problem that American scholars were grappling with, therefore, had substantially distanced itself from its original

94. On Allyn Young's interpretation of Smith's division of labor and increasing returns, see Ramesh Chandra, "Adam Smith, Allyn Young, and the Division of Labor," *Journal of Economic Issues* 38, no. 3 (September 2004), 787–805; Giorgio Colacchio, "Reconstructing Allyn A. Young's Theory of Increasing Returns," *Journal of the History of Economic Thought* 27, no. 3 (September 2005), 321–44; Roger J. Sandilands, "Perspectives on Allyn Young in Theories of Endogenous Growth," *Journal of the History of Economic Thought* 22, no. 3 (September 2000), 309–28.

95. Jacob Hollander, "The Dawn of a Science," in *Adam Smith, 1776–1926: Lectures to Commemorate the Sesquicentennial of the Publication of the "Wealth of Nations"* (Chicago, IL: University of Chicago Press, 1928), 1–21 at 20.

96. Viner, "Adam Smith and Laissez-Faire," 201; Glen R. Morrow, "Adam Smith: Moralist and Philosopher," in *Adam Smith, 1776–1926: Lectures to Commemorate the Sesquicentennial of the Publication of the "Wealth of Nations,"* 156–179 at 167.

formulation that was concerned with Smith's intellectual development and the philosophical compatibility of sympathy and self-interest. By the 1920s, American scholars had begun thinking about the Adam Smith Problem in terms of whether and how to critically reclaim Smith's legacy from methodological factionalism and opposing ethical viewpoints. In his essay entitled "Adam Smith and the Currents of History," John Maurice Clark (son of the famed neoclassical economist John Bates Clark) argued that Smith's "genetic economics"—a method that took seriously the real, historical forces that shaped economic doctrine—was the most relevant aspect of Smith's thought and "the most fundamental thing to preserve" from his works. The modern economist who might try to follow in Smith's footsteps, Clark posited, would not be a "doctrinaire democrat" or a socialist, nor would he "despise government" or "idealize it as some all-sufficient social agency." Instead, the true Smithian economist would rise above political divisions by studying the historical persistence and transformation of economic ideas as well as the institutions that expressed them.[97] In his reinterpretation of Das Adam Smith Problem, philosopher Glenn Morrow argued that Smith's economic treatise was hardly an apology for "naked individualism." Rather, Smith's notion of a "natural order" was an ideal of ethical individualism that presupposed the workings of social morality which Smith had stipulated in *The Theory of Moral Sentiments*.[98] Most famously, Jacob Viner, who would become one of the most influential figures of the so-called Chicago School of Economics, demonstrated how different conceptions of natural order in Smith's two major works made room for conflict between private and public interest, and, therefore, admitted a "wide and elastic range of activity for government."[99] Viner's reading of Smith showed how it was possible to forge a path of political economic analysis that avoided the twin vices of American political economy in

97. John Maurice Clark, "Adam Smith and the Currents of History," in *Adam Smith: 1776–1926*, 75.

98. Morrow, "Adam Smith: Moralist and Philosopher," 178.

99. Viner, "Adam Smith and Laissez-Faire," 231. I discuss Viner's essay and his position in the Chicago School in more detail in Chapter 5.

his day and age: the doctrinaire worship and the uncritical condemnation of laissez-faire. Viner wrote,

> In these days of contending schools, each of them with the deep, though momentary, conviction that it, and it alone, knows the one and only path to economic truth, how refreshing it is to return to the *Wealth of Nations* with its eclecticism, its good temper, its common sense, and its willingness to grant that those who saw things differently from itself were only partly wrong.[100]

It had been only fifty years since the lavish, free-trade banquet celebrated the centenary of *The Wealth of Nations* at Delmonico's, but the resulting image of Smith at the sesquicentennial could not have been more different. The Smith at Delmonico's had been simplified and sloganized, his ideas taken as eternal political commandments in the name of free trade. But the Smith that emerged by the time of the sesquicentennial was knotty, multidimensional, and complex. The later image was the culmination of continual attempts to make sense of the profound economic and social changes of the previous half century, and it was the product of a dynamic relationship between Smith's readers and Smith's ideas. For someone like Richard T. Ely, the diversity of Smith's moral and political commitments combined with his recognizable intellectual authority served as a holding pen for Ely's own progressive political commitments. That Smith saw labor as the sole source of value, for example, was evidence that even his economic theory was more than a collection of scientific axioms; it was also a set of ethical commitments aligned with mass labor movements. At the same time, discoveries about Smith's life and ideas, and especially the discovery of the *Lectures on Jurisprudence*, provided new opportunities to reflect on the significance of Smith in history, as well as the significance of history on Smith. Smith could be studied as a historical object and placed in a great line of predecessors and successors, but he could also be treated as a live interlocutor within contemporary debates over the importance of history for economic analysis. Smith's importance lay in the fact that he

---

100. Viner, "Adam Smith and Laissez-Faire," 232.

was a bottomless reservoir for drawing out questions—questions whose answers provided the method, content, or pattern of thinking that belonged to his contemporary reader.

These thinkers experienced an age of extremes, ideological and methodological alike. Some, like Ely, even suffered the consequences of activating those ideas in the public sphere. In searching for a corrective to the excesses of the time, they turned back to a time-worn, but somewhat unexpected source: Adam Smith. They found in Smith's methodological eclecticism a powerful counterpoint to the exclusivity of both the "old" and "new" schools of economics. If there was anything like a scholarly consensus around Smith, it was loose at best, but it was held together by shared interest in using Smith to illuminate the ethical and economic possibilities that existed between complete laissez-faire on the one hand and socialism on the other. The cataclysmic events of the coming years, however, all but shattered the prospects for its survival.

5

Economics Must Be
Political Economy

THREE YEARS after the Wealth of Nations Sesquicentennial the U.S. stock market crashed, and what followed was one of the worst economic collapses in American history. By 1930, about 4 million workers were unemployed—roughly eight percent of the labor force. By 1933, when the Great Depression was at its worst, nearly a quarter of the labor force was unemployed. More than 5,000 banks had closed; customers saw their lifetime's worth of savings vanish. During the four-year period of the Depression, the value of exports and imports plummeted almost seventy percent, and gross national product fell some thirty percent. Behind these impersonal statistics were the personal stories of dislocation and despair, of families seeking shelter in shantytowns, of workers migrating across vast drought-stricken plains desperately seeking opportunity.

The Depression fundamentally altered economic and political thinking. Who or what was responsible for the crash? Did the government have a responsibility to guarantee employment or to correct the distortions in market activity? Was the reign of free markets over? Economists from different intellectual pedigrees all came under fire for failing to predict the plummeting prices and skyrocketing unemployment of the era, and beliefs about the autonomous workings of the market system to correct itself were seriously challenged. Policy makers and academic economists scrambled to expand social welfare programs; they mounted new arguments in favor of raising tariffs; and they theorized anew the abstract, general principles by which the national economy could be prudently managed.[1] The rise of the New Deal order in the United States was thus accompanied by a loose academic consensus that markets could function only with expert oversight, all but confirming John Maynard Keynes's predictions that the end of laissez-faire was nigh. Pushed to the margins of the economics profession, market advocates were forced to reconsider assumptions about market processes and to reimagine the political and social possibilities of their time. As they did, they transformed Adam Smith into the unmistakable face of free market politics in America.

This chapter and Chapter 6 investigate the history of that transformation. The chapters show how and why free-market advocates in and around the so-called "Chicago School" of economics repeatedly turned to Smith and placed his ideas at the center of their ideological battles over the content and future of liberalism from the Great Depression onward.[2] Key figures—Frank Knight, Jacob Viner, Friedrich Hayek, George Stigler, and Milton Friedman—reimagined Smith as the original author of the price mechanism in order to unify and defend the substantive propositions of economics that had come under assault after the Depression: that free markets, under specific conditions, could be self-regulating and self-stabilizing; and that the freedom to pursue one's rational self-interest underpinned the automaticity of markets. Smith and Smithian concepts were thus reconceptualized in the language

1. In the words of David Ciepley, the Great Depression "completely wiped out the intellectual respectability of laissez-faire." David Ciepley, *Liberalism in the Shadow of Totalitarianism* (Cambridge, MA: Harvard University Press, 2007), 86; Burgin, *The Great Persuasion*, 4–5, 8–9, 14–15.

2. There is a large body of scholarship surrounding the chronology, evolution, and consistency of the "Chicago School." For general introductions, see Ross B. Emmett, ed., *The Chicago Tradition in Economics 1892–1945* (London: Routledge, 2001); Ross B. Emmett, *Frank Knight and the Chicago School in American Economics* (London: Routledge, 2009); Emmett, *The Elgar Companion to the Chicago School of Economics* (Cheltenham: Elgar, 2012); Johan Van Overtveldt, *The Chicago School: How the University of Chicago Assembled the Thinkers Who Revolutionized Economics and Business* (Chicago, IL: Agate, 2007). On the origins of the Chicago School developing alongside transnational intellectual networks like the Mont Pèlerin Society, see Burgin, *The Great Persuasion*; Philip Mirowski and Dieter Plehwe, *The Road from Mont Pèlerin: The Making of the Neoliberal Thought Collective* (Cambridge, MA.: Harvard University Press, 2009).

of twentieth-century price theory. "Self-interest" and "the invisible hand" became synonymous with not only the market itself, but also with an entire way of thinking about society as being organized through the natural, automatic, and self-generating actions of individual economic actors.

Yet this image of Smith was not monolithic, nor did it emerge all at once.[3] Different generations' interpretations of Smith were linked to diverse views about the scope of economic science and varying degrees of market advocacy. Early Chicago figures such as Frank H. Knight and Jacob Viner, for instance, contributed to an interpretive framework for reading Smith as an early theorist of price and a cautious defender of free markets who left substantial room for state intervention. This interpretation underwrote later uses of Smith and served as an important methodological link across different generations of thinkers. Moreover, the rise of the Chicago School as an intellectual epicenter of market advocacy in the United States was but one instance of a much wider transnational movement to revive, codify, and disseminate principles of classical liberalism that challenged the postwar consensus around socialism and state planning.[4] Concomitant with the founding of the Mont Pèlerin Society in 1947 and the conception of the Chicago Free Market Study in the early 1940s, thinkers on the edges of Chicago's economics department, such as Friedrich Hayek, Henry Simons, and Aaron Director, coalesced around economic and political precepts that appealed to a burgeoning Chicago sensibility and a nascent identity as defenders of free markets. In doing so, these scholars created the intellectual conditions for inventing and propounding one of the most prominent and enduring interpretations of Smith both within the economics profession and among the broader American public, that is, Smith as a free-market economist. Economists of the later generation—notably George Stigler and Milton Friedman—inherited the essence of the earlier Smith, but they also streamlined their image of Smith to be more in line with the ascendancy of rational choice theory and strident

3. Medema, "Adam Smith and the Chicago School."
4. Burgin, *The Great Persuasion*; Mirowski and Plehwe, *The Road from Mont Pèlerin*.

market advocacy. More than any other Chicago thinker, Friedman meshed scientific insights with political arguments in an ideologically consistent picture of Smith—one which Friedman propagated within his own political philosophy and policy recommendations from the 1960s on.

The story of the Chicago School is one of unexpected triumph and has been told in a number of important historical works.[5] Beyond its members' influence in the field of economics and in public policy, the Chicago School left an indelible mark on the interpretation, reception, and legacy of Adam Smith's ideas. Among Smith scholars, there is a general consensus that the Chicago School was culpable for propagating a version of Smith that is economistic at best, an outright misunderstanding at worst. This "Chicago Smith," in the words of Jerry Evensky, "uses *homo economicus* as the premise for analysis of human behavior and for modeling the human condition," and in turn, "has become the accepted identity of Adam Smith among most modern economists."[6] Chicago Smith, in other words, is an economist who believes in the social productiveness of self-interest alone, and whose master metaphor of the "invisible hand" illustrates how free markets—not government—protect and promote individual freedom. The enthusiasm with which some of Chicago's most illustrious figures touted this version of Smith is also the subject of much debate. Critics have found Chicago Nobel laureate George Stigler especially guilty for an infamous line he penned in 1971—that *The Wealth of Nations* was a "stupendous palace erected upon the granite of self-interest."[7] Stigler was by no means alone in claiming inheritance to Smith's authority in order to support a belief in the rationality of the profit motive, but his crime is often seen as

5. For example, Emmett, *The Chicago Tradition in Economics 1892–1945*; Burgin, *The Great Persuasion*; Emmett, *The Elgar Companion to the Chicago School of Economics*; Robert Van Horn, Philip Mirowski, and Thomas A Stapleford, eds., *Building Chicago Economics: New Perspectives on the History of America's Most Powerful Economics Program* (Cambridge: Cambridge University Press, 2011); Van Overtveldt, *The Chicago School.*

6. Jerry Evensky, "'Chicago Smith' versus 'Kirkaldy Smith,'" *History of Political Economy* 37, no. 2 (2005), 198.

7. George J. Stigler, "Smith's Travels on the Ship of State," *History of Political Economy* 3, no. 2 (September 1971), 265.

symbolic of a larger intellectual tide.[8] The philosopher Samuel Fleischacker wrote, "Thus George Stigler, and thus, with minor qualifications here and there, [emerge] two centuries of misinterpretations of
Adam Smith, especially by economists."[9]

Regardless as to the truth of the claim, many scholars have treated
the Chicago School's invention of the myth of Adam Smith as an
agreed-upon fact. Repudiating interpretations of Smith "as if he were a
co-conspirator of Chicago-style thinking" and attempting to "free [him]
from a 'reputation' as a Chicago-style economics professor *avant la
lettre*," continues to fuel much of contemporary Smith scholarship.[10]
But, as most agreed-upon facts go, this one merits further attention.
Adam Smith provides one lens through which we can understand the
processes of growth, contestation, and change within a particular institution and intellectual network. Moreover, given that the Chicago
School is often treated as one of the progenitors of what is now known
as postwar neoliberalism, we ought to understand how and why Chicago resuscitated the economic tenets of classical liberalism in the way
that they did, and what the consequences of those choices were—not
just for subsequent interpretations of Smith, but also for twentieth-
century political and economic thought more generally.[11]

8. Smith scholars who target this specific line include Samuel Fleischacker, *On Adam Smith's
Wealth of Nations: A Philosophical Companion* (Princeton, NJ: Princeton University Press,
2004), 84; Amartya Sen, "Uses and Abuses of Adam Smith," *History of Political Economy* 43, no. 2
(2011), 257–71; Dennis C. Rasmussen, "Adam Smith on What Is Wrong with Economic Inequality," *American Political Science Review* 110, no. 2 (2016), 342–52. See also Amartya Sen, "The
Contemporary Relevance of Adam Smith," in *The Oxford Handbook of Adam Smith*, ed. Christopher J. Berry et al. (Oxford: Oxford University Press, 2013), 581–91; Craig Smith, "Adam Smith
and the New Right," in *The Oxford Handbook of Adam Smith*, ed. Berry et al. 539–558.

9. Fleischacker, *On Adam Smith's Wealth of Nations*, 84.

10. Lisa Herzog, *Inventing the Market: Smith, Hegel, and Political Theory* (Oxford: Oxford
University Press, 2013), 6; Hont, *Jealousy of Trade*, 100.

11. The term "neoliberal" remains controversial and often tends to obfuscate and offend more
than clarify. The version of "neoliberalism" I am concerned with is best characterized in the
terms of Philip Mirowski and Dieter Plehwe as a "historical thought collective" that emerged
sometime in the late 1930s and early 1940s, though its origins are diverse (such as the famous
Lippman Colloquium of 1938 and the first meeting of the Mont Pèlerin Society in 1947). For
Mirowski and Plehwe, links to the Mont Pèlerin Society are a litmus test for whether a member

To be sure, the Chicago School was neither unprecedented nor alone in the way they taught, read, and reimagined Smith in the period following the Great Depression. Smith's ideas were featured prominently as the inspiration, if not the theoretical basis, for some of the most important contributions to mainstream economics and social philosophy concurrent with the rise of the Chicago School. Walter Lippman's *An Inquiry into the Principles of the Good Society*, for example, portrayed Smith as a prophet of liberalism—a liberalism that sought "to re-form the social order to meet the needs and fulfill the promise of a mode of production based on the division of labor."[12] First published in 1937, Lippman's *The Good Society* was met with popular success and quickly established Lippman's reputation as one of the foremost spokesmen for free markets as well as a leader of the charge against collectivism.[13] It also reinforced the idea that contemporary liberal economists were the inheritors of a classical liberal tradition that had

---

or a group falls within the realm of "neoliberal thought." However, I would underscore one of their central points, which is that neoliberalism is "anything but a '*pensée unique*,'" but instead draws on various strands of social, political, and economic thought that coexisted in the postwar period—including but not limited to Chicago Price Theory, German ordoliberalism, and Austrian economics. Though "flexible in its intellectual commitments," above all, as the neologism suggests, neoliberalism was "a quest for alternative intellectual resources to revive a moribund political project [i.e., liberalism]." Dieter Plehwe, "Introduction," in Mirowski and Plehwe, *The Road from Mont Pèlerin*, 1–42 at 15. Intellectual histories of neoliberalism abound. Angus Burgin's *The Great Persuasion* is a foundational intellectual history centered on the Mont Pèlerin and Milton Friedman. Related is Jones, *Masters of the Universe*; compared to Burgin, Jones ventures more into policy-oriented, think tank territory. Other major intellectual histories of neoliberalism include Taylor C. Boas and Jordan Gans-Morse, "Neoliberalism: From New Liberal Philosophy to Anti-Liberal Slogan," *Studies in Comparative International Development* 44, no. 2 (June 2009), 137–61; Gary Gerstle, "The Rise and Fall of the Neoliberal Order," *Transactions of the Royal Historical Society* 28 (2018), 241–64; David Harvey, *A Brief History of Neoliberalism* (Oxford: Oxford University Press, 2007); Niklas Olsen, *The Sovereign Consumer: A New Intellectual History of Neoliberalism*, Consumption and Public Life (Cham, Switzerland: Palgrave Macmillan, 2019); Quinn Slobodian, *Globalists: The End of Empire and the Birth of Neoliberalism* (Cambridge, MA: Harvard University Press, 2018). For a helpful overview of the historiography of neoliberalism, see Angus Burgin, "The Neoliberal Turn," (forthcoming).

12. Walter Lippmann, *The Good Society* (New York, NY: Grosset & Dunlap, 1936), 182.

13. Burgin, *The Great Persuasion*, 55.

been lost.[14] Twenty years later, two major works by philosophers continued to tackle the meaning of Smithian liberalism. In his *Polity and Economy* (1957), political philosopher Joseph Cropsey argued that Smith's defense of "liberal capitalism" and his rejection of a "virtuous society" were grounded in a belief that freedom from absolute civil and spiritual authority, rather than the attainment of moral excellence, were the true ends of society.[15] One year later, the German-Jewish philosopher Hannah Arendt's *The Human Condition* (1958) drew on a familiar image of Smith as a pivotal, if not tragic, figure who legitimized the expansion of the market economy, replacing the creative potential of *homo faber* with the isolated, alienated, productivity-seeking *animal laborans*.[16] Together, these different engagements with Smith's ideas capture the wider and enduring appeal of Smith's thought amidst the early twentieth century's "crisis of man."[17] For a generation of thinkers who witnessed the rise of Nazi Germany, the Second World War, and the rise of the Soviet Union, Smith's works offered responses to concerns about the demise of Western civilization and the changing of man's essential nature. Scholars questioned whether the philosophical premises of Smith's economic thought—self-love, value in labor, the propensity to exchange—were forces that might redeem or destroy liberal society.

The Chicago School was no less concerned about the prospects of liberal capitalist society, but they projected a degree of certainty about

14. For further discussion of Lippmann in relation to the Chicago School and post-Depression market advocacy, see Burgin, *The Great Persuasion*, chap. 2. For interesting discussions of Lippmann's brand of liberalism, see Ben Jackson, "Freedom, the Common Good, and the Rule of Law: Lippmann and Hayek on Economic Planning," *Journal of the History of Ideas* 73, no. 1 (2012), 47–68; Eric Schliesser, "Walter Lippmann: The Prophet of Liberalism and the Road Not Taken," *The Journal of Contextual Economics* 139 (2019), 349–64.

15. Joseph Cropsey, *Polity and Economy* (The Hague: Martinus Nijhoff, 1957).

16. Hannah Arendt, *The Human Condition, Second Edition* (Chicago, IL: The University of Chicago Press, 1958), 209–10. Arendt made much of Smith's distinction between "productive" and "unproductive" labor, arguing that Smith had "great contempt" for the kind of "menial service" and "performance-oriented" professions that ancient thinkers thought where the "highest and greatest activities." Arendt, *The Human Condition*, 207.

17. Mark Greif, *The Age of the Crisis of Man* (Princeton, NJ: Princeton University Press, 2015).

Smith's ideas that few others held at the time. Across their writings and teachings, one can glean a sense of an "apparently complete assurance that no other estimates of Adam Smith could ever be or would ever be made," to borrow a phrase from Richard Teichgraeber. The Chicago School, especially the later generation, looms so large in Smith's reception in America because its members self-consciously styled themselves as the bearers of Smith's mantle. Recovering Smith as his Chicago readers encountered him, then, reveals not only why one particular school of thought was so drawn to Smith, but also how and why their reinvention of Smith inevitably came to overwhelm other interpretations of the same thinker and texts.[18] What is more, the Chicago School's ideological uses of Smith's ideas often depended on a tenuous division between Smith's understanding of economics and his politics. By framing Smith's contribution and legacy in the pure, objective language of economics, his Chicago exponents constructed the social-scientific bases of their political outlook which privileged free enterprise over central planning, and market rationality over moral reasoning. Doing so, however, required that Smith's own approach to politics and moral philosophy be stripped away, or at least intentionally ignored.

Thus, what I call the "Chicago Smith Problem" was born. If the Chicago Smith embodied the definitive vocabulary of self-interest and the invisible hand of the market, the Chicago Smith *Problem* represents a set of thorny questions surrounding the political implications of Smith's economic analysis: how could Smith have "failed" to extend his insights in economic analysis into the realm of the political? Is government the antithesis of the market? And are politics and economics categorically distinct and oppositional spheres of human activity? Like Das Adam Smith Problem, the Chicago Smith Problem would eventually become an object of historical study, stimulating a seemingly endless stream of arguments about the significance and coherence of Smith's works writ large. And, like Das Adam Smith Problem, the Chicago Smith Problem emerged and evolved out of an historical period in

18. Teichgraeber III, "Adam Smith and Tradition: The Wealth of Nations before Malthus," 92.

which the reigning scientific and normative justifications for free markets no longer seemed tenable.

———

At the turn of the twentieth century, the economics profession bore the scars of multiple battles—from the trials that tested the limits of academic freedom, to the methodological controversies over what constituted scientific and social progress. Though American institutionalism and English marginalism had emerged as the dominant approaches to the social sciences, economists were heterogeneous in their methodological dispositions, research agendas, and policy recommendations. Plurality defined the profession. But the Depression was a shock to the system, and economists from all backgrounds began loosely coalescing around the idea that a completely unregulated economy was inadequate, and that some degree of reform-minded "planning" was necessary to overcome the problems of the social and economic order. "Planners" encompassed a wide range of forward-thinking people, everyone from those who wanted to scientifically manage business and industries to those who wanted to establish organizations to oversee production and pricing. In 1936, John Maynard Keynes's *General Theory of Employment, Interest, and Money* became the theoretical springboard for a scientific approach to planning in which the intervention of government was central to supplying investment and guaranteeing employment. Mushrooming government agencies such as the National Resources Planning Board, the US Chamber of Commerce, and the numerous programs of the New Deal all eagerly sought out planners to keep up with their initiatives. The real questions that divided economists, though, were about how *much* planning was necessary and *who* would do the planning.[19]

19. Ross, *The Origins of American Social Science*, chap. 6; Mary S. Morgan and Malcom Rutherford, "American Economics: The Character of the Transformation," in *From Interwar Pluralism to Postwar Neoclassism*, ed. Mary S. Morgan and Malcolm Rutherford (Durham, NC: Duke University Press, 1998), 2–4; Marcia L. Balisciano, "Hope for America: American Notions of Economic Planning between Pluralism and Neoclassicism, 1930–1950," *History of Political Economy 30 (supplement)*, 1998, 153–78. As Balisciano notes, "In this climate [after the Great

Debates about planning intensified against the backdrop of a second crisis: the Cold War. By the 1950s, economists and politicians began viewing the American economy and the newly erected welfare state in the shadow of European totalitarianism. Many such thinkers began to believe that the philosophical foundations of markets and democracy had to be fortified against the rising tides of communism and socialist planning. Economists who had the slightest inclinations towards pro-socialist projects were ostracized. Champions of Keynes's prescriptions faced increased suspicion as his macroeconomic policies increasingly looked dangerously close to a defense for a strong state. Amidst these warring economic ideologies, economists narrowed their methods and turned towards mathematics as their language of neutrality. This turn to mathematics was both a "self-defensive technocratic approach" as well as a demand from institutions seeking greater political correct-ness and scientific objectivity during this tense period.[20] Even Keynes-ians, once seen as near-heretics, could offer their propositions in a professionally-neutral, seemingly objective way by centering them on mathematics. The Cold War milieu thus enabled and reinforced the syn-thesis between Keynesian macroeconomic theory on the one hand, and the neoclassical assumptions about market foundations on the other; what emerged was a consensus about economics as a naturalistic social science. With its "scientific outlook, technical language, and political counsel," economics fashioned new tools to distance itself from its past

---

Depression], planning developed as a flexible and fluid concept. Forward actions of all kinds were proposed beneath the banner of planning in order, it was hoped, to define, shape, and ultimately improve economic outcomes. . . . Planning was a mirror for the pluralism of Ameri-can society in the 1930s and thus defied precise definition. As such, it was also a mirror for the pluralism of American economics and American economists during those years." Balisciano, "Hope for America," 155.

   20. This is obviously a very simplistic account of the impact of the Cold War on academic economics. For a more complete introduction to the subject of postwar neoclassicism, see Morgan and Rutherford, "American Economics: The Character of the Transformation," 14–17. See also Crauford D. Goodwin, "The Patrons of Economics in a Time of Transforma-tion," in *From Interwar Pluralism to Postwar Liberalism*, 53–81; Balisciano, "Hope for America."

and its contentious politics, thereby making possible new ways of analyzing the present and viewing the future.[21]

Thus, in the Anglo-American context, the intellectual milieu from the post-Depression era through the postwar period was overwhelmingly hostile to market sympathizers. Academics who advocated free markets and opposed government intervention clustered around just a few key institutions and were largely marginalized, but they actively worked to expand their intellectual network within the profession. On one side of the Atlantic was the London School of Economics (LSE). Leading figures such as Lionel Robbins and Edwin Canaan—the same Canaan who edited the *Lectures on Jurisprudence* and the then-standard edition of *The Wealth of Nations*—as well as the addition of Friedrich Hayek in 1931, turned the LSE into an academic incubator for the intellectual counterattack to Keynes. Robbins, Cannan, and Hayek brought together a diversity of intellectual traditions, but what united them was a shared antipathy towards Keynesian economic policies—from public works programs to modest tariffs to credit expansion—as well as a belief that laissez-faire economics could be soundly reconstructed.[22] On the other side of the Atlantic was the LSE's American counterpart: the University of Chicago.

In the first decades of the University of Chicago's existence, its economists were much less a unified "school" than a "mixed bag" of personalities and thinkers; however, beginning in the 1930s, the scholars self-consciously began developing a new identity.[23] They began cultivating a reputation as the most vocal opponents to New Deal economic policies as well as the modes of analysis which supported them—namely, institutional, historical, and Keynesian economics. Pioneering economists such as Jacob Viner and Frank Knight began constructing an economic method—price theory—that went against the grain of institutionalism, historicism, and Keynesianism and would eventually become the hallmark of their department. Both Viner and Knight had visited the LSE

21. Ross, *The Origins of American Social Science*, 468.

22. On the development of the LSE as an unlikely home for conservative, anti-Keynesian economics, see Burgin, *The Great Persuasion*, esp. 12–32.

23. Van Overtveldt, *The Chicago School*, 25–28; Melvin W. Reder, "Chicago Economics: Permanence and Change," *Journal of Economic Literature* 20, no. 1 (March 1982), 2–3.

in the 1930s, and Knight became close to Friedrich Hayek, who was later appointed in the Committee on Social Thought at Chicago. Those relationships started to produce results in the 1940s when Chicago's economics became associated with a broader movement to reconceptualize the virtues of free markets on both scientific and philosophical grounds.

The method and substance that defined Chicago Price Theory evolved over many years, but its central tenet is that prices transmit information about what consumers want to buy and what producers want to sell; prices also reveal the incentives on which people act. Analysis of prices—what determines them, what causes them to change—informs the baseline understanding of individual behavior and allocation in a competitive economy. Price theory, therefore, can be differentiated from both game theory and general equilibrium analysis in terms of the scale of its market context. On one end of the spectrum, game theory examines the outcomes of interactions between a small number of players; at the other end, general equilibrium tries to explain how all markets might equilibrate under certain special conditions. Price theory attempts to split the difference by reducing high-dimensional, complex interactions to simpler models, but does so with an eye towards explaining larger, aggregate outcomes.[24]

24. On the evolution of Chicago Price Theory, see Glen Weyl, "Price Theory," *Journal of Economic Literature*, Forthcoming, available at https://ssrn.com/abstract=2444233. See also Steven G. Medema, "Chicago Price Theory and Chicago Law and Economics: A Tale of Two Transitions," in *Building Chicago Economics: New Perspectives on the History of America's Most Powerful Economics Program*, eds. Robert Van Horn, Philip Mirowski, and Thomas A Stapleford, (Cambridge: Cambridge University Press, 2011) 151–79; Daniel Hammond, "The Development of Post-War Chicago Price Theory," in *The Elgar Companion to the Chicago School of Economics*, ed. Ross B. Emmett (Cheltenham: Elgar, 2010), 7–24. My attempt at explaining price theory here is cobbled together from "standard" definitions of price theory from Chicago economists themselves, as well as contemporary interpretations offered by self-proclaimed price theory economists such as Glen Weyl and Kevin Murphy. Milton Friedman's textbook on price theory describes the price mechanism in pieces: "Prices serve as guideposts to where resources are wanted most, and, in addition, prices provide the incentive for people to follow these guideposts. The use of factor prices to distribute the product makes it possible for other prices, namely product prices, to serve the functions of fixing standards and organizing production," and "Prices . . . transmit information, they provide an incentive to users of resources to be

Under the tutelage of Knight and Viner, Chicago's Price Theory courses in the 1930s became known as a hazing ritual of sorts, whereby scientists were trained and young minds initiated into a distinguished lineage.[25] The two scholars' specific emphases differed, as did their personalities. Viner's course was much more neoclassical in the English tradition, or, as one economic historian described it, "practically a walking tour of [Alfred] Marshall's *Principles* [of economics]."[26] Viner was known to cold-call and fail a large percentage of students, earning him a reputation for being "superb because he was extremely nasty."[27] Knight, on the other hand, probed into more philosophical and social territory and was prone to rambling. "We often remarked that two-thirds of his students never got anything from him, and the rest never got anything out of two-thirds of his remarks, but that remaining one-third of one-third [*sic*] was well worth the price of admission," recalled Rose Friedman (née Director).[28] Differences aside, both Knight and Viner adopted a deductive approach, and both emphasized economics' scientific theories as "tendency statements," as opposed to inviolable laws. In providing a "descriptive, objective explanation of the way in which prices come to be what they are," as Viner put it, both teachers drew on an example from Adam Smith's *The Wealth of Nations*, but not

guided by this information, and they provide an incentive to owners of resources to follow this information." Milton Friedman, *Price Theory* (New York, NY: Hawthorne, 1962), 9–10. Glen Weyl offers the following contemporary definition: price theory is "analysis that attempts to simplify a rich (high-dimensional heterogeneity, many agent, dynamics, etc.) and often incompletely specified model for the purposes of answering a simple (scalar or unidimensional) allocative question." Weyl, "Price Theory," 1.

25. Douglas A. Irwin and Steven G. Medema, eds., *Jacob Viner: Lectures in Economics 301* (New Brunswick, NJ: Transaction Publishers, 2013), 2.

26. Medema, "Chicago Price Theory and Chicago Law and Economics," 154.

27. Quoted in Van Overtveldt, *The Chicago School*, 80–81. Stories abound of Viner's imposing and intimidating style. Paul Samuelson recalled how "Viner added one new ingredient [to the Socratic method]: terror. George Stigler recalled how one poor student was victimized in front of the class when Viner asked him a question, Viner turned red and said, 'Mr. X, you do not belong in this class.'" George J. Stigler, *Memoirs of an Unregulated Economist* (New York, NY: Basic Books, 1988), 19–21.

28. Milton Friedman and Rose Friedman, *Two Lucky People: Memoirs* (Chicago, IL: University of Chicago Press, 1998), 38.

to prove Smith's correctness.[29] Instead, they chose a classic example from *The Wealth of Nations* because it illustrated Smith's misunderstanding of a core economic insight, which paved the way for the Chicago Price Theory's corrective.

The example in question is known as the "deer-beaver exchange" from Smith's *The Wealth of Nations* Book I Chapter VI, and it appears in Jacob Viner's 1930 lectures in Economics 301, in numerous iterations of Knight's version of Economics 301, in his related courses between 1930 and 1939, and in Knight's earlier article on "A Suggestion for Simplifying the Statement of the General Theory of Price" published in 1928. In Smith's original version, the cost of the deer is framed in terms of the number of beavers that could be caught in the same amount of time. If it takes twice as much labor to kill a beaver than it does a deer, for example, "one beaver should naturally exchange for, or be worth, two deer."[30] In modern terminology, this was a classic illustration of the doctrine of opportunity cost or cost-of-production theory—that the exchange value of a good depended on how much it cost (in terms of labor) to produce—but it was one with which neither Viner nor Knight were content.[31]

Smith's opportunity cost doctrine fell victim to "circular reasoning," according to Viner.[32] For Knight, Smith's primitive labor value theory was simply inadequate. "Go to Adam Smith, Chapter 6," one student noted in Knight's lecture, "and put in the distribution that is implied with the value theory step by step." Knight effectively walked students through Smith's variations on value-determination stemming from the initial deer-beaver exchange in which capital and land are not significant factors. "Now suppose that the land is fixed and significant," Knight instructed. "The land will begin to get a rent. What kind of cost curve

29. Jacob Viner, Lecture on June 17, 1930 in Economics 301, printed in Irwin and Medema, *Jacob Viner: Lectures in Economics 301*, 19.

30. *WN*, I.vi.1, 65.

31. One can reasonably argue that this is not a novel reading or use of Smith's example from *The Wealth of Nations*. In fact, Mark Blaug's monumental *Economic Theory in Retrospect* contains several pages of analysis centered on this "simple model in which only one factor of production is used to produce commodities." Mark Blaug, *Economic Theory in Retrospect*, 4th ed. (Cambridge: Cambridge University Press, 1985), 38–39.

32. Irwin and Medema, *Jacob Viner: Lectures in Economics 301*, 60.

will you get as soon as the land comes in? Can you say the two deer will necessarily exchange for one beaver regardless of the number produced? No."[33] From student notes, one often encounters Knight's Smith as a quaint and inconsistent thinker. Adam Smith's idea about the labor theory of value "has no historical or archaeological significance," according to Knight.[34] On Book I Chapter 11 ("Of the Produce of Land which always affords Rent"), Knight commented that Smith "gives Ricardian theory completely . . . forgetting all he said in Bk. I ch. 7," and by the time readers reached Book II Chapter 3 on the accumulation of capital, Smith "very definitely goes wrong, tho [sic] he started out right in Bk II ch. 11."[35]

This picture of Smith as an error-prone thinker was important for instructional purposes. Knight tied the fate of economics to the early errors of Smith. In Knight's view, David Ricardo, for example, adopted a labor theory of value and "followed the wrong one of two main lines of Smith."[36] The other (presumably correct line) was Book I Chapter VII of *The Wealth of Nations*, in which Smith stated something close to a general statement of equilibrium.[37] Smith was an economist who was "on verge of recognizing the equalization principle of Distribution," as one student noted in Knight's lectures on the History of Economic Thought.[38] Thus, showing how Smith's economic principles reached far, but ultimately fell short, enabled teachers like Knight and Viner to

33. Homer Jones, student notes. Econ 301: History of Economic Thought (Winter 1934). Frank Knight Papers, Box 8 Folder 10. Special Collections Research Center (SCRC) University of Chicago.

34. Student notes (unnamed). Econ 301: Price and Distribution Theory (Summer 1938). Frank Knight Papers, Box 8 Folder 18. SCRC, University of Chicago.

35. Student notes dated April 6, 1933 (unnamed). Econ 304: Economic Theory and Social Policy (Spring 1933). Frank Knight Papers, Box 8 Folder 4. SCRC, University of Chicago.

36. Student notes dated April 6, 1933 (unnamed). Econ 304: Economic Theory and Social Policy (Spring 1933). Frank Knight Papers, Box 8 Folder 4. SCRC, University of Chicago.

37. "The market price of every particular commodity is regulated by the proportion between the quantity which is actually brought to market, and the demand of those who are willing to pay the natural price of the commodity, or the whole value of the rent, labour, and profit, which must be paid in order to bring it thither. *WN* I.vii.8, 73.

38. Homer Jones, student notes. Econ 301: History of Economic Thought (Winter 1934). Frank Knight Papers, Box 8 Folder 10.

demonstrate how modern economists improved the science that Smith had founded.

This "textbook version" of Adam Smith is not unlike many versions of Smith in late-nineteenth century political economy. Smith was an artefact of political economy's past, and the purpose of studying the past was not to explain the "terms of the conditions existing at the time of [a theory's] ascendancy," as Knight put it, but rather to discover the economic truths.[39] The discovery of these economic truths—scientific, universal laws of human behavior—demanded an ahistorical perspective. Milton Friedman, one of Knight's students in the 1930s, wrote in an essay for Knight's class in 1933,

> I, for one, see little point in the history that aims solely to explain a theory in terms of the conditions existing at the time of its ascendancy. If there be any such a thing as truth, how a theory arose has little to do with the truth of it. And to me the primary interest of the economist is to find out the truth. Thus it is with the study of the labor theory of value.[40]

Only through this lens of scientific ahistoricism was it possible to assess the validity of economic theories. According to Friedman, Smith's labor theory of value was not just wrong; it was useless for understanding an "acceptable theory" of value.[41]

Friedman's early ruminations on Smith thus represent one way in which Chicago economists puzzled through the relationship between Smith's moral philosophy and his economics in the early twentieth century. Someone like Jacob Viner saw Smith's economics as an improvement on his moral philosophy whereas Friedman argued that Smith's economics, at least through the lens of price theory, was worsened precisely because of "the mixture in [Smith's] character of the moral

39. Student notes dated April 6, 1933 (unnamed). Economics 304: Economic Theory and Social Policy. Frank Knight papers, Box 8, Folder 4, SCRC, University of Chicago.

40. Milton Friedman, essay on "Labor Theory of Value in the Classical School" for Econ 302. 1933. Milton Friedman Papers, Box 5.13. Hoover Institution Archives, Stanford University.

41. Milton Friedman, essay on "Labor Theory of Value in the Classical School" for Econ 302. 1933. Milton Friedman Papers, Box 5.13. Hoover Institution Archives, Stanford University.

philosopher and the practical man." Friedman saw this most clearly in Smith's inability to reconcile the diamond-water paradox: that while water was one of the most useful substances, it purchased "scarce any thing;" diamonds, on the other hand, had little value in use but could exchange for many other goods.[42] What led Smith to this conclusion, according to Friedman, was that Smith's "mind [was] not free from ethical principles." Smith had been making a moral judgement on diamonds; this clouded his vision, and, as a consequence, Smith failed to see how the true value of a good was not in the labor it cost to produce it, but rather in its ability to satisfy a want. For Smith's economics to be true—or even useful—required a clear separation not just from his own moral philosophy, but also from external ethical judgments more generally.

The deer-beaver problem and the diamond-water paradox are clear examples of how Chicago economists could turn Smith into a negative example for economic theory and ultimately prove that their approach to economics was superior. Their theories were a correction to classical labor theories of value; they were more scientific than institutionalism, and more useful for illuminating social and political issues than abstract mathematical economics. But early Chicago economists also used Smith as a positive example, which had less to do with the validity of his economic theories, and more to do with his method and vision for political economy as a whole.

For someone like Frank Knight, Smith represented a way to navigate an uneasy relationship between politics and political economy. "The Wealth of Nations has been called a 'political pamphlet,'" a student noted in one of Knight's lectures, alluding to common misinterpretations of the eighteenth-century treatise. "Yet it gave great impetus to scientific price theory."[43] What was the issue with interpreting Smith as

42. "The things which have the greatest value in use have frequently little or no value in exchange; and, on the contrary, those which have the greatest value in exchange have frequently little or no value in use. Nothing is more useful than water: but it will purchase scarce any thing; scarce anything can be had in exchange for it. A diamond, on the contrary, has scarce any value in use; but a very great quantity of other goods may frequently be had in exchange for it." *WN* I.iv 13, 44–45.

43. Student notes dated April 11, 1933 (unnamed). Economics 304: Economic Theory and Social Policy. Frank H. Knight papers, Box 8, Folder 4. SCRC, University of Chicago.

a "political pamphlet?" Setting aside the impetus he gave to scientific price theory, was there a right way to read Smith's political economy? Knight's answers to these questions were far from explicit, but they reflected his beliefs about the appropriate scope of economics, as well as his preoccupation with the role that economics should play in a changing intellectual climate.

For Knight, to misinterpret Smith's *The Wealth of Nations* as propaganda was to misinterpret economics as propaganda. "Economics must be 'political economy,'" Knight underscored in his lectures.[44] What did that mean, though? First, it meant that economics was not a value-free science.[45] "I do not believe in the possibility of a value free political economy in any very strict sense," Knight commented. Mathematical economics (Knight spoke of "our mathematical economists" in vague terms) risked refining "elements of valuation" to the point where one approached "the absence of any kind of content." While not completely opposed to mathematical economics, Knight saw the rise of this approach as unfortunate; the assumptions mathematical economists made sometimes lacked "enough factual content to justify using the word economics, still less political economy."[46]

Second, Knight's insistence on "the connection of the word 'political' with the word 'economics'" reflected his belief that economics was, at its core, an inquiry whose "fundamental propositions have no meaning" if separated from social policy.[47] "Theoretical political economy as we

44. Frank H. Knight, lecture notes for Econ 301: Price and Distribution Theory (undated). Frank H. Knight papers, Box 9 Folder 19. SCRC, University of Chicago.

45. Frank H. Knight, lecture notes for Econ 301: Price and Distribution Theory (1943). Frank H. Knight papers, Box 9, Folder 6. SCRC, University of Chicago.

46. Frank H. Knight, lecture notes for Econ 301: Price and Distribution Theory (undated). Frank H. Knight papers, Box 9 Folder 19. SCRC, University of Chicago.

47. Frank H. Knight, lecture notes for Econ 301: Price and Distribution Theory (undated). Frank H. Knight papers, Box 9 Folder 19. SCRC, University of Chicago. Knight repeats this point a number of times: "I may point that a little by saying that I think that the change in name from 'political economy' to 'economics' is unfortunate." Gladys Hamilton, a student in Knight's class in 1934 noted the following: "Economic science is political. The change of name was very unfortunate. Economics as a science should be applied only to mathematical economics." Gladys Hamilton student notes. Econ 302: History of Economic Thought (Fall 1934). Frank Knight Papers, Box 8 Folder 14. SCRC, University of Chicago.

study it is a hundred and fifty years old, hardly existing before <u>The Wealth of Nations</u>," Knight declared. "The science arose out of the transformation of society and its problems of society."[48] In other words, Smith's magnum opus was the product of the author's direct engagement with the politics and society of his own times—hence, Smith's opposition to the mercantile system of the eighteenth century. Knight's point was that, from its urtext, political economy was a positive science with normative stakes. The study of political economy enabled scholars to understand the development of the modern social order, diagnose its ills, and improve upon it.

But there was a problem. As Knight put it, "The prime source of confusion in regard to economics has been this mixture of science and propaganda." Divorcing politics from economics to make economics more scientific and then recombining it with a predetermined ideology was exactly the wrong way to go. Again, Knight pointed to Adam Smith to illustrate his point. "Adam Smith's <u>Wealth of</u> Nations [*sic*] has been well called a political pamphlet," Knight stated. "The dominant interest in Smith's mind was political propaganda. The whole Classical economics has been called a system of political propaganda. This is largely false," he continued.[49]

Though never explicit and far from being hagiographic, Knight alluded to Smith as a model political economist who struck the ideal balance between detached scientist and political propagandist. Smith was "probably just as much interested in political policy as anyone else," and the science he founded was not one that merely preached ideology.[50] Instead, Smith uncovered the principles of "the kind of action required for producing a course of events which may [be] considered more desirable than that which would 'naturally' take place."[51] Smith's

48. Frank H. Knight, lecture notes for Econ 301: Price and Distribution Theory (undated). Frank H. Knight papers, Box 9 Folder 19. SCRC, University of Chicago.

49. Frank H. Knight, lecture notes for Econ 301: Price and Distribution Theory (undated). Frank H. Knight papers, Box 9 Folder 19. SCRC, University of Chicago.

50. Gladys Hamilton student notes. Econ 302: History of Economic Thought (Fall 1934). Frank Knight Papers, Box 9 Folder 14. SCRC, University of Chicago.

51. Frank H. Knight. Notes for Econ 301: Price and Distribution Theory (1943). Frank Knight Papers, Box 9, Folder 6. SCRC, University of Chicago.

political economy, according to Knight, modeled the way economic science could legitimately influence policy: by illuminating the principles of a social order in which institutions did not interfere with individual behavior. Thus, for Knight, Adam Smith not only represented the origins of political economy; he also represented political economy's proper aims as both a positive and normative science. Failing to see that was failing to understand the purpose political economy.

———

Knight never offered a thick, historically substantiated reading of Smith and his works, nor did he provide any guidelines for how, specifically, political economy in his own times might emulate Smith's. Instead, Knight imbued Smith with his own concerns about the political and ethical ends of economics and the prospects of a liberal society. The "obvious and simple system of natural liberty" outlined and developed "by its advocates from Adam Smith down" was "entirely sound" as a matter of economic theory. Knight had neatly summarized this theoretical proposition in his earlier and famous 1923 essay, "The Ethics of Competition:"

> a freely competitive organization of society tends to place every productive resource in that position in the productive system where it can make the greatest possible addition to the total social dividend as measured in price terms, and tends to reward every participant in production by giving it the increase in the social dividend which its cooperation makes possible.[52]

Yet this proposition was "not a statement of a sound ethical social ideal, the specification for a utopia."[53] Knight wanted to question not just the ethical bases of a competitive economic order, but also the ethical norms that a market society fostered. "An examination of the ethics of the economic system must consider the question of the kind of wants which it tends to generate or nourish as well as its treatment of wants as

---

52. Frank H. Knight, "The Ethics of Competition," *The Quarterly Journal of Economics* 37, no. 4 (1923), 588.

53. Knight, "The Ethics of Competition," 588.

they exist at any given time," he wrote.[54] In fact, in Knight's view, unhindered, competitive markets were not ethically neutral, and instead could undermine the existing ethical norms that held societies together.[55] Equally worrisome was the "exaggeration of the significance of freedom, or its overemphasis, to the neglect of other principles." The overestimation of economic freedom as the sole normative force of a liberal society was "the greatest error of the liberal age, and is partly responsible for the reaction we now witness, which threatens extinction of freedom and of all defensible values."[56]

Jacob Viner's work showed similar worries about the overestimation of economic freedom in a "natural order." A doctoral student of Frank Taussig's at Harvard, Viner's contributions as an economist were primarily in the realm of trade theory, but his publications on the history laissez-faire and mercantilism established his reputation as a formidable intellectual historian as well. The tensions inherent in Smith's ideas of a system of natural liberty and laissez-faire were the focal points of Jacob Viner's famous essay, "Adam Smith and Laissez-Faire," now considered a seminal contribution in Smith historiography. First presented at the Sesquicentennial Lectures in 1926, Viner's essay was, on the one hand, an attempt to reconcile Das Adam Smith Problem, and, on the other hand, an attempt to put to rest the notion that laissez-faire implied a politics of complete non-interventionism.

Viner rejected the formulation of the then-thirty-year-old Das Adam Smith Problem as a dichotomy between sympathy and self-interest. Viner believed a degree of irreconcilability existed between Smith's major works that stemmed from a "doctrine of a beneficent order in nature." The Theory of Moral Sentiments was characterized by its "unqualified doctrine of a harmonious order of nature, under divine guidance, which promotes the welfare of man through the operation of his individual propensities."[57] Drawing attention to what he noted as

54. Knight, "The Ethics of Competition," 586.

55. Burgin, The Great Persuasion, 113.

56. Frank H. Knight, "The Role of Principles in Economics and Politics," The American Economic Review 41, no. 1, (1951), 16.

57. Viner, "Adam Smith and Laissez-Faire," 202, 206.

Smith's "optimistic theology," Viner tried to show that Smith's social theory was not strictly empirical in nature, but also evoked a degree of providentialism. Yet this theological commitment was surprisingly absent in *The Wealth of Nations*.[58] Instead, the concept of a natural order was "partial and imperfect." Viner argued that flaws in the natural order manifested themselves as conflict between individual interest and the broader interests of the public—between merchant monopoly interests and consumers, manufacturers and farmers, or masters and apprentices. Left to its "natural course," the economic order was "marked by serious conflicts between private interests and interests of the general public:" masters and workmen fought over wages; the division of labor would ultimately lead to mental degradation and alienation; corn-dealers were motivated by greed and deceived the public; private interests could not be held accountable to maintain roads. This was a far cry from the harmonious order "designed and guided by a benevolent God" that permeated *The Theory of Moral Sentiments*. In fact, Viner thought that Smith's key contribution to political economy was made possible because of his later break with *The Theory of Moral Sentiments*. *The Wealth of Nations* abandoned the "absolutism, the rigidity, the romanticism" that had characterized Smith's former work and, therefore, was the better book.[59]

Thus, Viner simultaneously refuted and reformulated Das Adam Smith Problem and the basis of Smith's circumscribed notion of laissez-faire. Viner argued that Smith's conception of "natural order" in *The Wealth of Nations* not only deviated from *The Theory of Moral Sentiments*, but also belied any notion of laissez-faire as a stable, unified, self-correcting form of social organization that, if left alone, would regularly produce beneficial consequences. For Viner, Smith's version of laissez-faire foregrounded numerous instances in which government interference with private interests might actually promote rather than hinder the general interest: punishment for fraud, dishonesty, and violence; regulation of paper money and, notably, the establishment and maintenance of public works. It was wrong, in Viner's view, to conclude that

58. Viner, "Adam Smith and Laissez-Faire," 205, 206–8.
59. Viner, "Adam Smith and Laissez-Faire," 217, 201.

all government activity was Smith's greatest enemy. Smith made no "explicit condemnation[s] of government interference with individual initiative." Even when he admitted flaws in his system of natural liberty, Smith did not necessarily always arrive at the conclusion that "government intervention was preferable to laissez-faire."[60] Instead, Viner showed how Smith recognized the specific vulnerabilities of government interference and admitted that there would be "evils" that would be "beyond the competence" of even the best government to resolve.[61] Adam Smith and laissez-faire thus appeared to be full of contradictions, inconsistencies, and tensions. But rather than treating those as reasons to abandon Smith's thought, Viner saw these features as the source of Smith's value and uniqueness as a thinker. Acknowledging these tensions, Viner argued, enabled one to see the various areas in which government intervention might actually promote the general welfare. The final paragraph of Viner's essay beautifully captures the tension between individual freedom and government direction that he believed characterized Smith's political economy:

> Adam Smith was not a doctrinaire advocate of laissez faire. He saw a wide and elastic range of activity for government, and he was prepared to extend it even farther if government, by improving its standards of competence, honesty, and public spirit, showed itself entitled to wider responsibilities. He attributed great capacity to serve the general welfare to individual initiative applied in competitive ways to promote individual ends. He devoted more effort to the presentation of his case for individual freedom than to exploring the possibilities of service through government . . . But even in his own day, when it was not so easy to see, Smith saw that self-interest and competition were sometimes treacherous to the public interest they were supposed to serve, and he was prepared to have government exercise some measure of control over them where the need could be shown and the competence of government for the task demonstrated . . . [though he did not fully trust government, Smith

60. Viner, "Adam Smith and Laissez-Faire," 206, 221.
61. Viner, "Adam Smith and Laissez-Faire," 222.

saw] that it was necessary, in the absence of a better instrument, to rely upon government for the performance of many tasks which individuals as such would not do, or could not do, or could do only badly. He did not believe that laissez faire was always good, or always bad. It depended on circumstance; and as best he could, Adam Smith took into account all of the circumstances he could find.[62]

Thus, Knight's and Viner's readings of Smith speak to their "dispersed, concessionary, politically abstemious, and deeply conflicted" approach to free-market politics in the early decades of the twentieth century.[63] Knight was troubled by the prospects of liberalism's excesses, but he was far from being one of those "radical critics of competition" who, he believed, grossly underestimated the danger of liberalism's alternatives.[64] Similarly, Viner was unwilling to concede the notion of an unconditional laissez-faire economic order. Multiple Smiths coexisted. There was the textbook Adam Smith: the one who founded political economy, who proposed an incorrect theory of value, and who made inferences from close observations of everyday life. That version of Smith served as a pedagogical tool for illustrating the basic method and tools of economic science, especially in constructing Chicago Price Theory. On the other hand, there existed a more disembodied Smith that served a broader intellectual purpose. Characterizing Smith's works as balancing clear scientific insights with social policy, while questioning the ethics of a version of liberalism often attributed to his thought, was part of an ongoing effort to not only resuscitate the basic principles of markets, but also identify their limits.

By the 1940s Chicago's economics department and the wider intellectual community had begun to change. A cohort of thinkers in and around the economics department began actively promoting Chicago as a center for developing market-based solutions to social and political

62. Viner, "Adam Smith and Laissez-Faire," 231–32.

63. Burgin, *The Great Persuasion*, 44; Angus Burgin, "The Radical Conservatism of Frank H. Knight," *Modern Intellectual History* 6, no. 3 (2009), 513–38; Scott Gordon, "Frank Knight and the Tradition of Liberalism," *Journal of Political Economy* 82, no. 3 (1974), 571–77.

64. Knight, "The Ethics of Competition," 601.

problems.[65] Increasingly, Chicago would become synonymous with, first, a skepticism of socialist planning, and, later, an unapologetic free-market advocacy that belied the earlier generation's views. As a result, what was previously a kaleidoscopic and complicated view of Smith transformed into a much more coherent—and radically different—picture.

65. Ross B. Emmett writes, "Chicago economics was different by the 1940s, primarily because of the emergence of a contingent of economists committed to developing market-based solutions to social problems." Emmett, *The Chicago Tradition in Economics 1892–1945*, xviii.

6

Alive and Well and Living in Chicago

1946 WAS A WATERSHED YEAR at the University of Chicago. Jacob Viner left the department for Princeton, and Frank Knight was on his way to retirement. Friedrich Hayek, the Austrian émigré, was promoting his recent publication, *The Road to Serfdom*, with astonishing success. Henry Simons, an economist known more for his fiery polemics than for his academic publications, tragically committed suicide. Meanwhile, Milton Friedman had returned from brief stints teaching at the University of Wisconsin-Madison, Columbia University, and the University of Minnesota. Aaron Director—Friedman's brother-in-law—joined the Law School faculty, which fostered collaboration and ushered in a new movement between the law and economics departments. This symbolic changing of the guard brought about a dramatic shift in the way that Chicago economists did economics, and also the way they imagined Smith as their intellectual forbearer.[1]

---

1. It is common in the literature on the Chicago School to identify this divide as a "break" between the "old" and "new" Chicago Schools. See Steven G. Medema, "Adam Smith and the Chicago School." Medema draws up his account based on terms coined by Dierdre McCloskey in her "The Good Old Coase Theorem and the Good Old Chicago School," in *Coasean Economics: Law and Economics and the New Institutional Economics*, ed. Steven G. Medema (Dordrecht: Kluwer Academic Publishers, 1998), 239–48. Other works that identify this break include Smith, "Adam Smith and the New Right;" Jones, *Masters of the Universe*. In more recent work, Medema expands on his previous framework by identifying two "turning points" across *three* generations of the Chicago School. See Steven G. Medema, "Identifying a 'Chicago School' of Economics: On

One aspect of this shift was methodological. Whereas Knight and Viner had seen the relationship between price theory and liberalism as a philosophical as well as economic one, the rising generation of Chicago economists viewed it differently. Confronting theory with evidence to test a model's predictive capacity became the new hallmark of economics at Chicago.[2] Public finance studies as well as of monetary and regulatory policy, with an emphasis on prediction to validate hypotheses, replaced the focus on theoretical analysis that had defined the earlier generation. By 1953, Chicago had become a household name identified with a distinct school of thought; its members were recognized as a group of formidable public-minded scientists who employed a method of testing and prediction that Knight could not have anticipated. Jacob Viner later recalled his discovery that "The Chicago School" not only existed but, much to his surprise, was "ideologically loaded."[3] The shift also involved

the Origins, Evolution, and Evolving Meanings of a Famous Brand Name," 2018 Working Paper, permission to cite granted by author.

2. Friedman's "The Methodology of Positive Economics" (often referred to as F1953 or F53) emphasized the importance of predictive capacity in judging economic theories and is arguably one of the most influential essays on economic methodology in the twentieth century. On the impact and legacy of F1953, see Uskala Mäki, *The Methodology of Positive Economics: Reflections on the Milton Friedman Legacy* (Cambridge: Cambridge University Press, 2009); Eric Schliesser, "Friedman, Positive Economics, and the Chicago Boys," in *The Elgar Companion to the Chicago School of Economics* (Cheltenham: Elgar, 2010), 175–95.

3. Ross B. Emmett, *Frank Knight and the Chicago School in American Economics*; Steven G. Medema, "Identifying a 'Chicago School' of Economics." Viner wrote to Don Patinkin in November of 1969, describing his experience returning to the University for a conference, several years after he left the department in 1946. "I remained sceptical [*sic*] about this until I attended a conference sponsored by University of Chicago professors in 1951 . . . but the program for discussion, the selection of chairmen, and everything about the conference . . . were so patently rigidly structured, so loaded, that I got more amusement from the conference than from any other I ever attended. Even the source of the financing of the Conference, as I found out later, was ideologically loaded . . . From then on, I was willing to consider the existence of a 'Chicago School' (but one not confined to the economics department and not embracing all of the department) and that this 'School' had been in operation, and had won many able disciples, for years before I left Chicago. But at no time was I consciously a member of it, and it is my vague impression that if there was such a school it did not regard me as a member, or at least as a loyal and qualified member." The letter is reproduced in the appendix of Don Patinkin, "The Chicago Tradition, the Quantity Theory, and Friedman," *Journal of Money, Credit and Banking* 1, no. 1 (1969), 46–70.

the rhetorical mode that some of Chicago's most recognized figures adopted. The new generation of Chicago economists was much more self-referential and cognizant of being a part of a distinctive school with a publicly-recognized name, pedigreed history, and novel method. For example, in a speech to the Chicago Board of Trustees in 1974, Milton Friedman acknowledged the public perception of the Chicago School as "a belief in the efficacy of the free market as a means of organizing resources, for skepticism about government intervention into economic affairs, and for emphasis on the quantity theory of money." Friedman argued that Chicago stood for much more than free-market fundamentalism; it stood for an insistence on empirically testing theories with predictive capability. This approach not only made economics a science, but also legitimated policy perspectives. In Friedman's words, Chicago economics "takes seriously the use of economic theory as a tool for analyzing a startlingly wide range of concrete problems . . . [Chicago stands] for an approach that insists on the empirical testing of theoretical generalizations and that rejects alike facts without theory and theory without facts."[4]

This method, according to Friedman, unified different generations of economists at Chicago, and, more importantly, it connected Chicago to the very foundations of economics. Chicago economists were all students of Frank Knight and Jacob Viner's generation, Friedman declared, "and at a still longer remove, of Adam Smith—who but for the accident of having been born in the wrong century . . . would undoubtedly have been a Distinguished Service Professor at The University of Chicago."[5] George Stigler reinforced the association between Chicago and Smith in a banquet speech at the University of Glasgow's celebrations of the bicentenary of *The Wealth of Nations*: "I bring you greetings from Adam

4. Milton Friedman, speech at the 54th Annual Board of Trustees' Dinner for the Faculty. January 9, 1974. Milton Friedman Papers, Box 55.8. Hoover Institution Archives, Stanford University.

5. Milton Friedman, speech at the 54th Annual Board of Trustees' Dinner for the Faculty. January 9, 1974. Milton Friedman Papers, Box 55.8. Hoover Institution Archives, Stanford University.

Smith, who is alive and well and living in Chicago."[6] Though perhaps tongue-in-cheek, these nods to Smith revealed Chicago's underlying commitment to scientific rigor stemming from an invented Smithian tradition. In order to draw the direct line from Smith to Chicago, Stigler and Friedman turned Smith's ideas, particularly self-interest and the invisible hand, into positive, scientific—as opposed to normative and philosophical—insights that were foundational to their methodological and political projects. This often entailed a flattening of Smith's ideas in ways that smoothed over, or altogether obscured, the complexities, tensions, and other problematic aspects characteristic of earlier readings of Smith.

———

In the spring of 1945, Friedrich August von Hayek was on tour in the United States promoting his most recent publication, *The Road to Serfdom*. It was an unlikely scenario for the previously little-known Austrian scholar, who had first written the work with a British audience in mind and had struggled to find an American publisher. Hayek painted a harrowing picture of central planning and its tendencies. Not only did it abandon the principles of "individualist civilization," but, in Hayek's view, any social philosophy centered around planning—whether collectivist, communist, or fascist—led society down the dangerous road towards a totalitarian state. Though Hayek was careful to qualify his arguments and distance them from a "dogmatic laissez faire attitude," his rhetoric was at times apocalyptic and absolute. When Frank Knight reviewed the manuscript in 1943 he described it as an "able piece of work, but limited in scope and somewhat one-sided in treatment;" he doubted "whether it would have a very wide market in this country, or if it could change the position of many readers." Although the book experienced some success in its initial months of

6. As quoted in Ronald L. Meek, *Smith, Marx, & After: Ten Essays in the Development of Economic Thought* (London: Chapman & Hall, 1977), 3.

publication in 1944, in April of 1945, after *Readers Digest* published a condensed version, Hayek became a cultural sensation.[7]

The Road to Serfdom tour became an important springboard for establishing American channels for Hayek's ideas. During his visit to Detroit, Hayek met with Harold Luhnow, president of the Volker Fund, who was interested in converting his philanthropic organization into a "a foundation to promote a rethinking of liberal politics in America."[8] Luhnow wanted to fund a larger study around the core ideas of the work and, ideally, have Hayek write a version for an American audience—an American *Road to Serfdom*. Hayek took the opportunity to create something more ambitious. After several months of negotiation, he proposed the Chicago Free Market Study. Henry Simons had been a close ally of Hayek's since the 1930s and played a crucial role in orchestrating both institutional and personal support for the project. Chicago seemed to be the perfect home for Hayek's work. "A distinctive feature of 'Chicago economics,' as represented by Knight and Viner," Simons wrote, "is its traditional-liberal political philosophy—its emphasis on the virtues of dispersion of economic power (free markets) and of political decentralization."[9] Both Simons and Hayek hoped that such a program at Chicago, by "influencing the best professional opinions," would ultimately influence political action.[10]

7. F. A. Hayek, *The Road to Serfdom: Text and Documents—The Definitive Edition*, ed. Bruce Caldwell, (Chicago, IL: University of Chicago Press, 2007), 85. Frank Knight, reader's report, December 10, 1943. University of Chicago Press collection, box 230, folder 1, University of Chicago Library. Reprinted in the Appendix of F. A. Hayek, *The Road to Serfdom*, 249–50, 18–23. See also Burgin, *The Great Persuasion*, 87–94.

8. Rob Van Horn and Philip Mirowski, "The Rise of the Chicago School of Economics and the Birth of Neoliberalism," in *The Road from Mont Pèlerin: The Making of the Neoliberal Thought Collective*, eds. Philip Mirowski and Dieter Plehwe (Cambridge, MA: Harvard University Press), 139–178 at 141. Hayek's own recollection of his anxieties around the *Road to Serfdom* tour as well as subsequent developments can be found in his own book, F. A. Hayek, *Hayek on Hayek: An Autobiographical Dialogue*, ed. Stephen Kresge and Leif Wenar, The Collected Works of F.A. Hayek (Indianapolis, IN: Liberty Fund Inc., 2008).

9. As quoted in Van Horn and Mirowski, "The Rise of the Chicago School of Economics and the Birth of Neoliberalism," 145.

10. It is worth noting that from the standpoint of someone like Simons, one of the sites whereby professional opinion needed to be "influenced"—if not totally overturned—was the

Simons' death in 1946 left a void that was deeply felt among his colleagues, but there remained a number of critical allies who hoped to bring the project to fruition, Aaron Director and Friedman among them. Though the Free Market Study never reached its full potential and the American *Road to Serfdom* was never completed, Hayek and his associates established Chicago as an intellectual hub for distilling and disseminating the ideas of a "new, more economically oriented liberalism"—one in which the state's primary role was severely limited to fostering the conditions of economic competition and allowing markets to prosper.[11] Along with Hayek's founding of the Mont Pèlerin Society in 1947, the inception of the Chicago Free Market study represents the launching of an intellectual project that aimed to generate widespread ideological change in this direction.[12]

Several scholars have noted Hayek's intellectual debt to Smith and to the Scottish Enlightenment; Hayek's frequent references and citations to Smith date to the 1930s.[13] In his inaugural lecture at the LSE, "The Trend of Economic Thinking," Hayek portrayed Smith, Hume, and classical

---

Cowles Commission. The Commission was initially founded in 1932 to bring together statistically-minded economists to derive better models of the stock market, but was increasingly reviled for being a hotbed of self-declared socialists. It eventually relocated to a new home at Yale University in 1955. See Van Horn and Mirowski, "The Rise of the Chicago School of Economics," 146; for a more detailed background on the Cowles Commission see Till Düppe and E. Roy Weintraub, "Siting the New Economic Science: The Cowles Commission's Activity Analysis Conference of June 1949," *Science in Context* 27, no. 3 (2014), 453–83.

11. Van Horn and Mirowski, "The Rise of the Chicago School of Economics," 152.

12. For a detailed study of the negotiations, development, and impact of the Chicago Free Market Study, see Van Horn and Mirowski, "The Rise of the Chicago School of Economics and the Birth of Neoliberalism." For a discussion and critique of some of the central claims that Van Horn and Mirowski make, specifically about the nature of neoliberalism and the influence of the Volker Fund, see Bruce Caldwell, "The Chicago School, Hayek, and Neoliberalism," in *Building Chicago Economics: New Perspectives on the History of America's Most Powerful Economics Program*, eds. Robert Van Horn, Philip Mirowski, and Thomas A Stapleford, (Cambridge: Cambridge University Press, 2011), 301–34.

13. See for instance Smith, "Adam Smith and the New Right;" Leonidas Montes, "Is Friedrich Hayek Rowing Adam Smith's Boat?" in *Hayek, Mill and the Liberal Tradition*, ed. Andrew Farrant (London: Routledge, 2010), 7–38, Haakonssen and Winch, "The Legacy of Adam Smith;" and Van Horn and Mirowski, "The Rise of the Chicago School of Economics and the Birth of Neoliberalism."

economists in a typical fashion. From the time of Hume and Smith, Hayek claimed, "every attempt to understand economic phenomena" exposed the inadequacies and harms of excessive state activity and pointed to the beneficial possibilities of a doctrine of unintended consequences.[14] The "social enthusiasm" of the historical school and its successors, in Hayek's opinion, destroyed the usefulness that economics had once possessed "as a tool of interpretation" honed by "impeccable logic" and dedicated to producing mental models of economic phenomena.[15] Hayek treated Smith similarly in his famous 1945 lecture, "Individualism: True and False." Smith, alongside Locke, Mandeville, Hume, Josiah Tucker, and Adam Ferguson represented an intellectual tradition of true individualism, which stood in opposition not only to philosophical rationalism, but also collectivism and planning. Despite what the name suggests, true individualism was, according to Hayek, a theory of society—"an attempt to understand the forces which determine the social life of man"—as opposed to an axiomatic belief about "isolated or self-contained individuals."[16] Rationalist, or what Hayek called "Design theories," found their representatives in figures like the Encyclopedists, Rousseau, and the physiocrats. These were false theories because they not only assumed too much rationality in individuals, but also because they inevitably led to conclusions that "social processes can be made to serve human ends only if they are subjected to the control of individual human reason, and thus lead directly to socialism." On the other hand, theories of "true individualism" started with the assumption that human reason is not only severely limited but also fallible; they offered an explanation for how an individual's irrationalities and errors could be corrected "only in the course of a *social* process."[17] In the broad contours of Hayek's social thought, then, Adam Smith was a useful foil for both

14. F.A. Hayek, "The Trend of Economic Thinking," in *The Trend of Economic Thinking: Essays on Political Economists and Economic History*, ed. W.W. Bartley III and Stephen Kresge, vol. 3: The Collected Works of F.A. Hayek (London: Routledge, 1991),13–30 at 22.

15. Hayek, "The Trend of Economic Thinking," 21.

16. F.A. Hayek, "Individualism: True and False," in *Individualism and Economic Order* (Chicago, IL: University of Chicago Press, 1948), 1–32 at 6.

17. Hayek, "Individualism: True and False," 10, 8. Emphasis added.

the atomistic, perfectly rational "bogey of 'economic man,'" as well as for theories that relied too heavily on subjecting human reason to collectivist aims.[18] This effectively distanced Smith from neoclassical theories that assumed perfect knowledge of rational actors and rebutted the idea that Smith preached unvarnished egotism.[19] Smith's primary concern, Hayek argued, was "not so much with what man might occasionally achieve when he was at his best but that he should have as little opportunity as possible to do harm when he was at his worst."[20] But the economic and social system in which men did least harm could not be consciously designed or willed into being. For Hayek, acknowledging the limits of human knowledge—that "no person or small group of persons can know all that is known to somebody"—implied a practical and political conclusion: that all coercive or exclusive power had to be curtailed or placed under strict limitations.[21]

Hayek was still in the early stages of articulating his social and political theory of market society in the late 1940s, but his later work interwove his interpretation of Smith's epistemology and social theory with the neoliberal reverence for the price mechanism. In a 1976 essay marking the two hundredth anniversary of *The Wealth of Nations*, Hayek argued that Smith's "clear recognition of the central problem" of economic science made him the greatest economist; Smith had elucidated the simple and universal principles that enable social order to thrive with little to no central direction. Smith's famous illustration of the division of labor—the pin factory—revealed, for Hayek, how the productive powers of society were driven not by "known concrete needs and capacities" of brethren, but instead "by the abstract signals of the prices at which things were demanded and offered on the market."[22] Though

18. Hayek, "Individualism: True and False," 11.

19. Smith, "Adam Smith and the New Right," 550–51.

20. Hayek, "Individualism: True and False," 11.

21. Hayek, "Individualism: True and False," 16. For further discussion on Hayek's interpretation of individualism vis-à-vis Smith, see Montes, "Is Friedrich Hayek Rowing Adam Smith's Boat?"

22. F.A. Hayek, "Adam Smith (1723–1790), His Message in Today's Language," in *The Trend of Economic Thinking: Essays on Political Economists and Economic History*, ed. W.W. Bartley III and Stephen Kresge, vol. 3: 117–121. The Collected Works of F.A. Hayek (London: Routledge, 1991), 117.

Hayek noted that Smith did not (and could not) direct his arguments against socialism, he nevertheless portrayed Smith as a prophylactic against constructivist tendencies that carried hubristic assumptions about human knowledge and undermined individual liberty in their demands for social justice. Smith, in other words, perfectly encapsulated the epistemic liberalism that Hayek wanted to defend against the encroachments of central planning.

> The recognition that a man's efforts will benefit more people, and on the whole satisfy greater needs, when he lets himself be guided by the abstract signals of prices rather than by perceived needs, and that by this method we can best overcome our constitutional ignorance of most of the particular facts, and can make the fullest use of knowledge of concrete circumstances widely dispersed among millions of individuals, is the great achievement of Adam Smith.[23]

Though Hayek's readings of Smith may have been opportunistic, they were not inaccurate.[24] He was careful to distance his interpretation of Smith from those he found to be reductive or dogmatic. His interest in Smith's works and their prominence stemmed, above all, from his impulse to lay the epistemic foundations for a social theory of markets and how they worked to promote freedom. Knowledge was decentralized; order emerged spontaneously. These were the themes that Hayek claimed to inherit from Smith, but, more importantly, they were themes that resonated with his own version of neoliberal thought.

Though Hayek was arguably the most important link between Chicago and the international free-market advocacy efforts of the Mont Pèlerin Society (MPS), his influence waned as subtle shifts in the mental

---

23. Hayek, "Adam Smith (1723–1790), His Message in Today's Language," 116–122 at 118.

24. Peter Boettke, "F.A. Hayek as an Intellectual Historian," in *Historians of Economics and Economic Thought: the Construction of Disciplinary Memory*, eds. Steve Medema and Warren Samuels (London: Routledge, 2001), 117–128. Craig Smith also writes that Hayek's interest in Smith "is directed by what he takes from them and not necessarily by the chief themes of Smith's own work . . . He is quite explicitly tracing the emergence of ideas similar to his own in the works of a series of thinkers whose chief preoccupations might have been elsewhere. Smith, "Adam Smith and the New Right," 552.

landscapes of his colleagues slowly became wide rifts. In the 1950s, Hayek was becoming ever more disappointed with the level of intellectual engagement at MPS, especially at the apparent loss of interest in big, philosophical questions. In 1958, controversies surrounding the society's secretary, Albert Hunold, revealed fissures and personal animosities among some of the society's members, including a strong Chicago contingent represented by Milton Friedman and George Stigler. Additionally, Hayek found postwar America a frustrating environment for pursuing his ideas. Years of economic growth, a fairly stable political order, and toleration for modest regulation had made the need for an organization like MPS seem less urgent.[25] Hayek left Chicago for the University of Freiburg in 1962.

Hayek's departure was indicative of intellectual changes that had been occurring beneath the surface for nearly a decade. By the late 1940s and 1950s, the "economically oriented liberalism" that Hayek and Simons had sought to institutionalize became a defining feature of Chicago economics. This version of economically oriented liberalism encompassed a broad social theory: society was made up of autonomous, self-interested individuals; market mechanisms—specifically the price mechanism—facilitated the exchange of goods, services, ideas, and values; and market interactions were not just mutually beneficial but also globally stabilizing.[26] Combined with an anti-statist political outlook, this worldview shaped the methodological choices by which economists reached their scientific conclusions, which, in turn, reinforced their political and philosophical commitments. Thus, Adam Smith's ideas did more than simply lend "intellectual heft to the theories that contradicted the political assumptions of the postwar period."[27] By reworking Smithian concepts like "individualism," "self-interest," and

25. Burgin, *The Great Persuasion*, 123. For a more detailed historical account of the evolution of the MPS and its internal controversies in the 1950s, see Burgin's *The Great Persuasion*, chap. 4 "New Conservatisms."

26. Beatrice Cherrier, "The Lucky Consistency of Milton Friedman's Science and Politics, 1933–1963" in Van Horn, Mirowski, and Stapleford, *Building Chicago Economics: New Perspectives on the History of America's Most Powerful Economics Program*, 335–367 at 338.

27. Jones, *Masters of the Universe*, 101.

"the invisible hand," thinkers like Hayek, Stigler, and Friedman transformed Smith into an original way of thinking about an individualistic, market-oriented society that was justifiable on social-scientific grounds. Their substantive reinterpretation of Smith's social scientific insights, however, had consequences for subsequent understandings of the rationality—or irrationality—of politics, and the moral orientations of a free-market society.

———

George Stigler's first love was the history of economics. As one of Knight's students at Chicago in the 1930s, Stigler wrote his doctoral dissertation on the history of production and distribution theories in economics from 1870 to 1915. After holding various positions at Iowa State College, the University of Minnesota, Brown, and Columbia, he returned to Chicago in 1958 where he remained for the rest of his career. Over time, Stigler witnessed the field's declining interest in its own history. "The study of the history of economics has escaped all the forces that have transformed the character of economic research in the twentieth century," Stigler wrote in 1965. "It has escaped any serious quantification, and research assistants can seldom be used—why, even committees are scarce in the field!"[28] In 1972, the University of Chicago's department of economics abandoned the course requirement altogether.

Yet Stigler remained devoted to the history of economic ideas even as his own work took off in an unambiguously empirical direction. His interest in Smith in particular remained constant in spite of—or perhaps because of—the changing relationship between economics and its past. Stigler's views about the relevance of economics' past were complicated. On the one hand, he believed that studying the history of economic thought had "genuine and valuable" pedagogical benefits; one

28. George J. Stigler, *Essays in the History of Economics* (Chicago, IL: University of Chicago Press, 1965), v; Craig Freedman, *Chicago Fundamentalism: Ideology and Methodology in Economics* (Singapore: World Scientific, 2008), chap. 6; Nathan Rosenberg, "George Stigler: Adam Smith's Best Friend," *Journal of Political Economy* 101, no. 5, (1993), 835–36.

could learn to be a better reader and consumer of economics by starting to read the earlier economists, for example.[29] On the other hand, these "utilitarian functions" were insufficient justifications to keep reading the ideas of past thinkers. The history of economics could be useful insofar as it contributed to scientific progress. "The purpose in seeking to understand the man's theoretical system is not to be generous or malicious toward him," Stigler wrote in 1969, "but [rather] to maximize the probability that his work will contribute to scientific progress."[30] Once an analytical system was "well-defined and cleansed of irrelevant digression and inessential error," one could assess its scientific value. On this point Stigler did not see a difference between reading the past and reading the present. "The correct way to read Adam Smith is the correct way to read the forthcoming issues of a professional journal," he famously asserted.[31]

Stigler saw himself as Smith's distant (but not-so-secret) admirer and intellectual heir. As early as 1961, Stigler had been in contact with the University of Glasgow regarding its plans to publish a new edition of *The Wealth of Nations* for the bicentenary. At the end of the year, Professor Ronald Meek from the Department of Political Economy informed Stigler of Glasgow's Bicentenary Committee and their ambitions to compile and publish *The Collected Works of Adam Smith*, as well as "a commemorative volume of essays on Smith and his works, to be written by British and overseas scholars." Meek and his colleagues were "naturally anxious" to gather some American experts and support for the project, and even floated the idea of having Aaron Director be the editor of Smith's correspondence.[32] Two years later, in private

29. George J. Stigler, "Does Economics Have a Useful Past?" *History of Political Economy* 1, no. 2 (1969), 222.

30. Stigler, "Does Economics Have a Useful Past?" 221. Craig Freedman characterizes Stigler's approach as one that referred to historical systems and sets of ideas in order to "identify the progress of economic theory." See Freedman, *Chicago Fundamentalism*, 165.

31. Stigler, "Does Economics Have a Useful Past?," 221.

32. Letter from Ronald L. Meek to George J. Stigler, 28th December, 1961. See also Letter from A.S. Skinner to George J. Stigler, 22nd October, 1965. George Stigler Papers, University of Chicago Special Collections Research Center. The editorial role for Smith's correspondence eventually went to Professors E.C. Mossner and Ian Simpson Ross. For a first-hand account of the development of the Bicentenary Committee and the Glasgow Editions project, see

correspondence, Meek expressed even greater anxiety about the acqui-
sition of the Lothian manuscripts, the second set of student notes on
Smith's lectures on jurisprudence discovered in 1958. Stigler responded
with a mixture of genuine concern and expediency. The new manuscripts "seemed to be quite unimportant so far as intellectual history is
concerned," but Stigler, ever the pragmatist, urged the team at Glasgow
to "meet the bids of your rivals" to ensure the manuscripts were reunited
with Smith's other material. "Adam himself would surely both prefer to
be in Scotland and to be allocated by the price system."[33]

Stigler's reputation as "Adam Smith's Best Friend" betrayed the
imagined intellectual affinity between Smith's economic thought and
his own (see Fig. 6.1).[34] In his 1957 work on the theory of perfect competition, for example, Stigler presented Smith as one of the first in a line
of thinkers who provided a plausible theory of competition. Stigler reconstructed passages from Smith's *The Wealth of Nations* to illustrate a
very basic, "classical" definition of competition: a "process of responding to a new force and a method of reaching a new equilibrium."[35] The
remainder of the article explicated the various "analytical refinements"
made by Smith's critics and successors from Marx to Marshall to Knight
before presenting Stigler's own theory of competition. Not everyone

D.D. Raphael, "The Glasgow Edition of the Collected Works of Adam Smith," in Tribe and
Mizuta, *A Critical Bibliography of Adam Smith*, 50–60.

33. Stigler also added that "surely some loyal and prosperous son of Glasgow would come
to your rescue." Letter from George Stigler to Ronald L. Meek, undated, George Stigler Papers,
University of Chicago Special Collections Research Center.

34. Stigler recalls the origins of this epithet in an article published in 1976: "There is a game
I sometimes play with children; I call it 'Three Questions.' If all three questions are answered
correctly I promise $1 million. . . . The first two questions present no difficulty: perhaps the
number of brothers and sisters the child has, and the city in which it lives. The third question is
a different matter. Once I asked, 'Who was Adam Smith's best friend?' The reply from this child
was, 'You are, Uncle George.' I had someone like David Hume or James Hutton or Joseph Black
in Mind. Still I have long been a good friend of Smith, though I have no right to claim priority in
his circle." George J. Stigler, "The Successes and Failures of Professor Smith," *The Journal of Political
Economy* 84, no. 6 (1976), 1200. For a second-hand account, see Rosenberg, "George Stigler."

35. George J. Stigler, "Perfect Competition, Historically Contemplated," *Journal of Political
Economy* 65, no. 1 (1957), 2.

FIG. 6.1. George Stigler, "Adam Smith's Best Friend." Photo credit: Stephen Stigler.

was persuaded. The economist Paul J. McNulty, for example, rejected the pivotal importance that Stigler assigned to Smith, citing multiple instances where analyses of competition existed prior to *The Wealth of Nations.* "Any implication that [perfect competition's] transition from an element of common discourse to a concept of economic analysis was a contribution of Adam Smith must be rejected," McNulty wrote.[36]

36. Paul J. McNulty, "A Note on the History of Perfect Competition," *Journal of Political Economy* 75, no. 4 (1967), 395.

For Stigler, Smith's most important scientific accomplishment was one that defined modern economics: identifying the centrality of self-interest as the fundamental force of economic activity. Smith was a Promethean figure who stole the firepower of self-interest from the gods and bequeathed it to earthly economists. Self-interest was the "crown jewel" of *The Wealth of Nations* and "remains to this day, the foundation of the theory of the allocation of resources," Stigler wrote in 1976. Stigler hailed *The Wealth of Nations* as "a stupendous palace erected upon the granite of self-interest," which was an "immensely powerful force [that] guides resources to their most efficient uses, stimulates laborers to diligence and inventors to splendid new divisions of labor—in short, it orders and enriches the nation which gives it free rein."[37] Stigler made Smith's idea of self-interest into an axiom of modern economics, and, in doing so, he fashioned Smith into a modern economist like himself. Stigler characterized Smithian self-interest as a principle so ingenious that it was "Newtonian in its universality," a "theorem of almost unlimited power on the behavior of man."[38] This construction of self-interest stood in stark contrast with the readings of the previous generation. Jacob Viner, for instance, had identified Smith's notion of self-interest as being more than a narrow desire for wealth; it was a multifaceted concept of "self-love" that was simultaneously the basis for other virtues. Appealing to the self-love of the butcher, baker, and brewer in Smith's *The Wealth of Nations* may get us our dinner, but excessive self-interest also led to problematic self-preference, excessive toil, and injustice.[39] Stigler, on the other hand, glossed over these different connotations, arguing that

37. George Stigler, "The Successes and Failures of Professor Smith," *The Journal of Political Economy* 84, no. 6 (1976), 1201; Stigler, "Smith's Travels on the Ship of State," 265.

38. Stigler, "The Successes and Failures of Professor Smith," 1212.

39. For analysis on the concept of self-interest and self-love in Smith's works, see Maria Pia Paganelli, "The Adam Smith Problem in Reverse: Self-Interest in *The Wealth of Nations* and *The Theory of Moral Sentiments*" *History of Political Economy* 40, no. 2 (2008), 365–382; Fleischacker, *On Adam Smith's Wealth of Nations*, chap. 5; Pratap Bhanu Mehta, "Self-Interest and Other Interests," in *The Cambridge Companion to Adam Smith*, ed. Knud Haakonssen (Cambridge: Cambridge University Press, 2006), 246–69.

"much of the time, most of the time in fact, the self-interest theory (as [he] interpreted it on Smithian lines) will win."[40]

Whereas the earlier generation embraced the ambiguities, complexities, and tensions in Smith's ideas, Stigler stripped those features away. In identifying a single concept in Smith's analysis that was contiguous with his own approach to economics, Stigler gave rational self-interest a degree of infallibility, ultimately leading him to drive a wedge between *The Wealth of Nations* and *The Theory of Moral Sentiments*, between economics and other fields. For Stigler, Smith's moral philosophy bore "scarcely any resemblance to his economics," and thus proved that economics and moral psychology were—and always would be—at odds with one another.[41] Indeed, Stigler denied that any work in related fields could inform the development of groundbreaking economic theory, and even suggested that contemporary economic imperialism had its roots in Smith's economics.[42] Stigler made Smith vulnerable to Das Adam Smith Problem yet again.

The most lasting consequence of Stigler's interpretation of Smith was political—that is, Stigler tried to account for the failure of the "high priest of self-interest" to explain political outcomes. This was the subject of Stigler's 1971 essay, "Smith's Travels on the Ship of State." He asked, if self-interest is the dominant motivation in market contexts, why not also in politics? Stigler expressed his bewilderment—albeit somewhat sarcastically—at Smith's apparent oversight.

> The "uniform, constant, and uninterrupted effort of every man to better his condition"—why was it interrupted when a man entered Parliament? The man whose spacious vision could see the Spanish War of 1739 as a bounty and who attributed the decline of feudalism to changes in consumption patterns—how could he have failed to see the self-interest written upon the faces of politicians and

40. George Stigler, "Economics or Ethics?" *The Tanner Lectures on Human Values*, delivered at Harvard University. April 24, 25, and 28, 1980, 143–91, available at https://tannerlectures.utah.edu/lecture-library.php#s.

41. George J. Stigler, "The Influence of Events and Policies on Economic Theory," *The American Economic Review* 50, no. 2 (1960), 44.

42. Medema, "Adam Smith and the Chicago School," 42–43.

constituencies? The man who denied the state the capacity to conduct almost any business save the postal—how could he give to the sovereign the task of extirpating cowardice in the citizenry? How so, Professor Smith?[43]

If Smith had failed to apply his economic analysis in political contexts, it was because he was being too much of a moral and political scientist who believed too much in the power of moral suasion to effect reform, Stigler argued. Admitting such a failure by the high priest of self-interest was, in Stigler's words, "uncomfortable . . . for he is a better man than everyone else."[44]

Public choice economists such as James Buchanan and Gordon Tullock set out to prove that Smith's economic theory could and did apply to the analysis of political outcomes.[45] Stigler, however, saw the arena of politics as a black box of irrationality that produced unexpected outcomes. Smith, he argued, "gave a larger role to emotion, prejudice, and ignorance in political life than he ever allowed in ordinary economic affairs."[46] The Wealth of Nations, according to Stigler, was replete with examples of how individuals failed to make decisions that served their self-interest. Sometimes these errors were failures to anticipate the consequences of an action. Greedy landlords, for example, who demanded improvements on their lands at the expense of the tenant's capital stock instead of their own, removed incentives that would have otherwise yielded a higher rate of return. Other times these errors were those of a principal-agent problem. Monopolies were "the great enemy of good management," and company employees traded their own interest for that of their employer. Stigler used these examples, among others, to

43. Stigler, "Smith's Travels on the Ship of State," 274. Stigler quotes from WN II.iii.31, 343.

44. Stigler, "Smith's Travels on the Ship of State," 274.

45. On the uses of Smith in public choice theory, see, for example, S. M. Amadae, *Rationalizing Capitalist Democracy: The Cold War Origins of Rational Choice Liberalism*, 2nd edition (Chicago, IL: University of Chicago Press, 2003); Smith, "Adam Smith and the New Right;" Gordon L. Brady and Francesco Forte, "George J. Stigler's Relationship to the Virginia School of Political Economy," in *George Stigler: Enigmatic Price Theorist of the Twentieth Century*, ed. Craig Freedman (London: Palgrave Macmillan UK, 2020), 519–50.

46. Stigler, "Smith's Travels on the Ship of State," 270.

illustrate how the means of an actor's behavior were often inappropriate to his ends.[47]

Stigler argued that the contrast between the pure rationality of Smithian economics on the one hand and the irrationality of politics on the other underpinned "Smith's strong preference for private economic activity" and his deep distrust of the state. More specifically, Smith distrusted the state's motives more than its competence.[48] But this is where Stigler, as heir and admirer, saw a need to depart from the "venerable master," as he called Smith in his 1964 Presidential Address to the AEA.[49] While Smith was correct in arguing that freely choosing, independent individuals would allocate resources and skills more efficiently than the state, and that sometimes—indeed quite often—the state would become "the creature of organized, articulate, self-serving groups," Stigler argued that Smith still placed too much faith in the fundamental competence of the state. Smith did not provide much compelling evidence that states consistently achieve the goals of their policies, Stigler argued. Moreover, Smith appeared to merely assert, rather than prove, the harms of the mercantile system and state capture by "partial interest." These shortcomings were not unique to Smith. Even economists like Marshall, Jevons, and Pigou were guilty of asserting, with no empirical validation, that state management of certain economic activities was desirable. Thus, for Stigler, the chief error of economics, including of its founding father, was an "undocumented assumption that the state was efficient in achieving mistaken ends," whether public goods provisions or regulation of private businesses.[50] The economic competence of the state was an empirically unsound assumption made by economists from 1776 onward, and it was one that Stigler wanted to overturn.

Stigler's mark in economics centered on the economic competency—or rather incompetency—of state power. Once man's behavior was reduced to utility-maximizing self-interest, economists were able

47. Stigler, "Smith's Travels on the Ship of State," 275.

48. George J. Stigler, "The Economist and the State," *The American Economic Review* 55, no. 1/2 (1965), 3.

49. Stigler, "The Economist and the State," 1.

50. Stigler, "The Economist and the State," 4.

to tear down the edifices of government intervention in the economy; they sought "a large role for explicit or implicit prices in the solution of many social problems" and advanced the "modest policy" of deregulation in certain sectors of economic life.[51] Stigler's work in the early 1960s studying the effects of regulation on utilities and financial markets, as well as his culminating essay, "The Theory of Economic Regulation," concluded that regulation was not only ineffective, but often detrimental from the standpoint of the consumer. Regulation had little effect on prices, but more troublingly, states regulated at the bidding of the industries they were supposed to oversee—in effect, creating monopolies and destroying competition, rather than preventing them.[52] Such findings gave credence to the phenomenon of "regulatory capture" and a movement for greater economic deregulation.

Ironically, as far as Stigler's theory of regulatory capture is concerned, the conditions of capture were hidden in plain sight within Smith's works. His theory of political authority, grounded in his social-psychological theory of sympathy with the rich, explained the "problem of regulation" in which Stigler was so interested. Merchants and manufactures leveraged their epistemic advantage to influence legislators. The merchant class employed its skills at knowing and pursuing its own interests, as well as its wealth, as a "psychological lever with which to dazzle those who made state policy."[53] The striking thing about Stigler's reading of Smith, then, is not so much that he reinterpreted Smith

51. Stigler, "Economics or Ethics?" 171.

52. George J. Stigler and Claire Friedland, "What Can Regulators Regulate? The Case of Electricity," *The Journal of Law & Economics* 5 (1962), 1–16; George J. Stigler, "Public Regulation of the Securities Markets," *The Journal of Business* 37, no. 2 (1964), 117–42; Stigler, "The Theory of Economic Regulation," *The Bell Journal of Economics and Management Science* 2, no. 1 (1971), 3–21.

53. Smith notes that merchants "have frequently more acuteness of understanding than the greater part of country gentlemen." *WN* I.xi.p.10, 266. For a contemporary exploration of Smith's analysis of state capture, see Sankar Muthu, "Adam Smith's Critique of International Trading Companies: Theorizing 'Globalization' in the Age of Enlightenment," *Political Theory* 36, no. 2 (April 2008), 185–212; Paul Sagar, "We Should Look Closely at What Adam Smith Actually Believed," *Aeon*, January 16, 2018, available at https://aeon.co/essays/we-should-look-closely-at-what-adam-smith-actually-believed; Sagar, "Adam Smith and the Conspiracy of the Merchants," *Global Intellectual History* 6, no. 4 (2021), 463–83.

in a way that suited his own view of economic rationality, but that he insisted Smith's contribution to modern thought was not political in nature. Indeed, Stigler suggested that it was precisely the *apolitical* nature of Smith's economics that made his works transcendent. Smith's successes as an economist were due to his "impact . . . on other scholars, not his impact upon public thinking or policy."[54] For Stigler, having policy-oriented goals was tertiary to having scholarly influence and earning the general acceptance of one's theory. "In economics, the ultimate goal is to increase the understanding of economic life: What happens and why," Stigler wrote in his memoir. The second goal was to persuade other scholars that one was right.[55] Smith did both of these things, and this was evident in his identification of the centrality of self-interest and also in his critique of mercantilism that "rested squarely on his theory of competitive prices," rather than on a specific political agenda.[56] Policy ought to be beholden to science, not ideology, and that science had to be based on empirical proof, not the uncritical acceptance and "infinite repetition" of time-worn assertions.[57] Stigler harnessed Smith's concept of self-interest as the scientific basis of a broader commitment to economic decentralization and deregulation. But to do that, he first had to stipulate that Smith's economics was not only unrelated to his moral philosophy but also in conflict with the very nature of politics.

Thus, the consequence of Stigler's interpretation was that certain aspects of Smith's ideas were amplified and glorified, while others deemed irrelevant or unsatisfactory. On the one hand, Stigler declared Smith's discovery of self-interest to be absolute, universal, and timeless. On the other hand, he characterized Smith's account of political behavior as insufficient for policy advocacy. Stigler criticized Smith's view of politics as paternalistic and moralistic—or, in Stigler's words, reminiscent of a parent correcting a child: "the child was often mistaken and sometimes

---

54. Stigler, "The Successes and Failures of Professor Smith," 1201.
55. Stigler, *Memoirs of an Unregulated Economist*, 64.
56. Stigler, "The Successes and Failures of Professor Smith," 1201.
57. Stigler, "The Economist and the State," 4.

perverse, but normally it would improve in conduct if properly instructed." However, the problem, according to Stigler, was not simply one of Smith's patronizing tone; it was that Smith engaged in policy advocacy without "taking account of the political forces which confine and direct policy," which resulted in unpersuasive and unsound advice.[58] If economists, whether in the eighteenth century or in the twentieth century, wanted to turn their empirical claims into normative ones, they needed to better account for the political forces that constrained and determined policy. In this respect, Smith failed. This was the argumentative thread that tied Stigler's analysis of Smith's "failures" to his own work on regulatory capture and to his exhortations in his 1964 AEA Presidential address. Economists, in other words, needed a better political theory than what the "normative literature for 2,300 years before Smith" could provide.[59]

Stigler had no desire to be involved in the messy politicking of economic ideas. He hoped that economists would "develop a body of knowledge essential to intelligent policy formulation" and create channels for their ideas to enter the stream of public policy indirectly.[60] Economists were to be prophets, not preachers. But where Stigler stopped short of advocating for his ideas in the public arena, there was another Chicago economist whose rise was defined by his public influence: Milton Friedman. His rise "portended, and precipitated, the triumphant return of laissez-faire," Angus Burgin has argued; moreover, it promulgated what would become one of the most recognizable and influential images of Adam Smith—the symbol of unbridled markets.[61]

Milton Friedman arrived on the national and international stage the very year that Friedrich Hayek left Chicago. In 1962, Friedman's first

58. Stigler, "Smith's Travels on the Ship of State," 272–73.

59. Stigler, "Smith's Travels on the Ship of State," 274. I am grateful to Eric Schliesser for helping me clarify and sharpen these insights on Stigler's reading of Smith qua political theorist.

60. Stigler, "The Economist and the State," 17.

61. Burgin, *The Great Persuasion*, 185.

major public-facing work, *Capitalism and Freedom*, debuted, and it was soon recognized as a streamlined, codified presentation of his political positions on a variety of topics, from education to international trade policy. The work sought to demonstrate that competitive capitalism was a "system of economic freedom and a necessary condition for political freedom."[62] Freedom, in the negative sense, was simply the absence of interference from others. The basic problem of social organization was the coordination of economic activities across large numbers of people, and the solution was two-pronged: expand the market, and whittle down the state. The role of government was simply to enforce contracts, protect private property, and guarantee individual rights. Friedman argued that market logic could be applied to an astonishing array of issues. Education ought to be privatized, for example, and vouchers would be given to families who sent their children to private schools. Corporate social responsibility was illusory; the sole social responsibility of businesses was to maximize its profits. In addition to Friedman's fervent opposition to regulatory agencies, he called for the abolition of agricultural subsidies, occupational licensing, minimum wage laws, and the Food and Drug Administration among other things. *Capitalism and Freedom* was a daring work of free-market economic analysis intentionally packaged for popular consumption and policy advocacy.

Around the time *Capitalism and Freedom* appeared, Friedman's reputation as a formidable—albeit contrarian—economist was on the rise. He had already won the John Bates Clark Medal in 1951, which recognized his outstanding contributions to the field as a young scholar. One year later, his groundbreaking publication with Anna Schwartz, *A Monetary History of the United States, 1867–1960*, brought together different strands of his research and teaching interests, but, more importantly, cast significant doubt on Keynesian and mainstream theories of money. Using historical data, Friedman and Schwartz argued that the Great Depression was caused not by the lack of regulation, but in fact by over

---

62. Milton Friedman, *Capitalism and Freedom*, 40th Anniversary Edition (Chicago, IL: University of Chicago Press, 2002), 4.

regulation. The Federal Reserve's tight control of the money supply trig-gered the recession of 1928, which led to the Depression in 1929, which was further exacerbated by the Federal Reserve's failure to stabilize the supply of money between 1929 and 1931. By the late 1960s, Friedman's studies of monetarism and inflation were being widely circulated in the profession and were seen as a challenge to Keynesian presuppositions about trade-offs between inflation and unemployment. Friedman con-tended that attempts to manage unemployment would not just increase inflation but also necessitate accelerating rates of inflation. When the stagflation of the 1970s hit, Friedman "suddenly stood out as a seer in a kingdom of the blind."[63]

Open about his efforts to directly influence public policy, Friedman insisted that he could maintain a separation between his roles as an advocate and as a scientist. He saw his actions in the public sphere as animated not through his "scientific capacity but in [his] capacity as a citizen, an informed one."[64] In truth, however, Friedman's scientific achievements and political activism from the 1960s onward blurred the boundaries between those two roles. His devotion to empirically testing scientific hypotheses provided the means by which he probed ques-tions, but those hypotheses were themselves shaped by an overarching worldview of free-markets and limited government.[65] In 1964, he be-came the lead economic advisor for Barry Goldwater's presidential cam-paign, and though Friedman never served in any formal capacity in their administrations, he became one of the most sought-after public policy advisors for Presidents Richard Nixon and Ronald Reagan. Between 1966 and 1984, Friedman penned over four hundred op-eds for major media outlets such as *The Wall Street Journal* and *Newsweek*. With his prolific writ-ing ability, unassailable debating skills, and earnest open-mindedness,

63. Daniel T. Rodgers, *Age of Fracture* (Cambridge, MA: Belknap Press of Harvard Univer-sity, 2012), 52; Burgin, *The Great Persuasion*, 203–4.

64. Roger W. Spencer and David A. Macpherson, *Lives of the Laureates: Thirty-Two Nobel Economists*, 7th edition. (Cambridge, MA: The MIT Press, 2020), 60.

65. Cherrier, "The Lucky Consistency of Milton Friedman," 362.

Friedman positioned himself to be America's leading public intellectual in the second half of the twentieth century.

In contrast to his predecessors Knight, Viner, and even Hayek, Friedman abandoned the cautious, anti-dogmatic, and moderate approach to laissez-faire that they had carefully cultivated. Instead, he embraced a more polemical approach and a rhetorical mode that appealed to populist sympathies, and he did not shy away from controversy. His primary role as an economist, Friedman believed, was to "inform the public, to give the public a better idea of what is in the public's interest."[66] To that end, he mastered the art of distilling and repackaging abstract and complex academic theories into more palatable, usable language for a wider audience. Among the rhetorical tools at his disposal were the ideas of Adam Smith, which Friedman used to construct his "market-centered world."[67]

Friedman's repetitious invocations of Smith's words and ideas has not gone unnoticed by scholars.[68] Often Friedman's use of Smith was ornamental. In his *Newsweek* columns and other opinion pieces, Friedman used Smith as a mouthpiece to scorn bureaucrats, criticize government policy, or express his distaste for cheap invocations of the "public good." Quoting from *The Wealth of Nations*, Friedman scoffed at national primaries, describing them as performances of "that insidious and crafty animal, vulgarly called a statesman or politician, whose councils are directed by the momentary fluctuations of affairs."[69] In response to the Humphrey-Hawkins Bill (introduced in 1977 and passed in 1978 to encourage full employment), Friedman wrote that "the best critique of this bill that [he had] come across was published 200 years ago in that

---

66. Milton Friedman, "Economics and Economic Policy," *Economic Inquiry* 24, no. 1 (1986), 4.

67. Burgin, *The Great Persuasion*, 188.

68. See, for example, Evensky, "'Chicago Smith' versus 'Kirkaldy Smith';" Medema, "Adam Smith and the Chicago School;" Jones, *Masters of the Universe*; Smith, "Adam Smith and the New Right."

69. *WN* IV.ii.39, 468. Friedman repurposes the same quotation in his "The Invisible Hand," in *The Business System: A Bicentennial View* (Hanover, NH: Amos Tuck School of Business Administration, 1977), 2–13, available at https://miltonfriedman.hoover.org/objects/57602; Milton Friedman, "Humphrey-Hawkins," *Newsweek*, August 2, 1976, 55; Milton Friedman, "Adam Smith's Relevance for Today," *Challenge* 20, no. 1 (March 1977), 8.

great book, 'The Wealth of Nations' by Adam Smith." As Friedman related it to his readers, Smith wrote:

> "The statesman, who should attempt to direct private people in what manner they ought to employ their capitals, would not only load himself with a most unnecessary attention, but assume an authority which could safely be trusted, not only to no single person, but to no council or senate whatever, and which would nowhere be so dangerous as in the hands of a man who had folly and presumption enough to fancy himself to exercise it."[70]

Other times Friedman quoted *The Wealth of Nations* the way someone quotes the Bible, reciting passages from a sacred text in the hopes that unbelievers and wayward followers might atone for their sins. Not even *The Wall Street Journal* could escape Friedman's proselytizing. After it ran an editorial arguing that a secure world economy could be run "only through international cooperation," Friedman responded in a typical fashion: "Please Reread Your Adam Smith," his column was titled. If *The Wall Street Journal* was to prove itself a worthy Smith acolyte, Friedman taunted, "it might ponder Adam Smith's famous remark:

> "People of the same trade seldom meet together, even for merriment and diversion, but the conversation ends up in a conspiracy against the public, or in some contrivance to raise prices. It is impossible indeed to prevent such meetings, by any law which either could be executed, or would be consistent with liberty and justice. But though the law cannot hinder people of the same trade from sometimes assembling together, it ought to do nothing to facilitate such assemblies; much less to render them necessary."[71]

70. Adam Smith as quoted by Friedman, "Humphrey-Hawkins," 55. The quotation from *The Wealth of Nations* is from Book IV.ii.10. Friedman repurposes the same text in a similar critique of Humphrey-Hawkins in his essay "Adam Smith's Relevance for Today," 8.

71. Adam Smith as quoted by Milton Friedman, "Please Reread Your Adam Smith," *The Wall Street Journal*, June 24, 1987, available at https://miltonfriedman.hoover.org/objects56898. The quotation from *The Wealth of Nations* is found in I.x.c.27, 145.

Of all of the ideas, passages, and one-liners that Friedman drew from Smith, the metaphor of the invisible hand became the most frequent entry in his political lexicon. Like Stigler, Friedman honed in on what he believed was Smith's central insight and made it the core message of his own free-market advocacy. In line with the tradition set by Viner, Knight, and Hayek, Friedman's view of Smith's contributions was also mediated through the lens of price theory. The price mechanism manifested in Smith's invisible hand, which, according to Friedman, was Smith's "greatest achievement," his "flash of genius," and a "key insight." In Friedman's words, the invisible hand represented "the way in which voluntary acts of millions of individuals each pursuing his own objectives could be coordinated, without central direction, through a price system," and it was "the achievement that [established] *The Wealth of Nations* as the beginning of scientific economics."[72] Friedman repeatedly described the invisible hand as Smith's "flash of genius," whereby

> the prices that emerged from voluntary transactions between buyers and sellers—for short, in a free market—could coordinate the activity of millions of people, each seeking their own interest, in such a way as to make everyone better off.[73]

The logic of the invisible hand was essential to any successful defense of free markets and a free society. Individuals given free rein to pursue their own self-interest would "produce an orderly society benefiting everybody" without even intending to do so.[74]

The invisible hand is probably the most discussed and debated idea in Smith's works, even in the history of economic thought.[75] Yet Smith

72. Friedman, "The Invisible Hand."

73. Milton Friedman and Rose Friedman, *Free to Choose: A Personal Statement* (New York, NY: Houghton Mifflin Harcourt, 1990), 14. Friedman used similar language about Smith's "flash of genius" and "greatest achievement" in many instances, including in *Free to Choose* (television series) episode 2 ("The Tyranny of Control"); as well as in "The Case for Freedom," (March 27, 1980) as found in The Collected Works of Milton Friedman Project Records, Hoover Institution Archives, Stanford University, available at https://miltonfriedman.hoover.org/objects/57138.

74. Friedman, "The Case for Freedom."

75. It would be foolish of me to try to document all works that have tried to advance some interpretation of the invisible hand. At least among modern Smith scholars, one of the more

used the phrase exactly three times in the entirety of his corpus: first in his *History of Astronomy* essay, second in *The Theory of Moral Sentiments*, and lastly in *The Wealth of Nations*. The image was hardly noticed by his immediate successors—Ricardo, Malthus, and Mill—and virtually absent in debates on free trade in the nineteenth century. Buckle's *History of Civilization* briefly paraphrased Smith's idea but passed over any serious discussion of the metaphor itself.[76] At the time of the sesquicentennial, John Maurice Clark only briefly mentioned the need for a reassessment of the "teleology of his 'unseen hand,'" which echoed Jacob Viner's interpretation of the invisible hand within the framework of Smith's optimistic theology in *The Theory of Moral Sentiments*.[77] By the mid-twentieth century though, economists had begun assigning a level of significance to this idea of Smith's that exceeded past interpretations, and those attributions took place against the backdrop of abstract, mathematical, and neo-Keynesian models of markets.[78] In 1948, the

---

important revisionist interpretations of Smith's invisible hand comes from Emma Rothschild, who describes it as a "mildly ironic joke" and something that Smith himself would not have readily accepted as a normatively desirable feature of economic and moral life. See Emma Rothschild, "Adam Smith and the Invisible Hand," *The American Economic Review* 84, no. 2, (1994), 319–22; Emma Rothschild, *Economic Sentiments: Adam Smith, Condorcet, and the Enlightenment* (Cambridge, MA: Harvard University Press, 2001), chap. 5. William D. Grampp argues that the invisible hand is "more interesting than it is important," and explores ten possible interpretations in his "What Did Smith Mean by the Invisible Hand?" *Journal of Political Economy* 108, no. 3 (2000), 441–65. Shannon Stimson's account, contra Rothschild, is less focused on the rhetorical context than on the scientific one of classical economics. Shannon Stimson, "From Invisible Hand to Moral Restraint: The Transformation of the Market Mechanism from Adam Smith to Thomas Robert Malthus," *Journal of Scottish Philosophy* 2, no. 1 (March 2004), 22–47. For a more recent interpretation, see Schliesser, *Adam Smith*, chap. 10.

76. Gavin Kennedy, "Adam Smith and the Invisible Hand: From Metaphor to Myth," *Econ Journal Watch* 6, no. 2 (2009), 239–63; Kennedy, "Paul Samuelson and the Invention of the Modern Economics of the Invisible Hand."

77. John Maurice Clark, "Adam Smith and the Currents of History," in *Adam Smith, 1776–1926: Lectures to Commemorate the Sesquicentennial of the Publication of the "Wealth of Nations"* (Chicago, IL: University of Chicago Press), 53–76.

78. In addition to Gavin Kennedy's work, Warren J. Samuels has written authoritative accounts of uses of the invisible hand metaphor in twentieth-century economics. For an introduction, see the conversation, "Adam Smith's Invisible Hand," documented and published in Sandra Peart and David M. Levy, eds., *The Street Porter and the Philosopher: Conversations on Analytical*

MIT economist Paul Samuelson published his landmark economics textbook, *Economics: An Introductory Analysis*, in which he portrayed the "mystical principle" of the invisible hand as a precursor of foundational theories in modern economics such as perfect competition and general equilibrium. Though Samuelson tried to clarify his somewhat muddled presentation of the invisible hand in subsequent editions, he could not fully retract his original statement that Smith's invisible hand anticipated some of the most important theories in modern economics.[79]

Samuelson's textbook would eventually become the best-selling economics textbook of all time. Now in its twentieth edition, Samuelson's *Economics* has sold over 5 million copies and has been translated into some forty different languages. In 1977, Samuelson declared that he had "vindicated" Adam Smith from the criticisms of Ricardo, Marx, and later neoclassical thinkers who treated the Scotsman as "unoriginal . . . logically fuzzy and eclectically empty." A quick, formal mathematical proof identified a "valid element in Smith's INVISIBLE HAND doctrine:" that *self-interest, under perfect conditions of competition, can organize a society's production efficiently.*[80] No less important was Kenneth Arrow and Frank Hahn's 1971 *General Competitive Analysis*. Built upon Arrow and Gerard Debreu's 1954 work, *General Competitive Analysis* was a pathbreaking work of economic theory. In their 1971 work, Arrow and Hahn claimed that the special conditions under which general equilibrium was obtained were mathematical proof of Smith's invisible hand, a "poetic expression of the most fundamental of economic

Egalitarianism (Ann Arbor, MI: University of Michigan Press, 2008), 179–201; Samuels, Johnson, and Perry, *Erasing the Invisible Hand.*

79. Gavin Kennedy has studiously traced Samuelson's use and subsequent abuse of the invisible hand metaphor. See, for example, Kennedy, "Adam Smith and the Invisible Hand;" Kennedy, "Paul Samuelson and the Invention of the Modern Economics of the Invisible Hand." For a deeper treatment of Samuelson's intellectual development, specifically the role of mathematical modeling in economics, see Roger E. Backhouse, *Founder of Modern Economics: Paul A. Samuelson: Volume 1: Becoming Samuelson, 1915–1948*, Illustrated edition (New York, NY: Oxford University Press, 2017).

80. Paul A. Samuelson, "A Modern Theorist's Vindication of Adam Smith," *The American Economic Review* 67, no. 1, (1977), 42, 47. Emphasis in original.

balance relations."[81] Even outside of economics, philosophers used the metaphor to make sense of processes or explanations for outcomes that appeared spontaneous, natural, and mostly—but not always—harmonious. Robert Nozick's *Anarchy, State, and Utopia* identified some sixteen examples of "invisible hand explanations" in everything from trade to religion.[82]

Thus, the prevailing approach to wrestling with the invisible hand, at least among economists, stripped markets and the invisible hand of their human and institutional contexts and presented them as pure, immaterial, scientific models. In this respect, Friedman was less interested in furnishing a scientific proof of what the invisible hand was (or was not) than in making an academic contribution. The basis of his interpretation of the invisible hand—the price mechanism—had precedent in the works of Hayek and others. But as the economic crises of the 1970s unfolded, Friedman's predictions of spiraling unemployment and inflation provided further reason to question the reigning neo-Keynesian assumptions about the government's managerial role in the economy. Friedman's ingenuity lay in the fact that he took the scientific validity of the invisible hand for granted, and then transformed it into an overt political argument about the virtues of markets and the harms of government interference in economic life.

Friedman's invisible-hand waving culminated in a much-anticipated television series, *Free to Choose*, which debuted on public television and as a book in 1980. The timing and context in which the series was conceived and delivered were crucial. Four years earlier, Friedman had retired from the University of Chicago to take up a temporary post at the Federal Reserve Bank of San Francisco, and soon thereafter he

81. Kenneth J. Arrow and F.H. Hahn, *General Competitive Analysis* (San Francisco, CA: Holden-Day, 1971), 1–2.

82. Robert Nozick, *Anarchy, State, and Utopia*, Reprint edition (New York: Basic Books, 2013); Nozick, "Invisible-Hand Explanations," *The American Economic Review* 84, no. 2 (1994), 314–18; for further analysis on Nozick's invisible hand theories, see Gerald Gaus, "Explanation, Justification, and Emergent Properties: An Essay on Nozickian Metatheory," in *The Cambridge Companion to Nozick's Anarchy, State, and Utopia*, eds. Ralf M. Bader and John Meadowcroft (Cambridge: Cambridge University Press, 2011), 116–142; Kennedy, "Adam Smith and the Invisible Hand."

took a permanent position at the conservative Hoover Institution at Stanford University. Free from his routine academic obligations, Friedman had much more latitude as a public intellectual. In addition, *Free to Choose* was following on the heels of another television series which also featured a celebrity economist, John Kenneth Galbraith of Harvard: *The Age of Uncertainty*. For a number of reasons, the success of *The Age of Uncertainty* was lukewarm at best. Despite high expectations, viewers seemed unconvinced by Galbraith's attempts at a grand historical narrative, impartiality, and professional detachment. After only a small amount of persuasion from the show's producer and his wife, Rose, Friedman agreed to be a part of a documentary series that put free-market ideas—specifically, *his* free-market ideas—on television.[83]

Free To Choose had no pretense of political neutrality. It was not a history of economic ideas; instead, it was Friedman's "personal statement of [his] own social, economic, and political values," illustrated with stories from real people and organizations.[84] Each episode featured Friedman in a different location—New York, Hong Kong, India, Tokyo—exploring a specific dimension of free markets or confronting the problems of government interference with economic life. Each episode also included a post-documentary debate between supporters and opponents of Friedman's views—scholars, politicians, businessmen, and activists. Every one of these elements was intentional and calculated to maximize the public impact of Friedman's message. Real-world footage, stories of ordinary people engulfed in transformative market processes, and economists engaged in verbal jousting would appeal to a public that craved both "anecdotal validations" of abstract ideas and lively intellectual debate.[85]

83. For a rich and colorful analysis on the production and reception of Galbraith's *The Age of Uncertainty* compared to *Free to Choose*, see Angus Burgin, "Age of Certainty: Galbraith, Friedman, and the Public Life of Economic Ideas," *History of Political Economy* 45, Supplementary Volume 1 (2013), 191–219. For the Friedmans' personal account of the making of *Free to Choose*, see Milton Friedman and Rose D. Friedman, *Two Lucky People*, chap. 28.

84. As quoted in Burgin, "Age of Certainty," 211–12.

85. Burgin, "Age of Certainty," 212.

The central message of *Free to Choose* was that economic freedom, enshrined in free markets, was essential for political freedom, and Smith first articulated this argument in his famous metaphor of the invisible hand. "Adam Smith's flash of genius was to see how prices had emerged in the market," Friedman stated, echoing a familiar line. Famously, Friedman performed a version of Leonard Read's famous 1958 essay, "I, Pencil," to illustrate the common sense and scientific truth that markets realized. "Literally thousands of people cooperated to make this pencil," Friedman explained. "People who don't speak the same language, who practice different religions, who might hate one another if they ever met . . . what brought them together and induced them to make this pencil?" he asked. Nothing other than the "magic of the price system, the impersonal operation of prices."[86] Friedman's statement of the invisible hand was so abundantly clear and simple in *Free to Choose* in part because he recognized how difficult it might be for ordinary readers and viewers to grasp the full meaning of Smith's "greatest achievement." The invisible hand was, after all, invisible. It operated silently, and "people are seldom aware of a complicated machine as long as it is working," Friedman once explained in a 1977 speech. It might go unappreciated not only because of "how complicated and subtle the price system is" but also because it was often misunderstood as a system "based on egotism and selfishness."[87] Friedman was intent on correcting this misunderstanding of the price mechanism. In a later episode, the authoritative, Scottish voice of Adam Smith read from *The Wealth of Nations*, and Friedman stepped in as Smith's interpreter: "The invisible hand is a phrase introduced by Adam Smith in his great work *The Wealth of Nations*, in which he talked about the way in which individuals who intended only to pursue their own interest were led by an invisible hand

86. *Free to Choose*, Episode 1. Many viewers would have recognized this illustration from Leonard Read's famous essay, "I, Pencil," first published in 1958. Friedman does not reference Read in *Free to Choose*, but he does in a speech in 1977 called "The Invisible Hand," delivered at the Tuck School of Business at Dartmouth. On the influence of Read's essay and the development of free enterprise rhetoric, see Lawrence B. Glickman, *Free Enterprise: An American History* (New Haven, CT: Yale University Press, 2019), chap. 6.

87. Friedman, "The Invisible Hand," 6.

to promote the public welfare which was no part of their intention."[88] The version of self-interest underlining the price mechanism, according to Friedman, needn't be "selfish and narrow;" it could be "broad and far reaching." What Smith's invisible hand demonstrated was simply how the market mechanism "will often be more effective than the visible hand," and that insight could apply across innumerable contexts.[89]

One of Friedman's signature rhetorical maneuvers repurposed the logic of the invisible hand to reinforce the idea that the market and the state were frequently at odds with one another. Just as Stigler had found that industries would end up capturing the regulatory bodies intended to regulate them, and just as James Buchanan and Gordon Tullock concluded that democratic processes tended to produce outcomes against the interests of the broader public, Friedman argued that politicians could be "led by an invisible hand to promote an end which was no part of their intention."[90] This was the "invisible hand in politics." A (perhaps) well-meaning politician who intended only to serve the public interest ended up promoting his own private interests; the invisible hand of the government sphere, therefore, operated "in precisely the opposite direction from Adam Smith's."[91] Friedman contended that the "failure to understand this central insight of Smith" led to the heavy hand of government squeezing individual freedom wherever it could.

Though Free to Choose drew on global examples, Friedman's target audience was American, and he appealed to traditional American political ideals to amplify his message about the centrality of economic freedom. "Smith and Jefferson alike had seen concentrated government power as a great danger to the ordinary man," Friedman argued in Free to Choose. "They saw the protection of the citizen against the tyranny of government as the perpetual need."[92] Friedman painted a picture of

88. Free to Choose, Episode 2, "The Tyranny of Control."

89. Friedman, "The Invisible Hand," 7.

90. Friedman and Friedman, Free to Choose, 292. The same language is also used in Free to Choose (television series), episode 10, "How to Stay Free." On the influence of Stigler and Buchanan on Friedman, see Burgin, The Great Persuasion, 191.

91. Free to Choose, episode 2, "The Tyranny of Control."

92. Friedman and Friedman, Free to Choose, 4.

America as a country whose founding values—above all, freedom—were under threat; welfare was expanding, and, with it, people were losing "their human feeling of independence and dignity."[93] The U.S. public school system, for example, was inimical to its ends, taking away freedom from parents, jeopardizing educational opportunity, and exacerbating inequality. Consumer protection laws were burdensome, delivered shoddy products, and stifled innovation. Placing Smith and Jefferson side by side enabled Friedman to cast the relationship between economic freedom and political freedom as founding—and revolutionary—ideals worth fighting for. The Friedmans even described Jefferson's Declaration as "in many ways the political twin of Smith's economics."[94] Beyond providing a revolutionary battle cry, Friedman's message carried a moral argument as well. Markets not only guaranteed personal freedom, they also fostered conditions for virtuous behavior and an ethic of capitalism centered around individual responsibility, self-reliance, and innovation.[95]

Smith's iconic status thus became entangled with the free market politics of Milton Friedman in a way that exceeded the ambitions and intentions of the postwar generation. In the age of Friedman, reference to Smith was an unmistakable bow to the ideology of freer markets and less government. Even Smith-themed sartorial choices were politicized. Friedman was one of many public figures caught sporting various shades of an Adam Smith necktie (see Fig. 6.2). The tie had its origins with Donald Lipsett and his wife, Norma, who popularized the Smith tie among members of the conservative Philadelphia Society, which Lipsett founded in 1964. "The proverbial old-school tie is being put to ideological use in Washington these days," *Time* observed in 1981. "The most popular neckpiece around the Reagan White House is one bearing tiny cameo profiles of Adam Smith, the 18th century Scot whose An Inquiry into the Nature and Causes of the Wealth of Nations lined the

93. *Free to Choose*, Episode 4, "From Cradle to Grave."

94. Milton Friedman and Rose Friedman, "The Tide in the Affairs of Men," Collected Works of Milton Friedman Project records, Hoover Institution Archives, Stanford University. Reprinted in *Thinking about America: The United State in the 1990s*, ed. Annelise Anderson and Dennis L. Bark, (Stanford, CA: Hoover Institution Press, 1988), 455–68.

95. Burgin, *The Great Persuasion*, chap. 6.

FIG. 6.2. Milton Friedman sporting his famous Adam Smith necktie.
Hanna Holborn Gray Special Collections Research Center,
University of Chicago Library.

classic argument for getting government off the back of business."[96] By
1982, the Lipsetts had sold some 10,000 Adam Smith ties.[97]

96. "A Cravat for Conservatives." *Time Magazine*, 118, no. 1 (July 6, 1981), 60.
97. Clyde H. Farnsworth, "Neckties with an Economics Lesson," *The New York Times*, July 7,
1982, https://www.nytimes.com/1982/07/07/us/neckties-with-an-economics-lesson.html.
The Lipsetts had not yet come up with a women's line, though Dodi Kazanjian, the deputy press

That Smith appeared to be little more than the totem of free-market proselytizers like Friedman would be the complaint of Friedman's critics for decades to come. "People who wear the Adam Smith tie are not doing so to honor literary genius," wrote Herbert Stein, a former chairman of the Council of Economic Advisers. "They are doing so to make a statement of their devotion to the idea of free markets and limited government."[98] Democratic Socialist critic Michael Harrington ridiculed Friedman's Smith-laden rhetoric as something that "really comes down to an intellectual exercise whose practical political effect is to rationalize conservative power in America." How, Harrington wondered, "can you have a mystical belief in the invisible hand of Adam Smith" in a world so different than the one in which Smith lived? Neither Stein nor Harrington sought to combat Friedman's agenda with a fully fleshed out interpretation of Smith's works, though. Instead, their discomfort was with Friedman's overt ahistoricism and conviction that certain ideas—especially Smith's ideas—were objectively true and, therefore, entitled to inform twentieth-century public policy. The problem with Friedman's version of the invisible hand as a right-wing political agenda was not that it was a complete misinterpretation of Smith's text. The problem, as Michael Harrington put it, was that it was "essentially a mythic, non-historical presentation of an abstract solution taken out of time which does not look to the tremendous evolution of capitalist society."[99]

Yet Friedman's reinvention of Smith's invisible hand served an altogether different purpose. Friedman was not interested in a historical reconstruction of what the invisible hand meant to *Smith*; Friedman was simply interested in exploiting its rhetorical power for his own message. While there was a loose academic consensus around the idea that the invisible hand represented some aspect of the autonomous working of markets, Friedman took the scientific proposition for granted. For him, the invisible hand did more than furnish academics with a historical

---

secretary for Nancy Reagan, expressed her desire to get "soft fluffy Adam Smith bow ties for women" someday.

98. Herbert Stein, "Remembering Adam Smith," *The Wall Street Journal*, April 6, 1994.

99. *Free to Choose*, Episode 1, "The Power of the Market."

trinket for their proofs and theorems; it legitimized and represented an entire worldview oriented around the political and moral necessity of free markets. A tireless believer in the power of ideas, Friedman found in Smith an idea that could shift the terms of debate around economic freedom in a way that was "simple in concept, populist in tone, empirical in methodology, and capable of solving the great problems of the modern world."[100] And while he was not the originator of this version of Smith, Friedman catalyzed its broader public reception. *Free to Choose* sold over a million copies in print, and an estimated three million viewers watched the television program. The Americanism Educational League purchased copies of the video series and loaned them out to hundreds of colleges and universities.[101] Friedman even bought back the rights of *Free to Choose* so that he could keep the price of video cassettes as low as possible with the hopes of reaching younger audiences. So central was the idea of the invisible hand to him that, if Friedman had gotten his way, *Free to Choose* would have been named *The Invisible Hand*.[102]

———

Stigler and Friedman transformed Adam Smith into an American icon in the twentieth century. They took him out of esoteric philosophical debates about the consistency of his *oeuvre* and the abstract modeling of economic phenomena. Instead, they turned him into an economic everyman. Stigler and Friedman made Adam Smith available to the mass consumer as the symbol of self-interest, choice, and freedom. "Adam Smith was a radical and revolutionary in his time—just as those of us who preach laissez-faire are in our time," wrote Milton Friedman in an essay titled, "Adam Smith's Relevance for Today."[103] Friedman's article was actually based on a paper he presented at the Mont Pèlerin

100. Burgin, "Age of Certainty," 215.

101. As Burgin documents, within a few years, the Americanism Educational League informed Friedman that the video cassettes were "out on loan all of the time." Burgin, "Age of Certainty," 214.

102. Friedman and Friedman, *Two Lucky People*, 502, 495–96.

103. Friedman, "Adam Smith's Relevance for Today," 6.

Society's twenty-first general meeting in August of 1976, held in St. Andrews, and which suitably included a field trip to Kirkcaldy, the place of Smith's birth.[104] Around the same time, think tanks like the Adam Smith Institute in London as well as the Cato Institute and the Heritage Foundation, both in Washington, sprouted on both sides of the Atlantic, bearing Smith's name and staking claims to Smith's legacy by welding free-market economics to a new brand of conservative policymaking.[105]

On one level, such additions to Smith's modern legacy mark no new story. To turn Smith into a slogan, a logo, or a "symbolic figure who bestows authority on the particular policies adopted by a given political faction" simply appears to be a continuation of a much longer history of politicizing Smith for partisan purposes.[106] And this usually prompts some sort of reaction from those seeking to "rescue" Smith from misinterpretation or political abuse. But on another level, these past engagements with Smith are much more than verbal—and sometimes literal—embroidery. They are hallmarks of a distinctive, substantive argument about the essence of Smith's contribution to economics and its political implications. They are the markers of influence.

The Chicago Smith was neither accidental nor inevitable, but rather the deliberate construction of key figures who were part of an intellectual movement. It was the product of various minds that were continually searching for, questioning, and defending the content and structure of a liberal society at a time when that society appeared to be under threat. In addition, the Chicago Smith did not spring out of economists' heads, fully formed and fully armed. The Smith of Knight and Viner

104. "Newsletter of the Mont Pèlerin Society," no. 11 (December 1976). George Stigler Papers, University of Chicago Special Collections Research Center.

105. On the history of conservative think tanks in the United States and Great Britain, see Richard Cockett, *Thinking the Unthinkable: Think-Tanks and the Economic Counter-Revolution 1931–1983* (London: HarperCollins, 1995); James A. Smith, *Idea Brokers: Think Tanks And The Rise Of The New Policy Elite* (New York: The Free Press, 1991); Alice O'Connor, "Financing the Counterrevolution," in *Rightward Bound: Making America Conservative in the 1970s*, eds. Bruce Schulman and Julian Zelizer (Cambridge, MA: Harvard University Press, 2008), 148–68; Jones, *Masters of the Universe*.

106. Smith, "Adam Smith and the New Right."

embodied the fundamental tensions of market advocacy in the 1930s and early 1940s. As Knight's and Viner's readings show, recalling Smith's original intentions as a political economist and reestablishing the link between Smith's moral philosophy and political economy furthered a vision of economics as a pluralistic, positive science with normative commitments that was also resistant to reductive, ideological appropriations of laissez-faire. This earlier and often overlooked version of the Chicago Smith thus captures the way in which early free-market liberalism was an intellectual project full of conflict and compromise over its moral and political boundaries.

Later developments began more forcefully retrojecting the distinct Chicagoan methodological and political aims onto Smith. This became the foundation of Stigler's and Friedman's Smith from the 1950s onward: the Smith who represented a positive methodology based on the social productiveness of self-interest alone, whose conceptualization of markets unequivocally aligned with a political program of deregulation and hostility towards any attempt by the government to direct economic activity. But even this version of the Chicago Smith came in a variety of shades. Hayek, for instance, found in Smith an epistemic theory that supported a social philosophy of markets and a dogged anti-rationalism. Friedman and Stigler, by contrast, found in the Scotsman a mode of analysis which proved the irrationality and counterproductive nature of politics, whilst also proving the orderly and natural outcomes of self-interested, independent, and freely choosing individuals in the market. For Friedman, Smith's invisible hand was an "instrumental device" whose direct opposite was government. Government operated through coercion, clumsiness, and deceptive intention; the invisible hand of the market, however, was the realm of freedom, choice, and possibility.[107] Reading Smith through the "mystique of science" as Robert van Horn and Philip Mirowski dubbed it, Stigler and Friedman smoothed over the tensions, instabilities, and inconsistencies that were central features of the earlier generation's engagements with Smith; in doing so, they emphasized a single-minded, "economized" reading of Smith that fit

107. Rodgers, *Age of Fracture*, 42.

with their intellectual and political projects. Consequently, Friedman and Stigler assumed gatekeeping roles of Smith's legacy both in formal and informal capacities. Jerry Evensky, a widely-published Smith scholar, recalls submitting a manuscript to *The Journal of Political Economy*, and receiving a curt rejection letter from Stigler (who served as chief editor from 1972–1991) that stated, "This is not the Adam Smith I know."[108]

Perhaps the greatest consequence of the Chicago Smith was the way it served to reframe the problems of modern American capitalism and modern society as problems that stemmed from government, rather than the market itself. Smith was "no apologist for merchants and manufacturers, or, more generally, for other special interests," Friedman wrote in his 1976 retrospective, rather, Smith "regarded them as the great obstacles to laissez-faire, just as we do today." The critical but almost imperceptible move that Friedman made was extending Smith's critique of this monopolizing, merchant mindset to what Friedman believed to be the most important and dangerous monopoly of all: government. Friedman admitted that the interests of private monopolies exerted undue influence in government—"like an overgrown standing army," to use Smith's words. However—and this is crucial—Friedman also argued that "we must broaden the 'tribes' of 'monopolists' to include not only enterprises protected from competition, but also trade unions, school teachers, welfare recipients, and so on and on."[109] The invisible hand of politics was debilitating to the invisible hand of the market; only by restraining the former could the latter reign freely.

Though authoritative in its character, the Chicago Smith did not go unchallenged. Even as Friedman was reaching his apogee in the mid–1970s, a disparate group historians, political theorists, and public intellectuals began to repudiate Chicago's economized version of Smith. The Scotsman had always been alive and well, but, as a growing number of readers tried to free him from the confining halls of the University of

108. This anecdote was told to me by historian of economic thought Ross Emmett. Ross Emmett, email to author, March 27, 2021. Evensky does not have the original correspondence but recalls the specific comment, which he corroborated over email. Jerry Evensky, email message to author, July 16, 2021.

109. Friedman, "Adam Smith's Relevance for Today," 7.

Chicago, they began to ask new questions about the specific and historical nature of his politics and the moral preconditions of his vision of
commercial society. In doing so, they not only brought together different strands of Smith's thought in new ways, but also reignited debates
about whether Smith's commercial society—and at a longer remove,
American capitalism—was defensible on moral grounds.

7

Turning Smith Back
on the Present

1976 WAS THE YEAR of the American bicentennial. It was also the bi-centenary of *The Wealth of Nations*. Celebrations were held all over the world in cities from Glasgow to Tokyo, but few were filled with as much color and comedy as one particular event held in Cambridge, Massachusetts. On April 12, the Graduate Economics Association of MIT hosted a roast celebrating the two hundredth anniversary of *The Wealth of Nations*. George "Jerry" Goodman, a popular economics broadcaster and journalist who went by the pen name Adam Smith, found himself in the improbable scenario of accepting the "The Invisible Hand Award" in front of a throng of economists singing a Smith-themed hymn to the tune of "Rock of Ages."

> Wealth of Nations! Writ for me!
> Let me hide myself in Thee!
> Not the Profits, nor the Rent,
> But the Labour Time that's spent,
> Be of Value the true source.
> Make me better; no one worse
>
> . . .
>
> Hand invisible whose love
> We believe that we can prove!

With thy panoply of saints,
Mill, Ricardo, Marshall, Keynes,
Save us all from Marxist sins.
Keep us gaily making pins![1]

Just ten days earlier, on the other side of the Atlantic, the University of Glasgow had hosted its conference in honor of the bicentenary of *The Wealth of Nations*, a gathering which attracted award-winning scholars from around the world including George Stigler and Friedrich Hayek. The most important outcome of the conference was the release of the Glasgow Editions of the Works of Adam Smith, more than doubling the volume of Smith's published works. *The Wealth of Nations* and *The Theory of Moral Sentiments* were republished in 1976, followed shortly by an even fuller edition of the *Lectures on Jurisprudence* thanks to the discovery of a second set of student notes in 1958. In addition, Smith's correspondence was meticulously compiled and a new *Lectures on Rhetoric* featuring not one but two sets of student notes debuted. This marked a new high point for Smith fans worldwide. "These materials," the American historian Gary Willis heartily proclaimed in 1978, would provide the much-needed tools to "break Smith out of the prison of his popular reputation as the rationalizer of greed."[2] Intellectual historian Donald Winch wrote that 1976 marked "the point in time when scholarship relating to Smith came of age."[3]

---

1. These are the first and third (of four) verses of the "Wealth of Nations!" hymn. Program from the 200th Anniversary of Wealth of Nations Roast of Adam Smith at MIT, April 12, 1976. Text by William N. Parker. "Economics in the Rear-View Mirror," by Irwin Collier. http://www.irwincollier.com/from-the-200th-anniversary-of-wealth-of-nations-roast-of-adam-smith-at-mit-1976/. Goodman's account of the Roast is told in Adam Smith [Jerry Goodman], "The Invisible Hand Strikes Again," *New York Magazine*, May 3, 1976.

2. Garry Wills, "Benevolent Adam Smith," *The New York Review of Books*, February 9, 1978, available at http://www.nybooks.com/articles/1978/02/09/benevolent-adam-smith/; Donald Winch, "Not by Economics Alone," *The Times Literary Supplement*, March 12, 1976.

3. Winch, "Not by Economics Alone." See also Horst Claus Recktenwald, "An Adam Smith Renaissance Anno 1976? The Bicentenary Output-A Reappraisal of His Scholarship," *Journal of Economic Literature* 16, no. 1 (1978), 56–83, 56. Recktenwald estimated the number of "scientific publications in and about this [1976] anniversary year" to be about 350. See also Jonathan B. Wight,

Smith scholarship was coming of age just as the epoch of American industrial might was coming to a close. The golden era of the U.S.'s manufacturing boom was fading as a new service economy was on the rise, but the changes extended well beyond the structural composition of the economy. The rise of neoliberal policymaking in the 1970s and 1980s seemed to announce the victory of the New Right on both sides of the Atlantic, extending the logic of the market into public and private arenas at a feverish pace and permeating visions of an integrated world economy. The oil and energy crises resulting from the Arab-Israeli conflict in 1973 sent the global economy into shock, bringing forth new economic terminology like "stagflation"—the simultaneous spiraling of inflation and unemployment—and the political weaponization of Arthur Okun's "misery index" (the combination of unemployment and inflation rates).[4] While the ascendancy of the Reagan and Thatcher regimes reinforced the narrative that, in Reagan's famous words, "Government is not the solution to our problem. Government is the problem," by the 1980s, a counterforce of left-tilting academics and the vestiges of the 1960s' New Left brought Marxism into the philosophical mainstream. Anglophone philosophers such as G.A. Cohen and Ronald Dworkin reappropriated the ideas of choice, ownership, and markets in new defenses of liberal egalitarian distributive justice. However, as Katrina Forrester has shown in her revisionist history of twentieth-century political philosophy, these attempts to grapple with the philosophical

---

"The Rise of Adam Smith: Articles and Citations, 1970–1997," *History of Political Economy* 34, no. 1 (2002), 55–82.

4. For representative works on the economic and political transformations of the 1970s on, see Mark Blyth, *Great Transformations: Economic Ideas and Institutional Change in the Twentieth Century* (New York, NY: Cambridge University Press, 2002); Gerstle, "The Rise and Fall of the Neoliberal Order;" Jonathan Levy, *Ages of American Capitalism: A History of the United States* (New York, NY: Random House, 2021) especially chap. 18 and 19; Alice O'Connor, Gary Gerstle, and Nelson Lichtenstein, eds. *Beyond the New Deal Order: U.S. Politics from the Great Depression to the Great Recession*, Politics and Culture in Modern America (Philadelphia, PA: University of Pennsylvania Press, 2019); Rodgers, *Age of Fracture*; Bruce J. Schulman and Julian E. Zelizer, eds. *Rightward Bound: Making America Conservative in the 1970s* (Cambridge, MA: Harvard University Press, 2008).

and practical possibilities of socialism in some respects were evidence of marketized liberalism's allure.[5] A neoconservative intellectual movement was poised to respond. American capitalism was under threat, neoconservatives believed, not only from social justice "dogmatists" on the academic left, but also and more worryingly, from the erosion of traditional values such as the ethic of hard work, delayed gratification, individual responsibility, and the model of the two-parent family.[6] No matter which way one looked at it—from the left or the right, from an economic, political, or moral perspective—American capitalism was in crisis. In 1975, the July 14th cover of *Time* magazine blared: "Can Capitalism Survive?" as Adam Smith's characteristically stoic face gazed into the distance. "Don't count me out!" he cartoonishly exclaimed.

The crises of capitalism in the final quarter of the twentieth century led American academics and public intellectuals to "raise anew the question of alternatives to capitalism," as the economist Ken Arrow wrote in 1978. In that light, many returned to Adam Smith with a new set of demands and questions.[7] Stigler and Friedman's version of Smith showed how capitalism rested on the unshakeable foundations of rational self-interest and the economic logic of the price mechanism, but it elided—if not intentionally downplayed—any political and moral prerequisites. Could capitalism be defensible on political and moral

---

5. Katrina Forrester, *In the Shadow of Justice: Postwar Liberalism and the Remaking of Political Philosophy* (Princeton, NJ: Princeton University Press, 2019), chap. 7.

6. For "dogmatists," See Irving Kristol, "What is Social Justice?" (1976), in his *Neoconservatism: The Autobiography of an Idea* (Chicago, IL: Ivan R. Dee, 1995), 256. Select works on neoconservatism include Gary Dorrien, *The Neoconservative Mind: Politics, Culture, and the War of Ideology*, Reprint edition (Philadelphia, PA: Temple University Press, 1993); Jean-François Drolet, *American Neoconservatism: The Politics and Culture of a Reactionary Idealism*, Reprint edition (New York, NY: Oxford University Press, 2014); Justin Vaïsse, *Neoconservatism: The Biography of a Movement*, trans. Arthur Goldhammer, (Cambridge, MA.: Belknap Press, An Imprint of Harvard University Press, 2011); Mark Gerson, *The Neoconservative Vision: From the Cold War to the Culture Wars* (Lanham: Madison Books, 1995). On the synthesis of neoliberalism and the "family values" of social conservatism, see Melinda Cooper, *Family Values: Between Neoliberalism and the New Social Conservatism* (New York, NY: Zone Books, 2017).

7. Kenneth J. Arrow, "A Cautious Case for Socialism," (Lionel Trilling Seminar of the academic year 1977–1978 delivered at Columbia University) republished in *Dissent Magazine* 25, no. 4 (1978), 472–480 at 477.

grounds, too? What was Smith's political and institutional vision that made his "system of natural liberty" viable? And what, if any, were its moral promises and pitfalls?

Various thinkers tried to answer these questions through engaging with Smith's ideas in the wake of the bicentenary. In the wider context of late-twentieth century anxieties about capitalism's political and moral moorings, two parallel intellectual trends sought to recover what was believed to be lost in the Chicago School's version of Smith. The first of these trends was a forceful set of arguments about Smith as a political thinker in his own right, evident in influential works such as A.O. Hirschman's *The Passions and the Interests* (1977), Donald Winch's *Adam Smith's Politics* (1978), and István Hont and Michael Ignatieff's essay, "Needs and Justice in the *Wealth of Nations*" (1983). Though varied in their historical methods, these works offered re-readings of Smith that not only disassociated him from the "Chicago-style" and "liberal-capitalist" traditions constructed around him, but also introduced new interpretive categories and questions about the politics that made market-oriented modernity possible. Ironically though, these early efforts to restore the contingencies of Smith's politics resulted in a different version of Smith as an anti-political thinker of sorts.[8] Smith was no longer a Chicago-style economist who predicted the failure of self-interest in the political realm; he had become a thinker whose political economy was at best skeptical, pessimistic, and suspicious.

The second, and arguably more influential, trend was the development of a separate but related set of propositions about Smith's significance as a moral philosopher, or, more specifically, a moral theorist of commercial society and, at a longer remove, capitalism. The roots of this trend can be found in the intellectual history of American neoconservatism, especially in the writings of prominent public intellectuals and

8. Eric Schliesser, "Adam Smith on Political Leadership," in R. J. W. Mills and Craig Smith, *The Scottish Enlightenment: Human Nature, Social Theory and Moral Philosophy: Essays in Honour of Christopher J. Berry* (Edinburgh: University Press, 2021), 132–63; Craig Smith, "Adam Smith: Left or Right?" *Political Studies* 61, no. 4 (December 2013), 784–98.

scholars such as Irving Kristol, Gertrude Himmelfarb, James Q. Wilson, and Francis Fukuyama.[9] Kristol and Himmelfarb's writings offered an alternative to the Chicago School's economistic Smith through an idiosyncratic interpretation of his moral philosophy. Capitalism understood in economic terms alone, in their view, stood "helpless before any moralistic assault," so they turned to Smith for a new line of defense.[10] This preoccupation with Smith's defense of market society has resurfaced in more recent scholarship.

The interpretation of Smith as a moral theorist of capitalism, I argue, has become a convenient ideological holding pen for beliefs on opposite sides of the political spectrum, with those on the "Right" appealing to Smith in order to defend conservative moral sensibilities, and those on the "Left" appealing to Smith in order to defend a view of capitalism that also promoted social justice.[11] Both sides have found common ground in the idea that Smith's vision of capitalism was and is defensible on moral bases. Thus, Smith has become the locus of an unexpected

9. Antti Lepistö has recently and much more extensively documented the history of neoconservatism and their transformation of Scottish Enlightenment moral theory, specifically in the writings of the four writers mentioned here. For reasons of length and scope, my account covers just a tiny sliver of Lepistö's detailed study. See Antti Lepistö, *The Rise of Common-Sense Conservatism: The American Right and the Reinvention of the Scottish Enlightenment*, (Chicago, IL: University of Chicago Press, 2021).

10. Kristol, "On Conservatism and Capitalism," in Kristol, *Neoconservatism*, 234.

11. I do not intend to treat "left" and "right" as stable, coherent ideologies. Rather, I adopt Samuel Fleischacker's approach to using "left" and "right" as "cluster terms" that encompass political and moral beliefs about the role of tradition, trust in state power, and balancing conceptions of equality and freedom. Broadly speaking, interpretations of a "right" Smith emphasize Smith's decentralist political-economic thinking, his trust in individual agency and freedom, skepticism of interventionist government; meanwhile, interpretation of the "left" draw out Smith's commitment to the moral equality of individuals, his suspicion of the Church and monarchy, his opposition to slavery and the Corn Laws. For more on the use of the Left-Right designation in Smith scholarship see Samuel Fleischacker, "Adam Smith and the Left," in *Adam Smith*, ed. Hanley, 478–93; James R. Otteson, "Adam Smith and the Right" in the same volume, 594–511. See also Rothschild, "Adam Smith and Conservative Economics;" Smith, "Adam Smith: Left or Right?;" Smith, "Adam Smith and the New Right;" Iain McLean, *Adam Smith, Radical and Egalitarian: An Interpretation for the 21st Century* (Edinburgh: Edinburgh University Press, 2006), 139–40.

convergence of divergent political views: having been refashioned as the moral philosopher par excellence of capitalism, Smith provides a way for his interpreters, past and present, to articulate their anxieties about American capitalism's supposed moral faults without conceding its basic economic premises.

My concern here is not exclusively an American one. In the last quarter of the twentieth century, Smith scholarship had already attained a global reach, and it continues to grow today. However, the central problematics that began to emerge in the late 1970s and 1980s were direct responses to—if not straightforward refutations of—Smith's association with the Friedmanite Chicago School that had come to dominate the public and academic consciousness. That stubborn legacy of his, according to the late Cambridge historian and eminent Smith scholar István Hont, obfuscated serious attempts to understand Smith's politics, leaving revisionist writers to "rediscover repeatedly . . . and explain again and again to successive generations of economists that their 'Smith' is a simplistic, quasi-physiocrat, in contrast to the far more complex and often anti-physiocratic ideas of the real historical figure."[12] These early revisionist contributions, which came primarily though not exclusively from scholars in Great Britain, then served as a platform from which a later generation of thinkers (an increasing number of whom were and are American) would continue to build and advance Smith scholarship. The important point here is that, even having achieved international reach, Smith scholarship across the globe was and has been centered on debates shaped in and for distinctively American circumstances. The latest—but surely not the last—inflection point in Smith's story shows how even the most recent debates about what Smith might have actually said or meant have an ongoing vitality. Contending interpretations and reimaginations of Smith's thought reveal just how ambiguous and slippery notions of Smith's politics and moral vision are. Yet those ambiguous and slippery qualities are what enable Smith to be such a useful, ubiquitous, and powerful device

12. Hont, *Jealousy of Trade*, 110.

for expressing a wide range of hopes and fears about capitalism in the twentieth and twenty-first centuries.

———

Scholarship on Smith surged from 1976 onward—and not only in economics.[13] In addition to the Glasgow Editions of Smith's works, editors Andrew Skinner and Thomas Wilson also produced a 647-page collection of commemorative essays from an astonishing array of scholars and backgrounds: a landmark treatment of Smith's theory of the "impartial spectator" by D.D. Raphael; a comparative essay on Marxian themes of alienation and corruption by E.G. West; a reprisal of Cropsey's Straussian placement of Smith in the "liberal capitalist" tradition; and the Cambridge historian Duncan Forbes's work on "scientific" and "vulgar" forms of Whiggism in Smith and Hume's thought, to name a few. George Stigler's essay, "Smith's Travels on the Ship of State," was a standout and provocative contribution. As Winch described it, Stigler reigned as "one of Smith's most knowledgeable Chicago admirers," and though his views were perhaps a bit "extreme," they were unquestionably "influential . . . among economists and those historians who mainly write with economists in mind." Far from being the only economist contributor, Stigler nonetheless epitomized an interpretive mode whereby Smith's ideas could be judged against clear criteria of success and failure, and historical context and intention could be casually and conveniently set aside in favor of the weight of the tradition of economic thought that appeared "unbroken to our own day." Economists, especially economists like Stigler, were the victors. They were, in Winch's words, "legatees of the enterprise founded by Smith . . . the custodians and the prize-givers."[14] Who would dare challenge such guardians of Smith's legacy?

13. For different analyses of the post-bicentenary Smith scholarship trends, see Recktenwald, "An Adam Smith Renaissance Anno 1976?;" Wight, "The Rise of Adam Smith;" Keith Tribe, "Adam Smith: Critical Theorist?" *Journal of Economic Literature* 37, no. 2 (1999), 609–32.

14. Winch, "Not by Economics Alone."

An early challenger was an insider of the profession. Albert Otto Hirschman, better known as A.O. Hirschman, was an erstwhile developmental economist with a penchant for political theory. The German-Jewish émigré arrived in the United States in 1941, and he began his intellectual career as a Rockefeller Fellow at the University of California, Berkeley, from 1941–1943. At Berkeley's Doe Library, Hirschman fell in love with the works of Adam Smith, and he craved reading Smith and other classic works throughout his long and itinerant career as an economist and private economic counselor for the Colombian government. In 1973, Hirschman found some time to return to the works of Adam Smith, and, by the time he arrived at Princeton's Institute for Advanced Study in 1974, he was already revising a draft of his latest book project, *The Passions and The Interests: Political Arguments for Capitalism Before Its Triumph*. Hirschman immersed himself in the writings of Aristotle, the French physiocrats, Machiavelli, and the major figures of the Scottish Enlightenment—Hume, Hutcheson, Ferguson, Smith, and Millar. While at the Institute, he had the great fortune of being in close intellectual company with distinguished Cambridge historians Quentin Skinner, John Dunn, and J.G.A. Pocock, as well as the eminent historian of economic thought Donald Winch. Collectively, the Cambridge historians brought about a major reexamination of key concepts in early modern intellectual history—such as liberty, commerce, and virtue—with unrivalled historical gravitas. Hirschman was quickly drawn into their circle.

The Passions and the Interests was Hirschman's retreat into history. Having recently returned from a number of trips to South America, Hirschman had become disenchanted with the dicta of balanced-growth modernization theories that had become the consensus since the Bretton Woods era. Chile, in particular, was about to be set on a course of "radical free-market reconstruction" under the dictatorship of Augusto Pinochet, thanks in no small part to a scholarship exchange program between the University of Chicago's Department of Economics and the Catholic University in Santiago.[15] In 1974, Hirschman wrote

15. On the origins and role of the "Chicago Boys" in Chile see Jamie Peck's "Orientation" essay in *Building Chicago Economics: New Perspectives on the History of America's Most Powerful*

that he was "deeply disturbed by what, so it seemed, we [economists] had wrought or at least helped bring about."[16] By returning to the intellectual groundworks of capitalism, he hoped to "renew the sense of wonder about the genesis of the 'spirit of capitalism,'" and uncover the discursive shifts around the human motivations, behavior, and life in market societies.[17]

At the heart of *The Passions and The Interests* lay one question: how did the *passions* of money-making, the love of lucre, avarice, greed—once believed to be a deadly sin and the source of human corruption—transform into mere *interests* that could promote private and public good? If the passion for money-making connoted danger and impurity, reconceptualizing it as interest created a "comparatively neutral, and colorless term" which "permitted lifting or attenuating the stigma attached to the old labels." How, then, did such a private vice suddenly become the very bridle that restrained "those passions that had long been thought to be much less reprehensible?"[18]

For Hirschman, Adam Smith's "triumphal formulation" of passions *as* interests marked a turning point in the history of Western thought. Thinkers like Montesquieu and James Steuart conceived of passions and interests as oppositional forces; not only did commerce "polish and soften," it also acted as a safeguard against attempts to violently seize power. Both the love of lucre and the love of power were "self-propelling and insatiable," but only the latter could have dire political consequences.

Economics Program, eds. Van Horn, Mirowski, and Stapleford, (Cambridge: Cambridge University Press, 2011), xxv–lii. See also J. Daniel Hammond, "Markets, Politics, and Democracy at Chicago: Taking Economics Seriously," in the same volume, 36–63. For further critical commentary on the "Chicago Boys" experiment in relation to global neoliberalism, see Harvey, *A Brief History of Neoliberalism*; Naomi Klein, *The Shock Doctrine: The Rise of Disaster Capitalism*, (New York, NY: Metropolitan Books and Henry Holt, 2007).

16. Quoted in Jeremy Adelman, *Worldly Philosopher: The Odyssey of Albert O. Hirschman* (Princeton, NJ: Princeton University Press, 2014), 502.

17. A.O. Hirschman, *The Passions and the Interests: Political Arguments for Capitalism before Its Triumph* (Princeton, NJ: Princeton University Press, 2013), 9. Jeremy Adelman provides detailed investigations into Hirschman's abiding interests in classical texts of political theory in his magisterial biography, *Worldly Philosopher*. See also Michele Alacevich, *Albert O. Hirschman: An Intellectual Biography* (New York, NY: Columbia University Press, 2021).

18. Hirschman, *The Passions and the Interests*, 42.

Calm, self-centered acquisitiveness acted as "bulwarks against despotism and *les grand coups d'autorité*."[19] Interest tamed the passions. According to Hirschman, Montesquieu and Steuart championed commerce and industry first and foremost for their political effects; commerce limited, if not eliminated, the exercise of "arbitrary and authoritarian decision-making."[20] Smith, however, synonymized the passions and the interests. Hirschman argued that Smith reconceived of man's motivations as "actuated entirely by the 'desire of bettering [their] condition,'" as Smith wrote in *The Theory of Moral Sentiments*. Humans were animated by a whirlwind of economic and non-economic passions alike; sympathy, the desire for approval, and recognition were the basic preoccupations of man, and the love of lucre was but one way of obtaining them. By eliminating the distinction between passions and interests, Smith took "the final reductionist step of turning two into one," Hirschman argued. Passion could not be pitted against passion. Economic interests were no longer autonomous forces but rather the means of garnering sympathy and approbation, while noneconomic drives "are all made to feed into the economic ones and do nothing but reinforce them, being thus deprived of their erstwhile independent existence." This underhanded conceptual move of Smith's was at the center of *The Wealth of Nations*'s revolutionary contribution: an unambiguous, powerful economic— as opposed to political—rationale for the untrammeled pursuit of self-interest.[21]

On the one hand, Hirschman seemed to accentuate the Chicago Smith of Friedman and Stigler. His Smith was the alpha and omega of economic thinking, the man who took passionate greed and transformed it into rational self-interest which governed the modern world. Smith affirmed that "economics can go it alone," Hirschman wrote, and that under many circumstances, political progress was neither a prerequisite for nor a consequence of economic progress.[22] Yet Hirschman also managed to pry open room for a different reading of Smith, one

19. Hirschman, *The Passions and the Interests*, 78.
20. Hirschman, *The Passions and the Interests*, 87.
21. Hirschman, *The Passions and the Interests*, 109, 100.
22. Adelman, *Worldly Philosopher*, 519; Hirschman, *The Passions and the Interests*, 103–4.

who was deeply ambivalent about material progress, who shared the classical republican concerns about "debilitating luxury and corruption," and who saw the need to avert the disasters of the modern commercial age.[23] It was a Smith who, in Book III of *The Wealth of Nations* showed how feudal lords "*unwittingly* relinquished their power" as they traded away their authority over other people for mere trinkets and baubles.[24] In other words, it was a Smith who had a peculiar politics of irrationality. Compared to Montesquieu and Steuart, Hirschman's Smith was not as certain that commerce would "deliver mankind from ancient evils, such as abuses of power, wars, and the like." Hirschman did see some positive outcomes (for example, Smith's famous dicta that "commerce and manufactures gradually introduced order and good government, and with them, the liberty and security of individuals"), but Smith did not condone the chaotic "chain of events and motivations that brought about this happy result."[25] In Hirschman's account, Smithian politics was "the province of the 'folly of men,'" but this hardly made Smith the minimal-state advocate that market fundamentalists made him out to be. Rather, Hirschman posited that "Smith advocated less a state with minimal functions than one whose capacity for folly would have some ceiling."[26] In other words, the political sphere was full of clumsy, irrational, and opportunistic actors, but it was not so beyond redemption that it had to be cannibalized by economics going it alone.

As his biographer Jeremy Adelman has noted, Hirschman's views of Smith were "at times confused and confusing." This is hardly surprising for anyone who has tried to work out a thinker as complex as Smith.[27] However, as Adelman has suggested, there was an intentionality behind this portrait of Smith. Hirschman deposed Smith from his founder and

---

23. Hirschman, *The Passions and the Interests*, 106–7.

24. Hirschman, *The Passions and the Interests*, 102 (emphasis original). *WN* III.iv.10, 419.

25. *WN* III.iv.4, 412; Hirschman, *The Passions and the Interest*, 105.

26. Hirschman, *The Passions and the Interest*, 104.

27. Adelman reports that Hirschman had started working through Smith's writings in the spring of 1973, and that "his first impressions were of an author 'contradicting himself in the most *effronté* manner' which 'spoilt a neat ideological classification with which I had set out on this whole thing.'" As quoted in Adelman, *Worldly Philosopher*, 512.

hero's pedestal, turning the Scotsman instead into a "transitional, possibly tragic figure" of capitalism who reluctantly ushered in *homo economicus*. Smith was not the first in a line of thinkers who prophesied capitalism's triumph, but he was the last among those "still enmeshed in a moral economy but aware of and even predicting the emerging norms and practices of the capitalist world."[28]

Thus, while Chicago figures like Stigler and Friedman tried to sever Smith's politics from his economics, Hirschman began making space to reconsider what "Smith's politics" actually meant and what the consequences of it were for modern capitalist societies. Unfortunately, Hirschman's answer was not exactly clear. At least in *The Passions and the Interests*, Smith's politics didn't amount to a positive program of advocacy, nor was it a negative program of stripping away the state. Hirschman's twist on Smith's most famous metaphor—that Smith had "overplayed his Invisible Hand"—was meant to underscore the "politics of folly" but it never caught on. And while he hinted at Smith having civic republican sympathies, Hirschman did not attempt to fully recover Smith's own political positions or his outlook on the nature of politics in his own time; that was the task of Donald Winch.

In fact, it was Winch who had introduced Hirschman to Smith's *Lectures on Jurisprudence*, which had a profound effect on both scholars. In a way similar to Hirschman's *The Passions and the Interests*, Winch's seminal work, *Adam Smith's Politics: An Essay in Historiographic Revision*, emerged out of the intersection of changing intellectual currents. Winch had earned his PhD in economics at Princeton in 1960, where Jacob Viner's presence drew him close to studies in the history of economic thought. Winch evinced strong historical sensibilities and a distaste for presentist histories of economics in his first work, *Classical Political Economy and Colonies* (1965), which was closely followed by a study on Keynesian policy-making in Britain and the United States. From 1974 to 1975, Winch was on sabbatical at the Institute for Advanced Studies, where he intended to write a book on themes in the history of the social sciences. However, amidst the high tide of the Cambridge School's civic

28. Adelman, *Worldly Philosopher*, 520.

humanism and the Glasgow *festschrift* on the horizon, Winch found himself swept up by a project exclusively on Smith's politics.[29] Andrew Skinner, one of the lead editors of the Glasgow Editions, had passed Winch a copy of the Cambridge historian Duncan Forbes's essay, "Skeptical Whiggism, Commerce, and Liberty," and Quentin Skinner encouraged Winch to catch up on recent literature on civic humanism, virtue, and corruption. In correspondence, Forbes helped Winch shore up power to take aim at his primary target, what Winch called "the dominant liberal capitalist perspective on Smith."[30] This perspective, according to Winch, placed Smith on a spectrum between Locke and Hobbes on one end, and Marx and Mill on the other. Overall, it gave Smith pride of place as the "upholder of a system of natural liberty within which individuals possess certain natural rights and pursue selfish ends of an economic character."[31] Interestingly, economists and philosophers alike were responsible for this mischaracterization. There was of course, George Stigler, whose "counter-factual approach" in his "Ship of State" essay audaciously concluded that Smith had failed to apply economic reasoning to politics, and as a result, "consigned Smith . . . to the role of mere preacher in political matters."[32] There were also the American political philosophers like Joseph Cropsey and Sheldon Wolin, who were just as guilty for boxing in Smith too narrowly. Cropsey's *Polity and Economy* (1957), for instance, began with an explicit statement of the "axiomatic premise" that "capitalism is an

29. The "Cambridge School" is a ubiquitous and contested term. For a brief primer, see Richard Bourke's short document, "The Cambridge School," available at https://www.qmul.ac .uk/history/media/ph/news/The-Cambridge-School.pdf, accessed July 12, 2021. For a sample of more recent treatments, see Richard Bourke, "Revising the Cambridge School: Republicanism Revisited," *Political Theory* 46, no. 3 (2018), 467–77; J. G. A. Pocock, "On the Unglobality of Contexts: Cambridge Methods and the History of Political Thought," *Global Intellectual History* 4, no. 1 (January 2019), 1–14; Danielle Charette and Max Skjönsberg, "State of the Field: The History of Political Thought," *History* 105, no. 366 (July 1, 2020), 470–83.

30. Donald Winch, letter to Duncan Forbes, April 17, 1975. *Intellectual History Archive*, available at https://intellectualhistory.net/thousand-manuscripts-blog/item-no-7-the-winch-forbes -exchange.

31. Donald Winch, *Adam Smith's Politics: An Essay in Historiographic Revision* (Cambridge: Cambridge University Press, 1978), 13.

32. Winch, *Adam Smith's Politics*, 166.

embodiment of Smithian principles" and somewhat plaintively con-cluded that the moral imperfections of capitalist society were simply the price of political freedom in modernity.[33] Meanwhile, Wolin's *Politics and Vision* (1960) placed Smith at the turning point of Western political thought, a point where economy and society supplanted politics.[34] Though each of these thinkers approached Smith from different methodological angles, Winch contended that they all had the same effect. They all portrayed Smith as an "a-political economic liberal" and obscured his "views on a range of topics which are properly described as 'political.'"[35]

Making the negative case—what Smith's politics was *not*—was a fairly straightforward task, and Winch had no shortage of examples of the "spectacularly crass exhibits from self-styled historians of economic liberalism."[36] The much more daunting task was proving what Smith's politics *was* in terms of what Smith could "legitimately be said to have intended, rather than with what he might be said to have anticipated or foreshadowed."[37] To start, Winch drew upon the bourgeoning historiography on eighteenth-century Anglo-American political thought. The revolutionary-era political debates were steeped in the terminology, categories, and ideas of classical republicanism and civic humanism, Winch granted. So how might someone like Smith have harnessed those very ideas—of virtue, commerce, polity, and economy—in order to "activate or legitimate specific courses of political action?"[38] Winch did not necessarily want to establish Smith as a civic humanist; in fact, Winch resisted the idea of being in the "labeling and bottling business"

33. Cropsey, *Polity and Economy*, vii . For Winch's critique, see Winch, *Adam Smith's Politics*, 16–17, 20–22, 84.

34. Winch, *Adam Smith's Politics*, 21–22. Winch also uses Wolin's *Polity and Economy* as an illustration of a liberal capitalist view (albeit, a slightly more nuanced one) in his initial letter to Forbes. Donald Winch, letter to Duncan Forbes, April 17, 1975.

35. Donald Winch, letter to Duncan Forbes, April 17, 1975.

36. John Dunn, "Winch, Donald. Adam Smith's Politics: An Essay in Historiographic Revision," *Times Literary Supplement*, no. 3 (1978), 1279.

37. Winch, *Adam Smith's Politics*, 1.

38. Winch, *Adam Smith's Politics*, 28–34. On the scholarship of the "republican synthesis," see note 12 in Chapter 1.

altogether.[39] Winch considered it more important to equip and familiar-ize readers with the language that would have been available to Smith at his time, and from there determine Smith's views on a given theme. For instance, Winch adopted Forbes's distinction between the "sceptical" or "scientific Whiggism" of David Hume and "vulgar Whiggism" in order to highlight the wildly different interpretations and political implications of Smith's concept of liberty. For "sceptical" Whigs like Hume and Smith, liberty meant security under the rule of law and the regular and impartial administration of justice. What this implied, then, was that personal and civil liberties could be guaranteed even under monarchies and in the ab-sence of mass democracy. This was a far cry from the widespread and indiscriminate use of Smith's concept of liberty to imply a set of liberal democratic values. No, Winch argued. Smith's political values were "pre-capitalist and pre-industrial as well as pre-democratic."[40]

Over the course of *Adam Smith's Politics*, Winch scrupulously exca-vated multiple dimensions of Smith's political thinking using the tools of historical contextualism. A close reading of Smith's *Lectures on Juris-prudence* showed how Smith modified the normative political vision of his teacher Francis Hutcheson by grounding the study of law and government in "coolly historical" and "experimental" analysis.[41] On the

39. "At least, I don't think of myself as being in the labelling and bottling business. I am un-happy about the inaccuracies and stultifying effect on Smith scholarship of the dominant (among economists and social scientists at least) liberal capitalist perspective, but I am far too concerned with Smith himself to want to erect another stereotype for purely polemical pur-poses," Winch wrote to Duncan Forbes. Donald Winch, Letter to Duncan Forbes, May 6, 1975. Intellectual History Archive, Accessed July 20, 2021, available at https://intellectualhistory.net /thousand-manuscripts-blog/item-no-7-the-winch-forbes-exchange. See also Winch, *Adam Smith's Politics*, 3–5. Duncan Forbes also warned Winch about wandering too far into the weeds of civic humanism and boxing Smith into any one tradition. Some thinkers, Forbes wrote, are "ex-ceedingly complex, and too big to be bottled in any way . . . Don't sell yourself to this 'civic human-ism' business. (Smith is BIG!)" he wrote in a reply to Winch. Duncan Forbes, letter to Donald Winch, April 25, 1975, *Intellectual History Archive*, accessed July 20, 2021, available at https:// intellectualhistory.net/thousand-manuscripts-blog/item-no-7-the-winch-forbes-exchange.

40. Duncan Forbes, "Sceptical Whiggism, Commerce and Liberty," in *Essays on Adam Smith*, ed. Andrew S. Skinner and Thomas Wilson (Oxford: Clarendon Press, 1975), 179–201; Winch, *Adam Smith's Politics*, 39–41, 181.

41. Winch, *Adam Smith's Politics*, 65.

charged topic of standing armies, Winch insisted that Smith's position was not a straightforward rejection of the radical Whig view (Smith infamously defended standing armies over militias). On the contrary, Winch saw Smith's position as an extension of his analysis of state capacity in Book V of *The Wealth of Nations*, in which the sovereign's duty of defense took priority over justice, and where the security of modern commercial states depended on aligning the incentives of those who held political, economic, and military power.[42] On the hairy subject of public debts, Winch displayed Smith as a less-alarmist, calmer version of David Hume, the latter of whom in his 1752 essay "Of Public Credit," opined that "either the nation must destroy public credit, or public credit will destroy the nation."[43] For Hume, public debt would lead to oppressive taxation, encourage the growth of an idle rentier class, and leave a nation vulnerable to foreign debt holders. By contrast, while Smith was critical of what he called a "ruinous experiment" of public debt, he also stressed that modern commercial nations had to borrow money in order to fight wars, and that they had greater capacity to do so on account of the willingness of merchants to lend money. Smith's politics was not optimistic, but his analytical rigor and undogmatic character enabled him to maintain a "balance between serious concern and complacent contemplation of ruin."[44]

42. Winch, *Adam Smith's Politics*, chap. 5. For additional treatments of Smith on the standing army versus militia debate, see Leo Damrosch, *The Club: Johnson, Boswell, and the Friends Who Shaped an Age* (New Haven, CT: Yale University Press, 2019); Leonidas Montes, "Adam Smith on the Standing Army versus Militia Issue: Wealth over Virtue?" in *The Elgar Companion to Adam Smith*, ed. Jeffrey T. Young (Cheltenham: Elgar, 2010), 315–334; Richard B. Sher, "Adam Ferguson, Adam Smith, and the Problem of National Defense," *The Journal of Modern History* 61, no. 2 (1989), 240–68.

43. David Hume, "Of Public Credit," in *Essays Moral, Political, Literary*, edited and with a Foreword, Notes, and Glossary by Eugene F. Miller, with an appendix of variant readings from the 1889 edition by T.H. Green and T.H. Grose, revised edition (Indianapolis, IN: Liberty Fund 1987), 360–361.

44. Winch, *Adam Smith's Politics*, 135–36. For further reading on Hume and Smith on public debt, see Hont, *Jealousy of Trade*, 325–353; John Christian Laursen and Greg Coolidge, "David Hume and Public Debt: Crying Wolf?," *Hume Studies* 20, no. 1 (1994), 143–49; Maria Pia Paganelli, "David Hume on Public Credit," *History of Economic Ideas* XX, no. 1 (2012), 31–43; Maria Pia Paganelli and Reinhard Schumacher, "Do Not Take Peace for Granted: Adam Smith's

John Dunn described Winch's style as "teasingly restrained," but the effect of *Adam Smith's Politics* was unapologetic disruption. By "turning Smith's back on the present," as he put it, Winch forced contemporary Smith readers—particularly those who might consider themselves the rightful custodians of Smith's legacy—to confront a gaping discontinuity between Smith's time and their own.[45] An unbroken tradition of liberal individualism no longer existed that tied Locke to Hume to Smith to Mill, only to be challenged by Karl Marx. But the larger interpretive move Winch made was establishing that Smith's politics circumscribed his political economy. The contours of the political in Smith's works were porous, fluid, and attenuated, but undeniably there. Smith's politics operated at the level of legal and constitutional frameworks, rather than at the level of political leadership and judgment.[46] Moreover, Smith's politics represented an "underlying spirit," a particular disposition or orientation toward the study of politics, economy, and society. Smith's politics required diligence and clarity in considering controversial, confusing, and sometimes conflicting opinions. "Smith may have intended many things when writing on politics, some of which may be inconsistent with one another, confused, and just plain wrong," Winch admitted. It demanded patience and tolerance for the range and untidiness of human sentiments—ambition, pride, resentment, fear, enthusiasm—those very sentiments for which George Stigler had appeared to have no patience.[47] Smith's politics called for resilience in the face of "world-weariness;" it resisted the temptation to fall into convenient categories—Tory or Whig, Court or Country, Liberal or Conservative. It resolved to be "infuriatingly balanced." As Winch wrote, "There is certainly something to be said for a science of politics which finds

Warning on the Relation between Commerce and War," *Cambridge Journal of Economics* 43, no. 3 (April 2019), 785–97.

45. Dunn, "Winch, Donald. Adam Smith's Politics," 1279; Winch, *Adam Smith's Politics*, 184.

46. Winch, *Adam Smith's Politics*, 177. For more recent views on political judgment and political leadership in Smith's works, see Hont, "Adam Smith's History of Law and Government as Political Theory;" Oprea, "Adam Smith on Political Judgment;" Schliesser, "Adam Smith on Political Leadership."

47. Winch, *Adam Smith's Politics*, 168–70.

itself with work to do, rather than simply standing as the monument to a philosophical stance."[48] That Smith's politics could not be found pre-packaged with clear labels was precisely what defined it.

Adam Smith's Politics marked a pivotal moment in Smith studies. Winch pulled back the curtain on the dynamic between what Smith had written and what had been retrojected onto him. By locating Smith in the discursive, political, and cultural context of the eighteenth century, Winch crafted a reading of Smith as a thoroughgoing political thinker in his own right, rather than as a proto-Chicagoan economist or liberal-capitalist philosopher who anticipated and legitimized the hegemony of markets over the state. Of course, Winch was by no means the only scholar at the time to lean on this contextual approach, but with *Adam Smith's Politics*, he planted a proverbial flag in the sand. Winch marked out the territory once thought to belong to economists alone, and re-vealed how vast the landscape of Smith's ideas was once its study was properly historical.

A number of influential publications soon followed. Knud Haakons-sen's *The Science of a Legislator* (1981) was a highly technical work that deepened Winch's brief foray into the *Lectures on Jurisprudence* and ex-pounded on Smith's commitments as a legal and political theorist.[49] Subsequent works by J.G.A. Pocock, Christopher J. Berry, Nicholas Phillipson, and John Robertson expanded the study of sociability, his-tory, and theories of human-driven progress in the Scottish Enlighten-ment.[50] In 1983, the publication of István Hont and Michael Ignatieff's

48. Winch, *Adam Smith's Politics*, 176, 180, 45.

49. Knud Haakonssen, *The Science of a Legislator: The Natural Jurisprudence of David Hume and Adam Smith* (Cambridge: Cambridge University Press, 1981).

50. Christopher J. Berry, *The Idea of Luxury: A Conceptual and Historical Investigation* (Cambridge: Cambridge University Press, 1994); Berry, *Social Theory of the Scottish Enlightenment*; Nicholas Phillipson, "Culture and Society in the Eighteenth-Century Province: The Case of Edinburgh and the Scottish Enlightenment," in *The University in Society*, ed. Lawrence Stone (Princeton, NJ: Princeton University Press, 1974), 407–48; Nicholas Phillipson, "Adam Smith as Civic Moralist," in *Wealth and Virtue*, ed. István Hont and Michael Ignatieff, 1983, 137–38; J.G.A. Pocock, *Virtue, Commerce, and History* (Cambridge: Cambridge University Press, 1985); John Robertson, "Scottish Political Economy Beyond the Civic Tradition: Government and Economic Development in the 'Wealth of Nations,'" *History of Political Thought* 4, no. 3 (1983),

Wealth & Virtue (the product of a conference held at King's College, Cambridge, in 1979 on Scottish political economy and the civic humanist tradition), introduced another problematic that would be a central feature of Smith scholarship for years to come. Hont and Ignatieff called it the paradox of commercial society: "How was extreme inequality of distribution in modern society compatible with the satisfaction of the needs of its poorest working members?"[51] In their account, Smith denied that the neediness of the poor constituted a claim of right against the property of the rich, but this was hardly a denial of justice. By approaching Smith's political economy through this lens, Hont and Ignatieff ignited a debate about the extent to which Smith believed government had to play a role in protecting the basic rights of the poor.

According to their reading, Smith's contribution to modern thought was the transposition of the question of justice from jurisprudence to political economy. Hont and Ignatieff argued that Smith transferred the ancient jurisprudential discourse of natural rights, property, and claims of need and desert into the language of political economy. The purpose of civil government was to protect the security of property and provide for "the defence [*sic*] of the rich against the poor," Smith wrote in *The Wealth of Nations*.[52] But this did not mean Smith was unconcerned with the needs of the poor. Here, the natural jurisprudential distinction between perfect and imperfect rights, strict justice and distributive justice was critical. Civil government was in the business of protecting the "perfect rights" of citizens and rigidly enforcing strict justice—that which "only hinders us from hurting our neighbor."[53] Law and government, in other words, could not command men to be benevolent, nor were they responsible for achieving the aims of distributive justice; that was the function of markets. Smith's arguments, according to Hont and

---

451–82. For further context surrounding the revival of interest in the Scottish Enlightenment, see Colin Kidd, "The Phillipsonian Enlightenment," *Modern Intellectual History* 11, no. 1 (April 2014), 175–90.

51. István Hont and Michael Ignatieff, eds., *Wealth and Virtue: The Shaping of Political Economy in the Scottish Enlightenment* (Cambridge: Cambridge University Press, 1983), 4.

52. *WN* V.i.b.12, 715.

53. *TMS* II.ii.1.10, 82.

Ignatieff, were purposefully crafted to show "how an economy of abundance could be created," thereby exploding the tension between needs and rights and precluding the need to resort to redistributing property. In Hont and Ignatieff's reading, then, Smith's politics and economics were mutually constitutive, and *The Wealth of Nations*, therefore, could be read as a work "centrally concerned with the issue of justice."[54]

"Needs and Justice" was an agenda-setting essay. Hont would continue to shape historical scholarship with a series of densely packed and penetrating articles on seventeenth-and eighteenth-century political economy published between 1983 and 1994.[55] With regard to Smith specifically, Hont introduced an idiosyncratic historical method and categories of analysis that would become ubiquitous. On the one hand, Hont adopted the position of historiographic revisionism that spurned presentist anachronisms and "jealously [defended] the autonomy of the past."[56] On the other hand, Hont believed that a commitment to rigorous contextualism was not incompatible with finding lessons for the present. Take, for example, one of his most significant categories of analysis, namely, "commercial society." This was a deliberate word choice to avoid the anachronistic term, "capitalism."[57] Hont was intent on abandoning the "dreary nineteenth-and early twentieth-century confusions about Smith" and revealing the ways in which the language of eighteenth-century political economists transformed understandings of modern politics and the economy. In the seventeenth and eighteenth centuries, as international commerce expanded to become not just a matter of individual enrichment but also of national aggrandizement,

54. Hont and Ignatieff, *Wealth and Virtue*, 24–25, 2.

55. Hont later republished those essays with a new introduction in his landmark single volume, *The Jealousy of Trade* (2005). His lectures on Smith and Rousseau were published posthumously after his untimely death in 2013 as István Hont, *Politics in Commercial Society*, ed. Béla Kapossy and Michael Sonenscher (Cambridge, MA: Harvard University Press, 2015).

56. Paul Cheney, "István Hont, the Cosmopolitan Theory of Commercial Globalization, and Twenty-First-Century Capitalism," *Modern Intellectual History*, March 2021, 1–29 at 3.

57. The historian Paul Cheney has recently offered an interesting critique of Hont's use of the term "commercial society" by historicizing Hont in the context of the world-systems theories and dependency economics of the 1980s and 1990s. Cheney, "István Hont, the Cosmopolitan Theory of Commercial Globalization, and Twenty-First-Century Capitalism."

managing market competition became one of the primary functions of states and signaled that "the economy had become political."[58] The emergence of commercial society, therefore, entailed a shift in thinking about theories of human sociability, the nature of political organization, and the determinants of social change. Such were the themes and questions that "Smith himself faced" and, Hont argued, were "often identical with our own predicament today."[59]

Hont's command of history and his attention to contextual and conceptual detail was extraordinary, but his works were (and still are) quite challenging. He assumed a strong grasp of seventeenth-and eighteenth-century history and terminology, and his writing intermingled analytically dense historical and philosophical reconstruction with his own parochial interpretation.[60] However, for Hont and for others like him, participating in the project of historiographic revision, this kind of historical recovery was the bulwark against present-minded misreadings and polemical interpretations of Smith's politics. Once historically understood and critically repossessed, Smith's politics would anchor him in the past, preventing his ideas from being loosened into the turbulent waters of nineteenth-and twentieth-century constructions of liberal traditions. But these scholars had different degrees of tolerance for drawing out the contemporary lessons from history. Hirschman's dismay with the present state of capitalism had led him to reassess Smith in the past in the first place, while Winch's and Hont's scrutiny of Smith in the past was intended to question present categories of political

58. Hont, *Jealousy of Trade*, 111, 4–5.

59. Hont, *Jealousy of Trade*, 111. Hont expresses a similar attitude about reading the past in *Politics in Commercial Society*, 24. Hont was quite critical of what he saw as the dominance of "analytical political thought" in "North American republicanism," that is, the type of liberal-egalitarian political theory associated primarily with John Rawls, but also Ronald Dworkin, Joseph Raz, Amartya Sen, and countless others. On Hont's methodological approach and substantive contributions as a political theorist, see Paul Sagar, "István Hont and Political Theory," *European Journal of Political Theory* 17, no. 4 (October 2018), 476–500. See also the editors' introduction to Hont's *Politics in Commercial Society*. Additionally, Sagar has offered both a revision and an extension of Hont's ideas about the modes of political theorizing suited for commercial modernity in *The Opinion of Mankind* and *Adam Smith Reconsidered*.

60. Sagar, "István Hont and Political Theory."

analysis. Winch took the most stringent position: it was "difficult, and strictly necessary," he argued, to imagine what the "direct normative or scientific significance" of Smith's political positions would be in the twentieth century.[61]

Finally, there is a tension, or perhaps irony, in the version of Smith that collectively emerged from these readings. In the effort to recover his politics, early revisionists ended up inadvertently portraying Smith as an anti-political thinker of sorts. This is not to say that Hirschman, Winch, Haakonssen, and Hont fell into the trap that Stigler and Friedman had laid out, that is, treating Smith as an economic thinker who predicted the failure of self-interest in politics and saw political activity as anathema to the market. Rather, it was a more general approach that treated politics with suspicion. Hirschman's "politics of folly" may have had a ceiling, but it was folly nonetheless and did little to inspire faith in what Smith called that "insidious and crafty animal, vulgarly called a statesman or politician."[62] If one took Winch's interpretation seriously, Smith's politics was focused on constitutional principles, but when considering Smith's views of the human motivations underlining political action, Smith's attitude towards politics was at best "sceptical, pessimistic, or realistic, according to the reader's taste."[63] Hont and Ignatieff argued that *The Wealth of Nations* answered an essentially political question, but ultimately showed how Smith promoted "political ends (e.g., the alleviation of poverty) through expansion of markets."[64] None

61. Winch, *Adam Smith's Politics*, 183. It is not entirely clear why Winch took up this position in *Adam Smith's Politics*, though his later writings suggest that his preoccupations were primarily with systematically refuting the anachronistic and ahistoric tendencies of contemporary economists, including not only figures like Stigler, but also general equilibrium theorists like Frank Hahn. Some of Winch's views on method can be gleaned in Donald Winch, "Adam Smith's Problems and Ours," *Scottish Journal of Political Economy* 44, no. 4 (1997), 384–402; Winch, "Intellectual History and the History of Economic Thought: A Personal Account," *Journal of Interdisciplinary History of Ideas* 6, no. 12 (2017), item 6, 1–18.

62. WN IV.2.39, 468.

63. Winch, *Adam Smith's Politics*, 182.

64. Schliesser, "Adam Smith on Political Leadership," 133; see also James A. Harris, "The Protection of the Rich against the Poor: The Politics of Adam Smith's Political Economy," *Social Philosophy and Policy* 37, no. 1 (2020), 138–58 at 140.

of this, however, foreclosed on the possibility of a different conception of Smith's politics and a different image of Smith himself to emerge— one in which morality might play a decidedly positive, ameliorative, and active role, and one in which Smith's contributions as a moral philosopher rivalled his reputation as an economist and political theorist. For that to happen, though, it was not enough to simply turn Smith's back on the present. Smith had to be turned back *on* the present, too.

———

"It is not an exaggeration to apply the term 'crisis' to the events of recent decades," wrote Irving Kristol in 1976. The problems of capitalism were acutely felt in the 1970s, but Americans had become "so critically detached from them," Kristol argued, that they found it "difficult to perceive the *intentions* of the system—and, in light of these intentions, its accomplishments." Most Americans understood and accepted capitalism's economic success, but what they had failed to appreciate, according to Kristol, was the "kind of *society* capitalism is supposed to create." The answer, Kristol wrote, was that "there is no better way than to turn back to the writings of Adam Smith."[65]

Published in 1976, Kristol's essay, "Adam Smith and the Spirit of Capitalism" encapsulated the neoconservative turn to Adam Smith in the 1970s and its reinvention of the Scottish Enlightenment's moral philosophy. As Antti Lepistö has shown, prominent figures of the American neoconservative movement, Kristol preeminent among them, drew upon the vocabulary of Scottish common sense philosophy and appealed to the idea of an innate moral sense among "the people" in order to forge a conservative moral and political consensus.[66] From the neoconservative point of view, the crises of the 1970s were not purely economic, but rather the result of a "moral anarchy" that stemmed from the

———

65. Irving Kristol, "Adam Smith and the Spirit of Capitalism," in his *Neoconservatism: The Autobiography of an Idea* (Chicago, IL: Ivan R. Dee, 1995), 258–299 at 260. Initial emphasis in original. Latter emphasis added.

66. Lepistö, *The Rise of Common-Sense Conservatism*, 15.

liberal virtues of toleration, pluralism, and moral relativism.[67] These views had infected and "ruthlessly corrupted" the American people due to twin forces: the growing contingent of leftward-drifting academics who espoused the virtues of socialism, and the extended counterculture movement stemming from the fight for Civil Rights and The Great Society of the 1960s. Secularism, rationalism, and utopianism pervaded American culture and left people "utterly unprepared for such existential-spiritual spasms," as Kristol put it.[68] At stake for neoconservatives, then, was not only the health of the economy, but also a set of moral values that delineated the boundaries between the right and wrong sides of politico-cultural cleavages. By returning to thinkers like Adam Smith, neoconservatives found a powerful vocabulary with which they could explain "why they were right in the context of cultural debates over the family, crime, race, poverty, and multiculturalism."[69]

Kristol's reinterpretation of Adam Smith in his 1976 essay elevated Smith's moral philosophy above the standing of his economic theory. He saw Smith's view of human nature in *The Theory of Moral Sentiments* as providing the moral presuppositions for capitalism and grounding Smith's promise of universal opulence.[70] As the most famous member of what Kristol dubbed the "Anglo-Scottish Enlightenment," Smith was best known for writing the "founding text of modern capitalism," but he also represented a particular set of moral persuasions for modern society.[71] Smith showed how the human desire for sympathy and social esteem was checked by the impartial spectator—a "kind of vulgarized version of the Protestant idea of conscience," as Kristol put it. The central role of the conscience, therefore, revealed how Smith valued the role of moral and political community. The desire to better one's condition

67. Irving Kristol, "Countercultures," in Kristol, *Neoconservatism*, 139–147 at 145.

68. Kristol, "Countercultures," 139.

69. Lepistö, *The Rise of Common-Sense Conservatism*, 5. On the place of neoconservatism in the culture wars, see Dorrien, *The Neoconservative Mind*; Vaïsse, *Neoconservatism*. For exemplary historical works on the culture wars, see James Davison Hunter, *Culture Wars: The Struggle to Define America* (New York, NY: Basic Books, 1991); Andrew Hartman, *A War for the Soul of America: A History of the Culture Wars*, 2nd edition (Chicago, IL: University of Chicago Press, 2019).

70. Kristol, "Adam Smith and the Spirit of Capitalism," 288.

71. Kristol, "Adam Smith and the Spirit of Capitalism," 258.

was not aimed solely at the satisfaction of selfish, hedonistic interests, but more importantly at the "creation of a more humane and elevated bourgeois community, one with powerful feelings of fraternity and fellowship."[72] This conception of the moral constitution of individuals did two things. First, it provided an alternative to the rational, secular, and pessimistic conception of human nature that defined the theories of the French Enlightenment—an idea which Kristol used as a foil and not-so-subtle metaphor for the rebellious rationalism of his liberal counterparts. Whereas the French assumed a "low" view of human nature in which men had to be manipulated, persuaded, even coerced into being virtuous, the Anglo-Scottish tradition believed that the "inclination toward virtue" resided somewhere within man himself.[73] Virtue and an innate sense of right and wrong came from within, not from without. Second and more importantly, Kristol believed Smith's moral philosophy showed how capitalism, from its very inception, could not be indifferent to traditional and distinctly bourgeois virtues, especially those that were instilled and reinforced in the family, organized religion, and a strong educational system. This was a far cry from the defenses of capitalism advanced by economists, who, according to Kristol, relied on a conception of man as the "ultimate atom with measurable desires." In his rereading of Smith's *The Theory of Moral Sentiments*, Kristol set out to show how bourgeois man was defined not by his "self-centered hedonism," but rather by his ability to defer gratification. It was bourgeois man, not economic man, who pursued praiseworthiness, rather than simple praise. These virtues were not only the prerequisites for material improvement, but also for moral improvement and even true happiness.[74]

With his interpretation of Smith's moral philosophy, Kristol attempted to persuade Americans that something had been lost, or at least was missing, in the present view of American capitalist society. Smith had taken for granted the restraining role of "wholesome" institutions—organized

72. Kristol, "Adam Smith and the Spirit of Capitalism," 279, 280.
73. Kristol, "Adam Smith and the Spirit of Capitalism," 269.
74. Kristol, "Adam Smith and the Spirit of Capitalism," 297.

religion, the family, education—because their place in eighteenth-century life was so pervasive. Smith's vision of a prosperous, free, and flourishing society, therefore, was embedded in—rather than liberated from—"traditional moral virtues," Kristol argued.[75] Smith thus furnished Kristol with the philosophical underpinnings and intellectual authority for a neoconservative argument about capitalism's lost possibilities: the embeddedness of economic self-interest within "wholesome" institutions and "bourgeois" virtues, and the idea that capitalism needed moral, not just economic, advocates. This was the great task of neoconservatism: to give traditional conservatism "an intellectual dimension that goes beyond economics to reflections on the roots of social and cultural stability," Kristol wrote in a later autobiographical essay.[76] Bourgeois society was Smith's legacy, and it was a legacy that was America's to lose.

The argument that Smith's vision of capitalist society was rooted in a coherent and consistent set of moral commitments echoed in the works of other neoconservative thinkers, especially Gertrude Himmelfarb. Himmelfarb and Kristol had met in New York, where they were part of the New York Intellectuals, a circle of mostly Jewish, Trotskyist, American writers and literary critics, though they eventually abandoned Trotskyism. They were well-met minds. They shared a love of the philosophy of Leo Strauss, a disappointment with academics' contempt for the masses, and a reverence for the lost art of living a life guided by practical virtues. As Kristol later recounted, the two scholars were "bourgeois to the core." They married in 1942, an occasion which their good friend, the conservative sociologist Daniel Bell, famously described as "the best marriage of our generation."[77] Where Kristol showed a flair for public writing and provocation, Himmelfarb lent

75. Kristol, "Adam Smith and the Spirit of Capitalism," 298, 275.

76. For "wholesome" institutions and "traditional" values, see Kristol, "Adam Smith and the Spirit of Capitalism," 298, 275. As Antti Lepistö writes, Kristol's "Smith-informed vision of capitalism and the bourgeois way of life offered free market advocates useful moral arguments in favor of capitalism at a time of serious economic crisis." Lepistö, The Rise of Common-Sense Conservatism, 44. Irving Kristol, "An Autobiographical Memoir," in Kristol, Neoconservatism, 37.

77. Kristol, "An Autobiographical Memoir," 12.

serious historical substantiation to many of her husband's ideas. And, like Kristol, Himmelfarb found in Smith the philosophical bases for a neoconservative moral sensibility. Nowhere is this more apparent than in her history, *The Idea of Poverty: England in the Early Industrial Age*, first published in 1984.

Himmelfarb masterfully blended social and intellectual history in her account of the history of ideas about the poor, the nature of poverty, and the type of responses they generated. Smith played a pivotal role in Himmelfarb's account. His works marked a chasm in the history of social thought, but not for the reasons typically attributed to him as the father of economics. Himmelfarb questioned the idea that *The Wealth of Nations* was wholly novel, revolutionary, and disproportionately responsible for the coming of the industrial revolution.[78] While *The Wealth of Nations* might have been unoriginal in its economic theories, Himmelfarb argued that "it was genuinely revolutionary in its view of poverty and its attitude toward the poor." Crucially, Smith's attitude was not revolutionary in the way most people might expect. Smith did not propose the "de-moralization of the economy" along with the "de-moralization of man" in the image of *homo economicus*, nor did he subject the poor to "forces over which they had no control" in the new political economy of *The Wealth of Nations*. Himmelfarb argued that such interpretations were mistaken because they presupposed that Smith's vision of a market economy was "devoid of a moral purpose," and they failed to account for Smith's identity as a moral philosopher—a fact that was as much a matter of "conviction as well as profession."[79]

A number of important claims supported Himmelfarb's treatment of Smith. First, like Kristol, she pitted the sentimentalism and optimism of Smith's Scottish Enlightenment heritage against the rationalism and pessimism of the French *philosophes*. For Himmelfarb as for Kristol,

78. On this point, Himmelfarb referenced a wide range of texts and thinkers who antedated Smith or anticipated his ideas—James Steuart, the physiocrats, the *Encylclopédie* which contained the famous illustration of the pin-factory, and Adam Ferguson, among others. She also nods to Walter Bagehot and Joseph Schumpeter's unimpressed assessment of Smith. Gertrude Himmelfarb, *The Idea of Poverty* (New York, NY: Vintage, 1985), 42–43.

79. Himmelfarb, *The Idea of Poverty*, 46.

Smith's moral philosophy offered an emancipatory and democratic view of human nature. Where the French looked to enlightened rulers to "do for society what the people could not do for themselves," Himmelfarb contended, Smith's down-to-earth view of human nature posited that the street porter and the philosopher shared the same innate capacities to truck, barter, trade, and also acquire and exhibit the same virtues.[80] This view of Smith's moral and analytic egalitarianism is standard currency among scholars today.[81] Second, this optimistic view of human nature supported Smith's positive outlook for the modern economy in which the "liberal reward for labour," as Smith called it, guaranteed productivity, and a growing economy sustained a steady demand for labor met with high wages. Smith made the condition of the working poor "decisive," according to Himmelfarb. Against the doctrine of mercantilism, which held that wages needed to be low out of economic necessity and that the poor would only work if they were compelled by dire need, Smith showed that rich and poor alike were individually motivated to better their condition, and that in doing so, "the general interest would emerge without any intervention, regulation, or coercion."[82] Third, Himmelfarb reinterpreted Smith's proposal for public education as a preventative measure against the degrading effects of labor in early industrial society. This was neither a rudimentary theory of "state-administered, state-supported, state-enforced" social control, nor was it a paternalistic imposition of "alien 'middle-class' virtues" upon the poor in order to stave off social unrest. Rather, according to Himmelfarb, Smith's concern with public education revealed the extent to which he credited the poor with the same amount of moral agency

80. Himmelfarb, *The Idea of Poverty*, 53–54. Lepistö, *The Rise of Common-Sense Conservatism*, 46–47.

81. On Smith's analytic and moral egalitarianism, Peart and Levy, *The Street Porter and the Philosopher*; Samuel Fleischacker, *A Short History of Distributive Justice* (Cambridge, MA: Harvard University Press, 2004); Fleischacker, "Adam Smith on Equality," in *The Oxford Handbook of Adam Smith*, ed. Christopher J. Berry et al., 485–500; Elizabeth Anderson, "Adam Smith on Equality," in *Adam Smith: His Life, Thought, and Legacy*, ed. Ryan Patrick Hanley (Princeton, NJ: Princeton University Press, 2016), 156–72.

82. Himmelfarb, *The Idea of Poverty*, 51, 53.

as the rich. Smith believed the poor could become "better citizens, better workers, and better human beings," and this was clear evidence of his faith in human nature and the formative project baked into his political economy.[83]

A new conception of the moral economy thus emerged out of Himmelfarb's treatment of Smith in *The Idea of Poverty*. The term moral economy is significant, first, because it concatenated the two main prongs of Smith thought—moral philosophy on the one hand, political economy on the other—into a composite concept. Second, the term had gained currency with the publication of the British Marxist historian E.P. Thompson's *The Making of the English Working Class* (1963) and his later essay, "The Moral Economy of the English Crowd in the Eighteenth Century" (1971). Using the food riots of the seventeenth and eighteenth centuries as his historical setting, Thompson argued that those riots reflected a popular moral consensus about "essential rights" and much older notions of fair prices and just wages. Crowds were the heroes of Thompson's social history (as Himmelfarb noted in her prologue to *The Idea of Poverty*); crowds were the embodiment of a moral economy that pushed back against the impersonal and amoral market forces of Smith's political economy. Smith was, on Thompson's account,

---

83. Himmelfarb, *The Idea of Poverty*, 59, 60. Himmelfarb's discussion on Smith's defense of public education was an extended response to then-recent debates on Smith's "Marxian" conceptions of alienation, progress, and decay. Key contributions to that debate include Robert L. Heilbroner, "The Paradox of Progress: Decline and Decay in *The Wealth of Nations*," *Journal of the History of Ideas* 34, no. 2 (1973), 243–62; Robert Lamb, "Adam Smith's Concept of Alienation," *Oxford Economic Papers* 25, no. 2 (1973), 275–85; Edwin George West, "The Political Economy of Alienation: Karl Marx and Adam Smith," *Oxford Economic Papers* 21, no. 1 (1969), 1–23; Nathan Rosenberg, "Adam Smith on the Division of Labour: Two Views or One?," *Economica* 32, no. 126 (1965), 127–39. For recent assessments on Smith and education, see Edward J. Harpham, "Liberalism, Civic Humanism, and the Case of Adam Smith," *The American Political Science Review* 78, no. 3 (September 1984), 764–74; Andrew S. Skinner, "Adam Smith and the Role of the State: Education as a Public Service," in *Adam Smith's Wealth of Nations: New Interdisciplinary Essays*, eds. Stephen Copley and Kathryn Sutherland (Manchester: Manchester University Press, 1995), 70–96; Jack Russell Weinstein, "Introduction: Adam Smith's Philosophy of Education," in *The Adam Smith Review*, ed. Vivienne Brown, vol. 3 (Abingdon: Routledge, 2007), 63–86; Weinstein, *Adam Smith's Pluralism: Rationality, Education, and the Moral Sentiments* (New Haven, CT: Yale University Press, 2013).

the intellectual adversary.[84] But the neoconservative conception of the moral economy was different. Kristol had reworked the idea of bourgeois man to show how capitalism, though nascent in Smith's time, required strong socio-moral institutions; Himmelfarb then enlarged this perspective by showing how Smith's political economic vision reinforced a humane, democratic, and even liberatory view of human nature. The moral economy was not a vestige of history that periodically reasserted itself against the ever-widening reach of the market. For Himmelfarb, Smith's twin subjects introduced a "new kind of moral economy," one in which its economic bases—an advanced division of labor, the complementary growth of agriculture and manufacturing, and high wages and productivity—were not merely prescriptions for economic growth, but also transcendent normative claims to a "higher standard of living, a higher rank in life," and a common moral standing in that very economy.[85]

Importantly, neither Himmelfarb nor Kristol's interpretation of Smith's moral economy implied that the state had an obligation to raise its citizens' standard of living. In fact, quite the opposite was true. Yes, Smith's proposal for public education was state-administered, state-supported, and state-enforced, but Himmelfarb's emphasis was on the purpose, not on the mechanism. Himmelfarb argued that the logic of Smithian moral egalitarianism justified a neoconservative position that favored private charity over public assistance and rationalized the contraction of social welfare programs.[86] Crucially, however, keeping the state out of the moral economy was not a capitulation to market forces. Neoconservatives were as wary of leaving people at the mercy of the free market as they were of subjecting them to the paternalistic hand of the welfare state. To resist the pathologies of both neoliberal atomism and liberal paternalism, then, neoconservatives prescribed the practice of certain virtues—prudence, temperance, frugality, responsibility, and

84. Tim Rogan provides a far more detailed and perspicuous treatment of E.P. Thompson's "moral economy" in his recent book, *The Moral Economists: R. H. Tawney, Karl Polanyi, E. P. Thompson, and the Critique of Capitalism* (Princeton, NJ: Princeton University Press, 2017).

85. Himmelfarb, *The Idea of Poverty*, 48, 63.

86. Lepistö, *The Rise of Common-Sense Conservatism*, 133.

the like—and an attitude of compassion that affirmed the innate moral sense of ordinary people.[87] This epistemic viewpoint and social ethic were apparent in Smith's moral philosophy and fully realized during the Victorian era, the latter of which was the subject of Himmelfarb's later works such as *Poverty and Compassion* (1991), and *The De-Moralization of Society: From Victorian Virtues to Modern Values* (1995). Whatever egalitarian or democratic ethos suffused the neoconservative conception of Smithian moral agency, though, was strictly limited. If everyone had the capacity for moral and material improvement, this not only delegitimized the expansion of state welfare, but also denied special treatment for historically marginalized groups.[88] Put another way, if one of the main concerns of neoconservatives was who or what might regulate the market's "aggressive animus against bourgeois society," their answer appeared to be, as Gary Gerstle pithily stated, "the individual must regulate himself."[89]

Neoconservatives like Irving Kristol and Gertrude Himmelfarb showed that there was another side to Adam Smith. Where Friedman and Stigler had drawn a picture of a Smith who represented freedom under the pure rationality of markets with an indifference to morality and lifestyle, Kristol and Himmelfarb's version made freedom conditional on a narrow conception of morality for American society. Friedman, for instance, was famously in support of the decriminalization of marijuana; the "moral problem" associated with drugs was not with its use, he argued, but rather "that the government is making into criminals

87. Gary Gerstle characterizes this Victorian ethic as such: "He (and I am using the male pronoun deliberately) would acquire self-discipline and self-control, and thus self-respect, a 'pre-condition for the respect and approbation of others', Himmelfarb wrote. Such an individual would not consume mindlessly, or beyond his means; nor indulge in an excess of alcohol, drugs or sex. He would live by the golden rule; he would infuse his own life and the world beyond with 'moral and civic virtue.'" Gerstle, "The Rise and Fall of the Neoliberal Order," 259. Quoting Gertrude Himmelfarb, *The De-Moralization of Society: From Victorian Virtues to Modern Values* (New York, NY: Knopf, 1994), 256, 257.

88. On the limits of the "color-blindness" of neoconservative views on poverty reduction, see Lepistö, *The Rise of Common-Sense Conservatism*, chap. 4.

89. For "aggressive animus" see Kristol, "The Cultural Revolution and the Capitalist Future," 127; Gerstle, "The Rise and Fall of the Neoliberal Order," 258.

people, who may be doing something you and I don't approve of, but who are doing something that hurts nobody else."[90] The neoconservatives, on the other hand, used Smith's moral philosophy to formulate a populist logic and an epistemology that underwrote their belief in capitalism's moral prerequisites; yet the content of that morality was far less universal than their arguments, inundated with Smithian idioms, would suggest.[91] At the uneasy junction of neoliberal and neoconservative ideology, Adam Smith became a symbol of capitalism's bourgeois character, not the symbol of its economic prowess.

Thus, throughout the 1970s and 1980s, multiple Smiths coexisted. There was the Smith of the early revisionist scholars like Hirschman, Winch, and Hont. This Smith was historically contingent, politically complex, and inconvenient for polemical usage. Revisionist historiography revealed Smith's unique orientation toward the study of commercial modernity in and as the study of modern politics. There was also the Smith of the American neoconservative writers like Kristol and Himmelfarb. Not unlike the historical revisionists, neoconservative thinkers pushed back on the de-politicized, de-moralized version of Smith associated with Chicago neoliberalism, but they also exposed the artificiality of the older, but no less significant Adam Smith Problem that presupposed the incompatibility between moral sentiments and economic drives. By welding Smith's moral theory to his political economy, they proposed a vision of American capitalism whereby market forces were reigned in not by political forces, but by moral agency. The *Time* magazine cover from 1976 is thus an emblematic artifact of a remarkable convergence onto Smith during the late-twentieth century's crises of capitalism. Rather than admitting the possibility that capitalism might not survive, though, thinkers were reluctant to count Smith out. Instead, they returned to him with new hopes of resuscitating capitalism and stabilizing its political and moral foundations.

90. Milton Friedman, "America's Drug Forum," interview by Randy Paige, *America's Drug Forum*, 1991, https://www.aei.org/carpe-diem/milton-friedman-interview-from-1991-on-americas-war-on-drugs/.

91. For an interesting discussion of neoconservatism as a form of white identity politics, see Lepistö, *The Rise of Common-Sense Conservatism*.

Epilogue

WE ARE NOW DECADES into the Smith renaissance whose beginnings were announced in 1976. Scholarship on Smith is more diverse than ever, and our understanding of Smith's significance is thicker, more multidimensional, and more complicated. It has become instinctive to assert that "Smith did not try to develop a science of economics free of moral judgments or ethical considerations," that Smith was not "an extreme dogmatic defender of laissez-faire capitalism," and that a Stigler/Friedman-style interpretation of Smith as a defender of amoral, self-correcting, and unregulated markets was misguided.[1] Smith's most famous metaphor of the invisible hand is now widely regarded as but one instance—and a minor one at that—of the socially beneficial unintended consequences of individual liberty, not as a synonym for "the market" *tout court*. Emma Rothschild, one of the most influential contemporary Smith scholars, demoted the invisible hand to the humble status of a "trinket" and "mildly ironic joke" that expresses sardonic contempt toward the motivations and intentions of individual agents.[2]

1. Muller, *Adam Smith in His Time and Ours*, 197; Spencer J. Pack, *Capitalism as a Moral System: Adam Smith's Critique of the Free Market Economy* (Aldershot: Edward Elgar, 1991), 1; Patricia Hogue Werhane, *Adam Smith and His Legacy for Modern Capitalism* (Oxford: Oxford University Pres, 1991), 5–6.

2. Scholarship on the invisible hand is overwhelming. Rothschild goes further in arguing that the invisible hand is "un-Smithian" in that it "presupposes the existence of a theorist (if not of a reformer), who can see more than any ordinary individual can." This presupposition of an omniscient theorist seems in tension with the "independence and idiosyncrasy [*sic*] of individuals" that Smith champions throughout his works. Rothschild, "Adam Smith and the

In a head-on assault of the Friedman-style invocation of the invisible hand, Paul Sagar has recently argued that, at least in its most famous appearance in *The Wealth of Nations*, the invisible hand was invoked "not to draw attention to the problem of state *intervention*, but of state *capture*."[3] Scholars have dramatically expanded the intellectual terrain on which Smith traversed. Aesthetics, a theory of language and poetics, the philosophy of science, empire and colonialism, the role of women, religion—all these subjects have received extraordinarily rich and sophisticated treatments by scholars from around the world.[4] Evocative titles such as *The Authentic Adam Smith*, *The Other Adam Smith*, *An Authentic Account of Adam Smith*, *The Real Adam Smith*, and even a

---

Invisible Hand," 319–22; Rothschild, *Economic Sentiments*, chap. 5. See also Kennedy, "Adam Smith and the Role of the Metaphor of an Invisible Hand;" Shannon Stimson, "From Invisible Hand to Moral Restraint;" Schliesser, *Adam Smith*, chap. 10.

3. Sagar, "We Should Look Closely at What Adam Smith Actually Believed." Emphasis in original.

4. While I cannot possibly hope to capture every contribution here, some helpful introductory and survey works on these topics bear mentioning. On Smith's aesthetics, see Catherine Labio, "Adam Smith's Aesthetics," in *The Oxford Handbook of Adam Smith*, eds. Christopher J. Berry et al. (Oxford: Oxford University Press, 2013), 105–25; Charles L. Griswold, *Jean-Jacques Rousseau and Adam Smith: A Philosophical Encounter* (New York, NY: Routledge, 2017); Peter Jones, "The Aesthetics of Adam Smith," *Adam Smith: International Perspectives*, ed. H. Mizuta and C. Sugiyama (London: Palgrave Macmillan, 1993), 43–62; Samuel Fleischacker, *Adam Smith* (New York, NY: Routledge, 2021), chap. 2. On Smith's theory of language, rhetoric, and poetics, see Vivienne Brown, *Adam Smith's Discourse: Canonicity, Commerce, and Conscience* (New York, NY: Routledge, 1994); C. Jan Swearingen, "Adam Smith on Language and Rhetoric: The Ethics of Style, Character, and Propriety," in *The Oxford Handbook of Adam Smith*, eds. Berry, Smith, and Paganelli, 159–74; Mark Salber Phillips, "Adam Smith, Belletrist," in *The Cambridge Companion to Adam Smith*, ed. Knud Haakonssen, Cambridge Companions to Philosophy (Cambridge: Cambridge University Press, 2006), 57–78; Marcelo Dascal, "Adam Smith's Theory of Language," in the same volume, 79–111. On Smith's philosophy of science, see Fleischacker, *Adam Smith*, chap. 2; Schliesser, *Adam Smith*; Berry, Smith, and Paganelli, eds. *The Oxford Handbook of Adam Smith*, 36–53. On empire, see Onur Ulas Ince, "Adam Smith, Settler Colonialism, and Limits of Liberal Anti-Imperialism," *The Journal of Politics* 83, no. 3 (July 2021), 1080–96; Jennifer Pitts, *A Turn to Empire: The Rise of Imperial Liberalism in Britain and France* (Princeton, NJ: Princeton University Press, 2006); Muthu, "Adam Smith's Critique of International Trading Companies;" Edwin Van der Haar, "Adam Smith on Empire and International Relations," in *The Oxford Handbook of Adam Smith*, eds. Berry, Smith, and Paganelli, 417–39. On women, see Henry C. Clark, "Women and Humanity in Scottish Enlightenment Social Thought: The Case of Adam Smith," *Historical Reflections/Réflexions Historiques* 19, no. 3 (1993),

novel, *Saving Adam Smith* suggest that whoever this other, authentic, real Adam Smith is, he has something approaching a cult following.[5]

One of the most prominent lines of scholarship within the last twenty years or so has revitalized the image of Smith as a moral and cultural critic of capitalism. While some works continue beating the drum to the tune of "Adam Smith was not a laissez-faire dogmatist," a more recent wave of scholarship has drawn out the complexities of reading Smith as both a moral critic and a defender of commercial society.[6] Scholars have long noticed Smith's worries about the debilitating effects of the division of labor and anxieties attached to the insatiable desire

335–61; Maureen Harkin, "Smith's the Theory of Moral Sentiments: Sympathy, Women, and Emulation," *Studies in Eighteenth-Century Culture* 24, no. 1 (1995), 175–90; Maureen Harkin, "Adam Smith and Women: Introduction," in *The Adam Smith Review*, ed. Fonna Forman, vol. 7 (New York, NY: Routledge, 2013), 29–33; Harkin, "Adam Smith on Women," in *The Oxford Handbook of Adam Smith*, eds. Berry, Smith, and Paganelli, 501–20; and Jacqueline Taylor, "Adam Smith and Feminist Ethics: Sympathy, Resentment, and Solidarity," in *Adam Smith*, ed. Hanley, 354–70. On religion, see Gavin Kennedy, "Adam Smith on Religion," in *The Oxford Handbook of Adam Smith*, eds. Berry, Smith, and Paganelli, 464–84; Fleischacker, *Adam Smith*, chap. 8; Charles L. Griswold, *Adam Smith and the Virtues of Enlightenment* (Cambridge: Cambridge University Press, 1998), chap. 7; Lisa Hill, "The Hidden Theology of Adam Smith," *The European Journal of the History of Economic Thought* 8, no. 1 (March 2001), 1–29; Paul Sagar, "Adam Smith's Genealogy of Religion," *History of European Ideas* 47, no. 7 (2021), 1061–1078; Craig Smith, "Adam Smith on Philosophy and Religion," *Ruch Filozoficzny* 74, no. 3 (September 2018), 23–39; Schliesser, *Adam Smith*, chap. 14.

5. James Buchan, *The Authentic Adam Smith: His Life and Ideas*, Reprint edition (New York, NY: W. W. Norton & Company, 2007); Mike Hill and Warren Montag, *The Other Adam Smith: Popular Contention, Commercial Society, and the Birth of Necro-Economics* (Stanford, CA: Stanford University Press, 2014); Gavin Kennedy, *An Authentic Account of Adam Smith* (New York, NY: Palgrave Macmillan, 2017); Jonathan B. Wight, *Saving Adam Smith: A Tale of Wealth, Transformation, and Virtue*, (Upper Saddle River, NJ: Financial Press, 2001). The premise of Wight's novel is rather amusing: Adam Smith assumes the form of a Virginian truck driver and visits a university professor to teach him what Smith *actually* said.

6. Two works that represent the former genre are Pack, *Capitalism as a Moral System*; Werhane, *Adam Smith and His Legacy for Modern Capitalism*. Among the most notable works that cast Smith as both moral critic as well as champion of commercial society Muller, *Adam Smith in His Time and Ours*; Hanley, *Adam Smith and the Character of Virtue*; Dennis C. Rasmussen, "Does 'Bettering Our Condition' Really Make Us Better Off? Adam Smith on Progress and Happiness," *The American Political Science Review* 100, no. 3 (August 2006), 309–18; Rasmussen, *The Problems and Promise of Commercial Society*; Michelle A. Schwarze and John T. Scott, "Mutual Sympathy and the Moral Economy: Adam Smith Reviews Rousseau," *The Journal of Politics* 81, no. 1 (2019), 66–80.

"better one's condition." This more recent trend has constructed a new problematic that has become impossible to ignore. What appears to be one of the central, orienting questions for reading Smith in the twenty-first century is a new version of the old Adam Smith Problem: how do we reconcile Smith's advocacy of the material benefits of the market society he envisioned with his worries about its heavy moral costs? This moves well beyond questions about the textual (in)consistency between *The Theory of Moral Sentiments* and *The Wealth of Nations*, or whether Smith had changed his mind. Indeed, one of the central insights of recent scholars rests on the fact that Smith returned to *The Theory of Moral Sentiments* multiple times after the publication of *The Wealth of Nations*, and that the 1790 revision included the crucial addition of the entirety of Part VI ("Of the Character of Virtue") and the striking chapter in Part I, "Of the corruption of our moral sentiments, which is occasioned by this disposition to admire the rich and great, and to despise or neglect persons of poor and mean condition."[7] A much deeper concern about the fundamental moral status of market societies as a whole appears to drive the central question scholars have raised.[8] Perhaps István Hont put it most aptly in his Carlyle Lectures in 2009: "Can and should we regard commercial society and any analysis of it as fundamentally moral? How did Adam Smith manage to squeeze in morality on such unpromising foundations?"[9]

An outpouring of scholarship speaks to the magnitude and urgency of this interpretive problem. One especially important line of scholarship born within this framework has focused on the connections between Jean-Jacques Rousseau and Adam Smith. This literature has been

7. *TMS* I.iii.3.1, 61. For helpful summaries on reading the connections between *The Wealth of Nations* and the 1790 edition of *The Theory of Moral Sentiments*, see Fleischacker, *On Adam Smith's Wealth of Nations*, chap. 6; Hanley, *Adam Smith and the Character of Virtue*, introduction and chap. 1.

8. I should note that my wise and prescient colleague Paul Sagar has also independently arrived at this way of characterizing the central question of contemporary Smith scholarship, which he outlines in his forthcoming book, *Adam Smith Reconsidered: History, Liberty, and the Foundations of Modern Politics* (Princeton, NJ: Princeton University Press, forthcoming).

9. Hont, *Politics in Commercial Society*, 18.

the source of a bold and now-widespread claim that Smith shared the same concerns as Rousseau, the Enlightenment's arch-critic of commercial society.[10] Dennis Rasmussen, for instance, has amplified an earlier argument that Rousseau was "an important if unavowed interlocutor" for Smith and that Smith was "to some extent responding to Rousseau," or at very least "responding to the Rousseau*ian* critique of commercial society."[11] Similarly, Ryan Hanley has argued that Smith was "particularly sympathetic to Rousseau's insistence that commercial society is fundamentally driven by a vanity that threatens to corrupt its participants."[12] István Hont also claimed that the affinity between Rousseau and Smith is to be found in their "shared moral foundations," even though their political theories ultimately diverged.[13]

To be sure, there remains substantial scholarly disagreement over the extent of Rousseau's influence on Smith (the two never corresponded,

10. Among the most influential works that have argued for Rousseau's importance for Smith are Rasmussen, *The Problems and Promise of Commercial Society*; Ryan Patrick Hanley, "Commerce and Corruption: Rousseau's Diagnosis and Adam Smith's Cure," *European Journal of Political Theory* 7, no. 2 (April 2008), 137–58; Hanley, *Adam Smith and the Character of Virtue*; Hont, *Politics in Commercial Society*; Schwarze and Scott, "Mutual Sympathy and the Moral Economy." See also Charles L. Griswold, "Smith and Rousseau in Dialogue: Sympathy, Pitié, Spectatorship and Narrative," in *The Adam Smith Review*, eds. Vivienne Brown, Samuel Fleischacker, vol. 5 (New York, NY: Routledge, 2010), 69–94; Michael Ignatieff, "Smith, Rousseau and the Republic of Needs," in *Scotland and Europe 1200–1850*, ed. T.C. Smouth (Edinburgh: Edinburgh University Press, 1986), 187–206. For a helpful summary of recent literature exploring connections between Smith and Rousseau, see the editor's introduction in Maria Pia Paganelli, Dennis C. Rasmussen, and Craig Smith, eds., *Adam Smith and Rousseau: Ethics, Politics, Economics*, Edinburgh Studies in Scottish Philosophy (Edinburgh: Edinburgh University Press, 2018), 4–15. Griswold's *Jean-Jacques Rousseau and Adam Smith*: takes a slightly different approach. Griswold is more interested in Rousseau and Smith's answer to "questions of the self," as opposed to proving that Smith and Rousseau were responding to the same question about commercial society's morality.

11. The earlier claim referenced here appeared in István Hont and Michael Ignatieff, "Needs and Justice in the *Wealth of Nations*," in their *Wealth and Virtue*, 1–44 at 10. Rasmussen, *The Problems and Promise of Commercial Society*, 59. Emphasis in original.

12. Hanley, "Commerce and Corruption," 137–38. Hanley discusses the Rousseau-Smith affinity further in Hanley, *Adam Smith and the Character of Virtue*, 24–52.

13. For helpful clarification and analysis of the significance of Hont's analysis, see Ryan Hanley, "On the Place of Politics in Commercial Society," in *Adam Smith and Rousseau*, eds. Paganelli, Rasmussen, and Smith, as well as Sagar, *Adam Smith Reconsidered*.

to say the least).[14] However, the broader significance of this interpretive angle is that Smith has emerged as a moral theorist who, vis-à-vis Rousseau, harbored a normative suspicion of commercial society, but defended it nonetheless.[15] What is more, Smith's defense rested on moral grounds. Smith's moral theory, unlike Rousseau's, encouraged "mutual accommodation and equal recognition of persons," and it is this "positive-sum understanding of the moral economy" which undergirds Smith's "measured optimism about the possibility of moral and economic progress and his embrace of commercial society."[16] In spite of his concerns about the corruption of our moral and cognitive capacities,

14. There are some rather serious intellectual detractors to this interpretive framework and its conclusions. Paul Sagar and Mark Huilling are two of the most vocal critics of the view that Smith was *primarily* concerned with responding to Rousseau and that the two shared the same moral concerns about commercial society. Sagar's *Smith Reconsidered* is a book-length refutation of the importance of Rousseau for Smith and the idea that Smith can be thought of as primarily concerned with the *morality* of commercial society. Huilling calls the Rousseau-Smith connection an "extremely dubious argument" and maintains that scholars have overemphasized the historical and intellectual connections between the two thinkers. Even more aggressively, Huilling contends that Rousseau is often used simply as a convenient foil for Smith, which leads to "indulging in anachronistic reasoning, reading back into the eighteenth-century and nineteenth-century debate between liberals and socialists." See Paul Sagar, "Smith and Rousseau, after Hume and Mandeville," *Political Theory* 46, no. 1 (February 2018), 29–58; Sagar, *The Opinion of Mankind*; Mark Huilling, "Rousseau and the Scottish Enlightenment: Connections and Disconnections," in *Adam Smith and Rousseau*, ed. Paganelli, Rasmussen, and Smith, 32–52. In other works, Sagar and Robin Douglass contend that Smith's primary intellectual target was not Rousseau, but rather Bernard Mandeville. See Sagar, "Smith and Rousseau;" Robin Douglass, "Morality and Sociability in Commercial Society: Smith, Rousseau—and Mandeville," *The Review of Politics* 79, no. 4 (2017), 597–620; Robin Douglass, "A Moral Philosophy for Commercial Society? Or, How to Misread *The Theory of Moral Sentiments*," in *Interpreting Adam Smith: Critical Essays* (Cambridge: Cambridge University Press, forthcoming).

15. Jesse Norman writes, "As we have seen, Adam Smith was one of the great defenders of the emergent commercial society of his day. For him what existed then fell some way short of his preferred 'system of natural liberty,' but he celebrated such a society even so: as an antidote to the servility and personal dependency of feudalism, for the way in which it often improved morals and manners, and above all for its capacity to create 'universal opulence,' that is general wealth and prosperity. In relation to civic republicanism, Smith's celebration of commercial society is, precisely, a repudiation of slavery and the classical idea that a virtuous citizenry could be built upon slavery." Jesse Norman, *Adam Smith: Father of Economics* (New York: Basic Books, 2018), 315.

16. Schwarze and Scott, "Mutual Sympathy and the Moral Economy," 68.

Smith's revisions to *The Theory of Moral Sentiments*, especially Part VI, provided an ethical framework for the cultivation of virtue that might ameliorate and ward off the vices of commercial society.[17] And perhaps most importantly, the capacity for commercial society to generate universal opulence meant not only the alleviation of poverty, but also the introduction of social relations based on equal standing, authority, and esteem, rather than conditions of servility and dependence.[18] What we have, then, are several substantial and compelling accounts of Smith's "moral balance" sheet of commercial society in which the ledger reads decidedly positive.[19]

Superficial similarities to the neoconservative version of a Smithian moral economy are apparent in recent scholarship. This is not to suggest any influence from one to the other nor is it to suggest any unspoken

17. The theme of "corruption" in Smith's works has been well documented. Ryan Hanley and Dennis Rasmussen have provided some of the most serious treatments of the theme of corruption in commercial society, specifically the idea that inequality of wealth and income "distorts of our sympathies," and that the constant striving in commercial society threatens "precisely those aspects of the soul and mind that distinguish human beings as human, aspects which include not only the sentiments but also the capacity for the cultivation of intellectual virtues." Rasmussen, "Adam Smith on What Is Wrong with Economic Inequality;" Hanley, *Adam Smith and the Character of Virtue*, 34. For further commentary on the theme of corruption, see Lisa Hill, "Adam Smith and the Theme of Corruption," *The Review of Politics* 68, no. 4 (October 2006), 636–62; Hanley, "Commerce and Corruption."

18. There is almost unanimous agreement that, for Smith, the most important feature of commercial society was that it improved the condition of the poor. As discussed in Chapter 7, Hont and Ignatieff's essay, "Needs and Justice in the *Wealth of Nations*" was among the first major contributions on this topic. For other works that support this claim, see Hanley, *Adam Smith and the Character of Virtue*, 15–24; Winch, *Adam Smith's Politics*, 88–90; Muller, *Adam Smith in His Time and Ours*, 72–76; Hanley, *Adam Smith*, 281–302. On the emancipatory social relations of commercial society, see Fleischacker, *On Adam Smith's Wealth of Nations*, 55–57; Hanley, *Adam Smith and the Character of Virtue*, chap. 1; Muller, *Adam Smith in His Time and Ours*, 8; Rasmussen, *The Problems and Promise of Commercial Society*, chaps. 3 and 4; Elizabeth Anderson, *Private Government: How Employers Rule Our Lives (And Why We Don't Talk about It)* (Princeton, NJ: Princeton University Press, 2017), 4.

19. Jerry Muller uses the idea of a "moral balance sheet" for commercial society in Muller, *Adam Smith in His Time and Ours*, 10. Dennis Rasmussen echoes this moral balance sheet in *The Problems and Promise of Commercial Society*. Samuel Fleischacker also has a brief discussion of what he calls "A Moral Assessment of Capitalism?" in Fleischacker, *On Adam Smith's Wealth of Nations*, 55–57.

political agendas, but rather that taking stock of these views can be illuminating. At least one politician, the British Conservative MP Jesse Norman, has described Smith's vision of commercial society as "astonishingly egalitarian."[20] This assessment is echoed among scholars who, at least professionally, are not in the business of policy advocacy. Philosopher Samuel Fleischacker, for example, has provided the most thoroughgoing case for aligning Smith closer to the values of the contemporary left.[21] Closely following Himmelfarb, Fleischacker has argued that Smith "almost single-handedly . . . *changed the attitudes* that underwrote the restrictive, disdainful policies by which the poor were kept poor," and that the "greatest triumph" of *The Wealth of Nations* was not some proof of the socially-beneficial consequences of self-interest, but its call for a "shift in our moral imaginations."[22] To his credit, Fleischacker proceeds with caution and philosophical scrupulousness as he makes the case for Smith on "the Left."[23] Fleischaker's Smith advocated modest redistributivist policies, he disdained traditional forms of private power (the Church, the mercantile elite), and most importantly, he left sufficient room for the state to pursue the ends of distributive justice. In a similar vein, the egalitarian philosopher Elizabeth Anderson has argued that, for Smith, the "leading virtues of market society" were not growth and efficiency, but rather freedom from relationships of private domination and dependence. The market, therefore, was a sphere for both freedom and equality; this was a "deeply humane vision" of market society and a "huge advance for equality," to quote Anderson, but one that was lost after the Industrial Revolution.[24]

20. Norman, *Adam Smith*, 186–87.

21. Fleischacker, *A Short History of Distributive Justice*, 64. See also Fleischacker, "Adam Smith on Equality;" Fleischacker, *On Adam Smith's Wealth of Nations*, 72–80, 145–69, 203–26; Fleischacker, "Adam Smith and the Left," in *Adam Smith: His Life, Thought, and Legacy*, ed. Ryan Patrick Hanley (Princeton: Princeton University Press, 2016), 478–93.

22. Fleischacker, *A Short History of Distributive Justice*, 64; Fleischacker, *On Adam Smith's Wealth of Nations*, 208. Emphasis in original.

23. "Claiming Smith for these camps [social democrats and welfare state liberals] would also be intellectually irresponsible," writes Fleischacker. Fleischacker, "Adam Smith and the Left."

24. Anderson, *Private Government*, 4, 18, 22.

So while the neoconservative thinkers used a version of Smith's moral theory to justify a scaling back of the state in economic life, a more recent line of "Left Smith" interpretations suggests that Smith's "moral approval of the economic system we call 'capitalism' (what he called 'commercial society')" was conditional on its ability to promote—potentially through state power—greater political and socioeconomic equality.[25]

It should be fairly unsurprising at this point that both the contemporary Left and Right can lay claim to Smith, or that contending historical meanings have been attached to Smith's "politics," his "moral economy," and his "defense" of a humane capitalism. No single version of Smith has gone uncontested. But we still should ask: what is the significance of these repeated and ongoing appeals to Smith's moral assessment of capitalism? Why do we still need Adam Smith's moral approval in the twenty-first century?

Recent history might help us make some sense of these questions, and two events in particular can partly explain the hyper-salience of Smith's reputation as a moral theorist of capitalism. The first of these events was the embrace of market fundamentalism by the American Left beginning in the 1990s, most evident in the policies of the Clinton Administration. Between 1993 and 1999, the Clinton Administration implemented a staggering amount of market-based reforms in both domestic and international policy. In 1993 President Clinton signed the North American Free Trade Agreement; he signed the Personal Responsibility and Work Opportunity Reconciliation Act of 1996, fulfilling his campaign promise to "end welfare as we know it." Perhaps of greatest consequence was the repeal of the New Deal-era Glass-Steagall Act in 1999, which effectively deregulated the banking industry by no longer mandating the separation of commercial and investment banking in the United States. Historian Gary Gerstle has argued that Clinton, far more than Reagan, solidified the ideology of market fundamentalism of the 1970s and 1980s into the "political order" of neoliberalism, and the

25. Fleischacker, *On Adam Smith's Wealth of Nations*, 55.

Democratic embrace of Friedmanite market advocacy was both a cause and consequence of that order.[26] In brief, if markets could be made to work on the left, surely Adam Smith could be reimagined in a way that made this degree of market expansionism compatible with a progressive political agenda.

The second event was the Great Recession. Triggered by the Financial Crisis in 2007 and 2008, Americans lost an estimated $9.8 trillion in wealth during the worst economic downturn since the Great Depression. By 2009 some 15 million people were unemployed.[27] In 2011, a group of protestors gathered in New York City under the slogans "We are the 99%" and "Occupy Wall Street," drawing attention to the enormous disparities in wealth and income in the United States. Within a month, Occupy protests were happening all over the world. In 2013, Thomas Piketty's magnum opus, *Capital in the 21st Century*, was published, and President Obama famously declared economic inequality to be the "defining challenge of our time."[28] Successive waves of economic, intellectual, and political upheavals threw concerns about poverty, inequality, and the moral foundations of capitalist democracies into high relief, and their ripples could still be felt during the chaotic presidency of Donald Trump.

Smith's relevance has always been political, but it's no stretch to say that the events of the last decade alone have led readers to rediscover his immediate relevance with even more urgency. Studies on Smith's views on economic inequality, the normative stakes of economic growth, and

26. Gerstle, "The Rise and Fall of the Neoliberal Order," 256–57. See also Lily Geismer, *Don't Blame Us: Suburban Liberals and the Transformation of the Democratic Party*, (Princeton, NJ: Princeton University Press, 2014); Lily Geismer, *Left Behind: The Democrats' Failed Attempt to Solve Inequality* (New York, NY: Public Affairs, 2022); Joseph E. Stiglitz, *The Roaring Nineties: A New History of the World's Most Prosperous Decade*, Reprint edition (New York, NY: W. W. Norton & Company, 2004).

27. "Great Recession, great recovery? Trends from the Current Population Survey," Bureau of Labor Statistics, April 2018. https://www.bls.gov/opub/mlr/2018/article/great-recession-great-recovery.htm.

28. "Remarks by the President on Economic Mobility," December 4, 2013. The White House, Office of the Press Secretary, https://obamawhitehouse.archives.gov/the-press-office/2013/12/04/remarks-president-economic-mobility.

his conception of the "moral economy" reveal just how saturated public and academic discourses have become with questions concerning the morality of capitalism.[29] What appears to be at stake in this moment, however, is more than the extent to which we can distance Smith's reputation from his past admirers—neoliberal, neoconservative, or otherwise—it is our very ability to defend capitalism on moral grounds yet again. However, the image of Adam Smith that has emerged from these crises is steeped in political and historical contingency and fraught with ambiguity. Two examples from recent memory provide illustration.

In his now-famous speech on economic mobility in 2013, President Obama complicated the familiar picture of Smith as the patron saint of free markets and the apologist for inequality, and instead, portrayed the founding father of economics as a progressive friend of capitalism. "This shouldn't be an ideological question." Referring to his ambitions to raise the federal minimum wage, Obama asserted,

> It was Adam Smith, the father of free-market economics, who once said, "They who feed, clothe, and lodge the whole body of the people should have such a share of the produce of their own labor as to be themselves tolerably well fed, clothed, and lodged." And for those of you who don't speak old-English, let me translate. It means if you work hard, you should make a decent living. If you work hard, you should be able to support a family.[30]

29. For example, Deborah Boucoyannis, "The Equalizing Hand: Why Adam Smith Thought the Market Should Produce Wealth Without Steep Inequality," *Perspectives on Politics* 11, no. 04 (2013), 1051–70; Lisa Herzog, "Adam Smith on Markets and Justice," *Philosophy Compass* 9, no. 12 (December 2014), 864–75; Rasmussen, "Adam Smith on What Is Wrong with Economic Inequality;" Schwarze and Scott, "Mutual Sympathy and the Moral Economy."

30. Barak Obama, "Remarks by the president on economic mobility," December 4, 2013, https://obamawhitehouse.archives.gov/the-press-office/2013/12/04/remarks-president -economic-mobility. The full passage from which Obama quoted is from *The Wealth of Nations* I.viii.36, 96. "Is this improvement in the circumstances of the lower ranks of the people to be regarded as an advantage or as an inconveniency to the society? The answer seems at first sight abundantly plain. Servants, labourers, and workmen of different kinds, make up the far greater part of every great political society. But what improves the circumstances of the greater part can never be regarded as an inconveniency to the whole. No society can surely be flourishing and happy, of which the far greater part of the members are poor and miserable. It is but equity,

Even without appealing to Smith as the author of *The Theory of Moral Sentiments*, the implication is fairly straightforward: if even Adam Smith believed that everyone ought to earn their fair share in a free market society, then taking federal action to ensure the conditions of prosperity and fairness is not only authorized but obligatory.

Of course, conservatives were ready to reclaim the moral high ground with Adam Smith, too. In a 2015 White House Summit on Poverty, Arthur Brooks, then-president of the conservative American Enterprise Institute, described his intellectual debt to Adam Smith.

> Capitalism is nothing more than a system, and it must be predicated on right morals. It must be. Adam Smith taught me that. Adam Smith, the father of modern economics—he wrote "The Wealth of Nations," in 1776—17 years before he wrote "The Theory of Moral Sentiments," which was a more important book because it talked about what it meant as a society to earn the right to have free enterprise, to have free economics. And it was true then, and it's still true today . . . This conversation with the President of the United States is so important . . . because we're talking about the right morality toward our brothers and sisters, and built on that, that's when we can have an open discussion to get our capitalism right. And then the distribution of resources is only a tertiary question.[31]

For Brooks, Smith's *The Theory of Moral Sentiments* is less a work of Enlightenment moral science and more a work of moral precepts that underwrites *The Wealth of Nations*, and, by extension, twenty-first-century capitalism. Concerns about the distribution of wealth in society ought to be secondary to concerns about protecting free enterprise, in Brooks's view; but even free enterprise itself is predicated on "the right

---

besides, that they who feed, clothe, and lodge the whole body of the people, should have such a share of the produce of their own labour as to be themselves tolerably well fed, clothed, and lodged."

31. Arthur Brooks, "Remarks by the President in Conversation on Poverty at Georgetown University," May 12, 2015, https://www.whitehouse.gov/the-press-office/2015/05/12/remarks-president-conversation-poverty-georgetown-university.

morality." With hindsight, the resemblance to Kristol and Himmelfarb's neoconservative ideal of the Smithian "bourgeois man" is obvious. However, the effect of Brooks's argument is to so closely juxtapose capitalism with morality and the father of economics with *The Theory of Moral Sentiments* that it becomes automatic to believe that capitalism *is* morally justifiable, however vague those terms may be.

If such whiplash-inducing uses of Smith is indicative of a crisis, it is a crisis of the imagination. They reveal how much we have come to depend on Smith for ways to think our way out of predicaments. We have become so confined by our hope that capitalism must survive, that we have to "get it right," that, rather than seeking out its alternatives, we insist that its lifelines lay in the body of work that Adam Smith created more than two and a half centuries ago. We find ourselves caught within conceptual ambiguity and have become captive to what Angus Burgin has identified as a "familiar linguistic paradox:" the ambiguity, slipperiness, and under-specificity of the meaning of Smith's politics, his moral economy, and his defense of capitalism have inspired endless contestation and frustration, but those very qualities are also what enable Smith to be so readily adopted, used, and weaponized.[32] Saying that Smith's politics or his moral vision of capitalism is ambiguous is not to say that it is meaningless or empty. Rather, it suggests that their meanings are being continually reshaped and reinvented by Smith's interpreters who bring their own set of beliefs and preoccupations to bear on his ideas.

This, then, might be the ultimate Adam Smith Problem: can the historical recovery of Adam Smith's thought—"what he can legitimately be said to have intended, rather than with what he might be said to have anticipated or foreshadowed" to quote Winch again—ever be truly separated from recruiting him to serve our present political and intellectual needs? The history I have documented here reveals that not only is the historical recovery of Smith compatible with his enduring political resonance, but also that belief in Smith's enduring political resonance is

32. Burgin, "The Neoliberal Turn."

perhaps the reason why so many people are seeking deeper inquiry into his works in the first place.[33] We turn to Smith time and time again because we believe the history of political thought might help us "tease apart the different sorts of political vision that are currently relevant to us," or because "*We need a new master-narrative for our times.*"[34] Yet as soon as we have created a new master narrative around Smith or identified a suitable political and moral vision from his works, history renders Smith elusive again.

At the beginning of this book, I asked: Who is Adam Smith? Who *was* Adam Smith? Adam Smith is a thinker who has been compartmentalized countless times, yet manages to escape each time. Who he *was* in the minds of his past readers has shaped who he *is* to us today. As scholars before me have argued, the history of reading Smith is a history of unhistorical readings, selective interpretations, even political appropriations. It is a history riddled with foreshortening, attenuating, and misreading, yet it is also a history that proves why Smith's ideas were—and are—worth reading, contemplating, defending, and criticizing. Of greater consequence have been the hesitancy, unwillingness, and even inability of Smith's readers to see and treat his works *only* as products of their historical moment. Perhaps, then, we might be better off admitting that we are not immune to the missteps of the past, and that we cannot fully shed our prejudices, and that our political and intellectual expectations when reading (and re-reading) Adam Smith's works will inevitably shape our view of him, despite our best attempts to do otherwise. If nothing else, we stand to gain a greater self-consciousness— not in the sense of whether we have the correct reading of Smith, or whether we are better or worse than those interpreters who came before us, but in the sense that we learn more about *why* we are reaching for

33. Again, I borrow from Stefan Collini's model. Collini suggests that even when a thinker has "no current political resonance, but is recognized as having acquired some kind of classic status or to have become an object of purely scholarly enquiry," we should be wary of thinking that "becoming the object of detailed scholarly enquiry is incompatible with an enduring political resonance." Collini, *Public Moralists*, 318.

34. Hont, *Politics in Commercial Society*, 1; Norman, *Adam Smith*, 324, emphasis in original.

Adam Smith's ideas in the first place. What are *our* conditions of possibility that are drawing us to Smith, now? What are we asking Smith to do for our political, moral, and economic thinking in the twenty-first century? If we can answer these questions and do our thinking for ourselves, perhaps we will be worthy of learning from Adam Smith after all.

ACKNOWLEDGMENTS

"I AM A SLOW a very slow workman, who do and undo everything I write at least half a dozen of times before I can be tolerably pleased with it," wrote Adam Smith to Thomas Cadell in 1788. Versions of this book have been done and undone, written and rewritten at least half a dozen of times, or so it feels. I can be tolerably pleased with it—perhaps barely—only because of the gracious and unwavering support of so many colleagues, mentors, friends, and family.

This project first came to life at the nexus of the Departments of Political Science and History at Stanford University, where Alison McQueen, Josh Ober, Barry Weingast, and Caroline Winterer were and still are the pillars of my academic life. Alison showed me what it means to think and teach clearly about politics; her gift for breaking down arguments and close reading without ever losing sight of the perennial questions sharpens the minds of all who have the privilege of learning from her. Josh is single-handedly responsible for not only converting me to political theory but for keeping me there. His acumen, sagacity, and truly boundless knowledge of history have shown me what's possible as a political theorist working between the ancient and modern worlds. Barry is a colleague unlike any other. We have read, written, and travelled the world together thinking about and with Adam Smith, and Barry has been a bottomless reservoir of support—whether in the form of footnotes, provocations, a glass of wine, or fixing dangling modifiers. Caroline showed me that intellectual history could be beautiful, grand, and fun at the same time. Her vision of American intellectual history on the scale of deep space and time, her ability to speak in magisterial paragraphs in every conversation big or small, and her appreciation for the humorous and whimsical has enabled me to see the world in richer colors, more light, and with a few more T-Rexes. My honorary dissertation committee member, Jennifer Burns, has been an invaluable mentor who helped me navigate not just my first archival trip, but also the intersections of American history and the history of economic thought. Finally, Claire Rydell Arcenas is the reason why I pursued a reception history of Smith in the first place. Claire was an endlessly patient sounding board, an archival coach, and most of all, a steadfast friend; I can only hope that *Adam Smith's America* will be half as good as *America's Philosopher*. Collectively, these incredible scholars and human beings helped bring this book into its first incarnation as a doctoral dissertation. But more than that, they taught me how to be a scholar, a writer, a teacher, and a citizen.

A large portion of the book was written (and rewritten) while I was at Brown University. I owe an enormous amount of gratitude to Angus Burgin, Ryan Hanley, Jennifer Ratner-Rosenhagen, and Eric Schliesser, each of whom read an earlier version of this book at my manuscript workshop in January of 2020. This book is sharper and clearer because of their probing questions, constructive criticism, and their willingness to help me work out ideas as I continued to revise the work. Of course, bringing these heavyweights of intellectual history and political theory together would not have been possible without the tremendous support I received from the Political Theory Project at Brown, where I was a postdoctoral associate for two years. Dan D'Amico, Emily and David Skarbek, and John Tomasi challenged my thinking every day and Aly Laughlin made everything possible. David Estlund, Alex Gourevitch, and Sharon Krause read early drafts of chapters as I was still working out what I was up to, and they salvaged my arguments when I could barely articulate them. Arthur Ghins, Danilo Freire, Natalya Naumenko, Antong Liu, and Julia Netter made the monastic life of a postdoctoral researcher bearable and infinitely more interesting.

I completed the book while starting my new position as a College Fellow and tutor in Social Studies at Harvard, and during the COVID–19 pandemic no less. My colleagues Amy Alemu, David Armitage, Eric Beerbohm, Anya Bassett, Andrew Brandel, Bo-Mi Choi, Charles Clavey,

Katrina Forrester, Sean Gray, Jonathan Hansen, Ana Keilson, Gili Klieger, Abbie Modaff, Nicole Newendorp, Nicolas Prevelakis, Justin Reynolds, Tracey Rosen, Bonnie Talbert, Brandon Terry, Don Tontiplaphol, Rosie Wagner, William Whitham, and Rob Willison provided more encouragement and support than they can possibly know during the most challenging academic year I have ever experienced. Their collective brilliance, generosity, and sense of humor radiated even through Zoom and our KN–95 masks in the classroom, and I have been so lucky to be surrounded by them as I finished this book.

Rob Tempio is a dream editor. His early enthusiasm and clear vision for this project were a constant source of energy, while his calm reassurance, good humor, and ability to find words when I had none left were trusted tonics. Matt Rohal, Chloe Coy, Michelle Garceau Hawkins, Karen L. Carter, Silvia Benvenuto, and the entire team at Princeton University Press deserve acknowledgement for making everything come together despite a global pandemic, supply chain disruptions, and my first-time author anxiety. The help and insight of two anonymous reviewers provided me with clarity and insight I could not have discovered on my own and reshaped the book. I also want to thank Claire Arcenas, Luke Mayville, Alison McQueen, Josh Ober, Rob Reich, and John Tomasi for all of their helpful advice on metamorphosizing a dissertation into a book.

Countless individuals have read and commented on sections of this book and contributed to its development at different stages and in different forms: Pete Boettke, Bruce Caldwell, Irwin Collier, Ross Emmett, Fonna Forman, Judith Goldstein, Sam Haselby, Doug Irwin, Gavin Kennedy, Sarah Igo, Jacob Levy, Luke Mayville, Leonidas Montes, Maria Pia Paganelli, Rob Reich, Paul Sagar, Shannon Stimson, Richard Whatmore. In-person and virtual conversations with Rebecca Brenner Graham, Larry Glickman, Andrew Hartman, Benjamin Hein, Antti Lepistö, Marc-William Palen, Seth Rockman, Emma Rothschild, Lukas Rieppel, and Lyle Rubin made the intersection of the history of ideas and the histories of capitalism a welcoming and endlessly fascinating space to work. I am also grateful to the many audiences and respondents who have provided lively and productive discussions of my work, no matter how half-baked my arguments were: the Brown Political Philosophy Workshop; the Center for the History of Political Economy at Duke; the Dartmouth Political Economy Project; the Mercatus Center Workshop in Philosophy, Politics and Economics; the Institute for Liberal Studies; the Philosophy, Politics, and Economics Research Seminar Series at Arizona State University; the Society for US Intellectual History; the Stanford U.S. History Workshop; the Stanford Ethics and Politics Ancient and Modern Workshop; the Stanford Humanities Center; the Stanford Seminar on the Enlightenment and Revolution; and the Political Science workshop at SUNY-Albany.

A heartfelt thank you to the research librarians and library staff who made this research possible: the John Hay Library at Brown University, the Columbia University Archives, the Harvard University Archives and Houghton Library, the Baker Library at Harvard Business School, the Hoover Institution Archives, the New York Public Library, and the Hanna Holborn Gray Special Collections Research Center at the University of Chicago. Special thanks to Ben Stone, the curator of American and British history at the Stanford library, who was one of the first experts I consulted and who helped me locate critical bibliographic sources and newspaper databases. I would also like to thank Stephen Stigler for granting me access to George Stigler's papers at Chicago while they were not yet catalogued.

I have often joked that the number of hours I spend dancing equals the number of hours I can tolerate writing. A company of dancers, dance teachers, body workers, and artists therefore deserves my deepest gratitude: Christian Burns, Becky Chaleff, Sandra Chinn, Cora Cliburn, Robert Dekkers, Katie Faulkner, Diane Frank, Zvi Gotheiner, Alex Ketley, Christopher Lam, Arthur Leeth, Muriel Maffre, Jay Markov, Dana Mills, Robert Moses, Asami Odate, Jenny Oliver, Mindy Phung, Nailah Randall-Bellinger, Summer Lee Rhatigan, Marcus Schulkind, Sydney Skybetter, Holly Stone, Kristine Tom, Erik Wagner, Adam Weinert, Katrina Wisdom, Aline Wachsmuth, Devin Wu, and the many dance communities I have called home. These movers, shakers, and healers have radically shaped me as a physical researcher, not just a disembodied mind, and I am so honored to have shared space with every single one of them.

As Adam Smith writes in *The Theory of Moral Sentiments*, there are certain friends "upon whose wisdom and virtue we can . . . entirely depend." Lily Lamboy has been by my side from Day Zero—grad school admit weekend—to graduation and beyond. She has been my confidante and collaborator; whenever I lost my way in a sea of ideas and arguments, I could rely on her firm conviction to ground me. Her relentless pursuit of justice inspires me to be a better human being every day. Shing Shing Ho is my chosen sister. We have navigated life's smallest and biggest decisions together—everything from which limited edition seasonal boba tea to buy, to family, relationships, and careers. Matt Ware brought determination and levity to everything we did together from board games to design challenges, camping to debates about the merits of the Bohr Model. Sara Malik has been a steadfast friend whose tenacity, compassion, and wit know no bounds and are matched only by her voracious appetite for books and love of animals. Dozens of loops around the Stanford Dish with Sara Kwasnick—one of the few friends who didn't complain about my uphill pace—kept me energized and clear-minded, and I thank her for welcoming me into the wonderful extended Kwasnick family. Countless drives from Palo Alto to San Francisco and from Providence to Boston for ballet class were worth it because of the company and companionship of Cora Cliburn and Asami Odate.

Finally, to my family. Stewart Koppell is my dearest friend and partner without whom this work and my life would be incomplete. No amount of verbiage can convey the gratitude I have for his sympathy, love, and support over the years. He has been a steadfast impartial spectator, and he inspires wonder in me about the natural and human world. His inimitable "gaiety of temper" is—as Smith saw in Hume—"attended with the most severe application, the most extensive learning, the greatest depth of thought, and a capacity in every respect the most comprehensive." As much as my own frailty will permit, I consider him as close to the idea of a perfectly wise and virtuous human being as possible. My parents Don and Helen, and my siblings David, Grace, and Daniel, have taught me what it means to be truly loved and to be lovely. They will, I hope, forgive me for my inability to express what they mean to me as I paraphrase Smith once more—for they have certainly loved me more than any other person ever has or ever will love me, and I love and respect them more than I shall either love or respect any other person.

REFERENCES

Manuscript Collections

John Hay Library, Brown University, Providence, RI
  Francis Wayland Family Papers, 1754–1941
  Student Lecture Notes
Rare Books and Manuscripts Library, Columbia University, New York, NY
  Columbia College Papers, 1703–1964
  Columbiana Manuscripts, 1572–1986
  Edwin Robert Anderson Seligman Papers, 1750–1939
  John Bates Clark Papers, 1848–1955
  John Maurice Clark Papers, 1920–1963
  Lecture Notes Collection, 1817–1969
Pusey Library and Houghton Library, Harvard University, Cambridge, MA
  Harvard University Archives
  North American Review Papers, 1831–1843
  Papers of Edward Everett
  Papers of Francis Bowen, 1850–1890
Hoover Institution Archives, Stanford, CA
  Milton Friedman Papers
New York Public Library, New York, NY
  Noah Webster Papers, 1764–1843
Hanna Holborn Gray Special Collections Research Center, University of Chicago, Chicago, IL
  Aaron Director Papers
  Frank Knight Papers
  Henry Simons Papers
  George Stigler Papers (with permission of Stephen Stigler)

Digital Collections

This work was made possible through the vast amounts of digital resources available online. Most were accessed through the Stanford, Brown, and Harvard University libraries, while others are available to the public.

Archive of European Intellectual Life—Institute of Intellectual History, University of St. Andrews

https://arts.st-andrews.ac.uk/intellectualhistory/

America's Historical Newspapers

www.readex.com/content/americas-historical-newspapers

A Century of Lawmaking for a New Nation: U.S. Congressional Documents and Debates

http://memory.loc.gov/ammem/amlaw/lawhome.html

Annals of Congress

Register of Debates

Congressional Globe

Congressional Record

The Collected Works of Milton Friedman, Hoover Institution Archives, Stanford University

https://miltonfriedman.hoover.org/collections

Economics in the Rear-View Mirror: Archival Artifacts from the History of Economics. Transcribed and curated by Irwin Collier.

www.irwincollier.com

Founders Online—National Archives

https://founders.archives.gov

Papers of Alexander Hamilton

Papers of Benjamin Franklin

Papers of James Madison

Papers of Thomas Jefferson

Free to Choose TV

www.freetochoose.tv

Free to Choose: Original 1980 TV Series

Massachusetts Historical Society

http://masshist.org/digitaladams

Adams Family Papers: An Electronic Archive

ProQuest Congressional

http://congressional.proquest.com

Annals of Congress

Register of Debates

Congressional Globe

Congressional Record

Rotunda—The American Founding Era

https://rotunda.upress.virginia.edu/founders

The Adams Papers Digital Edition

The Papers of Alexander Hamilton Digital Edition

The Papers of Thomas Jefferson Digital Edition

Founders Early Access

Works Cited

"A Cravat for Conservatives." *Time Magazine* 118, no. 1 (July 6, 1981), 60.

Adair, Douglass. "'That Politics May Be Reduced to a Science': David Hume, James Madison, and the Tenth Federalist." *Huntington Library Quarterly* 20, no. 4 (1957): 343–60.

Adair, Douglass G. *The Intellectual Origins of Jeffersonian Democracy: Republicanism, the Class Struggle, and the Virtuous Farmer.* Edited by Mark E. Yellin. Landham: Lexington Books, 2000.

Adam Smith, 1776–1926: Lectures to Commemorate the Sesquicentennial of the Publication of the "Wealth of Nations." Chicago, IL: University of Chicago Press, 1928.

Adams, Henry Carter. "Sibley College Lectures XI. 'The Labor Problem.'" *Scientific American Supplement*, no. 555 (August 21, 1886): 8861–63.

Adams, Henry Carter et al. *Science Economic Discussion.* New York, NY: Science Co., 1886.

Adams, John. *Discourses on Davila; A Series of Papers on Political History. By an American Citizen,* in *The Works of John Adams, Second President of the United States: with A Life of the Author, Notes and Illustrations, by his Grandson Charles Francis Adams,* vol. 6. Boston, MA: Charles C. Little and James Brown, 1851.

Adelman, Jeremy. *Worldly Philosopher: The Odyssey of Albert O. Hirschman.* Princeton, NJ: Princeton University Press, 2014.

Alacevich, Michele. *Albert O. Hirschman: An Intellectual Biography.* New York, NY: Columbia University Press, 2021.

Albertone, Manuela. *National Identity and the Agrarian Republic: The Transatlantic Commerce of Ideas between America and France.* Surrey, England: Ashgate, 2014.

Amadae, S. M. *Rationalizing Capitalist Democracy: The Cold War Origins of Rational Choice Liberalism.* 2nd edition. Chicago, IL: University of Chicago Press, 2003.

Amory, Hugh, and David D. Hall, eds. *A History of the Book in America, Volume 1: The Colonial Book in the Atlantic World.* Chapel Hill, NC: University of North Carolina Press, 2009.

Anderson, Annelise and Dennis L. Bark, eds. *Thinking about America: The United States in the 1990s.* Stanford, CA: Hoover Institution Press, 1988.

Anderson, Elizabeth. *Private Government: How Employers Rule Our Lives (And Why We Don't Talk about It).* Princeton, NJ: Princeton University Press, 2017.

Appleby, Joyce. *Liberalism and Republicanism in the Historical Imagination.* Cambridge, MA: Harvard University Press, 1992.

Arcenas, Claire Rydell. *America's Philosopher: John Locke in American Intellectual Life.* Chicago, IL: forthcoming.

Arendt, Hannah. *The Human Condition,* 2nd Edition. Chicago, IL: University of Chicago Press, 1958.

Arrow, Kenneth J. "A Cautious Case for Socialism." *Dissent* 25, no. 4 (1978): 472–480.

Arrow, Kenneth J. and F.H. Hahn. *General Competitive Analysis.* San Francisco, CA: Holden-Day, 1971.

Ashraf, Nava, Colin F. Camerer, and George Loewenstein. "Adam Smith, Behavioral Economist." *Journal of Economic Perspectives* 19, no. 3 (2005): 131–45.

Avrich, Paul. *The Haymarket Tragedy.* Princeton, NJ: Princeton University Press, 1984.

Backhouse, Roger E. *Founder of Modern Economics: Paul A. Samuelson: Volume 1: Becoming Samuelson, 1915–1948*. Illustrated edition. New York, NY: Oxford University Press, 2017.

Backhouse, Roger E. and Keith Tribe. *The History of Economics: A Course for Students and Teachers*. Newcastle upon Tyne: Agenda Publishing, 2017.

Bader, Ralf M. and John Meadowcroft. *The Cambridge Companion to Nozick's Anarchy, State, and Utopia*. Cambridge: Cambridge University Press, 2011.

Bailyn, Bernard. *The Ideological Origins of the American Revolution*. Cambridge, MA: Harvard University Press, 1967.

Balisciano, Marcia L. "Hope for America: American Notions of Economic Planning between Pluralism and Neoclassicism, 1930–1950." *History of Political Economy* 30 (supplement) (1998): 153–78.

Banning, Lance. *The Sacred Fire of Liberty: James Madison and the Founding of the Federal Republic*. New York, NY: Cornell University Press, 1995.

Barber, William J., ed. *Breaking the Academic Mould: Economists and Higher Learning in the Nineteenth Century*. New Brunswick, NJ: Transaction Publishers, 1993.

Beckert, Sven and Christine Desan, eds. *American Capitalism: New Histories*. Columbia Studies in the History of U.S. Capitalism. New York, NY: Columbia University Press, 2018.

Beckert, Sven and Seth Rockman, eds. *Slavery's Capitalism: A New History of American Economic Development*. Reprint edition. Philadelphia, PA: University of Pennsylvania Press, 2018.

Bergés, Sandrine and Eric Schliesser, eds. *Sophie de Grouchy's Letters on Sympathy: A Critical Engagement with Adam Smith's The Theory of Moral Sentiments*. New York, NY: Oxford University Press, 2019.

Berry, Christopher J. *Social Theory of the Scottish Enlightenment*. Edinburgh: Edinburgh University Press, 1997.

———. *The Idea of Commercial Society in the Scottish Enlightenment*. Edinburgh: Edinburgh University Press, 2013.

———. *The Idea of Luxury: A Conceptual and Historical Investigation*. Cambridge: Cambridge University Press, 1994.

Berry, Christopher J., Craig Smith, and Maria Pia Paganelli, eds. *The Oxford Handbook of Adam Smith*. Oxford: Oxford University Press, 2013.

Blaug, Mark. *Economic Theory in Retrospect*. 4th ed. Cambridge: Cambridge University Press, 1985.

Blyth, Mark. *Great Transformations: Economic Ideas and Institutional Change in the Twentieth Century*. New York, NY: Cambridge University Press, 2002.

Boas, Taylor C. and Jordan Gans-Morse. "Neoliberalism: From New Liberal Philosophy to Anti-Liberal Slogan." *Studies in Comparative International Development* 44, no. 2 (June 2009): 137–61.

Boettke, Peter. "F.A. Hayek as an Intellectual Historian." In *Historians of Economics and Economic Thought: The Construction of Disciplinary Memory*. Edited by Steve Medema and Warren Samuels. 117–128. London: Routledge, 2001.

Boucoyannis, Deborah. "The Equalizing Hand: Why Adam Smith Thought the Market Should Produce Wealth Without Steep Inequality." *Perspectives on Politics* 11, no. 4 (2013): 1051–70.

Bourke, Richard. "Revising the Cambridge School: Republicanism Revisited." *Political Theory* 46, no. 3 (2018): 467–77.

Bourne, Edward G. "Alexander Hamilton and Adam Smith." *The Quarterly Journal of Economics* 8, no. 3 (April 1894): 328–44.

Bowen, Francis. *The Principles of Political Economy Applied to the Condition: The Resources, and the Institutions of the American People.* Boston, MA: Little, Brown, and Company, 1856.

Brady, Gordon L. and Francesco Forte. "George J. Stigler's Relationship to the Virginia School of Political Economy." In *George Stigler: Enigmatic Price Theorist of the Twentieth Century.* Edited by Craig Freedman. 519–50. London: Palgrave Macmillan UK, 2020.

Branson, Roy. "James Madison and the Scottish Enlightenment." *Journal of the History of Ideas* 40, no. 2 (1979): 235–50.

Bréban, Laurie and Jean Dellemotte. "From One Form of Sympathy to Another: Sophie de Grouchy's Translation of and Commentary on Adam Smith's Theory of Moral Sentiments." Working Paper. HAL, April 4, 2016. https://econpapers.repec.org/paper/halwpaper/hal-01435828.htm.

Broadie, Alexander and Craig Smith, eds. *The Cambridge Companion to the Scottish Enlightenment.* 2nd ed. Cambridge Companions to Philosophy. Cambridge: Cambridge University Press, 2019.

Brown, Roger H. *Redeeming the Republic: Federalists, Taxation, and the Origins of the Constitution.* Baltimore, MD: The Johns Hopkins University Press, 1993.

Brown, Vivienne. *Adam Smith's Discourse: Canonicity, Commerce, and Conscience.* New York, NY: Routledge, 1994.

Bryson, Gladys. *Man and Society: The Scottish Inquiry of the Eighteenth Century.* Princeton, NJ: Princeton University Press, 1945.

Buchan, James. *The Authentic Adam Smith: His Life and Ideas.* Reprint edition. New York, NY: W. W. Norton & Company, 2007.

Buckle, Henry Thomas. *History of Civilization in England, Vol. 2.* London: Parker, Son, and Bourn, West Strand, 1861.

Burgin, Angus. "Age of Certainty: Galbraith, Friedman, and the Public Life of Economic Ideas." *History of Political Economy* 45, Supplementary Volume 1 (2013): 191–219.

———. *The Great Persuasion: Reinventing Free Markets since the Depression.* Cambridge, MA: Harvard University Press, 2012.

———. "The Neoliberal Turn." Working paper presented at the Political Theory Project. Brown University, January 30, 2020.

———. "The Radical Conservatism of Frank H. Knight." *Modern Intellectual History* 6, no. 03 (2009): 513–38.

Caldwell, Bruce. *Hayek's Challenge: An Intellectual Biography of F.A. Hayek.* Chicago, IL: University of Chicago Press, 2004.

Caldwell, William. "Review of *Lectures on Justice, Police, Revenue, and Arms, Delivered in the University of Glasgow,* by Edwin Cannan and Adam Smith." *Journal of Political Economy* 5, no. 2 (1897): 250–58.

Calhoun, John C. *Union and Liberty: The Political Philosophy of John C. Calhoun.* Edited by Ross M. Lence. Indianapolis, IN: Liberty Fund, 1992.

Cannan, Edwin. *A History of the Theories of Production and Distribution in English Political Economy, from 1776 to 1848.* London: Percival and Co., 1893.

Cappon, Lester J., ed. *The Adams-Jefferson Letters: The Complete Correspondence between Thomas Jefferson and Abigail and John Adams*. Chapel Hill, NC: University of North Carolina Press, 1959.

Carson, Mina Julia. *Settlement Folk: Social Thought and the American Settlement Movement, 1885–1930*. Chicago, IL: University of Chicago Press, 1990.

Chandra, Ramesh. "Adam Smith, Allyn Young, and the Division of Labor." *Journal of Economic Issues* 38, no. 3 (September 2004): 787–805.

Charette, Danielle and Max Skjönsberg. "State of the Field: The History of Political Thought." *History* 105, no. 366 (July 2020): 470–83.

Cheney, Paul. "István Hont, the Cosmopolitan Theory of Commercial Globalization, and Twenty-First-Century Capitalism." *Modern Intellectual History* (March 2021): 1–29, available at https://doi.org/10.1017/S147924432100007X.

Chernow, Ron. *Alexander Hamilton*. New York, NY: Penguin Books, 2005.

Ciepley, David. *Liberalism in the Shadow of Totalitarianism*. Cambridge, MA: Harvard University Press, 2007.

Clark, Henry C. "Women and Humanity in Scottish Enlightenment Social Thought: The Case of Adam Smith." *Historical Reflections/Reflexions Historiques* 19, no. 3 (1993): 335–61.

Clark, John Maurice. "Adam Smith and the Currents of History." In *Adam Smith, 1776–1926: Lectures to Commemorate the Sesquicentennial of the Publication of the "Wealth of Nations"* (Chicago, IL: University of Chicago Press), 53–76.

Clay, Henry. "The American System." In *The Senate: 1789–1989. Classic Speeches: 1830–1993*. Edited by Wendy Wolff, Vol. 3, 83–116. Washington, D.C.: U.S. Government Printing Office, n.d.

Cockett, Richard. *Thinking the Unthinkable: Think-Tanks and the Economic Counter-Revolution 1931–1983*. London: Harper Collins, 1995.

Colacchio, Giorgio. "Reconstructing Allyn A. Young's Theory of Increasing Returns." *Journal of the History of Economic Thought* 27, no. 3 (September 2005): 321–44.

[Collin, Nicholas.] A Foreign Spectator, "An Essay on the Means of Promoting Federal Sentiments in the United States" XV. Reprinted in *Friends of the Constitution: Writings of the "Other" Federalists, 1787–1788*. Edited by Colleen E. Sheehan and Gary L. McDowell. 406–440. Indianapolis, IN: Liberty Fund, 1998. Available at https://oll.libertyfund.org/titles/2069.

Collini, Stefan. *Public Moralists: Political Thought and Intellectual Life in Britain, 1850–1930*. Oxford: Clarendon Press, 1991.

Collini, Stefan, Richard Whatmore, and Brian Young, eds. *Economy, Polity, and Society: British Intellectual History 1750–1950*. Cambridge: Cambridge University Press, 2000.

Conkin, Paul Keith. *Prophets of Prosperity: America's First Political Economists*. Bloomington, IN: Indiana University Press, 1980.

Cooper, Melinda. *Family Values: Between Neoliberalism and the New Social Conservatism*. New York: Zone Books, 2017.

Cooper, Thomas. *Lectures on the Elements of Political Economy*. Columbia, S.C.: M'Morris & Wilson, 1829.

Cropsey, Joseph. *Polity and Economy*. The Hague: Martinus Nijhoff, 1957.

Cunningham, W. "Review of *A History of the Theories of Production and Distribution in English Political Economy, from 1776 to 1848*, by Edwin Cannan." *The Economic Journal* 3, no. 11 (1893): 493–94.

Cushing, Caleb. *Summary of the Practical Principles of Political Economy: With Observations on Smith's Wealth of Nations and Say's Political Economy*. Cambridge: Hilliard and Metcalf, 1826.

Damrosch, Leo. *The Club: Johnson, Boswell, and the Friends Who Shaped an Age*. New Haven, CT: Yale University Press, 2019.

Denslow, Van Buren. "American Economics." *The North American Review*, 139 no. 332 (Jul 1884): 12–29.

Destutt de Tracy, Antoine Louis Claude Comte. *A Treatise on Political Economy*. Translated by Thomas. Georgetown: Joseph Milligan, 1817.

Dew, Thomas Roderick. *Lectures on the Restrictive System*. Richmond, VA: Samuel Shepherd & Company, 1829.

Dorfman, Joseph. *The Economic Mind in American Civilization*. Vols. 1–5. New York, NY: The Viking Press, 1946–1959.

———. *The Economic Mind in American Civilization*. Vol. 2, Reprint edition. New York, NY: August M. Kelley, 1966.

———. "The Role of the German Historical School in American Economic Thought." *The American Economic Review* 45, no. 2 (1955): 17–28.

Dorrien, Gary. *The Neoconservative Mind: Politics, Culture, and the War of Ideology*. Reprint edition. Philadelphia, PA: Temple University Press, 1993.

Douglass, Frederick. "A Friendly Word to Maryland: An Address Delivered in Baltimore, Maryland, on 17 November 1864." In *The Frederick Douglass Papers. Series One: Speeches, Debates, and Interviews*. Edited by John W. Blassingame and John R. McKivingan. Vol. 4 (1864–80). 38–50. New Haven, CT: Yale University Press, 1991.

———. *My Bondage and My Freedom*. Edited by David W. Blight. New Haven, CT: Yale University Press, 2014.

Douglass, Robin. "Morality and Sociability in Commercial Society: Smith, Rousseau—and Mandeville." *The Review of Politics* 79, no. 4 (2017): 597–620.

Dowbiggin, Ian Robert. *Keeping America Sane: Psychiatry and Eugenics in the United States and Canada, 1880–1940*. Ithaca, NY: Cornell University Press, 1997.

Drolet, Jean-François. *American Neoconservatism: The Politics and Culture of a Reactionary Idealism*. Reprint edition. New York, NY: Oxford University Press, 2014.

Drucker, H.M. *The Political Uses of Ideology*. London: Palgrave Macmillan, 1974.

Dunbar, Charles F. "Economic Science in America, 1776–1876." *The North American Review* 122, no. 250 (January 1876): 124–54.

———. "The Academic Study of Political Economy." *The Quarterly Journal of Economics* 5, no. 4 (1891): 397–416.

———. "The Reaction in Political Economy." *The Quarterly Journal of Economics* 1, no. 1 (1886): 1–27.

Dunn, John. "Winch, Donald. Adam Smith's Politics: An Essay in Historiographic Revision." *Times Literary Supplement* no. 3 (1978): 1279.

Düppe, Till and E. Roy Weintraub. "Siting the New Economic Science: The Cowles Commission's Activity Analysis Conference of June 1949." *Science in Context* 27, no. 3 (2014): 453–83.

Easterly, William. "Progress by Consent: Adam Smith as Development Economist." *The Review of Austrian Economics* 34 (2021): 179–201.

Edling, Max. *A Hercules in the Cradle: War, Money, and the American State, 1783–1867*. Chicago, IL: Chicago University Press, 2014.

Edwards, Rebecca. *New Spirits: Americans in the Gilded Age, 1865–1905*. New York, NY: Oxford University Press, 2006.

Edwards, Richard C. "Economic Sophistication in Nineteenth Century Congressional Tariff Debates." *The Journal of Economic History* 30, no. 4 (1970): 802–38.

Eiffe, Franz F. "Amartya Sen Reading Adam Smith." *History of Economics Review* 51, no. 1 (January 2010): 1–23.

Eliot, Thomas D. "The Relations between Adam Smith and Benjamin Franklin before 1776." *Political Science Quarterly* 39, no. 1 (1924): 67–96.

Elkins, Stanley, and Eric McKitrick. *The Age of Federalism: The Early American Republic, 1788–1800*. New York, NY: Oxford University Press, 1995.

Ely, Richard T. "Ethics and Economics." *Science* 7, no. 175 (1886): 529–33.

———. *The Past and the Present of Political Economy*. Baltimore, MD: N. Murry, The Johns Hopkins University, 1884.

———. "Political Economy in America." *The North American Review* 144, no. 363 (Feb. 1887): 113–119.

Emmett, Ross B. *Frank Knight and the Chicago School in American Economics*. London: Routledge, 2009.

———., ed. *The Elgar Companion to the Chicago School of Economics*. Cheltenham: Elgar, 2012.

———., ed. *The Chicago Tradition in Economics 1892–1945*. London: Routledge, 2001.

Evensky, Jerry. "'Chicago Smith' versus 'Kirkaldy Smith.'" *History of Political Economy* 37, no. 2 (2005): 197–203.

Faccarello, Gilbert, and Heinz D. Kurz. *Handbook on the History of Economic Analysis. Volume II, Schools of Thought in Economics*. Cheltenham: Elgar, 2016.

Faccarello, Gilbert, and Philippe Steiner. "The Diffusion of the Work of Adam Smith in the French Language: An Outline History." *Économies et Sociétés*, no. 10 (1995): 5–30.

Ferguson, E. James. *The Power of the Purse: A History of American Public Finance, 1776–1790*. Published for the Omohundro Institute of Early American History and Culture, Williamsburg, Virginia. Chapel Hill, NC: The University of North Carolina Press, 2014.

Fink, Leon. *The Long Gilded Age: American Capitalism and the Lessons of a New World Order*. Philadelphia, PA: University of Pennsylvania Press, 2015.

Fleischacker, Samuel. *Adam Smith*. New York, NY: Routledge, 2021.

———. "Adam Smith's Reception among the American Founders, 1776–1790." *The William and Mary Quarterly* 59, no. 4 (2002): 897–924.

———. *On Adam Smith's Wealth of Nations: A Philosophical Companion*. Princeton, NJ: Princeton University Press, 2004.

———. *A Short History of Distributive Justice*. Cambridge, MA: Harvard University Press, 2004.

Foner, Eric. *Free Soil, Free Labor, Free Men: The Ideology of the Republican Party before the Civil War*. Oxford: Oxford University Press, 1995.

———. *Reconstruction: America's Unfinished Revolution, 1863–1877*. New York, NY: Harper & Row, 1988.

Forrester, Katrina. *In the Shadow of Justice: Postwar Liberalism and the Remaking of Political Philosophy*. Princeton, NJ: Princeton University Press, 2019.

Freeden, Michael. "Eugenics and Ideology." *The Historical Journal* 26, no. 4 (1983): 959–62.

———. "Eugenics and Progressive Thought: A Study in Ideological Affinity." *The Historical Journal* 22, no. 3 (1979): 645–71.

Freedman, Craig. *Chicago Fundamentalism: Ideology and Methodology in Economics*. Singapore: World Scientific, 2008.

Freeman, Joanne. *The Field of Blood: Violence in Congress and the Road to Civil War*. New York, NY: Farrar, Straus and Giroux, 2018.

Friedman, Milton. "Adam Smith's Relevance for Today." *Challenge* 20, no. 1 (March 1977): 6–12.

———. *Capitalism and Freedom*. 40th Anniversary Edition. Chicago, IL: University of Chicago Press, 2002.

———. "Economics and Economic Policy." *Economic Inquiry* 24, no. 1 (1986): 1–10.

———. "The Invisible Hand." In *The Business System: A Bicentennial View*. 2–13. Hanover, NH: Amos Tuck School of Business Administration, 1977. Available at https://miltonfriedman.hoover.org/objects/57602.

———. *Price Theory*. New York, NY: Hawthorne, 1962.

Friedman, Milton and Rose Friedman. *Free to Choose: A Personal Statement*. New York, NY: Houghton Mifflin Harcourt, 1990.

———. *Two Lucky People: Memoirs*. Chicago, IL: University of Chicago Press, 1998.

Gaus, Gerald. "Explanation, Justification, and Emergent Properties: An Essay on Nozickian Metatheory." In *The Cambridge Companion to Nozick's Anarchy, State, and Utopia*. 116–142. Edited by Ralf M. Bader and John Meadowcroft. Cambridge: Cambridge University Press, 2011.

Geiger, George Raymond. *The Philosophy of Henry George*. New York, NY: The Macmillan Company, 1933.

Geismer, Lily. *Don't Blame Us: Suburban Liberals and the Transformation of the Democratic Party*. Princeton, NJ: Princeton University Press, 2014.

———. *Left Behind: The Democrats' Failed Attempt to Solve Inequality*. New York, NY: Public Affairs, 2022.

George, Henry. *Progress and Poverty: An Enquiry into the Cause of Industrial Depressions, and of Increase of Want with Increase of Wealth*. New York, NY: Sterling Publishing Company, 1879.

Georgini, Sara et al., eds. *The Papers of John Adams. Vol. 20: June 1789–February 1971*. Cambridge, MA: Belknap, 2020.

Gerson, Mark. *The Neoconservative Vision: From the Cold War to the Culture Wars*. Lanham: Madison Books, 1995.

Gerstle, Gary. "The Rise and Fall of the Neoliberal Order." *Transactions of the Royal Historical Society* 28 (2018): 241–64.

Giocoli, Nicola. "The Intellectual Legacy of Progressive Hubris: A Review Essay of Thomas C. Leonard, *Illiberal Reformers: Race, Eugenics & American Economics in the Progressive Era*." *History of Economic Ideas* 25, no. 3 (2017), 157–69.

Glickman, Lawrence B. *Free Enterprise: An American History*. New Haven, CT: Yale University Press, 2019.

Goldstein, Judith L. *Ideas, Interests, and American Trade Policy*. Ithaca, NY: Cornell University Press, 1993.

Goldstein, Judith and Robert O. Keohane. *Ideas and Foreign Policy: Beliefs, Institutions, and Political Change*. Ithaca, NY: Cornell University Press, 1993.

Gordon, Scott. "Frank Knight and the Tradition of Liberalism." *Journal of Political Economy* 82, no. 3 (1974): 571–77.

Grampp, William D. "What Did Smith Mean by the Invisible Hand?" *Journal of Political Economy* 108, no. 3 (2000): 441–65.

Green, James R. *Death in the Haymarket: A Story of Chicago, the First Labor Movement, and the Bombing that Divided Gilded Age America*. New York, NY: Pantheon Books, 2006.

Greif, Mark. *The Age of the Crisis of Man*. Princeton: Princeton University Press, 2015.

Griswold, Charles L. *Adam Smith and the Virtues of Enlightenment*. New York, NY: Cambridge University Press, 1999.

———. *Jean-Jacques Rousseau and Adam Smith: A Philosophical Encounter*. New York, NY: Routledge, 2017.

———. "Smith and Rousseau in Dialogue: Sympathy, Pitié, Spectatorship and Narrative." *The Adam Smith Review* Vol 5: 69–94. Edited by Vivienne Brown and Samuel Fleischacker. New York, NY: Routledge, 2010.

Haakonssen, Knud. *The Science of a Legislator: The Natural Jurisprudence of David Hume and Adam Smith*. Cambridge: Cambridge University Press, 1981.

———, ed. *The Cambridge Companion to Adam Smith*. Cambridge: Cambridge University Press, 2006.

Hacker, Louis M. (Louis Morton). *Alexander Hamilton in the American Tradition*. New York, NY: McGraw-Hill, 1957.

Haeffele-Balch, Stefanie, Virgil Henry Storr, and Peter J. Boettke, eds. *Mainline Economics: Six Nobel Lectures in the Tradition of Adam Smith*. Arlington, VA: Mercatus Center at George Mason University, 2016.

Hahn, Steven. *A Nation under Our Feet: Black Political Struggles in the Rural South from Slavery to the Great Migration*. Cambridge, MA: Harvard University Press, 2003.

Hanley, Ryan Patrick. *Adam Smith and the Character of Virtue*. Cambridge: Cambridge University Press, 2009.

———., ed. *Adam Smith: His Life, Thought, and Legacy*. Princeton, NJ: Princeton University Press, 2016.

———. "Commerce and Corruption: Rousseau's Diagnosis and Adam Smith's Cure." *European Journal of Political Theory* 7, no. 2 (April 2008): 137–58.

———. *Our Great Purpose: Adam Smith on Living a Better Life*. Princeton: Princeton University Press, 2019.

Haraszti, Zoltan. *John Adams and the Prophets of Progress*. Cambridge, MA: Harvard University Press, 1952.

———. "The 32nd Discourse on Davila." *The William and Mary Quarterly* 11, no. 1 (1954): 89–92.

Harkin, Maureen. "Adam Smith and Women: Introduction." In *The Adam Smith Review*. Vol. 7: 29–33. Edited by Fonna Forman New York, NY: Routledge, 2013.

———. "Smith's the Theory of Moral Sentiments: Sympathy, Women, and Emulation." *Studies in Eighteenth-Century Culture* 24, no. 1 (1995): 175–90.

Harpham, Edward J. "Liberalism, Civic Humanism, and the Case of Adam Smith." *The American Political Science Review* 78, no. 3 (September 1984): 764–74.

Harris, James A. "The Protection of the Rich against the Poor: The Politics of Adam Smith's Political Economy." *Social Philosophy and Policy* 37, no. 1 (2020): 138–58.

Hartman, Andrew. *A War for the Soul of America, Second Edition: A History of the Culture Wars.* Chicago, IL: University of Chicago Press, 2019.

Hartz, Louis. *The Liberal Tradition in America.* New York, NY: Houghton Mifflin Harcourt, 1955.

Harvey, David. *A Brief History of Neoliberalism.* Oxford: Oxford University Press, 2007.

Hasbach, W. "Adam Smith's Lectures on Justice, Police, Revenue and Arms." *Political Science Quarterly* 12, no. 4 (1897): 684–98.

Hayek, F. A. "Adam Smith (1723–1790): His Message in Today's Language." In *The Trend of Economic Thinking: Essays on Political Economists and Economic History*. Edited by W.W. Bartley III and Stephen Kresge. Vol. 3: 11–121. The Collected Works of F.A. Hayek (London: Routledge, 1991)

———. *Hayek on Hayek: An Autobiographical Dialogue.* Edited by Stephen Kresge and Leif Wenar. The Collected Works of F.A. Hayek. Indianapolis, IN: Liberty Fund, 2008.

———. *The Road to Serfdom: Text and Documents—The Definitive Edition.* Edited by Bruce Caldwell. Chicago, IL: University of Chicago Press, 2007.

———. *The Trend of Economic Thinking: Essays on Political Economists and Economic History.* Edited by W.W. Bartley III and Stephen Kresge. London: Routledge, 1991.

———. "Individualism: True and False." In *Individualism and Economic Order*. 1–32. Chicago, IL: University of Chicago Press, 1948.

Heilbroner, Robert L. "The Paradox of Progress: Decline and Decay in *The Wealth of Nations*." *Journal of the History of Ideas* 34, no. 2 (1973): 243–62.

———. *The Worldly Philosophers: The Lives, Times, and Ideas of the Great Economic Thinkers.* Rev. 7th ed. New York, NY: Simon & Schuster, 1999.

Herzog, Lisa. "Adam Smith on Markets and Justice." *Philosophy Compass* 9, no. 12 (December 2014): 864–75.

———. *Inventing the Market: Smith, Hegel, and Political Theory.* Oxford: Oxford University Press, 2013.

Heyne, Paul. "Clerical Laissez-Faire: A Case Study in Theological Economics." In *Are Economists Basically Immoral? And Other Essays on Economics, Ethics, and Religion*. Edited by Geoffrey Brennan and A.M.C. Waterman. 238–64. Indianapolis, IN: Liberty Fund, 2008.

Hill, Lisa. "Adam Smith and the Theme of Corruption." *The Review of Politics* 68, no. 4 (October 2006): 636–62.

———. "The Hidden Theology of Adam Smith." *The European Journal of the History of Economic Thought* 8, no. 1 (2001): 1–29.

Hill, Mike and Warren Montag, *The Other Adam Smith: Popular Contention, Commercial Society, and the Birth of Necro-Economics*. Stanford, CA: Stanford University Press, 2014.

Himmelfarb, Gertrude. *The De-Moralization of Society: From Victorian Virtues to Modern Values*. New York, NY: Knopf, 1994.

———. *The Idea of Poverty*. New York, NY: Vintage, 1985.

Hirschman, A.O. *The Passions and the Interests: Political Arguments for Capitalism before Its Triumph*. Princeton, NJ: Princeton University Press, 2013.

Hirst, Francis W. *Adam Smith*. London: Macmillan & Company, 1904.

Hochstrasser, T.J. "Physiocracy and the Politics of Laissez-Faire." In *The Cambridge History of Eighteenth-Century Political Thought*. Edited by Mark Goldie and Mark Wokler. 419–42. Cambridge: Cambridge University Press, 2006.

Hollander, Jacob, ed. *Economic Essays, Contributed in Honor of John Bates Clark*. New York, NY: The Macmillan Company, 1927.

Holton, Woody. *Unruly Americans and the Origins of the Constitution*. New York, NY: Hill and Wang, 2007.

Hont, István. "Adam Smith's History of Law and Government as Political Theory." In *Political Judgement. Essays for John Dunn*. Edited by Richard Bourke and Raymond Geuss. 131–71. Cambridge: Cambridge University Press, 2009.

———. *The Jealousy of Trade: International Competition and the Nation State in Historical Perspective*. Cambridge, MA.: Belknap Press of Harvard University Press, 2005.

———. *Politics in Commercial Society*. Edited by Béla Kapossy and Michael Sonenscher. Cambridge, MA: Harvard University Press, 2015.

Hont, István and Michael Ignatieff, eds. *Wealth and Virtue: The Shaping of Political Economy in the Scottish Enlightenment*. Cambridge: Cambridge University Press, 1983.

Howe, Daniel Walker. *The Unitarian Conscience: Harvard Moral Philosophy, 1805–1861*. Cambridge, MA: Harvard University Press, 1970.

———. "Why the Scottish Enlightenment Was Useful to the Framers of the American Constitution." *Comparative Studies in Society and History* 31, no. 3 (July 1989): 572–87.

Hume, David. "Of Liberty and Necessity." In *Enquiries Concerning the Human Understanding and Concerning the Principles of Morals by David Hume*. Edited by L.A. Selby-Bigge, M.A., 2nd ed. 80–103. Oxford: Clarendon Press1902.

———. "Of Public Credit." In *Essays Moral, Political, Literary*. Edited and with a Foreword, Notes, and Glossary by Eugene F. Miller, with an appendix of variant readings from the 1889 edition by T.H. Green and T.H. Grose. Revised edition. 391–410. Indianapolis, IN: Liberty Fund 1987.

Hunter, James Davison. *Culture Wars: The Struggle to Define America*. New York, NY: Basic Books, 1991.

Hutchinson, William T. and William M. E. Rachal, eds. *The Papers of James Madison*. Vol. 6. 1 *January 1783–30 April 1783*. Chicago, IL: University of Chicago Press, 1969.

Huyssen, David. *Progressive Inequality: Rich and Poor in New York, 1890–1920*. Cambridge, MA: Harvard University Press, 2014.

Huzzey, Richard. "Free Trade, Free Labour, and Slave Sugar in Victorian Britain." *The Historical Journal* 53, no. 2 (2010): 359–79.

Ignatieff, Michael. "Smith, Rousseau and the Republic of Needs." In *Scotland and Europe 1200–1850*. Edited by T.C. Smouth. 187–206. Edinburgh: Edinburgh University Press, 1986.

Igo, Sarah E. "Toward a Free-Range Intellectual History." In *The Worlds of American Intellectual History*. Edited by Joel Isaac et al. 324–42.Oxford: Oxford University Press, 2016.

Ince, Onur Ulas. "Adam Smith, Settler Colonialism, and Limits of Liberal Anti-Imperialism," *The Journal of Politics* 83, no. 3 (July 2021): 1080–96.

Irwin, Douglas A. *Against the Tide: An Intellectual History of Free Trade*. Princeton, NJ: Princeton University Press, 1996.

———. *Clashing over Commerce: A History of US Trade Policy*. Chicago, IL: University of Chicago Press, 2017.

———. "The Welfare Cost of Autarky: Evidence from the Jeffersonian Trade Embargo, 1807–09." *Review of International Economics* 13, no. 4 (2005): 631–45.

Irwin, Douglas A. and Steven G. Medema, eds. *Jacob Viner: Lectures in Economics 301*. New Brunswick, NJ: Transaction Publishers, 2013.

Isaac, Joel et al. *The Worlds of American Intellectual History*. Oxford: Oxford University Press, 2016.

Jackson, Ben. "Freedom, the Common Good, and the Rule of Law: Lippmann and Hayek on Economic Planning." *Journal of the History of Ideas* 73, no. 1 (2012): 47–68.

———. "Intellectual Histories of Neo-Liberalism and their Limits." In *A Neo-Liberal Age? Britain Since the 1970s*. Edited by Alec Davies, Ben Jackson, and Florence Sutcliffe-Braithwaite. London: UCL Press, 2021.

Johnson, Donald Bruce and Kirk H. Porter, eds. *National Party Platforms, 1840–1968*. 4th ed. Urbana, IL: University of Illinois Press, 1970.

Jones, Daniel Stedman. *Masters of the Universe: Hayek, Friedman, and the Birth of Neoliberal Politics*. Princeton: Princeton University Press, 2012.

Jones, Emily. *Edmund Burke and the Invention of Modern Conservatism, 1830–1914: An Intellectual History*. Oxford: Oxford University Press, 2017.

Katz, Michael B. *In the Shadow of the Poorhouse: A Social History of Welfare in America, Tenth Anniversary Edition*. New York, NY: Basic Books, 1996.

Kaufmann, M. "Adam Smith and His Foreign Critics." *The Scottish Review* 10, no. 20 (1887): 387–411.

Kennedy, Gavin. "Adam Smith and the Invisible Hand: From Metaphor to Myth." *Econ Journal Watch* 6, no. 2 (2009): 239–63.

———. "Adam Smith and the Role of the Metaphor of an Invisible Hand." *Economic Affairs* 31, no. 1 (March 2011): 53–57.

———. *An Authentic Account of Adam Smith*. New York, NY: Palgrave Macmillan, 2017.

———. "Paul Samuelson and the Invention of the Modern Economics of the Invisible Hand." *History of Economic Ideas* 18, no. 3 (2010): 105–19.

Kidd, Colin. "The Phillipsonian Enlightenment." *Modern Intellectual History* 11, no. 1 (April 2014): 175–90.

Kirk, Russell. *The Conservative Mind from Burke to Eliot*. Washington, D.C.: Regnery Publications, 1986.

Klein, Daniel B. "Dissing the Theory of Moral Sentiments: Twenty-Six Critics, from 1765 to 1949." *Econ Journal Watch* 15, no. 2 (2018): 201.

Klein, Naomi. *The Shock Doctrine: The Rise of Disaster Capitalism*. New York, NY: Metropolitan Books and Henry Holt, 2007.

Kloppenberg, James T. *The Virtues of Liberalism*. New York, NY: Oxford University Press, 1998.

Knight, Frank H. "The Ethics of Competition." *The Quarterly Journal of Economics* 37, no. 4 (1923): 579–624.

———. "The Role of Principles in Economics and Politics." *The American Economic Review* 41, no. 1 (1951): 1–29.

Kristol, Irving. *Neoconservatism: The Autobiography of an Idea*. Chicago, IL: Ivan R. Dee, 1995.

Labaree, Leonard W., ed. *The Papers of Benjamin Franklin*. Vol. 4. *July 1, 1750, through June 30, 1753*. New Haven, CT: Yale University Press, 1961.

Lai, Cheng-Chung, ed. *Adam Smith Across Nations: Translations and Receptions of The Wealth of Nations*. Oxford: Clarendon Press, 2000.

Lamb, Robert. "Adam Smith's Concept of Alienation." *Oxford Economic Papers* 25, no. 2 (1973): 275–85.

Laursen, John Christian and Greg Coolidge. "David Hume and Public Debt: Crying Wolf?" *Hume Studies* 20, no. 1 (1994): 143–49.

Lears, T. J. Jackson. *No Place of Grace: Antimodernism and the Transformation of American Culture, 1880–1920*. Chicago, IL: University of Chicago Press, 1994.

———. *Rebirth of a Nation: The Making of a Modern America, 1877–1920*. New York: HarperCollins, 2009.

Lebovitz, Adam. *Colossus: Constitutional Theory in France and America, 1776–1799*. Cambridge, MA: Harvard University Press, forthcoming.

Leonard, Thomas C. *Illiberal Reformers: Race, Eugenics, and American Economics in the Progressive Era*. Princeton, NY: Princeton University Press, 2016.

———. "'More Merciful and Not Less Effective': Eugenics and American Economics in the Progressive Era." *History of Political Economy* 35, no. 4 (2003): 687–712.

Lepistö, Antti. *The Rise of Common-Sense Conservatism: The American Right and the Reinvention of the Scottish Enlightenment*. Chicago, IL: University of Chicago Press, 2021.

"Letters from William and Mary College, 1798–1801." *Virginia Magazine of History and Biography* 29, no. 2 (April 1921): 129–79.

Levy, David M. "How the Dismal Science Got Its Name: Debating Racial Quackery." *Journal of the History of Economic Thought* 23, no. 1 (March 2001): 5–35.

Levy, Jonathan. *Ages of American Capitalism: A History of the United States*. New York, NY: Random House, 2021.

Lew-Williams, Beth. *The Chinese Must Go: Violence, Exclusion, and the Making of the Alien in America*. Cambridge, MA: Harvard University Press, 2018.

Lippmann, Walter. *The Good Society*. New York, NY: Grosset & Dunlap, 1936.

List, Georg Friedrich. *Outlines of American Political Economy*. Philadelphia, PA: Samuel Parker, 1827.

Liu, Glory M. "'The Apostle of Free Trade:' Adam Smith and the Nineteenth-Century American Trade Debates." *History of European Ideas* 44, no. 2 (February 2018): 210–23.

———. "Rethinking the 'Chicago Smith' Problem: Adam Smith and the Chicago School, 1929–1980." *Modern Intellectual History* 17, no. 4 (2020): 1041–68.

Looney, J. Jefferson, ed. *The Papers of Thomas Jefferson.* Retirement Series. Vol. 10. *May 1816 to 18 January 1817.* Princeton, NJ: Princeton University Press, 2013.

Lundberg, David and Henry F. May. "The Enlightened Reader in America." *American Quarterly* 28, no. 2 (July 1976): 262–93.

Lutz, Donald S. "The Relative Influence of European Writers on Late Eighteenth-Century American Political Thought." *American Political Science Review* 78, no. 1 (March 1984): 189–97.

Madison, James. *Federalist 10.* In *The Federalist with Letters of "Brutus."* Edited by Terence Bell. 40–46. Cambridge: Cambridge University Press, 2003.

Magness, Phillip W. "The Progressive Legacy Rolls On: A Critique of Steinbaum and Weisberger on *Illiberal Reformers.*" *Econ Journal Watch* 15, no. 1 (2018): 20.

Mäki, Uskala. *The Methodology of Positive Economics: Reflections on the Milton Friedman Legacy.* Cambridge: Cambridge University Press, 2009.

May, Henry F. *The Enlightenment in America.* Oxford: Oxford University Press, 1978.

Mayville, Luke. *John Adams and the Fear of American Oligarchy.* Princeton, NJ: Princeton University Press, 2016.

McCloskey, Dierdre. "The Good Old Coase Theorem and the Good Old Chicago School." In *Coasean Economics: Law and Economics and the New Institutional Economics.* Edited by Steven G. Medema. 239–48. Dordrecht: Kluwer Academic Publishers, 1998.

McCoy, Drew R. *The Elusive Republic: Political Economy in Jeffersonian America.* Chapel Hill, NC: The University of North Carolina Press, 1996.

McCraw, Thomas K. *The Founders and Finance: How Hamilton, Gallatin, and Other Immigrants Forged a New Economy.* Cambridge, MA: Belknap Press, 2014.

McLean, Iain. "Adam Smith, James Wilson, and the US Constitutional Convention." In *The Adam Smith Review.* Edited by Fonna Forman. Vol. 8, 141–60. Abindon: Routledge, 2015.

———. *Adam Smith, Radical and Egalitarian: An Interpretation for the 21st Century* Edinburgh: Edinburgh University Press, 2006.

McNamara, Peter. *Political Economy and Statesmanship: Smith, Hamilton, and the Foundation of the Commercial Republic.* DeKalb, IL: Northern Illinois University Press, 1997.

McNulty, Paul J. "A Note on the History of Perfect Competition." *Journal of Political Economy* 75, no. 4 (1967): 395–99.

Medema, Steven G. "Identifying a 'Chicago School' of Economics: On the Origins, Evolution, and Evolving Meanings of a Famous Brand Name." 2018 Working Paper, permission to cite granted by author.

Meek, Ronald L. *Smith, Marx, & After: Ten Essays in the Development of Economic Thought.* London: Wiley, 1977.

———. "Smith, Turgot, and the 'Four Stages' Theory." *History of Political Economy* 3, no. 1 (March 1971): 9–27.

———. *Social Science and the Ignoble Savage.* Cambridge: Cambridge University Press, 1976.

———. *The Economics of Physiocracy: Essays and Translations.* Cambridge, MA: Harvard University Press, 1963.

Meyer, Donald H. *The Instructed Conscience: The Shaping of the American National Ethic.* Philadelphia, PA: University of Pennsylvania Press, 1972.

Miller, A. C. "A Catalogue of the Library of Adam Smith by James Bonar." *Journal of Political Economy* 3, no. 2 (1895): 242–43.

Miller, Thomas P. "John Witherspoon and Scottish Rhetoric and Moral Philosophy in America." *Rhetorica* 10, no. 4 (1992): 381–403.

Mills, R. J. W. and Craig Smith, eds. *The Scottish Enlightenment: Human Nature, Social Theory and Moral Philosophy: Essays in Honour of Christopher J. Berry.* Edinburgh: Edinburgh University Press, 2021.

Minutes and Proceedings of the Political Economy Club, 1821–1882. Vol. 3. London: Unwin Brothers, 1881.

Mirowski, Philip and Dieter Plehwe, eds. *The Road from Mont Pèlerin: The Making of the Neoliberal Thought Collective.* Cambridge, MA.: Harvard University Press, 2009.

Mitchell, Broadus. *Alexander Hamilton: The National Adventure, 1788–1804.* New York, NY: Macmillan, 1962.

Mizuta, Hiroshi and Chuhei Sugiyama, eds. *Adam Smith: International Perspectives.* London: Palgrave Macmillan UK, 1993.

Montes, Leonidas. "Das Adam Smith Problem: Its Origins, the Stages of the Current Debate, and One Implication for Our Understanding of Sympathy." *Journal of the History of Economic Thought* 25, no. 01 (2003): 63–90.

———. "Is Friedrich Hayek Rowing Adam Smith's Boat?" In *Hayek, Mill, and the Liberal Tradition.* Edited by Andrew Farrant. 7–38. London: Routledge, 2010.

Morgan, Edmund S. "Safety in Numbers: Madison, Hume, and the Tenth 'Federalist.'" *Huntington Library Quarterly* 49, no. 2 (1986): 95–112.

Morgan, Mary S. and Malcom Rutherford, eds. *From Interwar Pluralism to Postwar Neoclassism.* Durham, NC: Duke University Press, 1998.

Muller, Jerry Z. *Adam Smith in His Time and Ours: Designing the Decent Society.* Princeton, NJ: Princeton University Press, 1993.

Muthu, Sankar. "Adam Smith's Critique of International Trading Companies: Theorizing 'Globalization' in the Age of Enlightenment." *Political Theory* 36, no. 2 (April 2008): 185–212.

Newcomb, Simon. "Can Economists Agree upon the Basis of Their Teachings?" *Science* 8, no. 179 (1886): 25–26.

Nicholls, James C., ed. *Mme Riccoboni's letters to David Hume, David Garrick, and sir Robert Liston, 1764–1783.* Oxford: Voltaire Foundation at the Taylor Institution, 1976.

Nieli, Russell. "Spheres of Intimacy and the Adam Smith Problem." *Journal of the History of Ideas* 47, no. 4 (1986): 611–24.

Norman, Jesse. *Adam Smith: Father of Economics.* New York, NY: Basic Books, 2018.

Nozick, Robert. *Anarchy, State, and Utopia.* Reprint edition. New York, NY: Basic Books, 2013.

———. "Invisible-Hand Explanations." *The American Economic Review* 84, no. 2 (1994): 314–18.

O'Brien, Michael. *Conjectures of Order: Intellectual Life and the American South, 1810–1860.* Chapel Hill, NC: The University of North Carolina Press, 2004.

O'Connor, Alice. *Poverty Knowledge: Social Science, Social Policy, and the Poor in Twentieth-Century U.S. History.* Princeton, NJ: Princeton University Press, 2002.

O'Connor, Alice, Gary Gerstle, and Nelson Lichtenstein, eds. *Beyond the New Deal Order: U.S. Politics from the Great Depression to the Great Recession*. Politics and Culture in Modern America. Philadelphia, PA: University of Pennsylvania Press, 2019.

O'Connor, Michael Joseph Lalor. *Origins of Academic Economics in the United States*. New York, NY: Columbia University Press, 1944.

O'Driscoll, Gerald P., ed. *Adam Smith and Modern Political Economy: Bicentennial Essays on The Wealth of Nations*. Ames, IA: Iowa State University Press, 1979.

Olsen, Niklas. *The Sovereign Consumer: A New Intellectual History of Neoliberalism*. Consumption and Public Life Series. Cham, Switzerland: Palgrave Macmillan, 2019.

Oncken, August. "The Consistency of Adam Smith." *The Economic Journal* 7, no. 27 (1897): 443–50.

Oprea, Alexandra. "Adam Smith on Political Judgment: Revisiting the Political Theory of the *Wealth of Nations*." *The Journal of Politics* 84, no. 1 (January 2022): 18–32.

Pace Vetter, Lisa. *The Political Thought of America's Founding Feminists*. New York, NY: New York University Press, 2017.

Pack, Spencer J. *Capitalism as a Moral System: Adam Smith's Critique of the Free Market Economy*. Aldershot: Edward Elgar, 1991.

Paganelli, Maria Pia. "David Hume on Public Credit." *History of Economic Ideas* XX, no. 1 (2012): 31–43.

———. "The Adam Smith Problem in Reverse: Self-Interest in *The Wealth of Nations* and *The Theory of Moral Sentiments*." *History of Political Economy* 40, no. 2 (2008): 365–382.

Paganelli, Maria Pia, Dennis C. Rasmussen, and Craig Smith, eds. *Adam Smith and Rousseau: Ethics, Politics, Economics*. Edinburgh Studies in Scottish Philosophy. Edinburgh: Edinburgh University Press, 2018.

Paganelli, Maria Pia and Reinhard Schumacher. "Do Not Take Peace for Granted: Adam Smith's Warning on the Relation between Commerce and War." *Cambridge Journal of Economics* 43, no. 3 (April 2019): 785–97.

Palen, Marc-William. *The "Conspiracy" of Free Trade: The Anglo-American Struggle over Empire and Economic Globalization, 1846–1896*. Cambridge: Cambridge University Press, 2016.

The Papers of Thomas Jefferson. 45 Volumes. Princeton, NJ: Princeton University, 1950–2021 (ongoing).

Patinkin, Don. "The Chicago Tradition, the Quantity Theory, and Friedman." *Journal of Money, Credit and Banking* 1, no. 1 (1969): 46–70.

Peart, Daniel. "Looking Beyond Parties and Elections: The Making of United States Tariff Policy during the Early 1820s." *Journal of the Early Republic* 33, no. 1 (2013): 87–108.

Peart, Sandra and David M. Levy, eds. *The Street Porter and the Philosopher: Conversations on Analytical Egalitarianism*. Ann Arbor, MI: University of Michigan Press, 2008.

Phillipson, Nicholas. *Adam Smith: An Enlightened Life*. London: Penguin Books, 2010.

———. "Culture and Society in the Eighteenth-Century Province: The Case of Edinburgh and the Scottish Enlightenment." In *The University in Society*. Edited by Lawrence Stone. 407–48. Princeton, NJ: Princeton University Press, 1974.

Pitts, Jennifer. *A Turn to Empire: The Rise of Imperial Liberalism in Britain and France*. Princeton, NJ: Princeton University Press, 2006.

Pocock, J.G.A. *The Machiavellian Moment: Florentine Political Thought and the Atlantic Republican Tradition*. Princeton, NJ: Princeton University Press, 1975.

———. "On the Unglobality of Contexts: Cambridge Methods and the History of Political Thought." *Global Intellectual History* 4, no. 1 (January 2019): 1–14.

———. *Virtue, Commerce, and History*. Cambridge: Cambridge University Press, 1985.

Polkinghorn, Bette. *Adam Smith's Daughters: Eight Prominent Women Economists from the Eighteenth Century to the Present*. Cheltenham: Elgar, 1998.

Price, L. L. "Life of Adam Smith by John Rae." *The Economic Journal* 5, no. 19 (1895): 384–86.

Rader, Benjamin G. *The Academic Mind and Reform: The Influence of Richard T. Ely in American Life*. Lexington, KY: University of Kentucky Press, 1966.

Rae, John. *The Life of Adam Smith*. London: Macmillan, 1895.

Rashid, Salim. "Adam Smith's Rise to Fame: A Reexamination of the Evidence." *The Eighteenth Century* 23, no. 1 (1982): 64–85.

Rasmussen, Dennis C. "Adam Smith on What Is Wrong with Economic Inequality." *American Political Science Review* 110, no. 2 (2016): 342–52.

———. "Does 'Bettering Our Condition' Really Make Us Better Off? Adam Smith on Progress and Happiness." *The American Political Science Review* 100, no. 3 (August 2006): 309–18.

———. *The Infidel and the Professor: David Hume, Adam Smith, and the Friendship that Shaped Modern Thought*. Princeton, NJ: Princeton University Press, 2017.

———. *The Problems and Promise of Commercial Society: Adam Smith's Response to Rousseau*. University Park, PA: Penn State Press, 2008.

Ratner-Rosenhagen, Jennifer. *American Nietzsche: A History of an Icon and His Ideas*. Chicago, IL: University of Chicago Press, 2012.

Raymond, Daniel. *The Elements of Political Economy, in Two Parts*. 2nd ed. Baltimore, MD: Lucas, Jun. and E.J. Coale, 1823.

Recktenwald, Horst Claus. "An Adam Smith Renaissance Anno 1976? The Bicentenary Output-A Reappraisal of His Scholarship." *Journal of Economic Literature* 16, no. 1. (1978): 56–83.

Reder, Melvin W. "Chicago Economics: Permanence and Change." *Journal of Economic Literature* 20, no. 1 (March 1982): 1–38.

Reeder, John. *On Moral Sentiments: Contemporary Responses to Adam Smith*. Bristol: Thoemmes Press, 1997.

"Review: *Considérations sur l'Industrie et la Législation sous le Rapport de leur Influence sur la Richesse des Etats, et Examen Critique des Principaux Ouvrages, Qui ont paru sur l'Economie Politique* by Louis Say." *The North American Review* 17, no. 41 (1823): 424–436.

"Review of *A Manual of Political Economy, with Particular Reference to the Institutions, Resources and Condition of the United States*, by Willard Phillips." *The North American Review* 32, no. 70 (1831): 215–33.

"Review: Buckle's *History of Civilization in England* (volumes 1 and 2)." *The North American Review* 93 (1861): 519–559.

"Review of *Principles of Political Economy, with Some of Their Applications to Social Philosophy*." *The North American Review* 98, no. 202 (1864): 270–73.

"Review of *Principles of Political Economy, with Some of Their Applications to Social Philosophy* by John Stuart Mill." *The North American Review* 67, no. 141 (1848): 370–419.

"Review of *Principles of Political Economy. Part the First. Of the Laws of the Production and Distribution of Wealth* by Henry C. Carey." *The North American Review* 47, no. 100 (1838): 73–90.

"Review: *Summary of the Practical Principles of Political Economy, with Observations on Smith's Wealth of Nations, and Say's Political Economy* by A Friend of Domestic Industry." *The North American Review* 23, no. 53 (1826): 465–66.

Richardson, Heather Cox. *The Death of Reconstruction: Race, Labor, and Politics in the Post-Civil War North, 1865–1901*. Cambridge, MA: Harvard University Press, 2001.

Rieppel, Lukas. *Assembling The Dinosaur*. Cambridge, MA: Harvard University Press, 2019.

Robertson, John. "Scottish Political Economy Beyond the Civic Tradition: Government and Economic Development in the 'Wealth of Nations.'" *History of Political Thought* 4, no. 3 (1983): 451–82.

———. *The Case for the Enlightenment: Scotland and Naples, 1680–1760*. Cambridge: Cambridge University Press, 2005.

Rockman, Seth. "Negro Cloth: Mastering the Market for Slave Clothing in Antebellum America." In *American Capitalism: New Histories*. Edited by Sven Beckert and Christine Desan. Columbia Studies in the History of U.S. Capitalism. 170–194. New York: Columbia University Press, 2018.

Rodgers, Daniel T. *Age of Fracture*. Cambridge, MA: Belknap Press of Harvard University, 2012.

———. *As a City on a Hill: The Story of America's Most Famous Lay Sermon*. Princeton, NJ: Princeton University Press, 2018.

———. *Atlantic Crossings: Social Politics in a Progressive Age*. Cambridge, MA: Harvard University Press, 1998.

———. "Republicanism: The Career of a Concept." *The Journal of American History* 79, no. 1 (1992): 11–38.

Rogan, Tim. *The Moral Economists: R. H. Tawney, Karl Polanyi, E. P. Thompson, and the Critique of Capitalism*. Princeton, NJ: Princeton University Press, 2017.

Rosenberg, Nathan. "Adam Smith on the Division of Labour: Two Views or One?" *Economica* 32, no. 126 (1965): 127–39.

———. "George Stigler: Adam Smith's Best Friend." *Journal of Political Economy* 101, no. 5 (1993): 833–48.

Ross, Dorothy. *The Origins of American Social Science*. Cambridge: Cambridge University Press, 1991.

Ross, Ian Simpson. *The Life of Adam Smith*. 2nd ed. Oxford: Oxford University Press, 2010.

Rossiter, Clinton. *Alexander Hamilton and the Constitution*. New York, NY: Harcourt, Brace & World, 1964.

Rothschild, Emma. "Adam Smith and Conservative Economics." *The Economic History Review* 45, no. 1 (February 1992): 74–96.

———. "Adam Smith and the Invisible Hand." *The American Economic Review* 84, no. 2 (1994): 319–22.

———. *Economic Sentiments: Adam Smith, Condorcet, and the Enlightenment*. Cambridge, MA: Harvard University Press, 2001.

———. "Smithianismus and Enlightenment in 19th Century Europe," (Center for History and Economics, University of Cambridge). Working paper.

Rush, Benjamin. *An Inquiry into the Influence of Physical Causes upon the Moral Faculty delivered before a Meeting of the American Philosophical Society, Held at Philadelphia, on the Twenty-Seventh of February, 1786.* Philadelphia, PA: Haswell, Barrington, and Haswell, 1839.

———. *Medical Inquiries and Observations Upon the Diseases of the Mind.* 5th Edition Philadelphia, PA: Kimber and Richardson, 1835.

Sagar, Paul. "Adam Smith and the Conspiracy of the Merchants." *Global Intellectual History* 6, no. 4 (2021): 463–83.

———. *Adam Smith Reconsidered: History, Liberty, and the Foundations of Modern Politics.* Princeton, NJ: Princeton University Press, forthcoming.

———. "Adam Smith's Genealogy of Religion," *History of European Ideas* 47, no. 7 (2021): 1061–1078.

———. "István Hont and Political Theory." *European Journal of Political Theory* 17, no. 4 (October 2018): 476–500.

———. "Smith and Rousseau, after Hume and Mandeville." *Political Theory* 46, no. 1 (February 2018): 29–58.

———. *The Opinion of Mankind: Sociability and the Theory of the State from Hobbes to Smith.* Princeton, NJ: Princeton University Press, 2018.

———. "We Should Look Closely at What Adam Smith Actually Believed." *Aeon* January 16, 2018. https://aeon.co/essays/we-should-look-closely-at-what-adam-smith-actually-believed.

Sagar, Paul, ed. *Interpreting Adam Smith: Critical Essays.* Cambridge: Cambridge University Press, forthcoming.

Samuels, Warren J., Marianne F. Johnson, and William H. Perry, eds. *Erasing the Invisible Hand: Essays on an Elusive and Misused Concept in Economics.* Cambridge: Cambridge University Press, 2014.

Samuelson, Paul A. "A Modern Theorist's Vindication of Adam Smith." *The American Economic Review* 67, no. 1 (1977): 42–49.

Sanders, Valerie and Gaby Weiner, eds. *Harriet Martineau and the Birth of Disciplines: Nineteenth-Century Intellectual Powerhouse.* Abingdon: Routledge, 2017.

Sandilands, Roger J. "Perspectives on Allyn Young in Theories of Endogenous Growth." *Journal of the History of Economic Thought* 22, no. 3 (September 2000): 309–28.

Sawvel, Franklin B., ed. *Complete Anas of Thomas Jefferson.* New York: The Round Table Press, 1903.

Saxton, Alexander. *The Indispensable Enemy: Labor and the Anti-Chinese Movement in California.* Berkeley, CA: University of California Press, 1971.

Say, Jean-Baptiste. *A Treatise on Political Economy, or, the Production, Distribution and Consumption of Wealth, Translated from the Fourth Edition of the French.* Edited by Clement C. Biddle. Translated by C.R. Prinsep. 3rd ed. Philadelphia, PA: John Grigg, 1827.

Schliesser, Eric. "Adam Smith on Political Leadership." In *The Scottish Enlightenment: Human Nature, Social Theory and Moral Philosophy. Essays in Honour of Christopher J. Berry.* Edited by RJW Mills and Craig Smith. 132–163. Edinburgh: Edinburgh University Press, 2021.

———. *Adam Smith: Systematic Philosopher and Public Thinker.* Oxford: Oxford University Press, 2017.

———. "Walter Lippmann: The Prophet of Liberalism and the Road Not Taken." *The Journal of Contextual Economics* 139 (2019): 349–64.

Schoen, Brian D. *The Fragile Fabric of Union: Cotton, Federal Politics, and the Global Origins of the Civil War*. Baltimore, MD: The Johns Hopkins University Press, 2009.

Schulman, Bruce J. and Julian E. Zelizer, *Rightward Bound: Making America Conservative in the 1970s*. Cambridge, MA: Harvard University Press, 2008.

Schwarze, Michelle A., and John T. Scott. "Mutual Sympathy and the Moral Economy: Adam Smith Reviews Rousseau." *The Journal of Politics* 81, no. 1 (2019): 66–80.

Scurr, Ruth. "Inequality and Political Stability from Ancien Régime to Revolution: The Reception of Adam Smith's Theory of Moral Sentiments in France." *History of European Ideas* 35, no. 4 (December 2009): 441–49.

Seligman, E. R. A. "Review of *Life of Adam Smith*, by R. B. Haldane." *Political Science Quarterly* 3, no. 1 (1888): 179–179.

———. "Review of *Adam Smith, sa vie, ses travaux, ses doctrines*, by Albert Delatour. *Political Science Quarterly* 2, no. 1 (1887): 185–86.

———. "Review of *Die Allgemeinen Philosophischen Grundlagen der von François Quesnay und Adam Smith begründeten Politischen Oekonomie; Untersuchungen uber Adam Smith und die Entwicklung der Politischen Oekonomie*, by Wilhelm Hasbach." *Political Science Quarterly* 7, no. 3 (1892): 556–58.

Sen, Amartya. "Uses and Abuses of Adam Smith." *History of Political Economy* 43, no. 2 (2011): 257–71.

Shalhope, Robert E. "Toward a Republican Synthesis: The Emergence of an Understanding of Republicanism in American Historiography." *The William and Mary Quarterly* 29, no. 1 (1972): 49–80.

Sher, Richard B. "Adam Ferguson, Adam Smith, and the Problem of National Defense." *The Journal of Modern History* 61, no. 2 (1989): 240–68.

———. *The Enlightenment and the Book: Scottish Authors and Their Publishers in Eighteenth-Century Britain, Ireland, and America*. Chicago, IL: University of Chicago Press, 2010.

Sher, Richard B. and Jeffrey R. Smitten, eds. *Scotland and America in the Age of the Enlightenment*. Edinburgh: Edinburgh University Press, 1990.

Skinner, Andrew S. "Adam Smith and the American Revolution." *Presidential Studies Quarterly* 7, no. 2/3 (April 1977): 75–87.

Skinner, Andrew S. and Thomas Wilson, eds. *Essays on Adam Smith*. Oxford: Clarendon Press, 1975.

Sklansky, Jeffrey. *The Soul's Economy: Market Society and Selfhood in American Thought, 1820–1920*. Chapel Hill, NC: University of North Carolina Press, 2002.

Sloan, Douglas. *The Scottish Enlightenment and the American College Ideal*. New York, NY: Teachers College Press, Columbia University, 1971.

Slobodian, Quinn. *Globalists: The End of Empire and the Birth of Neoliberalism*. Cambridge, MA: Harvard University Press, 2018.

Small, Albion Woodbury. *Adam Smith and Modern Sociology: A Study in the Methodology of the Social Sciences*. Chicago, IL: University of Chicago Press, 1907.

Smith, Adam. *The Wealth of Nations* with an introduction by Prof. Edwin R.A. Seligman. Everyman's edition. Edited by Ernest Rhys. Vol. 1. London: J.M. Dent & Sons, 1910.

———. *Lectures on Justice, Police, Revenue and Arms*. Edited by Edwin Cannan. Oxford: Clarendon, 1896.

Smith, Craig. "Adam Smith: Left or Right?" *Political Studies* 61, no. 4 (December 2013): 784–98.

———. "Adam Smith on Philosophy and Religion." *Ruch Filozoficzny* 74, no. 3 (September 2018): 23–39.

———. *Adam Smith's Political Philosophy: The Invisible Hand and Spontaneous Order.* Routledge Studies in Social and Political Thought. New York, NY: Routledge, 2006.

Smith, James A. *Idea Brokers: Think Tanks and The Rise of The New Policy Elite.* New York, NY: The Free Press, 1991.

Smith, Vernon L. and Bart Wilson. *Humanomics: Moral Sentiments and the Wealth of Nations for the Twenty-First Century.* Cambridge: Cambridge University Press, 2019.

Somos, Mark. "'A Price Would Be Set Not Only upon Our Friendship, but upon Our Neutrality:' Alexander Hamilton's Political Economy and Early American State-Building." *Studies across Disciplines in the Humanities and Social Sciences, Helsinki Collegium for Advanced Studies* 10 (2011): 184–211.

———. *American States of Nature: The Origins of Independence, 1761–1775.* New York, NY: Oxford University Press, 2019.

Spencer, Mark G. *David Hume and Eighteenth-Century America.* Cambridge: Cambridge University Press, 2012.

Spencer, Roger W. and David A. Macpherson. *Lives of the Laureates: Thirty-Two Nobel Economists.* 7th edition. Cambridge, MA: The MIT Press, 2020.

Steinbaum, Marshall I. and Bernard A. Weisberger. "The Intellectual Legacy of Progressive Economics: A Review Essay of Thomas C. Leonard's Illiberal Reformers." *Journal of Economic Literature* 55, no. 3 (2017): 1064–83.

Steuart, James. *Inquiry into the Principles of Political Oeconomy.* London: A. Millar and T. Cadell, 1767.

Stigler, George. "Does Economics Have a Useful Past?" *History of Political Economy* 1, no. 2 (1969): 217–30.

———. "Economics or Ethics?" *The Tanner Lectures on Human Values*, delivered at Harvard University. April 24, 25, and 28, 1980. Available at https://tannerlectures.utah.edu/_resources/documents/a-to-z/s/stigler81.pdf.

———. *Essays in the History of Economics.* Chicago, IL: University of Chicago Press, 1965.

———. *Memoirs of an Unregulated Economist.* New York, NY: Basic Books, 1988.

———. "Perfect Competition, Historically Contemplated." *Journal of Political Economy* 65, no. 1 (1957): 1–17.

———. "Public Regulation of the Securities Markets." *The Journal of Business* 37, no. 2 (1964): 117–42.

———. "Smith's Travels on the Ship of State." *History of Political Economy* 3, no. 2 (September 1971): 265–77.

———. "The Economist and the State." *The American Economic Review* 55, no. 1/2 (1965): 1–18.

———. "The Influence of Events and Policies on Economic Theory." *The American Economic Review* 50, no. 2 (1960): 36–45.

———. "The Successes and Failures of Professor Smith." *The Journal of Political Economy* 84, no. 6 (1976): 1199–1213.

———. "The Theory of Economic Regulation." *The Bell Journal of Economics and Management Science* 2, no. 1 (1971): 3–21.

Stigler, George J. and Claire Friedland. "What Can Regulators Regulate? The Case of Electricity." *The Journal of Law & Economics* 5 (1962): 1–16.

Stiglitz, Joseph E. *The Roaring Nineties: A New History of the World's Most Prosperous Decade.* Reprint edition. New York, NY: W. W. Norton & Company, 2004.

Stimson, Shannon. "From Invisible Hand to Moral Restraint: The Transformation of the Market Mechanism from Adam Smith to Thomas Robert Malthus." *Journal of Scottish Philosophy* 2, no. 1 (March 2004): 22–47.

Stirling, J. H. "Review: *History of Civilization in England and France, Spain and Scotland* by Henry Thomas Buckle." *The North American Review* 115, no 236 (1872): 65–103.

Streeter, Ryan. "Free Trade and Decadence, Old and New." *American Enterprise Institute*, July 20, 2020, sec. Society and Culture. Available at https://www.aei.org/articles/free-trade-and-decadence-old-and-new/.

Su, Alastair. "Reading, and Misreading, Adam Smith: Recovering Herbert Somerton Foxwell's 'Really Historical Edition' of the Wealth of Nations." Working paper.

Summers, Mark W. *The Ordeal of the Reunion: A New History of Reconstruction.* The Littlefield History of the Civil War Era. Chapel Hill, NC: The University of North Carolina Press, 2014.

Sylla, Richard. "Hamilton and the Federalist Financial Revolution, 1789–1795." *The New York Journal of American History* 65, no. 2 (2004): 32–39.

Syrett, Harold C., ed. *The Papers of Alexander Hamilton.* Vol. 10, *December 1791–January 1792.* New York, NY: Columbia University Press, 1966.

Taylor, John. *Arator, Being a Series of Agricultural Essays, Practical and Political: In Sixty-Four Numbers.* Petersburg: Whitworth & Yancey, 1818.

Teichgraeber III, Richard F. "Adam Smith and Tradition: The Wealth of Nations before Malthus." In *Economy, Polity, and Society.* Edited by Stefan Collini, Richard Whatmore, and Brian Young, 85–104. Cambridge: Cambridge University Press, 2000.

———. "Rethinking Das Adam Smith Problem." *Journal of British Studies* 20, no. 2 (April 1981): 106–23.

———. " 'Less Abused than I Had Reason to Expect': The Reception of the Wealth of Nations in Britain, 1776–90." *The Historical Journal* 30, no. 2 (1987): 337–66.

Terrill, Tom E. *The Tariff, Politics, and American Foreign Policy, 1874–1901.* Westport, CT: Praeger, 1973.

Thomas, John L. *Alternative America: Henry George, Edward Bellamy, Henry Demarest Lloyd and the Adversary Tradition.* Cambridge, MA: Harvard University Press, 1983.

Thompson, C. Bradley. *John Adams and the Spirit of Liberty.* Lawrence, KS: University Press of Kansas, 1998.

Tribe, Keith. "Adam Smith: Critical Theorist?" *Journal of Economic Literature* 37, no. 2 (1999): 609–32.

———. *Continental Political Economy from the Physiocrats to the Marginal Revolution.* Cambridge: Cambridge University Press, 2003.

———. " 'Das Adam Smith Problem' and the Origins of Modern Smith Scholarship." *History of European Ideas* 34, no. 4 (2008): 514–25.

———. *Governing Economy: The Reformation of German Economic Discourse, 1750–1840.* Cambridge: Cambridge University Press, 1988.

———. *Strategies of Economic Order: German Economic Discourse, 1750–1950*. Cambridge: Cambridge University Press, 1995.

———. "The 'System of Natural Liberty': Natural Order in the *Wealth of Nations*." *History of European Ideas* 47, no. 4 (2021): 573–83.

Tribe, Keith and Hiroshi Mizuta, eds. *A Critical Bibliography of Adam Smith*. London: Pickering & Chatto, 2002.

Unger, Harlow G. *Noah Webster: The Life and Times of an American Patriot*. New York, NY: John Wiley & Sons, 1998.

Vaïsse, Justin. *Neoconservatism: The Biography of a Movement*. Translated by Arthur Goldhammer. Cambridge, MA: Belknap Press, An Imprint of Harvard University Press, 2011.

Van Horn, Robert, Philip Mirowski, and Thomas A Stapleford, eds. *Building Chicago Economics: New Perspectives on the History of America's Most Powerful Economics Program*. Cambridge: Cambridge University Press, 2011.

Van Overtveldt, Johan. *The Chicago School: How the University of Chicago Assembled the Thinkers Who Revolutionized Economics and Business*. Chicago, IL: Agate, 2007.

Viner, Jacob. "Adam Smith and Laissez-Faire." *Journal of Political Economy* 35, no. 2 (April 1927): 198–232.

Voltaire, *Oeuvres Complètes*. Edited by Beaumarchais. 70 vols. Kehl: Imprimerie de la Société Littéraire-Typographique, 1784–1789.

Walsh, Vivian. "Smith after Sen." *Review of Political Economy* 12, no. 1 (January 2000): 5–26.

Warner, Charles Dudley, ed. *Library of the World's Best Literature: Biographical Dictionary*. Vol. 23. New York, NY: R. S. Peale and J. A. Hill, 1898.

Wasserman, Janek. *The Marginal Revolutionaries: How Austrian Economists Fought the War of Ideas*. New Haven, CT: Yale University Press, 2019.

Wayland, Francis. *The Elements of Political Economy*. 2nd ed. New York, NY: Robinson and Franklin, 1838.

[Webster, Noah] A Citizen of America, "An Examination into the Leading Principles of the Federal Constitution." In *The Debate on the Constitution: Federalist and Antifederalist Speeches, Articles, and Letters During the Struggle over Ratification. Part 1*. Edited by Bernard Bailyn. 129–163. New York, NY: The Library of America, 1993.

Weinstein, Jack Russell. *Adam Smith's Pluralism: Rationality, Education, and the Moral Sentiments*. New Haven, CT: Yale University Press, 2013.

———. "Introduction: Adam Smith's Philosophy of Education." In *The Adam Smith Review*. Edited by Vivienne Brown. Vol. 3. 63–86. Abingdon: Routledge, 2007.

Werhane, Patricia Hogue. *Adam Smith and His Legacy for Modern Capitalism*. Oxford: Oxford University Pres, 1991.

West, Edwin George. "The Political Economy of Alienation: Karl Marx and Adam Smith." *Oxford Economic Papers* 21, no. 1 (1969): 1–23.

Weyl, Glen. "Price Theory." *Journal of Economic Literature*, Forthcoming. Available at https://ssrn.com/abstract=2444233.

Whatmore, Richard. "Adam Smith's Role in the French Revolution." *Past & Present*. no. 175 (2002): 65–89.

White, Richard. *Railroaded: The Transcontinentals and the Making of Modern America*. New York, NY: W.W. Norton and Company, 2012.

———. *The Republic for Which It Stands: The United States during Reconstruction and the Gilded Age, 1865–1896*. Oxford History of the United States. New York, NY: Oxford University Press, 2017.

Wight, Jonathan B. "The Rise of Adam Smith: Articles and Citations, 1970–1997." *History of Political Economy* 34, no. 1 (2002): 55–82.

———. *Saving Adam Smith: A Tale of Wealth, Transformation, and Virtue*. Upper Saddle River, NJ: Financial Press, 2001.

Willcox, William B., ed. *The Papers of Benjamin Franklin. Vol. 16. January 1 through December 31, 1769*. New Haven, CT: Yale University Press, 1972.

Willis, Kirk. "The Role in Parliament of the Economic Ideas of Adam Smith, 1776–1800." *History of Political Economy* 11, no. 4 (November 1979): 505–44.

Wills, Garry. *Explaining America: The Federalist*. New York: Penguin Books, 2001.

———. *Inventing America: Jefferson's Declaration of Independence*. 1st Mariner Books edition Boston, MA Houghton Mifflin, 2002.

Winch, Donald. *Adam Smith's Politics: An Essay in Historiographic Revision*. Cambridge: Cambridge University Press, 1978.

———. "Adam Smith's Problems and Ours." *Scottish Journal of Political Economy* 44, no. 4 (1997): 384–402.

———. "Intellectual History and the History of Economic Thought: A Personal Account." *Journal of Interdisciplinary History of Ideas* 6, no. 12 (January 2018): 1–18.

Winterer, Caroline. *American Enlightenments: Pursuing Happiness in the Age of Reason*. New Haven, CT: Yale University Press, 2016.

———. *The Culture of Classicism: Ancient Greece and Rome in American Intellectual Life, 1780–1910*. Baltimore, MD: The Johns Hopkins University Press, 2004.

———. "History." In *A Cultural History of Ideas in the Age of Enlightenment*. Cultural History of Ideas series. Vol. 4. Edited by Sophia Rosenfeld and Peter Struck. London: Bloomsbury Academic Press, forthcoming.

Witherspoon, John. *Lectures on Moral Philosophy*. Edited by Varnum Lansing Collins. Princeton, NJ: Princeton University Press, 1912.

Wood, Gordon S. *The Creation of the American Republic, 1776–1787*. Chapel Hill, NC: University of North Carolina Press, 1969.

Young, Jeffrey T., ed. *The Elgar Companion to Adam Smith*. Cheltenham: Elgar, 2010.

INDEX

abolitionism, 10, 130–32
academic political economy: Cold War and, 199–200; in the Depression era, 198–200 (*see also* Chicago School of Economics); early courses and textbooks on, 20–21, 75–78, 83–95, 92–93, 111; free trade debates and, 4, 122–29, 133–43; *idéologues* and, 75–77 (*see also* Say, Jean-Baptiste); *Methodenstreit* and, 157–58; origins of, 1, 71–75; in postbellum America, 97–111, 133, 146–47; in the Progressive Era, 2, 152–66, 169–75 (*see also* Ely, Richard T.; Seligman, E.R.A.)
Adam Smith Institute, 251
Adam Smith necktie, 247–49, *248*
Das Adam Smith Problem: "Chicago Smith Problem" and, 2, 196–98; contemporary scholarship on, 292, 301–2; in the nineteenth century, 148, 150; in the Progressive Era, 169, 184–86; sesquicentennial of *The Wealth of Nations* (Smith) and, 186–88; Viner on, 210–13, 230; Zeyss on, 168–69
Adams, Abigail, 58–59
Adams, Charles, 58–59
Adams, Henry Carter, 100, 174
Adams, John, 23, 28n48, 51–52; political thought of, 59–66; *The Theory of Moral Sentiments* (Smith) and, 17, 51–52, 59, 62–66, 67; *The Wealth of Nations* (Smith) and, 21, 59
Adams, John Quincy, 59

The Age of Uncertainty (television series), 244
agrarian republicanism, 50, 73
agriculture: antebellum free trade debates and, 132; Hamilton on, 39–40, 43–50; Jefferson on, 50; Madison on, 31–32; physiocrats on, 40–43; stadial theory and, 27–28; Taylor on, 73
Alison, Francis, 25–26, 55, 56
American Economics Association (AEA), 100, 156
American System, 81–82, 94–95, 116–22, 125, 129, 132–33. *See also* List, Friedrich; protectionism
anti-Chinese sentiment, 151–52
Anti-Cobden Club, 135–36
Anti-Corn Law League, 119
Arendt, Hannah, 196
Arrow, Kenneth, 242–43, 258
Association for the Protection of American Industries, 135–36
Austrian School, 157–58, 195n11

Bank of North America, 37
Bastable, Charles Francis, 182
Belford, Joseph, 142–43
Bell, Daniel, 281
Bellamy, Edward, 152
Bigelow, John, 112–14
Blackstone, William, 180n81
Blair, Hugh, 13
Böhm-Bawerk, Eugen, 157–58n23
Bonar, James, 147, 177–78

A NOTE ON THE TYPE

This book has been composed in Arno, an Old-style serif typeface in the classic Venetian tradition, designed by Robert Slimbach at Adobe.